The Black Family

Essays and Studies

The Black Family

Essays and Studies

Edited by
Robert Staples

University of California,
San Francisco Medical Center

Wadsworth Publishing Company, Inc.
Belmont, California

Library of Congress Catalog Card
Number: 71-141508
Printed in the United States of America

4 5 6 7 8 9 10 — 74

To my grandmothers, Daisy Ivory and Ella
Thompson, and to all the other courageous
Black women who are responsible
for the survival of the Black family

Preface

Many aspects of the Black family have long been ignored by social scientists and laymen. When it has been considered, people have been concerned primarily with its deviance from normal middle-class white family behavior. Such aspects of Black family life as premarital dating patterns, socio-sexual behavior, and socialization processes have generally been left out of most articles on this subject. A unique characteristic of *The Black Family* is that it offers a broader perspective on the dynamics of Black behavior. The selections included give the reader an opportunity to better understand the internal behavior processes and the psycho-social dimensions of the Black family; this book is designed to present a balanced view of the Black family.

The choice of readings reflects the dichotomous character of studies on the Black family. Some articles represent the scientific studies found in professional books and journals. Others are taken from popular literature. The articles look at the Black family as a unit but also consider the social, political, and economic factors that influence it. The Black family cannot be studied in a vacuum but must be seen in the context of the societal forces which influence its structure and dynamics. This contrast in selections exposes the reader to various viewpoints and types of literature. Thus he is free to be eclectic in his own interpretation of the nature of Black family life.

Many colleagues, students, and friends assisted in the preparation of this reader. I am grateful to the authors of the various selections in this book and, in particular, to Professor Barbara Rhodes of San Fernando Valley State College and Dr. Robert Bell of Temple University, who allowed me to print their previously unpublished papers. Miss Yvonne Walden and Miss Shirley Lavender were very helpful during the preparation of materials for publication. I am also indebted to Miss Jacqueline Luckett for her technical and clerical assistance.

Though many other people too numerous to mention have contributed to this volume, I would like to thank the following people for their interest and suggestions: Boone Hammond, Pennsylvania State University; Hyman Rodman, the Merrill-Palmer Institute; and Jack Arnold of Wadsworth Publishing Company, who went beyond the call of duty in helping me overcome the obstacles normally encountered in preparation of a book of this sort. For their helpful suggestions, thanks go to reviewers Edward Silva, University of Wisconsin, and Frederick L. Campbell, University of Washington. I am also grateful to the late Donald Bender, my mentor at the University of Minnesota, for although he did not contribute directly to this reader, without his earlier guidance I would have been incapable of undertaking such an effort.

Contents

Introduction 3

Selected Bibliography

The Black Family

Essays and Studies

Introduction

A book entitled *The Black Family*, by its very title, is subject to challenge. The Black Family, as a single model for study, does not exist. There are only individual family units, whose members are Black, who have both experiences unique to that group and experiences common to many other families, Black and white. However, we obviously cannot study each individual family, record its esoteric experiences, and simply let each family speak for itself.

Therefore, a book which purports to examine the Black family in all its dimensions does have certain limitations. The Black family is not a monolithic unit about which we can make definitive statements. Instead, it is a type of social organization whose form changes from social class to social class, region to region, country to country, and culture to culture. Nonetheless, one trait that Black families usually share is a history of racist oppression, whether under colonialism or slavery.

Because of this common history, Black families cannot be compared, objectively, with white families. There is no evidence to indicate that Black and white families share the same experiences, even if they belong to the same socioeconomic group. Studies which contrast Black and white families only serve to underscore the unique in the Black experience. No white family has faced the historical subjugation and contemporary racism that Black families have encountered and continue to encounter.

Most studies of the Black family have focused on the most deprived segment of the Black population and have made sweeping generalizations about its pathological character. (Unintentionally or not, these studies have thus provided the forces of racism with further propaganda to maintain the status quo level of white privilege–Black deprivation.) Such studies cannot provide the knowledge of Black family structure and dynamics that we need to develop a relevant sociology of Black family life. For example, instead of focusing on reducing the number of illegitimate Black children, social scientists should be concerned with bringing about the kind of public policy that will ensure all children, regardless of the legitimacy of their conception, an equal life chance in this society. This means a challenge to the basic value structure of American society, a challenge which gives primacy to humanist rather than ethnocentric and puritanical values.

A relevant sociology of the Black family will seek to discover the strengths in the Black community that have allowed any form of Black family life to exist under so many years of hardship. In pursuing the discovery of those strengths, the magnificent role of the Black woman in maintaining the Black family as a viable unit will stand out as one of the most positive forces responsible for the survival of the Black family.

This collection of essays and studies on the Black family will give the reader an idea of what exists in the literature, the gaps that need to be filled, and the conclusions that need to be refuted. Until a relevant sociology of the Black family becomes available, we must make do with what there is. This volume is, hopefully, an improvement on what already exists. It can serve as a framework on which we can build a relevant sociology of the Black family.

Part One

The Setting

The long travail of the Black family has its genesis in the vast continent of Africa. Because Africa is a land of diverse cultures and languages, it is difficult to generalize about African family life in the pre-slave period. However, most students of African history acknowledge that the African family was a stable, secure group subjected to the mores and folkways of its particular tribal unit. It was the forced removal of Blacks from Africa to the Americas that changed the Black family's structure, eroded its normative underpinnings, and exposed it to the most deculturating practices any group of people has ever experienced.

A historical analysis of the Black family is a necessary, although not sufficient, basis for understanding it today. The relative importance of the historical process in influencing the form of the Black family remains in dispute. Some social scientists contend that enough time has elapsed since slavery was abolished to uncover the basic etiological factors responsible for the problems faced by Black families. These theorists believe that we should study not the cultural transformation during the slave period but the socioeconomic forces that ordinarily sustain family life—and that have been disproportionately absent in the Black community.

Regardless of the currency of their .position, reviewing the past experiences of Black family members can be of some value. One of the best ways to comprehend the meaning of slavery for Afro-American family life is through a comparative analysis of slavery in North America and Latin

America. The selection from Stanley Elkins' *Slavery: A Problem in American Institutional and Intellectual Life* deals with the differences in the structure and consequences of Anglo-Saxon slavery.

According to Elkins, the principal differences between North and South American slavery were in Latin America's manumission process and legal basis of marriages between slaves. That is, slaves could become free citizens more easily there. Those that remained slaves were allowed to have a legal marriage ceremony, and the sanctity of the family was sanctioned in both law and the canons of the Catholic Church. The reverse was true of slavery in North America.

In reading the Elkins material, one might almost discern a humane form of slavery, which this writer considers a contradiction in terms. The Spanish slave code of 1789 forms much of the difference between Anglo and South American slavery, according to Elkins. However, this code was not only unenforced but never promulgated in any of the Spanish Caribbean colonies.[1] Most of the Spanish slave law deals with security measures to keep slaves confined to their respective plantations. In fact, some of the measures encouraging marriage among the slaves were designed to hold the slaves to the estates with family ties.

The selection by Frazier is probably the best available synopsis of his book *The Negro Family in the United States*. Using the natural history approach to the study of the Black family, Frazier saw it as the culmination of an evolutionary process, its structure strongly affected by the debilitating effects of slavery, racism, and economic exploitation. The Black family developed different forms according to the different situations it encountered, and variations in sexual and marital practices evolved out of the social heritage of slavery and the social class level of individual families in the Black community.

For those of us who regard Frazier as the most eminent sociologist of all time, the final paragraph is most disenchanting, as he writes that the survival of the Afro-American in American civilization is a measure of his success in adopting the culture of whites. But Frazier wrote that almost twenty years ago. In 1962, just before his death, he wrote:

> The African intellectual recognizes what colonialism has done to the African and he sets as his first task the mental, moral, and spiritual rehabilitation of the African.
>
> But the American Negro intellectual, seduced by dreams of final assimilation, has never regarded this as his primary task.[2]

Frazier's study is especially important not only because of his thorough research but also because it was one of the early works dealing with the Black family.

---

[1] Cf. Gwendolyn Midlo Hall, "The Myth of Benevolent Spanish Slave Law," *Negro Digest*, 19 (February 1970), pp. 31–38.

[2] E. Franklin Frazier, "The Failure of the Negro Intellectual," *Negro Digest* (February 1961), p. 35.

Some of the reasons for this neglect of the Black family in American scholarship are discussed in the excerpt from Billingsley's book *Black Families in White America*. He reports that scholars have ignored the Black family by virtue of their European ethnocentrism and the nature of their professional disciplines. In the studies that have been undertaken, the Black family has usually been examined in terms of a form of social pathology rather than in terms of the normal functioning of most stable Black families.

The selection by Daniel P. Moynihan could be viewed as the apotheosis of research on the Black family as a pathological form of social organization. The selection is taken from the famous and controversial Moynihan Report, *The Negro Family: The Case for National Action*, which was written during the period Billingsley describes as the era of emphasis on poverty; and since Blacks were conspicuous among the poor, researchers focused on them and searched for explanations of their poverty. As in the case of the ill-fated war on poverty, Moynihan and the poverty experts found the reasons for poverty residing in the maladaptation of the poor to the normative means for achieving the socially acceptable goals of American society. In Moynihan's case, his major theme was that "at the heart of the deterioration of the fabric of Negro society is the deterioration of the Negro family."

Moynihan attempts to document his major proposition by citing statistics on the dissolution of Black marriages, the high rate of Black illegitimate births, the prevalence of female-headed households among Blacks, and the way in which the deterioration of the Black family has led to an increase in welfare dependency.

Statistics aside, however, the larger implications of the Moynihan Report are ominous. Because it was an official government publication, it could be viewed as a reflection of the political state's stance on dealing with the effects of racism and exploitation of the Black community. In these terms, the Report makes the criminal the victim and the victim the criminal. For a society which has systematically denied equal opportunity to its Black citizens to then cite the results of its act as the cause of their oppression is hypocrisy in the grossest sense.

Two articles reprinted here, one by William Ryan and the other by Laura Carper, provide critiques of the Moynihan Report. According to Ryan, poor methodology is a principal weakness of the Report; it took at face value the Census Bureau statistics on illegitimacy rates for whites at about 3 percent and for Blacks at about 22 percent—a 7 to 1 difference. When racial differences in reporting illegitimate births, shotgun marriages, abortions, and contraception are taken into account, the ratio drops to a more realistic 2 to 1. In addition, he cites other fallacies in the Report, such as obvious misstatements of fact and the gross error of interpreting statistical relationships in cause-and-effect terms.

The article by Carper cites further weaknesses of the Moynihan Report. For instance, the increase in welfare dependency could easily be attributed to more liberal welfare laws rather than the putative breakdown of the Black family. She adds new dimension to criticisms of Moynihan's study in noting

Moynihan's description of the therapeutic effects of military service. His study does not contain a plan for action, but mass enlistment could hardly be one. With a Black casualty rate double that of whites in the war in Vietnam, increasing the number of Blacks in the Armed Services suggests that the solution for Black poverty is the elimination of the Black poor. While Moynihan's intentions are obviously not so nefarious, nor does Carper's article imply they are, it demonstrates his inability to comprehend the esoteric nature of Black family life and to put forth relevant suggestions for reducing or eliminating poverty in the Black community.

1

General Background

Stanley M. Elkins: Slavery in Capitalist and Noncapitalist Cultures

The four major legal categories which defined the status of the American slave may be roughly classified as "term of servitude," "marriage and the family," "police and disciplinary powers over the slave" and "property and other civil rights." The first of these, from which somehow all the others flowed, had in effect been established during the latter half of the seventeenth century; a slave was a slave for the duration of his life, and slavery was a status which he transmitted by inheritance to his children and his children's children.

It would be fairest, for several reasons, to view the remaining three categories in terms of the jurisprudence of the nineteenth century. By that time the most savage aspects of slavery from the standpoint of Southern practice (and thus, to a certain extent, of law) had become greatly softened. We may accordingly see it in its most humane light and at the same time note the clarity with which its basic outlines remained fixed and embodied in law, much as they had been laid down before the middle of the eighteenth century.

From *Slavery: A Problem in American Institutional and Intellectual Life* (Chicago: University of Chicago Press, 1968), pp. 52-55 and 72-74. Footnotes have been renumbered. Copyright © 1968, The University of Chicago. Stanley M. Elkins is Professor of History at Smith College. Reprinted by permission of the publisher and the author.

That most ancient and intimate of institutional arrangements, marriage and the family, had long since been destroyed by the law, and the law never showed any inclination to rehabilitate it. Here was the area in which considerations of humanity might be expected most widely to prevail, and, indeed, there is every reason to suppose that on an informal daily basis they did: the contempt in which respectable society held the slave trader, who separated mother from child and husband from wife, is proverbial in Southern lore. On the face of things, it ought to have been simple enough to translate this strong social sentiment into the appropriate legal enactments, which might systematically have guaranteed the inviolability of the family and the sanctity of the marriage bond, such as governed Christian polity everywhere. Yet the very nature of the plantation economy and the way in which the basic arrangements of Southern life radiated from it made it inconceivable that the law should tolerate any ambiguity, should the painful clash between humanity and property interest ever occur. Any restrictions on the separate sale of slaves would have been reflected immediately in the market; their price would have dropped considerably. Thus the law could permit no aspect of the slave's conjugal state to have an independent legal existence outside the power of the man who owned him: "The relation of master and slave is wholly incompatible with even the qualified relation of husband and wife, as it is supposed to exist among slaves . . . ."[1] Marriage, for them, was denied any standing in law. Accordingly, as T. R. R. Cobb of Georgia admitted, "The contract of marriage not being recognized among slaves, none of its consequences follow . . . ."[2] "The relation between slaves," wrote a North Carolina judge in 1858, "is essentially different from that of man and wife joined in lawful wedlock . . . [for] with slaves it may be dissolved at the pleasure of either party, or by the sale of one or both, depending on the caprice or necessity of the owners."[3]

It would thus go without saying that the offspring of such "contubernial relationships," as they were called, had next to no guaranties against indiscriminate separation from their parents.[4] Of additional interest is the fact that children derived their condition from that of their mother. This was not unique to American slavery, but it should be noted that especially in a system conceived and evolved exclusively on grounds of property there

---

[1] *Howard v. Howard*, 6 Jones N.C. 235 (December, 1858), quoted in Helen T. Catterall, *Judicial Cases concerning American Slavery and the Negro* (Washington: Carnegie Institution, 1926 ff.), II, 221.

[2] Thomas R. R. Cobb, *An Inquiry into the Law of Slavery in the United States of America* (Philadelphia: T. & J. W. Johnson, 1858), p. 246.

[3] Quoted in Catterall, *Judicial Cases*, II, 221.

[4] The few exceptions—none of which meant very much in practice, except perhaps the law of Louisiana—are discussed in Bancroft, *Slave-trading*, pp. 197–221. "Louisiana, least American of the southern States," writes Mr. Bancroft, "was least inhuman. In becoming Americanized it lost many a liberal feature of the old French *code noir*, but it forbade sale of mothers from their children less than ten years of age (and *vice versa*) and bringing into the State any slave child under ten years of age without its mother, if living. The penalty for violating either prohibition was from $1,000 to $2,000 and the forfeiture of the slave. That would have meant much if it had been strictly enforced" (p. 197). Louisiana's Spanish and French background, plus the fact that in both the legal and social senses slavery in Latin America generally was very different from slavery in North America, may furnish significant clues to some of the idiosyncrasies in the Louisiana code. See below.

could be little doubt about how such a question would be resolved. Had status been defined according to the father's condition—as was briefly the case in seventeenth-century Maryland, following the ancient common law—there would instantly have arisen the irksome question of what to do with the numerous mulatto children born every year of white planter-fathers and slave mothers. It would have meant the creation of a free mulatto class, automatically relieving the master of so many slaves on the one hand, while burdening him on the other with that many colored children whom he could not own. Such equivocal relationships were never permitted to vex the law. That "the father of a slave is unknown to our law" was the universal understanding of Southern Jurists.[5] It was thus that a father, among slaves, was legally "unknown," a husband without the rights of his bed,[6] the state of marriage defined as "only that concubinage . . . with which alone, perhaps, their condition is compatible,"[7] and motherhood clothed in the scant dignity of the breeding function.[8] . . .

Neither in Brazil nor in Spanish America did slavery carry with it such precise and irrevocable categories of perpetual servitude, *"durante vita"* and "for all generations," as in the United States. The presumption in these countries, should the status of a colored person be in doubt, was that he was free rather than a slave.[9] There were in fact innumerable ways whereby a slave's servitude could be brought to an end. The chief of these was the very considerable fact that he might buy his own freedom. The Negro in Cuba or Mexico had the right to have his price declared and could, if he wished, purchase himself in installments. Slaves escaping to Cuba to embrace Catholicism were protected by a special royal order of 1733 which was twice reissued. A slave unduly punished might be set at liberty by the magistrate. In Brazil the slave who was the parent of ten children might legally demand his or her freedom.[10] The medieval Spanish code had made a slave's service terminable under any number of contingencies—if he denounced cases of treason, murder, counterfeiting, or the rape of a virgin, or if he performed various other kinds of meritorious acts. Though all such practices did not find their way into the seventeenth- and eighteenth-century legal arrangements of Latin America, much of their spirit was perpetuated in the values,

---

[5] *Frazier* v. *Spear*, 2 Bibb (Ken.), 385 (Fall, 1811), quoted in Catterall, *Judicial Cases*, I, 287.

[6] "A slave has never maintained an action against the violator of his bed. A slave is not admonished for incontinence, or punished for fornication or adultery; never prosecuted for bigamy, or petty treason for killing a husband being a slave, any more than admitted to an appeal for murder." Opinion of Daniel Dulany, Esq., Attorney-General of Maryland, quoted in William Goodell, *The American Slave Code in Theory and Practice* (New York: American and Foreign Anti-Slavery Society, 1853), pp. 106–107.

[7] *State* v. *Samuel (a slave)*, 2 Dev. and Bat. (N.C.), 177 (December, 1836), quoted in Catterall, *Judicial Cases*, II, 77.

[8] The picturesque charge that planters deliberately "bred" their slave women has never been substantiated, and Avery Craven's point that white women bred about as young and as often as their black sisters is a sensible one. But with no law to prevent the separation of parents and children, and with the value of a slave being much in excess of what it cost to rear him, the temptation to think and talk about a prolific Negro woman as a "rattlin' good breeder" was very strong.

[9] "In the Cuban market freedom was the only commodity which could be bought untaxed; every negro against whom no one had proved a claim of servitude was deemed free . . . ." William Law Mathieson, *British Slavery and Its Abolition* (London: Longmans, Green, 1926), pp. 37–38.

[10] Johnston, *Negro in the New World*, p. 89.

customs, and social expectations of that later period. It is important to appreciate the high social approval connected with the freeing of slaves. A great variety of happy family events—the birth of a son, the marriage of a daughter, anniversaries, national holidays—provided the occasion, and their ceremonial was frequently marked by the manumission of one or more virtuous servitors. It was considered a pious act to accept the responsibility of becoming godfather to a slave child, implying the moral obligation to arrange eventually for its freedom. Indeed, in Cuba and Brazil such freedom might be purchased for a nominal sum at the baptismal font.[11] All such manumissions had the strong approval of both church and state and were registered gratis by the government.[12]

In extending its moral authority over men of every condition, the church naturally insisted on bringing slave unions under the holy sacraments. Slaves were married in church and the banns published; marriage was a sacred rite and its sanctity protected in law. In the otherwise circumspect United States, the only category which the law could apply to conjugal relations between slaves—or to unions between master and slave—was concubinage. But concubinage, in Latin America, was condemned as licentious, adulterous, and immoral; safeguards against promiscuity were provided in the law,[13] and in Brazil the Jesuits labored mightily to regularize the libertinage of the master class by the sacrament of Christian marriage.[14] Moreover, slaves owned by different masters were not to be hindered from marrying, nor could they be kept separate after marriage. If the estates were distant, the wife was to go with her husband, and a fair price was to be fixed by impartial persons for her sale to the husband's master.[15] A slave might, without legal interference, marry a free person. The children of such a marriage, if the mother were free, were themselves free, inasmuch as children followed the condition of their mother.[16]

[11] What I have said in this paragraph is virtually a paraphrase of the information which Mr. Tannenbaum has collected and so skillfully summarized on pp. 50, 53–54, 57–58 of *Slave and Citizen.*

[12] Johnston, *Negro in the New World,* p. 42.

[13] "The master of slaves must not allow the unlawful intercourse of the two sexes, but must encourage matrimony." Spanish slave code of 1789, quoted in *ibid.,* p. 44. Although slaves were allowed "to divert themselves innocently" on holy days, the males were to be kept apart from the females. *Ibid.,* p.44.

[14] Freyre, *The Masters and the Slaves,* p. 85.

[15] Johnston, *Negro in the New World,* pp. 44–45. A diocesan synod of 1680 in Cuba issued weighty regulations on this subject which were supposed to supplement and have equal force with civil law. "Constitution 5 established that 'marriage should be free' and ordered that 'no master prohibit his slaves from marriage, nor impede those who cohabit therein, because we have found that many masters with little fear of God and in grave danger of their consciences, proscribe their slaves from marrying or impede their cohabitation with their married partners, with feigned pretexts'; and also prohibited 'that they go away to sell them outside the city, without that they take together husband and wife.' " Ortiz, *Los Negros Esclavos,* p. 349. The church even made some concessions here to African tribal marriage arrangements, to the extent that a slave with multiple wives might—if the first-married wife's identity could not be ascertained—pick out the one he preferred and have his marriage with her solemnized under the sacraments. *Ibid.,* p. 349.

[16] Tannenbaum, *Slave and Citizen,* p. 56.

E. Franklin Frazier: The Negro Family in America

The evolution of the Negro family in the United States has a special significance for the science of culture. Within the short space of 150 years, the Negro family has telescoped the age-long evolution of the human family.[1] On the basis of concrete factual materials it is possible to trace the evolution of the Negro family from its roots in human nature to a highly institutionalized form of human association. During the course of its evolution, the Negro family has been forced to adjust itself to different forms of social organization and to the stresses and strains of modern civilization. In studying the adjustments which the Negro family has made to these changes, it is possible to gain a clearer understanding of the relation of human motivations to culture. Moreover, the evolution of Negro family life not only has provided additional evidence of the primary importance of the family in the transmission of culture but also has shown the role of the family in the building of new cultures.

Under the Institution of Slavery

As a result of the manner in which the Negro was enslaved, the Negro's African cultural heritage has had practically no effect on the evolution of his family life in the United States. The slave traders along the coast of Africa who were primarily interested in healthy young Negroes—generally males—had no regard for family relationships. In fact, the human cargo which they collected were the remnants of various tribes and clan organizations. The manner in which men and women were packed indiscriminately in slave ships during the Middle Passage tended to destroy social bonds and tribal distinctions. Then the process of "breaking" the Negroes into the slave system in the West Indies, where they often landed before shipment to the colonies and the United States, tended to efface the memories of their traditional culture. In the colonies and later in the southern United States, the slaves were widely scattered on comparatively small plantations where there was little opportunity to reknit social bonds or regenerate the African culture.

Doubtless memories of African culture regarding mating survived, but these memories became meaningless in the New World. The mating or sexual associations which Negroes formed on American soil were largely in response to their natural impulses and the conditions of the new environ-

From pp. 65–79, 82–84 in "The Negro Family in America" by E. Franklin Frazier. From *The Family: Its Function and Destiny*, Revised Edition, edited by Ruth N. Anshen. Copyright © 1949 by Harper & Brothers. Copyright © 1959 by Ruth Nanda Anshen. Reprinted by permission of Harper & Row, Publishers, Inc. Before his death in 1962, Dr. Frazier was Chairman of the Department of Sociology, Howard University, Washington, D.C.

[1] See the writer's *The Negro Family in the United States*, Chicago, University of Chicago Press, 1939.

ment. There was, first, a lack of females in the slave population until the 1830's, and this caused the slaves in some sections to seek satisfaction of their sexual hunger among Indian women. Then there was the discipline of the plantation or the arbitrary will of the masters which regulated sexual association and the selection of mates among the slaves. Thus it came about that sexual selection and mating were no longer culturally defined or regulated by African mores.

Nevertheless, there was selection of mates on the basis of spontaneous impulses and mutual attraction. There was the wooing of females by males who attempted to win their favor by gifts and expressions of affection. The stability of these matings was dependent largely upon the temperaments of the mates and the strength of the mutual attraction and affection. Where the mates were inclined or were permitted to live together as husband and wife, mutual sympathies and understanding developed as the result of habitual association. Pregnancy and offspring sometimes resulted in the breaking of bonds, but they often provided a new bond of sympathy and common interest. A common interest in the relationship was more likely to develop where there were mutual services and the sharing of benefits, as for example in the cultivation of a garden. Under such conditions the Negro family acquired the character of a natural organization in that it was based primarily upon human impulses and individual wishes rather than upon law and the mores.

Under favorable conditions the family as a natural organization developed considerable stability during slavery. The first requirement for stable family life among the slaves was, of course, that the family groups should not be broken up through sale or arbitrary action on the part of the masters. Where the plantation became a settled way of life and a social as well as an economic institution, the integrity of the slave family was generally respected by the masters. Moreover, the social relations which grew up facilitated the process by which the Negro took over the culture of the whites. The close association between whites and Negroes, often from childhood, enabled the slaves to take over the language, manners, and ideas of the masters. These close contacts were enjoyed by the slaves who worked in and about the master's house. On many plantations the masters provided religious and moral instruction for the slaves. The moral supervision included, in some cases at least, the chaperonage of the female slaves. It was through those channels that the white man's ideas and sentiments in regard to sex and family relations were communicated to the slaves. These cultural advantages, which were restricted mainly to the house servant, became the basis of social distinctions among the slaves. The house servants enjoyed a certain prestige in the slave society which grew up about the Negro quarters.

In the division of labor on the plantation there was some opportunity for the expression of talents and intelligence. This was especially true in regard to the black mechanics who were so necessary to the maintenance of self-sufficiency on the plantation. Often it was the son of a favored house servant who was apprenticed to a craftsman to learn a trade. In becoming a skilled craftsman or mechanic the intellectual powers as well as the manual dexterity of the slave were improved. In addition, because of his skill he was accorded recognition by the master and acquired a higher status among the slaves. The recognition which was accorded the personality of the skilled craftsman was reflected in his pride in his workmanship. What was more important was that it was a moralizing influence which was reflected in the family life of the skilled artisans. The skilled mechanic often assumed the conventional role of husband and father and was recognized as the head of his family. The fruits of his skill, so far as a premium was placed upon good performance, were often shared with his family. Consequently, these family groups, which were without the support of law, often achieved the solidarity and stability of a legally sanctioned family.

The development of family life described above represents the development of the slave family under the most favorable conditions. Among the vast majority of slaves, the Negro mother remained the most stable and dependable element during the entire period of slavery. Despite a benevolent master, the slave family was often dispersed when the plantation was sold or an estate was settled. With indifferent or cruel masters the slave family was constantly being broken up and its members scattered. But in either case some regard had to be shown for the bond between the Negro mother and her children. The masters' economic interest in the survival of the children caused them to recognize the dependence of the young children upon the mother. Then, too, the master, whether out of humanity or self-interest, was compelled to respect the mother's often fierce attachment to her children. Wherever the charge that slave mothers were indifferent to their offspring has any factual support it can be explained by the forced pregnancies and harsh experiences attending motherhood. Most of the evidence indicates that the slave mother was devoted to her children and made tremendous sacrifices for their welfare. She was generally the recognized head of the family group. She was the mistress of the cabin, to which the "husband" or father often made only weekly visits. Under such circumstances a maternal family group took form and the tradition of the Negro woman's responsibility for her family took root.

The development of the maternal family among the slaves was further encouraged by the sexual association between blacks and whites. In the cities, where slaves moved about freely and there were many free Negroes, the sexual relations between Negro women and white men were casual and often of a debased character. But it was not only in the cities that the races mixed. Although there is no way of measuring the extent of the sexual association between slaveholders and slaves, there is abundant evidence of concubinage and polygamy on the part of the masters. The character of the sexual associations between the two races ran the gamut of human relationships. At one extreme the slave woman or Negro woman was used to satisfy a fleeting impulse. At the other extreme the sexual association was supported by personal attachment and deep sentiment. In the latter case, the white father in rare instances might assume the role of a father which lacked only a legal sanction. Nevertheless, because of the ideas and sentiments embodied in the institution of slavery, the Negro or mulatto mother remained the responsible and stable head of the family group. On the other hand, it was from such associations that the free Negro population continued to increase until the Civil War.

The Family among the Free Negroes

The free Negro population increased steadily from the time when Negroes were first introduced into the Virginia colony in 1619. For three or four decades the servitude of the Negroes was limited to seven years, as in the case of white servants. Even after the status of the Negro servants became one of perpetual servitude, or slavery, the free Negro population continued to increase. The increase in the free Negro population came from five sources: (1) children born of free colored parents; (2) mulatto children born of free colored mothers; (3) mulatto children born of white servants and of free white women; (4) children of free Negro and Indian parentage; and (5) manumitted slaves.[2] Although it is not possible to know the increase in the free Negro population through each of these sources, it appears that the manumission of slaves was relatively the most important source. Slaves achieved freedom through manumission both because of the action of their owners and because of their own efforts. A large number of the white fathers emancipated their mulatto offspring; as a result about three-eighths of the free Negroes were mulattoes, as compared with only one-twelfth of the slave population. In numerous cases the white fathers provided for the economic welfare and education of their colored offspring. Slaves were able to become free through their own efforts especially in Maryland, Virginia, and North Carolina, where the economic basis of slavery was being undermined. In these areas skilled artisans were permitted to hire out their time and save enough money to buy their freedom. Whether they were freed because of their relation to their white masters or because of their own efforts, the free Negroes possessed certain cultural advantages which were reflected in their family life.

It was among the free Negroes that the family first acquired an institutional character. This was possible primarily because the free Negroes were able to establish family life on a secure economic foundation. In the southern cities the free Negroes had a secure position in the economic organization. Partly on the basis of wealth and occupation, a class system emerged among the free Negroes. Among the wealthier free colored families in Louisiana and in Charleston, some of whom were themselves slaveholders, the family was similar to that of the white slaveholders. It was patriarchal in organization and the status of women was similar to that of the women among the white slaveholding class. Moreover, these families were founded upon traditions which had been built up over several generations. Those traditions were a measure, in a sense, of the extent to which the Negro had assimilated the American cultural heritage.

[2] John H. Russell, *The Free Negro in Virginia*, Baltimore, Johns Hopkins University Press, 1913, pp. 40–41.

It has already been pointed out how the house servants and the slave artisans had been able because of their favored position to take over American culture. Here it should be pointed out how the free Negroes, who had come largely from these groups, incorporated the American culture and transmitted it through their families to succeeding generations. Because of their relationship to the white race the mulattoes generally had a conception of themselves different from that of the pure-blooded Negro. Where they were favored by their white fathers, the close association with their fathers or their position in the household enabled them to take over the attitudes and sentiments as well as the overt behavior of the father. As freedmen with some economic competence or with a mechanical skill which afforded a good income, they were able to maintain a way of life that accorded with their conception of themselves and with the patterns of behavior taken over from the whites. This led to the beginning of an institutional life within the free colored communities similar to that in the white communities. The free Negroes established schools, churches, literary societies, and organizations for mutual aid. The families with traditions formed the core of the organized social life in the free Negro communities. Not only did these families give support to the institutional life, but they were supported in turn by the institutions of the community. Although it is true that because of social isolation the culture of the free Negroes became provincial and ingrown, it nevertheless provided a heritage for their children.

Civil War and Emancipation

The Civil War and emancipation created a crisis in the family life of the Negro. This crisis affected the free Negro as well as the slave family. It tended to destroy whatever stability the slave family had achieved under the slave regime. It tore the free Negro family from its moorings in a society where it occupied a privileged position. The distinction between slave and free was wiped out. How did the Negro family meet this crisis? How was its organization and stability influenced by its new relation to American culture? How, specifically, was its role or function in mediating American culture to the Negro affected by the Negro's new relation to American life? These are some of the questions which we shall attempt to answer in the present chapter.

As the Union armies penetrated the South, the plantation regime was disrupted and the slaves were uprooted from their customary way of life. Thousands of Negroes flocked to army camps and to the cities; thousands joined the march of Sherman to the sea. The disorder and confusion were a test of the strength and character of family ties. In many cases the family ties which were supported only by habit and custom were broken. Negro men deserted their families and even some Negro mothers deserted their children. On the other hand, many fathers took their families with them when they went in search of freedom. Many Negroes went in search of relatives from whom they had been separated through sale while they were slaves. Throughout this chaotic situation, the Negro mother held the family group together and supported her children. This devotion was based partly upon her traditional role and partly upon the deep emotional attachment to her young that was evoked in the face of danger.

The northern missionaries who went south to establish schools and hospitals and to assist the Negro during his first steps in freedom were faced with the problems of the Negro family. They encouraged the Negro to get a legal sanction for his marital relations and to settle down to orderly monogamous marriage. They had to contend with the confusion which slavery had caused by the selling away of "husbands" who returned to claim "wives" who had "married" other men. Then there was the problem of giving the Negro husband and father a status in family relations which he had not enjoyed during slavery. The missionaries depended chiefly upon exhortation and moralizing to establish conventional marital and familial relations among the freedmen. These methods had some effect but they did not determine the future development of the Negro family. The course of that development was determined by the dominant economic and social forces in the South as well as by the social heritage of the freedmen.

When conditions became settled in the South the landless and illiterate freedman had to secure a living on a modified form of the plantation system. Concessions had to be made to the freedman in view of his new status. One of the concessions affected the family organization. The slave quarters were broken up and the Negroes were no longer forced to work in gangs. Each family group moved off by itself to a place where it could lead a separate existence. In the contracts which the Negroes made with their landlords, the Negro father and husband found a substantial support for his new status in family relations. Sometimes the wife as well as the husband made her cross for her signature to the contract, but more often it was the husband who assumed responsibility for the new economic relation with the white landlord. Masculine authority in the family was even more firmly established when the Negro undertook to buy a farm. Moreover, his new economic relationship to the land created a material interest in his family. As the head of the family he directed the labor of his wife and children and became concerned with the discipline of his children, who were to succeed him as owners of the land.

As the result of emancipation the Negro was thrown into competition with the poor whites. At the same time he became estranged from the former slaveholding class, and the sympathetic relations which had been built up during slavery were destroyed. Since the nature of the contacts between whites and blacks was changed, the character of the process of acculturation was changed. The estrangement between the whites and blacks was inevitable when the color caste was established in the South. If the democratic aims set up during the Reconstruction Period had been achieved, this estrangement would not have occurred. But where race was made the basis of status the Negroes in defense withdrew from the whites and suspected even their attempts to help the freedmen. Consequently, there came into existence two separate social worlds and, as far as spatial separation permitted, two separate communities. Since the Negro's personal life was oriented toward the separate Negro world, he derived his values from that world. The patterns of behavior and ideals which he took over from the white man were acquired generally through formal imitation of people outside his social world. In their social isolation the majority of Negroes were forced to draw upon the meager social heritage which they had acquired during slavery.

In the world of the Negro folk in the rural areas of the South, there grew up a family system that met the needs of the environment. Many of the ideas concerning sex relations and mating were carried over from slavery. Consequently, the family lacked an institutional character, since legal marriage and family traditions did not exist among a large section of the population. The family groups originated in the mating of young people who regarded sex relations outside of marriage as normal behavior. When pregnancy resulted, the child was taken into the mother's family group. Generally the family group to which the mother belonged had originated in a similar fashion. During the disorder following slavery a woman after becoming pregnant would assume the responsibility of motherhood. From time to time other children were added to the family group through more or less permanent "marriage" with one or more men. Sometimes the man might bring his child or children to the family group, or some orphaned child or the child of a relative might be included. Thus the family among a large section of the Negro population became a sort of amorphous group held together by the feelings and common interests that might develop in the same household during the struggle for existence.

From the standpoint of marriage statistics the rural Negro population has shown a large percentage of illegitimacy. But these statistics have little meaning if they are not related to the folkways regarding sex and marriage relations which have grown up in those isolated rural areas. The type of sex and marital relations which have been described does not indicate that sex relations have been promiscuous and free from controls. There has been, in the first place, the general recognition of the obligation of the mother to her children. In fact, pregnancy has been regarded as a phase of the maturing or fulfillment of the function of a woman. On the other hand, marriage meant subordination to a man or the formation of a new type of relationship. Often, therefore, when a girl became pregnant and the man wanted to marry her, the girl's mother objected. Later the girl might marry the father of her child or some other man. But this meant forming a partnership in working a farm together and assuming other obligations. In a society of this type the mother continued to occupy a dominant position in the family. The grandmother enjoyed an even more important position and has always been a leading figure in the Negro family.

Statistics have always shown a large number of Negro families with women as heads. These statistics have reflected the conditions described above. It appears that about 10 percent of the Negro families in the rural areas, as compared with about 30 percent in urban areas, have had women as heads. This difference is doubtless due to the fact that in the rural areas of the South the Negro man and the woman with her children need each other more in the struggle for existence than do those in the city. In fact, the stability of these family groups in the rural areas has depended largely upon the coöperation of man and woman in the struggle for a livelihood. As the result of this coöperation, deep sentiments and attachments have developed not only between spouses but also between the fathers and their children. This has caused these family groups to have on the whole the stability of conventional family groups.

Not all rural Negro communities in the South have been characterized by the simple mores described above. The rural Negro communities have differed greatly, the differences being dependent upon both economic and cultural factors. Where, outside the plantation area, the Negro has been able to acquire land and a higher economic status, the family has achieved an organization closely resembling the American pattern. The economic factor, however, has not been the sole determinant of this difference. In the areas outside the plantation region the Negro has never been so isolated biologically, mentally, and socially as in that section. Dating from the time of slavery, the Negro in those outside areas, as we have pointed out, has lived in closer association with the whites and has enjoyed some opportunity for self-development. When the Negro began his career as a freedman, therefore, he had a richer cultural heritage as well as a greater opportunity for economic development than the Negro in the plantation South. Nevertheless, the high percentage of landownership among the families outside the plantation area has provided a basis for a stable family life. As we have seen, it has encouraged the growth of a patriarchal family system. Moreover, the church and other institutions in these communities have supported conventional family mores. Illegitimacy and unlegalized marriage relations have not been tolerated as among the isolated plantation folk.

The progressive stabilization of Negro family life continued throughout the nineteenth century and during the first decade of the twentieth. This process was associated with a gradual increase in home and landownership and has involved the intermarriage of the stable elements among the descendants of free Negroes with the more ambitious and successful freedmen with a background of slavery. The descendants of the free Negroes brought to these unions a rich cultural heritage, and the ambitious descendants of slaves brought new aspirations and a new outlook on life. Out of this process there emerged a class stratification of the Negro population which was based largely upon social distinctions, the principal one of which was the tradition of a stable and conventional family life. In placing a high value upon a stable and conventional family life, these elements in the Negro population were safeguarding the chief means through which the gains of the Negro in civilization were preserved and transmitted to future generations.

Urbanization and Negro Family Life

So far the discussion of the Negro family has been concerned mainly with the family in the agricultural South, where nine-tenths of the Negro population was concentrated until the first decade of the present century. Around the opening of the century the drift of rural Negroes to southern cities had begun to attract attention. Then came the mass migrations to northern cities during and following the First World War, and these dramatized the accelerated urbanization of the Negro population.

In the hundreds of towns and cities of the South, the Negro family had taken shape and the rural folk culture was attempting to adjust itself to new conditions. Many Negro women had been attracted to these urban areas because of the chance to gain a living in domestic service. Sometimes they carried their illegitimate as well as their legitimate offspring with them. The freedom from familial and community controls sometimes meant the sloughing off of the responsibilities of motherhood, and the sexual freedom of the rural areas lost much of its harmless character. Sex expression tended to become a purely individualistic affair in which the hedonistic element became the chief end. Yet the family continued to survive among the majority of the population in these towns and cities. Here its maternal character was even more conspicuous than among the rural folk, not only as a result of the high rate of illegitimacy but also because of desertion on the part of the male head of the family. Amid the general demoralization of family life in these urban areas, there were enclaves of families which because of deeply rooted traditions maintained conventional family life and held themselves aloof from the masses.

The effects of an urban environment upon the Negro family were accentuated among the masses who migrated to the metropolitan areas of the North. The inadequacy of the sex and familial folkways and mores which had given stability to life in the rural South was revealed in the problems of the Negro family in the city. First, there was the problem of illegitimacy. As we have seen, illegitimacy was not necessarily a social problem among the isolated folk in the rural South. It did not violate the mores and the ideal of motherhood, for there women enjoyed a certain social sanction in any case. In an urban environment sex and motherhood were given a new social definition. The bearing of children was an economic burden which placed a handicap upon the mother as well as upon the family group in the severe struggle for existence. Then, too, the community, through neighbors, schoolteachers, social workers, and others, frowned upon unmarried motherhood and defined it as immoral. As a consequence the unmarried mother's behavior lost its naive character. Her growing sophistication with the ways of city life, together with the economic burden of childbearing and the moral disapproval of the community, changed her attitude toward motherhood. Although this resulted in much demoralization, it should not be overlooked that the new stimuli of the city awakened the imagination of men and women, and the romantic element became involved in the sex experience.

Desertion on the part of the husband and father has been another serious problem of the Negro family in the city. In the rural South fathers had often deserted their families when they had gone to work in turpentine and lumber camps or in the cities. When Negroes began migrating to the North, it was sometimes the man who went first, with the idea of sending for his wife and children. Once in the environment of the city, however, the father or husband developed new interests and formed new sexual associations. Even when the husband or father brought his wife or family to the city, he often deserted them. Though in many cases of desertion the couple had not been legally married, nevertheless desertion on the part of the man was equivalent to the breaking of marital ties. Desertion meant that the community of interests and the sympathies which had held families together in the rural South were dissolved in the cities. Moreover, the social control exercised by the church and lodge and neighborhood opinion no longer existed in the city. Desertion revealed one of the chief weaknesses of this type of family: the absence of family traditions deeply rooted in the mores of the group. The informal breaking of legal marriage ties and the confused notions concerning the marital status and divorce tended to emphasize how much the family folkways of the migrants differed from the American mores governing marital relations.

The inadequacy of the type of family organization to which the migrant was accustomed resulted in much juvenile delinquency. Although juvenile delinquency in our cities is primarily a community problem, the widespread juvenile delinquency among the children of Negro migrants has resulted largely from the failure of the family. The poverty of the Negro has required many mothers to seek employment outside the home. As we have pointed out, in a third of the Negro families in the cities the mother has been the sole head of the family. Consequently, Negro children have been denied the supervision of their parents. Even in families where the father has been present, there has been no cultural heritage that could be communicated to the children. The folk culture, which these families have brought from the South, lost its meaning in the cities of the North. However much these families attempted to isolate their children from the influences of the cities, they could not prevent them from being affected by the public school.

Although the public school has contributed to the disorganization of the Negro folk culture in the city, it has also brought the Negro into contact with the larger American culture and thereby helped in the reorganization of his family life. The reorganization of family life, however, has not been achieved merely by the acquisition of new ideas concerning family life. The new ideas have only become effective in behavior when they were related to changed economic and social conditions. In the northern metropolis the occupational differentiation of the Negro population has been accelerated. As the Negro man has become an industrial worker and has no longer been dependent entirely upon domestic service and casual unskilled labor, he has become subject to a discipline that has affected his home life. The fact that he has received a higher and a more steady remuneration has enabled him to assume full responsibility for the support of his family. As a consequence, he has received more recognition as the head of the family and as such has taken more interest in his children, whom he has wanted to see "get ahead" as a result of greater educational opportunities. . . .

The Negro Family and Modern Civilization

Although this discussion has been concerned with the Negro family in American civilization, it has a broader significance. The problems which the Negro family has encountered in its development involve problems of acculturation and assimilation which other peoples as well as Negroes must face today as a result of the impact of Western civilization. In the United States Negroes are placed in a peculiar position with reference to Western civilization because they were practically stripped of their traditional culture. Consequently, there was scarcely any opportunity for cultural conflicts to develop in the United States as in other parts of the world.[3] However, as the result of the emergence of a new middle class among American Negroes, their changing relation to American society involves problems of culture and personality which are related to the family.

The character of the Negro family during the various stages of its development has been affected by the social isolation of Negroes in American society. The lack of opportunity for the Negro male to participate freely in the economic organization and his subordination to whites as well as the general exclusion of Negroes from political activities have all affected the organization and the functioning of the Negro family. This has entailed a waste of human life and human energy. It represents in a sense the price which the Negro has been forced to pay in order to survive in American society. But this survival has not been the survival of a biological group but of a sociologically defined group. And it has been the family which has assured the survival of the Negro in American society.

The emergence of a new middle class is evidence of the increasing integration of the Negro in American society. However, the increasing integration of the Negro has brought into relief problems of culture and personality. The new middle class is without roots because it is increasingly cutting itself loose from its roots in the segregated Negro community. Moreover, it still has no social roots in the white community since it has not become identified with the white middle class. Consequently, middle-class Negroes are experiencing considerable conflict and frustration, and this is being reflected in Negro families. What social heritage can Negro parents pass on to their children? What group identification can they provide their children? Sociologically, these conflicts and frustrations are manifesting themselves in social disorganization and personal disorganization. Formerly social and personal disorganization was confined almost exclusively to lower-class Negroes but increasingly the problems resulting from disorganization are manifesting themselves among middle-class Negroes.

The survival of the Negro in American civilization is a measure, in a sense, of his success in adopting the culture of the whites or an indication of the fact that the Negro has found within the white man's culture a satisfying

[3] See for example, I. Schapera, *Western Civilization and the Natives of South Africa*, London, George Routledge & Sons, 1934.

life and a faith in his future. His future survival in a highly mobile and
urbanized society will be on a different basis. In the large metropolitan
communities of the North, Negroes are increasingly intermarrying with
whites. Thus the Negro family is incorporating new traditions, and the
children of mixed marriages have a new view on American life. As the result
of these developments the Negro will have to face greater stresses in his
personal life, and the segregated groups and institutions will no longer provide an adequate refuge in the white man's world. During all these changes
and crises the family will continue to play an important role in transmitting
the new conception which the Negro will acquire of himself and of his place
in American society.

Andrew Billingsley: The Treatment
of Negro Families in American
Scholarship

... The Negro family as an institution has been virtually ignored by
students of group life in America. The principal reason for this failure
seems to be associated with the fact that studies in this area, like those in
other areas of human life, are as highly influenced by the political, religious,
and philosophical ideologies of the authors, as by any concern with social
relevance or any more general spirit of scientific inquiry. Scholars have been
steered away from the study of the Negro family by their own European
ethnocentrism and by the nature of their professional disciplines. When
they have treated the Negro family, they have done so in a negativistic and
distorted fashion for the same reasons. In this chapter we examine some of
the sources of ignorance and distortion in the treatment of Negro families
by American scholarship. Our hope is that we may clear the way for more
accurate and meaningful perception. . . .

On the whole, scholars in each of these areas have found it convenient to
turn to matters other than the Negro family. Not that the family—or the
Negro people in general—has been ignored in such studies. On the contrary,
these are two of the most extensively researched and discussed areas of
American life. But for reasons both historical and contemporary in nature,
the two areas of study, the family and the Negro, have not come together for
more than minimal consideration. The reasons lie deeper than the selective
interests and rewards of individual scholars. They lie in the nature of these
broad fields of study themselves. . . .

It would seem most logical that studies of the American family include
some reference to Negro family life. However, a recent anthology contain-
ing fifty-two family studies has only one which treats the Negro family, and

Andrew Billingsley, *Black Families in White America*, © 1968. Reprinted by permission of Prentice-Hall,
Inc., Englewood Cliffs, New Jersey. Footnotes have been renumbered. Dr. Billingsley is Assistant Chancellor
for Academic Affairs and Associate Professor of Social Welfare at the University of California, Berkeley.

that one is Frazier's, written in 1939. It is not simply that only one article is devoted exclusively to Negro families; one reads all the other articles in vain (some of which are not bound by ethnic focus) looking for any reference to Negro families as part of the general discussion of American family patterns.[1]

An equally extensive, highly respected, and widely used compendium of case studies in family law has only one paper devoted to Negro families, and that one is focused almost exclusively on the problem of illegitimacy.[2] These two volumes are unusual in giving even that amount of attention to Negro families. Two tendencies, then, are current in studies of American families. The first, and most general, is to ignore Negro families altogether. The second is to consider them only insofar as they may be conceived as a social problem. In a symposium on The Negro Family at the University of California at Berkeley a few years ago, after a nationally known sociologist referred repeatedly to the "problem of the Negro family," a Negro wife and mother rose and took him to task. "Why do you always consider us a problem?" she demanded. "I don't consider myself a problem." The sociologist was undaunted. He didn't know why she needed to be so defensive. Thus, despite the fact that the vast majority of Negro families are stable, conforming, and achieving, and cause no problems to anybody, the tendency to view them in negative terms persists. The Negro historian Benjamin Quarles recently observed that "When we pick up a social science book, we look in the index under 'Negro,' it will read, 'see Slavery,' 'see Crime,' 'see Juvenile Delinquency,' perhaps 'see Commission on Civil Disorders'; perhaps see anything except the Negro. So when we try to get a perspective on the Negro, we get a distorted perspective"[3]. . . .

Family sociology in America was born in the late nineteenth century when social Darwinism held sway.[4] During this period the focus was not on contemporary family life at all, but on earlier more primitive forms. The underlying assumption was that contemporary European family forms represented a natural evolution and had reached a certain stage of perfection. The idea was to search among primitive peoples for the earlier forms of family life, so that the evolutionary process could be traced and the sources of such perfection established. Scholars argued about whether original family relationships were monogamous or polygamous, and found evidence for both in historical documents and oral traditions. They were concerned with whether earlier forms of family structure had been essentially matriarchal or patriarchal, and again found evidence for both.

However vigorously scholars pursued the study of the natural evolution of the family, and however vehemently they argued among themselves, it is

[1] Norman W. Bell and Ezra F. Vogel, eds., *A Modern Introduction to the Family* (New York: The Free Press, 1960).

[2] Caleb Foote, Robert J. Levy, and Frank E. A. Sander, *Case Studies and Materials on Family Law* (Boston: Little, Brown and Company, 1966).

[3] Benjamin Quarles, *Jet Magazine*, XXXIII, No. 12 (December 28, 1967), p. 32.

[4] Bell and Vogel, pp. 3–5.

strikingly clear that there was no room in such scholarship for concern with Negro family life. For in the United States in the latter part of the nineteenth century, the Negro family had no recognized institutional existence. Freshly released from slavery, the Negro people were struggling to find a place in the wider society, with various degrees of help and obstruction from that society. The dominant focus was on politics and economics in the most basic sense, with no appreciable concern for social integration in any form, and certainly none for family integration. Both Negroes and whites were concerned mainly with survival—the survival of the Negro people, the survival of the southern way of life, and the survival of the republic.

Because there was almost no focus on contemporary family life, and because the Negro people, as a free people, were considered to be extremely contemporary, it is little wonder that Negro family life was so completely ignored. And if some scholars saw that the origin of man was somewhat bound up with the origin and development of group life as represented by the family, it would certainly be the origin and development of the white man which would be studied, and not that of the "primitive" black people in their midst. For in the late nineteenth century, whatever the contribution of the abolitionists, the Civil War victors, and the reconstructionists, none of these liberal groups succeeded in comprehending the essential humanness shared by black and white people alike. All of "the liberals" proceeded on the assumption that the black people was another people, quite apart from the rest of society, though deserving of special help and a certain, though limited, degree of freedom.

A second phase of family studies, stimulated by conditions of *poverty*, focused on the conditions of life faced by contemporary families. These studies grew out of the early twentieth century liberal humanitarian movements, and are represented by the studies of Roundtree and the Webbs of England. Many surveys were conducted to document the conditions of "life and labor" of the working classes in the cities of Europe and America. Such studies were continued in the United States, particularly as economic adversity struck the industrial communities of America, which were being peopled by immigrant families from Europe.

While earlier family studies had focused on primitive groups, these focused on poverty groups and were almost exclusively concerned with economic conditions affecting family life. No attention was paid to the broader set of relationships between family life and community life, or to the place of family life in the wider society. These studies concentrated on the urban poor and consequently ignored Negro family life, for around the turn of the century Negroes were still not an urban industrial force. They were essentially rural peasants located in the deep South.

In many respects, many of the studies of family life conducted during this period were predecessors of some of the current commentary on Negro families. They depended on secondary rather than on first-hand data and were usually statistical in form. Moreover, they concentrated on various forms of deviant behavior which were believed to be results of breakdown in family life. These included divorce rates, crime rates, illegitimacy rates, death rates, and various health statistics. There are indeed some striking parallels between those early poverty studies focused on other ethnic minorities and current studies focused on Negroes.

The 1920s ushered in a third phase of family studies. Poverty seemed somewhat under control, or at least it was pushed from the headlines by the burgeoning prosperity. Scholars of family life began to turn their attention to some of the problems faced by *middle class families*. This period of inquiry may be termed the psychological phase, for many of these studies were concerned with the dominant themes of "adjustment" and "individual happiness." Despite the growth of the middle class in America, economic well-being was not sufficient to guarantee these psychological values. Middle class families began to discover that they had problems of personal—and particularly sexual—adjustment. The study of family life shifted dramatically during this period to the study of middle class family life, and the problems of psychological functioning associated with these families. Not only Freud, but also the social psychological studies of George H. Mead and the sociological studies of the Burgesses reflected this concern.

Again, Negro families were left out. For while they were becoming increasingly urban after the great migrations in 1914 to 1918, and while they were indeed concentrated in industrial towns and cities of the South and North, the industrial poverty phase of family studies had passed. The new thing was to study the problems of family life among the middle classes, and Negroes, alas, were not yet middle class in any appreciable numbers. Furthermore, and not unrelated to this fact, they were not yet perceived as having psychological and sexual problems to the extent and degree of refinement that white middle class families had them. The European emigrants had discovered that neither a certain degree of assimilation nor economic well-being solved all the problems of existence and family life. Native whites made a similar discovery, thanks to the insights of psychoanalysis. But Negroes were not yet to be admitted into these private circles of family life education lectures, private psychiatric treatment, and studies of family structure and function. For Negroes were still engaged in the struggle for economic survival, and students of family life had already passed through this stage, along with the more prosperous white segments of the society.

The years 1930 to 1940 were the golden age for studies of Negro life; the best studies of Negro family life available today were done during that period. These were years of tremendous political activity. For the first time in nonwar years, what happened in Washington vastly affected every segment of American life. For the first time since Reconstruction, Negroes became an important political force. Negroes were now so transplanted from the rural South and so concentrated in key industrial areas they could not be ignored in the political efforts to save American society from the economic disaster ushered in with 1929. Consequently, as the eyes of the nation turned to a reconstruction of the whole society, including the Negro elements, scholarship turned in a similar direction. Students of family life thus discovered the Negro family.

If the first factor which accounts for this discovery is broadly social—in the sense that the whole society, including all of its important elements, was in trouble and deserved to be studied—the second factor was the emergence of Negro scholars, who could not ignore the Negro family precisely for the same reasons that white scholars could and did. It was during these years, with generous support from white institutions, that Negro scholars, sometimes in active collaboration with white scholars, produced some of the most important studies of Negro family life. Chicago was the focus of sociological inquiry. during this period, and from there arrived E. Franklin Frazier's study of *The Negro Family in Chicago*,[5] to be followed toward the end of the decade by his *The Negro Family in the United States*.[6] A few years later there appeared the monumental study of Drake and Cayton, *Black Metropolis*,[7] which has large sections on Negro family life. In addition, the comprehensive series of studies on Negro youth commissioned by the American Council on Education[8] has not since been equaled. These studies, conducted in each of the major sections of the country, developed a great body of information on Negro family life. In addition to his work with the American Council on Education, Charles S. Johnson conducted a long series of studies of Negro life in rural America, making a significant contribution to the study of family life among Negroes.[9] Thus during this period a handful of Negro social scientisits, including W. E. B. DuBois, Charles S. Johnson, Allison Davis, St. Clair Drake, Horace Cayton, E. Franklin Frazier, and Ira Reid, joined by a dozen or so white scholars centered mainly around Chicago, including Louis Wirth, Munro Edmonson, John H. Roehr, Robert L. Park, John Dollard, and W. L. Warner, produced the bulk of social science scholarship about Negro family life.

But in the period running roughly from 1940 to 1960, students of American society had other matters demanding their attention. There was the war to explain, the unprecedented industrialization, the accompanying bureaucratization of society. Along with this, there was the new psychoanalytic revolution, a new and growing prosperity, social class considerations, mental health, and large interest in child rearing practices in the American family. Consequently, it was only with the new emphasis on poverty ushered in during the early 1960s that social scientists again discovered the Negro family. Now they became increasingly aware that not only war and prosperity, but poverty as well, seemed destined to be fixed factors in our social life.

[5] E. Franklin Frazier, *The Negro Family in Chicago* (Chicago: University of Chicago Press, 1932).

[6] E. Franklin Frazier, *The Negro Family in the United States* (Chicago: University of Chicago Press, 1939).

[7] St. Clair Drake and Horace R. Cayton, *Black Metropolis*, rev. ed. (New York: Harper & Row, Publishers, 1962).

[8] Allison Davis and John Dollard, *Children of Bondage* (New York: American Council on Education and Harper & Row, Publishers, 1940). Other studies in this series are: E. Franklin Frazier, *Negro Youth at the Crossway* (1940); Charles S. Johnson, *Growing Up in the Black Belt* (1941); W. Lloyd Warner, Buford H. Junker, and Walter A. Adams, *Color and Human Nature* (1941); Ira De Augustine Reid, *In a Minor Key: Negro Youth in Story and Fact* (1940).

[9] Charles S. Johnson, *Shadow of the Plantation* (Chicago: University of Chicago Press, 1934).

The incongruity of it all forced a reexamination, both of the social fabric of the larger and now international society and of the inner workings of our own pluralistic society.

When we took a fresh look at poverty, we observed that Negroes were conspicuous among the poor, though they constituted less than a third of the total poor people in this country. But by now we were armed with statistical techniques which helped us to see that Negroes were over-represented among the poor. We therefore focused on them, and searched for explanations. By now we also knew the connections between family life and the broader social context, including economic, political, and educational advancement.

It is perhaps a peculiarly American quality to look for single causes of complex phenomena. It was amazingly convenient to explain poverty by ignoring the total poverty picture and explaining only Negro poverty, for in this way one could avoid some of the more troubling aspects of the Negro experience, aside from poverty—namely, persistent prejudice and discrimination based on race. Seeking to explain only *Negro* poverty, one could conveniently ignore the mass of causal factors and focus on the Negro people themselves, their leadership, their psychological motivation and aspirations, their family structure, and, in a flash of superficial enlightenment, their history of slavery. The Negro family, therefore, came in for some scholarly attention. But this attention has been directed to only that "half" of Negro families in the lower class, and even more specifically, that "third" of Negro families below the poverty line, or that "quarter" of Negro families headed by women, or that "tenth" of Negro families with illegitimate children, or that even smaller proportion of Negro families which combine these three conditions and are supported by public welfare.

For it must be said with all candor that the social scientists who have recently discovered the Negro family have not yet produced a study of that 75 percent of Negro families who have stable marriages, or that half of Negro families who have managed to pull themselves into the middle class, or that 90 percent of all Negro families who are self-supporting, or that even larger portion who manage to keep out of trouble, often despite the grossest kinds of discrimination and provocation. It would be very instructive indeed to know how two thirds of all Negro families with less than $2,000 annual income in 1966 could manage to hold themselves together and meet the American test of family stability. For surely that is the statistic which needs explaining, rather than the minority of poor families where the man disappears in order to let the family survive economically. In addition, some understanding of how this majority of Negro families manages can help provide clues for the rehabilitation of other families, and at the same time can enlighten the society about the problems these Negro families still face.

The major reason for this selective focus on the negative aspects of Negro family life is that scholars do not yet seem to be interested in the Negro family as an institution for its own sake, and for what an understanding of it can tell us about our society. Studies so far which have focused on Negro family life in the lower class, problem-ridden sectors are not concerned at all with Negro family life. They are concerned, instead, with poverty, family breakdown, and illegitimacy, and somehow tie these phenomena to the Negro experience. This seems to obviate, for a time at least, the urgent need to explain these phenomena in the larger white society, where they are far more numerous. Perhaps if it can be said convincingly enough that people are in these conditions because they have been enslaved and still have a slave mentality, and because they have been discriminated against because of their race—all of which are true enough—then scholars and social reformers can avoid, for a few more years, looking for causes of these phenomena in the normal workings of our society—particularly in the workings of the upper reaches of our financial, industrial, military, educational, political, and religious institutions. This can postpone, for a time, the possible revelation that these pathologies may be endemic to our society, and are therefore normative and structural—not merely functions of individual, psychological, and subcultural hangups.

Fortunately, there is already emerging a small but growing literature on Negro families which takes these families seriously in their own right and does not treat them essentially as deviants from white norms. Outstanding among this new literature is the work of Jessie Bernard,[10] Hylan Lewis and his associates,[11] Lee Rainwater and his associates in St. Louis,[12] Joan Gordon in Harlem,[13] and a number of unpublished works.

[10] Jessie Bernard, *Marriage and Family among Negroes* (Englewood Cliffs, N.J.: Prentice-Hall, Inc., 1966).

[11] Hylan Lewis, "Changing Perceptions of Race, Class, Culture, and Social Welfare." Paper presented at Institute on Research toward Improving Race Relations, Airlie House, Warrenton, Va., August 1967. See also Lewis's introduction to Camille Jeffers' *Living Poor* (Ann Arbor: Ann Arbor Publishers, 1967), and Elliott Liebow, *Tally's Corner* (Boston: Little, Brown and Company, 1966).

[12] Lee Rainwater, "Crucible of Identity: The Negro Lower-Class Family," *Daedalus* (Winter 1966).

[13] Joan Gordon, *The Poor of Harlem: Social Functioning in the Underclass* (New York: Office of the Mayor, Interdepartmental Neighborhood Service Center, July 31, 1965).

2

The Moynihan Report:
Challenge and Response

Daniel P. Moynihan: The Tangle of
Pathology

That the Negro American has survived at all is extraordinary—a lesser people might simply have died out, as indeed others have. That the Negro community has not only survived, but in this political generation has entered national affairs as a moderate, humane, and constructive national force is the highest testament to the healing powers of the democratic ideal and the creative vitality of the Negro people.

But it may not be supposed that the Negro American community has not paid a fearful price for the incredible mistreatment to which it has been subjected over the past three centuries.

In essence, the Negro community has been forced into a matriarchal structure which, because it is so out of line with the rest of the American society, seriously retards the progress of the group as a whole, and imposes a crushing burden on the Negro male and, in consequence, on a great many Negro women as well.

There is, presumably, no special reason why a society in which males are dominant in family relationships is to be preferred to a matriarchal arrangement. However, it is clearly a disadvantage for a minority group to be

Reprinted from *The Negro Family: The Case for National Action*, by the Office of Policy Planning and Research, United States Department of Labor (U.S. Government Printing Office, March 1965), pp. 29–44. Daniel P. Moynihan is Urban Affairs Adviser to the President of the United States.

operating on one principle, while the great majority of the population, and the one with the most advantages to begin with, is operating on another. This is the present situation of the Negro. Ours is a society which presumes male leadership in private and public affairs. The arrangements of society facilitate such leadership and reward it. A subculture, such as that of the Negro American, in which this is not the pattern, is placed at a distinct disadvantage.

Here an earlier word of caution should be repeated. There is much evidence that a considerable number of Negro families have managed to break out of the tangle of pathology and to establish themselves as stable, effective units, living according to patterns of American society in general. E. Franklin Frazier has suggested that the middle-class Negro American family is, if anything, more patriarchal and protective of its children than the general run of such families.[1] Given equal opportunities, the children of these families will perform as well or better than their white peers. They need no help from anyone, and ask none.

While this phenomenon is not easily measured, one index is that middle-class Negroes have even fewer children than middle-class whites, indicating a desire to conserve the advances they have made and to insure that their children do as well or better. Negro women who marry early to uneducated laborers have more children than white women in the same situation; Negro women who marry at the common age for the middle class to educated men doing technical or professional work have only four-fifths as many children as their white counterparts.

Children Born per Woman Age 35 to 44: Wives of Uneducated Laborers who Married Young, Compared with Wives of Educated Professional Workers who Married after Age 21, White and Nonwhite, 1960*

	Children per Woman	
	White	Nonwhite
Wives married at age 14 to 21 to husbands who are laborers and did not go to high school	3.8	4.7
Wives married at age 22 or over to husbands who are professional or technical workers and have completed 1 year or more of college	2.4	1.9

*Wives married only once, with husbands present.
Source: 1960 Census, *Women by Number of Children Ever Born*, PC(2) 3A, Tables 39 and 40, pp. 199–238.

It might be estimated that as much as half of the Negro community falls into the middle class. However, the remaining half is in desperate and deteriorating circumstances. Moreover, because of housing segregation it is immensely difficult for the stable half to escape from the cultural influences of the unstable one. The children of middle-class Negroes often as not must grow up in, or next to the slums, an experience almost unknown to white

[1] E. Franklin Frazier, *Black Bourgeoisie* (New York, Collier Books, 1962).

middle-class children. They are therefore constantly exposed to the pathology of the disturbed group and constantly in danger of being drawn into it. It is for this reason that the propositions put forth in this study may be thought of as having a more or less general application.

In a word, most Negro youth are in *danger* of being caught up in the tangle of pathology that affects their world, and probably a majority are so entrapped. Many of those who escape do so for one generation only: as things now are, their children may have to run the gauntlet all over again. That is not the least vicious aspect of the world that white America has made for the Negro.

Obviously, not every instance of social pathology afflicting the Negro community can be traced to the weakness of family structure. If, for example, organized crime in the Negro community were not largely controlled by whites, there would be more capital accumulation among Negroes, and therefore probably more Negro business enterprises. If it were not for the hostility and fear many whites exhibit towards Negroes, they in turn would be less afflicted by hostility and fear and so on. There is no one Negro community. There is no one Negro problem. There is no one solution. Nonetheless, at the center of the tangle of pathology is the weakness of the family structure. Once or twice removed, it will be found to be the principal source of most of the aberrant, inadequate, or antisocial behavior that did not establish, but now serves to perpetuate the cycle of poverty and deprivation.

It was by destroying the Negro family under slavery that white America broke the will of the Negro People. Although that will has reasserted itself in our time, it is a resurgence doomed to frustration unless the viability of the Negro family is restored.

Matriarchy

A fundamental fact of Negro American family life is the often reversed roles of husband and wife.

Robert O. Blood, Jr., and Donald M. Wolfe, in a study of Detroit families, note that "Negro husbands have unusually low power,"[2] and while this is characteristic of all low income families, the pattern pervades the Negro social structure: "the cumulative result of discrimination in jobs . . . , the segregated housing, and the poor schooling of Negro men."[3] In 44 percent of the Negro families studied, the wife was dominant, as against 20 percent of white wives. "Whereas the majority of white families are equalitarian, the largest percentage of Negro families are dominated by the wife."[4]

The matriarchal pattern of so many Negro families reinforces itself over

---

[2] Robert O. Blood, Jr., and Donald M. Wolfe, *Husbands and Wives: The Dynamics of Married Living* (New York, The Free Press, 1960), p. 34.

[3] *Ibid.* p. 35.

[4] *Ibid.*

the generations. This process begins with education. Although the gap appears to be closing at the moment, for a long while, Negro females were better educated than Negro males, and this remains true today for the Negro population as a whole.

Educational Attainment of the Civilian Noninstitutional Population 18 Years of Age and Over, March 1964

Color and Sex	Median School Years Completed
White:	
Male	12.1
Female	12.1
Nonwhite:	
Male	9.2
Female	10.0

Source: Bureau of Labor Statistics, unpublished data.

The difference in educational attainment between nonwhite men and women in the labor force is even greater; men lag 1.1 years behind women.

The disparity in educational attainment of male and female youth age 16 to 21 who were out of school in February 1963, is striking. Among the nonwhite males, 66.3 percent were not high school graduates, compared with 55.0 percent of the females. A similar difference existed at the college level, with 4.5 percent of the males having completed 1 to 3 years of college compared with 7.3 percent of the females.

The poorer performance of the male in school exists from the very beginning, and the magnitude of the difference was documented by the 1960 Census in statistics on the number of children who have fallen one or more grades below the typical grade for children of the same age. The boys have more frequently fallen behind at every age level. (White boys also lag behind white girls, but at a differential of 1 to 6 percentage points.)

Percent of Nonwhite Youth Enrolled in School Who Are 1 or More Grades below Mode for Age, by Sex, 1960

Age	Male	Female
7 to 9 years old	7.8	5.8
10 to 13 years old	7.8	5.8
14 and 15 years old	35.5	24.8
16 and 17 years old	39.4	27.2
18 and 19 years old	57.3	46.0

Source: 1960 Census, *School Enrollment*, PC(2) 5A, Table 3, p. 24.

In 1960, 39 percent of all white persons 25 years of age and over who had completed 4 or more years of college were women. Fifty-three percent of the nonwhites who had attained this level were women.

However, the gap is closing. By October 1963, there were slightly more

Negro men in college than women. Among whites there were almost twice as many men as women enrolled.

There is much evidence that Negro females are better students than their male counterparts.

Daniel Thompson of Dillard University, in a private communication on January 9, 1965, writes:

> As low as is the aspirational level among lower class Negro girls, it is considerably higher than among the boys. For example, I have examined the honor rolls in Negro high schools for about 10 years. As a rule, from 75 to 90 percent of all Negro honor students are girls.

Dr. Thompson reports that 70 percent of all applications for the National Achievement Scholarship Program financed by the Ford Foundation for outstanding Negro high school graduates are girls, despite special efforts by high school principals to submit the names of boys.

Fall Enrollment of Civilian Noninstitutional Population in College by Color and Sex, October 1963 (in Thousands)

Color and Sex	Population, Age 14–34, Oct. 1, 1963	Number Enrolled	Percent of Youth, Age 14–34
Nonwhite			
Male	2,884	149	5.2
Female	3,372	137	4.1
White			
Male	21,700	2,599	12.0
Female	20,613	1,451	7.0

Source: U.S. Bureau of the Census, *Current Population Reports*, Series P-20, No. 129, July 24, 1964, Tables 1, 5.

The finalists for this new program for outstanding Negro students were recently announced. Based on an inspection of the names, only about 43 percent of all the 639 finalists were male. (However, in the regular National Merit Scholarship program, males received 67 percent of the 1964 scholarship awards.)

Inevitably, these disparities have carried over to the area of employment and income.

In 1 out of 4 Negro families where the husband is present, is an earner, and some one else in the family works, the husband is not the principal earner. The comparable figure for whites is 18 percent.

More important, it is clear that Negro females have established a strong position for themselves in white collar and professional employment, precisely the areas of the economy which are growing most rapidly, and to which the highest prestige is accorded.

The President's Committee on Equal Employment Opportunity, making a preliminary report on employment in 1964 of over 16,000 companies with nearly 5 million employees, revealed this pattern with dramatic emphasis.

In this work force, Negro males outnumber Negro females by a ratio of 4 to 1. Yet Negro males represent only 1.2 percent of the males in white collar occupations, while Negro females represent 3.1 percent of the total female white collar work force. Negro males represent 1.1 percent of all male professionals, whereas Negro females represent roughly 6 percent of all female professionals. Again, in technician occupations, Negro males represent 2.1 percent of all male technicians while Negro females represent roughly 10 percent of all female technicians. It would appear therefore that there are proportionately 4 times as many Negro females in significant white collar jobs than Negro males.

Although it is evident that office and clerical jobs account for approximately 50 percent of all Negro female white collar workers, it is significant that 6 out of every 100 Negro females are in professional jobs. This is substantially similar to the rate of all females in such jobs. Approximately 7 out of every 100 Negro females are in technician jobs. This exceeds the proportion of all females in technician jobs— approximately 5 out of every 100.

Negro females in skilled jobs are almost the same as that of all females in such jobs. Nine out of every 100 Negro males are in skilled occupations while 21 out of 100 of all males are in such jobs.[5]

This pattern is to be seen in the Federal government, where special efforts have been made recently to insure equal employment opportunity for Negroes. These efforts have been notably successful in Departments such as Labor, where some 19 percent of employees are now Negro. (A not disproportionate percentage, given the composition of the work force in the areas where the main Department offices are located.) However, it may well be that these efforts have redounded mostly to the benefit of Negro women, and may even have accentuated the comparative disadvantage of Negro men. Seventy percent of the Negro employees of the Department of Labor are women, as contrasted with only 42 percent of the white employees.

Among nonprofessional Labor Department employees—where the most employment opportunities exist for all groups—Negro women outnumber Negro men 4 to 1, and average almost one grade higher in classification.

The testimony to the effects of these patterns in Negro family structure is widespread, and hardly to be doubted.

Whitney Young

Historically, in the matriarchal Negro society, mothers made sure that if one of their children had a chance for higher education, the daughter was the one to pursue it.[6]

The effect on family functioning and role performance of this historical experience [economic deprivation] is what you might predict. Both as a husband and as a father the Negro male is made to feel inadequate, not because he is unlovable or

---

[5] Based on preliminary draft of a report by the President's Committee on Equal Employment Opportunity.

[6] Whitney Young, *To Be Equal* (New York, McGraw-Hill Book Company, 1964), p. 25.

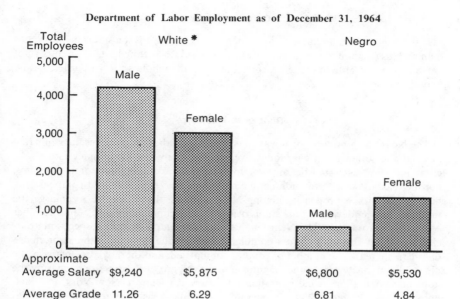

Department of Labor Employment as of December 31, 1964

Total Employees	White *		Negro	
Approximate Average Salary	$9,240	$5,875	$6,800	$5,530
Average Grade	11.26	6.29	6.81	4.84

*This is non-Negro and may include some nonwhites other than Negro.

unaffectionate, lacks intelligence or even a gray flannel suit. But in a society that measures a man by the size of his pay check, he doesn't stand very tall in a comparison with his white counterpart. To this situation he may react with withdrawal, bitterness toward society, aggression both within the family and racial group, self-hatred, or crime. Or he may escape through a number of avenues that help him to lose himself in fantasy or to compensate for his low status through a variety of exploits.[7]

Thomas Pettigrew

The Negro wife in this situation can easily become disgusted with her financially dependent husband, and her rejection of him further alienates the male from family life. Embittered by their experiences with men, many Negro mothers often act to perpetuate the mother-centered pattern by taking a greater interest in their daughters than their sons.[8]

Deton Brooks

In a matriarchal structure, the women are transmitting the culture.[9]

[7] *Ibid.*, p. 175.

[8] Thomas F. Pettigrew, *Profile of the Negro American* (New York: Van Nostrand, 1964), p. 16.

[9] Deton Brooks, quoted in *The New Improved American* by Bernard Asbell (New York, McGraw-Hill Book Company, 1965), p. 76.

Dorothy Height

If the Negro Woman has a major underlying concern, it is the status of the Negro man and his position in the community and his need for feeling himself an important person, free and able to make his contribution in the whole society in order that he may strengthen his home.[10]

Duncan M. MacIntyre

The Negro illegitimacy rate always has been high—about eight times the white rate in 1940 and somewhat higher today even though the white illegitimacy rate also is climbing. The Negro statistics are symptomatic of some old socioeconomic problems, not the least of which are underemployment among Negro men and compensating higher labor force propensity among Negro women. Both operate to enlarge the mother's role, undercutting the status of the male and making many Negro families essentially matriarchal. The Negro man's uncertain employment prospects, matriarchy, and high cost of divorces combine to encourage desertion (the poor man's divorce), increase the number of couples not married, and thereby also increase the Negro illegitimacy rate. In the meantime, higher Negro birth rates are increasing the nonwhite population, while migration into cities like Detroit, New York, Philadelphia, and Washington, D.C., is making the public assistance rolls in such cities heavily, even predominantly, Negro.[11]

Robin M. Williams, Jr., in a Study of Elmira, New York

Only 57 percent of Negro adults reported themselves as married—spouse present, as compared with 78 percent of native white American gentiles, 91 percent of Italian-American, and 96 percent of Jewish informants. Of the 93 unmarried Negro youths interviewed, 22 percent did not have their mother living in the home with them, and 42 percent reported that their father was not living in their home. One-third of the youths did not know their father's present occupation, and two-thirds of a sample of 150 Negro adults did not know what the occupation of their father's father had been. Forty percent of the youths said that they had brothers and sisters living in other communities; another 40 percent reported relatives living in their home who were not parents, siblings, or grandparents.[12]

The Failure of Youth

Williams' account of Negro youth growing up with little knowledge of their fathers, less of their fathers' occupations, still less of family occupational traditions, is in sharp contrast to the experience of the white child. The white family, despite many variants, remains a powerful agency not

---

[10] Dorothy Height, in the Report of Consultation on Problems of Negro Women, President's Commission on the Status of Women, April 19, 1963, p. 35.

[11] Duncan M. MacIntyre, *Public Assistance: Too Much or Too Little?* (New York, New York State School of Industrial Relations, Cornell University, Bulletin 53-1, December 1964), pp. 73–74.

[12] Robin M. Williams, Jr., *Strangers Next Door* (Englewood Cliffs, N.J., Prentice-Hall, Inc., 1964), p. 240.

only for transmitting property from one generation to the next, but also for transmitting no less valuable contracts with the world of education and work. In an earlier age, the Carpenters, Wainwrights, Weavers, Mercers, Farmers, Smiths acquired their names as well as their trades from their fathers and grandfathers. Children today still learn the patterns of work from their fathers even though they may no longer go into the same jobs.

White children without fathers at least perceive all about them the pattern of men working.

Negro children without fathers flounder—and fail.

Not always, to be sure. The Negro community produces its share, very possibly more than its share, of young people who have the something extra that carries them over the worst obstacles. But such persons are always a minority. The common run of young people in a group facing serious obstacles to success do not succeed.

A prime index of the disadvantage of Negro youth in the United States is their consistently poor performance on the mental tests that are a standard means of measuring ability and performance in the present generation.

There is absolutely no question of any genetic differential: Intelligence potential is distributed among Negro infants in the same proportion and pattern as among Icelanders or Chinese or any other group. American society, however, impairs the Negro potential. The statement of the HAR-YOU report that "there is no basic disagreement over the fact that central Harlem students are performing poorly in school"[13] may be taken as true of Negro slum children throughout the United States.

By the 8th Grade, Central Harlem Pupils' Average IQ Was 87.7 Compared to the National Norm of 100

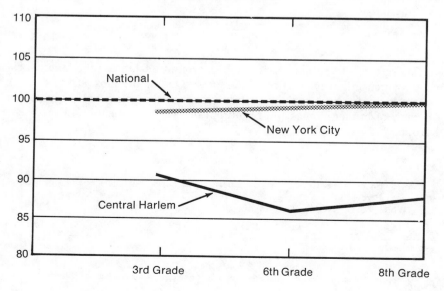

[13] *Youth in the Ghetto, op cit.*, p. 195.

Eighth grade children in central Harlem have a median IQ of 87.7, which means that perhaps a third of the children are scoring at levels perilously near to those of retardation. IQ *declines* in the first decade of life, rising only slightly thereafter.

The effect of broken families on the performance of Negro youth has not been extensively measured, but studies that have been made show an unmistakable influence.

Martin Deutch and Bert Brown, investigating intelligence test differences between Negro and white 1st and 5th graders of different social classes, found that there is a direct relationship between social class and IQ. As the one rises so does the other: but more for whites than Negroes. This is surely a result of housing segregation, referred to earlier, which makes it difficult for middle-class Negro families to escape the slums.

The authors explain that "it is much more difficult for the Negro to attain identical middle- or upper-middle-class status with whites, and the social class gradations are less marked for Negroes because Negro life in a caste society is considerably more homogeneous than is life for the majority group."[14]

Mean Intelligence Scores of Negro Children by School, Grade, Social Class, and by Presence of Father

Social Class and School Grade	Father Present	Father Absent
Lowest social class level:		
Grade 1	95.2	87.8
Grade 5	92.7	85.7
Middle social class level:		
Grade 1	98.7	92.8
Grade 5	92.9	92.0

Adapted from author's table.

Therefore, the authors look for background variables other than social class which might explain the difference: "One of the most striking differences between the Negro and white groups is the consistently higher frequency of broken homes and resulting family disorganization in the Negro group."[15]

Father Absent from Home

Lowest Social Class Level Percent of		Middle Social Class Level Percent of		Highest Social Class Level Percent of	
White	Negro	White	Negro	White	Negro
15.4	43.9	10.3	27.9	0.0	13.7

Adapted from authors' table.

[14] Martin Deutch and Bert Brown, "Social Influences in Negro-White Intelligence Differences," *Social Issues*, April 1964, p. 27.

[15] *Ibid.*, p. 29.

Further, they found that children from homes where fathers are present have significantly higher scores than children in homes without fathers.

	Mean Intelligence Scores
Father present	97.83
Father absent	90.79

The influence of the father's presence was then tested *within* the social classes and school grades for Negroes alone. They found that "a consistent trend within both grades at the lower SES [social class] level appears, and in no case is there a reversal of this trend: for males, females, and the combined group, the IQ's of children with fathers in the home are always higher than those who have no father in the home."[16]

Percent of Nonwhite Males Enrolled in School, by Age and Presence of Parents, 1960

Age	Both Parents Present	One Parent Present	Neither Parent Present
5 years	41.7	44.2	34.3
6 years	79.3	78.7	73.8
7 to 9 years	96.1	95.3	93.9
10 to 13 years	96.2	95.5	93.0
14 and 15 years	91.8	89.9	85.0
16 and 17 years	78.0	72.7	63.2
18 and 19 years	46.5	40.0	32.3

Source: 1960 Census, *School Enrollment*, PC(2) 5A, Table 3, p. 24.

The authors say that broken homes "may also account for some of the differences between Negro and white intelligence scores."[17]

The scores of fifth graders with fathers absent were lower than the scores of first graders with fathers absent, and while the authors point out that it is cross sectional data and does not reveal the duration of the fathers' absence, "What we might be tapping is the cumulative effect of fatherless years."[18]

This difference in ability to perform has its counterpart in statistics on actual school performance. Nonwhite boys from families with both parents present are more likely to be going to school than boys with only one parent present, and enrollment rates are even lower when neither parent is present.

When the boys from broken homes are in school, they do not do as well as the boys from whole families. Grade retardation is higher when only one parent is present, and highest when neither parent is present.

The loneliness of the Negro youth in making fundamental decisions about education is shown in a 1959 study of Negro and white dropouts in Connecticut high schools.

[16] *Ibid.*

[17] *Ibid.*, p. 31.

[18] *Ibid.*

Only 29 percent of the Negro male dropouts discussed their decision to drop out of school with their fathers, compared with 65 percent of the white males (38 percent of the Negro males were from broken homes). In fact, 26 percent of the Negro males did not discuss this major decision in their lives with anyone at all, compared with only 8 percent of white males.

A study of Negro apprenticeship by the New York State Commission Against Discrimination in 1960 concluded:

> Negro youth are seldom exposed to influences which can lead to apprenticeship. Negroes are not apt to have relatives, friends, or neighbors in skilled occupations. Nor are they likely to be in secondary schools where they receive encouragement and direction from alternate role models. Within the minority community, skilled Negro "models" after whom the Negro youth might pattern himself are rare, while substitute sources which could provide the direction, encouragement, resources, and information needed to achieve skilled craft standing are nonexistent.[19]

Percent of Nonwhite Males Enrolled in School Who Are 1 or More Grades below Mode for Age, by Age Group and Presence of Parents, 1960

Age Group	Both Parents Present	One Parent Present	Neither Parent Present
7–9 years	7.5	7.7	9.6
10–13 years	23.8	25.8	30.6
14–15 years	34.0	36.3	40.9
16–17 years	37.6	40.9	44.1
18–19 years	60.6	65.9	46.1

Source: 1960 Census, *School Enrollment*, PC(2) 5A, Table 3, p. 24.

Delinquency and Crime

The combined impact of poverty, failure, and isolation among Negro youth has had the predictable outcome in a disastrous delinquency and crime rate.

In a typical pattern of discrimination, Negro children in all public and private orphanages are a smaller proportion of all children than their proportion of the population although their needs are clearly greater.

On the other hand Negroes represent a third of all youth in training schools for juvenile delinquents.

Children in Homes for Dependent and Neglected Children, 1960

	Number	Percent
White	64,807	88.4
Negro	6,140	8.4
Other races	2,359	3.2
All races	73,306	100.0

Source: 1960 Census, *Inmates of Institutions*, PC(2) 3A, Table 31, p. 44.

[19] "Negroes in Apprenticeship, New York State," *Monthly Labor Review,* September 1960, p. 955.

It is probable that at present, a majority of the crimes against the person, such as rape, murder, and aggravated assault are committed by Negroes. There is, of course, no absolute evidence; inference can only be made from arrest and prison population statistics. The data that follow unquestionably are biased against Negroes, who are arraigned much more casually than are whites, but it may be doubted that the bias is great enough to affect the general proportions.

Number of Arrests in 1963

	White	Negro
Offenses charged total	31,988	38,549
Murder and nonnegligent manslaughter	2,288	2,948
Forcible rape	4,402	3,935
Aggravated assault	25,298	31,666

Source: *Crime in the United States* (Federal Bureau of Investigation, 1963), Table 25, p. 111.

Again on the urban frontier the ratio is worse: 3 out of every 5 arrests for these crimes were of Negroes.

In Chicago in 1963, three-quarters of the persons arrested for such crimes were Negro; in Detroit, the same proportions held.

In 1960, 37 percent of all persons in Federal and State prisons were Negro. In that year, 56 percent of the homicide and 57 percent of the assault offenders committed to State institutions were Negro.

Number of City Arrests in 1963*

	White	Negro
Offenses charged total	24,805	35,520
Murder and nonnegligent manslaughter	1,662	2,593
Forcible rape	3,199	3,570
Aggravated assault	19,994	29,357

*In 2,892 cities with population over 2,500.
Source: *Crime in the United States* (Federal Bureau of Investigation, 1963), Table 31, p. 117.

The overwhelming number of offenses committed by Negroes are directed toward other Negroes: the cost of crime to the Negro community is a combination of that to the criminal and to the victim.

Some of the research on the effects of broken homes on delinquent behavior recently surveyed by Thomas F. Pettigrew in *A Profile of the Negro American* is summarized below, along with several other studies of the question.

Mary Diggs found that three-fourths—twice the expected ratio—of Philadelphia's Negro delinquents who came before the law during 1948 did not live with both their natural parents.[20]

---

[20] Mary H. Diggs, "Some Problems and Needs of Negro Children as Revealed by Comparative Delinquency and Crime Statistics," *Journal of Negro Education*, 19, 1950, pp. 290–297.

In predicting juvenile crime, Eleanor and Sheldon Glueck also found that a higher proportion of delinquent than nondelinquent boys came from broken homes. They identified five critical factors in the home environment that made a difference in whether boys would become delinquents: discipline of boy by father, supervision of boy by mother, affection of father for boy, affection of mother for boy, and cohesiveness of family.

In 1952, when the New York City Youth Board set out to test the validity of these five factors as predictors of delinquency, a problem quickly emerged. The Glueck sample consisted of white boys of mainly Irish, Italian, Lithuanian, and English descent. However, the Youth Board group was 44 percent Negro and 14 percent Puerto Rican, and the frequency of broken homes within these groups was out of proportion to the total number of delinquents in the population.[21]

In the majority of these cases, the father was usually never in the home at all, absent for the major proportion of the boy's life, or was present only on occasion.

(The final prediction table was reduced to three factors: supervision of boy by mother, discipline of boy by mother, and family cohesiveness within what family, in fact, existed; it was, nonetheless, 85 percent accurate in predicting delinquents and 96 percent accurate in predicting nondelinquents.)

Researchers who have focussed upon the "good" boys in high delinquency neighborhoods noted that they typically come from exceptionally stable, intact families.[22]

Recent psychological research demonstrates the personality effects of being reared in a disorganized home without a father. One study showed that children from fatherless homes seek immediate gratification of their desires far more than children with fathers present.[23] Others revealed that children who hunger for immediate gratification are more prone to delinquency, along with other less social behavior.[24] Two psychologists, Pettigrew says, maintain that inability to delay gratification is a critical factor in immature, criminal, and neurotic behavior.[25]

[21] Maude M. Craig and Thelma J. Glick, "Ten Years Experience with the Glueck Social Prediction Table," *Journal of Crime and Delinquency*, July 1963, p. 256.

[22] F. R. Scarpitti, Ellen Murray, S. Dinitz, and W. C. Reckless, "The 'Good' Boy in a High Delinquency Area: Four Years Later," *American Sociological Review*, 25, 1960, pp. 555–558.

[23] W. Mischel, "Father-Absence and Delay of Gratification: Cross-Cultural Comparisons," *Journal of Abnormal and Social Psychology*, 63, 1961, pp. 116–124.

[24] W. Mischel, "Preference for Delayed Reinforcement and Social Responsibility," *Journal of Social and Abnormal Psychology*, 62, 1961, pp. 1–7. "Delay of Gratification, Need for Achievement, and Acquiescence in Another Culture," *Journal of Abnormal and Social Psychology*, 62, 1961, pp. 543–552.

[25] O. H. Mowrer and A. D. Ullman, "Time as a Determinant in Integrative Learning," *Psychological Review*, 52, 1945, pp. 61–90.

Finally, Pettigrew discussed the evidence that a stable home is a crucial factor in counteracting the effects of racism upon Negro personality.

A warm, supportive home can effectively compensate for many of the restrictions the Negro child faces outside of the ghetto; consequently, the type of home life a Negro enjoys as a child may be far more crucial for governing the influence of segregation upon his personality than the form the segregation takes—legal or informal, Southern or Northern.[26]

A Yale University study of youth in the lowest socioeconomic class in New Haven in 1950 whose behavior was followed through their 18th year revealed that among the delinquents in the group, 38 percent came from broken homes, compared with 24 percent of nondelinquents.[27]

The President's Task Force on Manpower Conservation in 1963 found that of young men rejected for the draft for failure to pass the mental tests, 42 percent of those with a court record came from broken homes, compared with 30 percent of those without a court record. Half of all the nonwhite rejectees in the study with a court record came from broken homes.

An examination of the family background of 44,448 delinquency cases in Philadelphia between 1949 and 1954 documents the frequency of broken homes among delinquents. Sixty-two percent of the Negro delinquents and 36 percent of white delinquents were not living with both parents. In 1950, 33 percent of nonwhite children and 7 percent of white children in Philadelphia were living in homes without both parents. Repeaters were even more likely to be from broken homes than first offenders.[28]

Juvenile Delinquents, Philadelphia, by Presence of Parents, 1949-54

	White			Negro		
	All Court Cases	First Offenders	Recidivists	All Court Cases	First Offenders	Recidivists
Number of cases	20,691	13,220	4,612	22,695	11,442	6,641
Number not living with both parents	7,422	4,125	2,047	13,980	6,586	4,298
Percent not living with both parents	35.9	31.2	44.4	61.6	57.6	64.7

Source: Adapted from Table 1, p. 255, "Family Status and the Delinquent Child," Thomas P. Monahan, *Social Forces*, March, 1957.

[26] Thomas F. Pettigrew, *op cit.*, p. 22.

[27] Erdman Palmore, "Factors Associated with School Dropouts on Juvenile Delinquency Among Lower Class Children," *Social Security Bulletin*, October 1963, p. 6.

[28] Thomas P. Monahan, "Family Status and the Delinquent Child," *Social Forces*, March 1957, p. 254.

The Armed Forces

The ultimate mark of inadequate preparation for life is the failure rate on the Armed Forces mental test. The Armed Forces Qualification Test is not quite a mental test, nor yet an education test. It is a test of ability to perform at an acceptable level of competence. It roughly measures ability that ought to be found in an average 7th or 8th grade student. A grown young man who cannot pass this test is in trouble.

Fifty-six percent of Negroes fail it.

This is a rate almost four times that of the whites.

The Army, Navy, Air Force, and Marines conduct by far the largest and most important education and training activities of the Federal Government, as well as provide the largest single source of employment in the nation.

Military service is disruptive in some respects. For those comparatively few who are killed or wounded in combat, or otherwise, the personal sacrifice is inestimable. But on balance service in the Armed Forces over the past quarter-century has worked greatly to the advantage of those involved. The training and experience of military duty itself is unique; the advantages that have generally followed in the form of the G.I. Bill, mortgage guarantees, Federal life insurance, Civil Service preference, veterans' hospitals, and veterans' pensions are singular, to say the least.

Although service in the Armed Forces is at least nominally a duty of all male citizens coming of age, it is clear that the present system does not enable Negroes to serve in anything like their proportionate numbers. This is not a question of discrimination. Induction into the Armed Forces is based on a variety of objective tests and standards, but these tests nonetheless have the effect of keeping the number of Negroes disproportionately small.

In 1963 the United States Commission on Civil Rights reported that "A decade ago, Negroes constituted 8 percent of the Armed Forces. Today . . . they continue to constitute 8 percent of the Armed Forces."[29]

In 1964 Negroes constituted 11.8 percent of the population, but probably remain at 8 percent of the Armed Forces.

	Percent Negro
Enlisted Men	
Army	12.2
Navy	5.2
Air Force	9.1
Marine Corps	7.6
Officers	
Army	3.2
Navy	.2
Air Force	1.2
Marine Corps	.2

[29] Report of the U.S. Commission on Civil Rights, September 1963, p. 173.

Almost Four Times as many Negroes as Whites Fail the Armed Forces Mental Test*
Percent Failed Mental Test

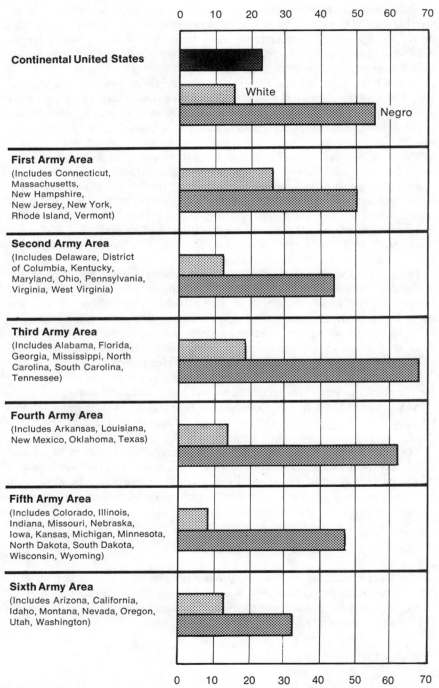

*Based on 1962 pre-induction examinations of draftees; does not include results of examinations of enlistees.

The significance of Negro under-representation in the Armed Forces is greater than might at first be supposed. If Negroes were represented in the same proportions in the military as they are in the population, they would number 300,000 plus. This would be over 100,000 more than at present (using 1964 strength figures). If the more than 100,000 unemployed Negro men were to have gone into the military the Negro male unemployment rate would have been 7.0 percent in 1964 instead of 9.1 percent.

In 1963 the Civil Rights Commission commented on the occupational aspect of military service for Negroes. "Negro enlisted men enjoy relatively better opportunities in the Armed Forces than in the civilian economy in every clerical, technical, and skilled field for which the data permit comparison."[30]

There is, however, an even more important issue involved in military service for Negroes. Service in the United States Armed Forces is the *only* experience open to the Negro American in which he is truly treated as an equal: not as a Negro equal to a white, but as one man equal to any other man in a world where the category "Negro" and "white" do not exist. If this is a statement of the ideal rather than reality, it is an ideal that is close to realization. In food, dress, housing, pay, work—the Negro in the Armed Forces *is* equal and is treated that way.

There is another special quality about military service for Negro men: it is an utterly masculine world. Given the strains of the disorganized and matrifocal family life in which so many Negro youth come of age, the Armed Forces are a dramatic and desperately needed change: a world away from women, a world run by strong men of unquestioned authority, where discipline, if harsh, is nonetheless orderly and predictable, and where rewards, if limited, are granted on the basis of performance.

The theme of a current Army recruiting message states it as clearly as can be: "In the U.S. Army you get to know what it means to feel like a man."

At the recent Civil Rights Commission hearings in Mississippi a witness testified that his Army service was in fact "the only time I ever felt like a man."

Yet a majority of Negro youth (and probably three-quarters of Mississippi Negroes) fail the Selective Service education test and are rejected. Negro participation in the Armed Forces would be less than it is, were it not for a proportionally larger share of voluntary enlistments and reenlistments. (Thus 16.3 percent of Army sergeants are Negro.)

Alienation

The term alienation may by now have been used in too many ways to retain a clear meaning, but it will serve to sum up the equally numerous ways in which large numbers of Negro youth appear to be withdrawing from American society.

[30] *Ibid.,* p. 174.

One startling way in which this occurs is that the men are just not there when the Census enumerator comes around.

According to Bureau of Census population estimates for 1963, there are only 87 nonwhite males for every 100 females in the 30-to-34-year age group. The ratio does not exceed 90 to 100 throughout the 25-to-44-year bracket. In the urban Northeast, there are only 76 males per 100 females 20-to-24-years of age, and males as a percent of females are below 90 percent throughout all ages after 14.

Ratio of Males per 100 Females in the Population, by Color, July 1, 1963

Age	Males per 100 Females	
	White	Nonwhite
Under 5	104.4	100.4
5–9 years	103.9	100.0
10–14 years	104.0	100.0
15–19 years	103.2	99.5
20–24 years	101.2	95.1
25–29 years	100.1	89.1
30–34 years	99.2	86.6
35–39 years	97.5	86.8
40–44 years	96.2	89.9
45–49 years	96.5	90.6

Source: *Current Population Reports*, Series P-25. No. 276, Table 1 (Total Population Including Armed Forces Abroad).

There are not really fewer men than women in the 20-to-40 age bracket. What obviously is involved is an error in counting: the surveyors simply do not find the Negro man. Donald J. Bogue and his associates, who have studied the Federal count of the Negro man, place the error as high as 19.8 percent at age 28; a typical error of around 15 percent is estimated from age 19 through 43.[31] Preliminary research in the Bureau of the Census on the 1960 enumeration has resulted in similar conclusions, although not necessarily the same estimates of the extent of the error. The Negro male *can* be found at age 17 and 18. On the basis of birth records and mortality records, the conclusion must be that he is there at age 19 as well.

When the enumerators do find him, his answers to the standard questions asked in the monthly unemployment survey often result in counting him as "not in the labor force." In other words, Negro male unemployment may in truth be somewhat greater than reported.

The labor force participation rates of nonwhite men have been falling since the beginning of the century and for the past decade have been lower than the rates for white men. In 1964, the participation rates were 78.0 percent for white men and 75.8 percent for nonwhite men. Almost one percentage point of this difference was due to a higher proportion of non-

[31] Donald J. Bogue, Bhaskar D. Misra, and D. P. Dandekar, "A New Estimate of the Negro Population and Negro Vital Rates in the United States, 1930-1960," *Demography*, Vol.1, No. 1, 1964, p. 350.

white men unable to work because of long-term physical or mental illness; it seems reasonable to assume that the rest of the difference is due to discouragement about finding a job.

If nonwhite male labor force participation rates were as high as the white rates, there would have been 140,000 more nonwhite males in the labor force in 1964. If we further assume that the 140,000 would have been unemployed, the unemployment rate for nonwhite men would have been 11.5 percent instead of the recorded rate of 9 percent, and the ratio between the nonwhite rate and the white rate would have jumped from 2:1 to 2.4:1.

Understated or not, the official unemployment rates for Negroes are almost unbelievable.

The unemployment statistics for Negro teenagers—29 percent in January 1964— reflect lack of training and opportunity in the greatest measure, but it may not be doubted that they also reflect a certain failure of nerve.

"Are you looking for a job?" Secretary of Labor Wirtz asked a young man on a Harlem street corner. "Why?" was the reply.

Richard A. Cloward and Robert Ontell have commented on this withdrawal in a discussion of the Mobilization for Youth project on the lower East Side of New York.

What contemporary slum and minority youth probably lack that similar children in earlier periods possessed is not motivation but some minimal sense of competence.

We are plagued in work with these youth, by what appears to be a low tolerance for frustration. They are not able to absorb setbacks. Minor irritants and rebuffs are magnified out of all proportion to reality. Perhaps they react as they do because they are not equal to the world that confronts them, and they know it. And it is the knowing that is devastating. Had the occupational structure remained intact, or had the education provided to them kept pace with occupational changes, the situation would be a different one. But it is not, and that is what we and they have to contend with.[32]

Narcotic addiction is a characteristic form of withdrawal. In 1963, Negroes made up 54 percent of the addict population of the United States. Although the Federal Bureau of Narcotics reports a decline in the Negro proportion of new addicts, HARYOU reports the addiction rate in central Harlem rose from 22.1 per 10,000 in 1955 to 40.4 in 1961.[33]

There is a larger fact about the alienation of Negro youth than the tangle of pathology described by these statistics. It is a fact particularly difficult to grasp by white persons who have in recent years shown increasing awareness of Negro problems.

The present generation of Negro youth growing up in the urban ghettos

[32]Richard A. Cloward and Robert Ontell, "Our Illusions about Training," *American Child*, January 1965, p. 7.

[33]*Youth in the Ghetto, op cit.*, p. 144.

has probably less personal contact with the white world than any generation in the history of the Negro American.[34]

Until World War II it could be said that in general the Negro and white worlds lived, if not together, at least side by side. Certainly they did, and do, in the South.

Since World War II, however, the two worlds have drawn physically apart. The symbol of this development was the construction in the 1940's and 1950's of the vast white middle- and lower-middle class suburbs around all of the Nation's cities. Increasingly, the inner cities have been left to Negroes—who now share almost no community life with whites.

In turn, because of this new housing pattern—most of which has been financially assisted by the Federal government—it is probable that the American school system has become *more*, rather than less segregated in the past two decades.

The Rate of Narcotic Users in Central Harlem Was 8 Times as High as That for New York City in 1961

RATE-Cases per 10,000 Population

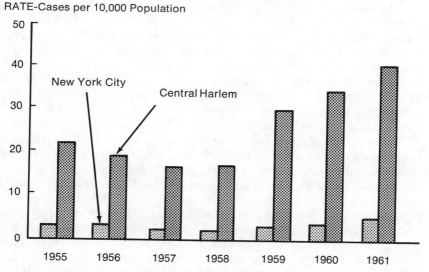

School integration has not occurred in the South, where a decade after *Brown* v. *Board of Education* only 1 Negro in 9 is attending school with white children.

And in the North, despite strenuous official efforts, neighborhoods and therefore schools are becoming more and more of one class and one color.

In New York City, in the school year 1957–58 there were 64 schools that

[34] Nathan Glazer and Daniel Patrick Moynihan, *op cit.*

were 90 percent or more Negro or Puerto Rican. Six years later there were 134 such schools.

Along with the diminution of white middle-class contacts for a large percentage of Negroes, observers report that the Negro churches have all but lost contact with men in the Northern cities as well. This may be a normal condition of urban life, but it is probably a changed condition for the Negro American and cannot be a socially desirable development.

The only religious movement that appears to have enlisted a considerable number of lower class Negro males in Northern cities of late is that of the Black Muslims: a movement based on total rejection of white society, even though it emulates white mores.

In a word: the tangle of pathology is tightening.

William Ryan: Savage Discovery—
The Moynihan Report

The Labor Department publication, *The Negro Family* (usually called "The Moynihan Report" in reference to its presumed chief author), has had an enormous impact on public discussion about the Negro in America. It contains frightening statistics about broken Negro families, illegitimate Negro children and Negro welfare recipients, and these have been seized on by journalists who proclaim in loud voices what the Moynihan Report states very quietly: Negro family instability is a basic cause of the Negro inequality and "pathology" that are reflected in unemployment statistics, census data and the results of sociological research.

In view of this influence, it is important to make public the serious shortcomings of the report that a careful analysis uncovers. Briefly, it draws dangerously inexact conclusions from weak and insufficient data; encourages (no doubt unintentionally) a new form of subtle racism that might be termed "Savage Discovery," and seduces the reader into believing that it is not racism and discrimination but the weaknesses and defects of the Negro himself that account for the present status of inequality between Negro and white. The document can be criticized on three levels: first, the methodological weaknesses; second, the manifest misstatements; and, finally, the naive error of interpreting statistical relationships in cause-and-effect terms; that is, of stating that, since A is associated with B, it follows that A causes B.

Among the methodological weaknesses is the use of such material as census data without apparent awareness either of its deficiencies or, more important, of the existence of other well-known or well-estimated data within whose context this material must be considered. The outstanding example of this failure is a highly sophomoric treatment of illegitimacy.

Reprinted from *The Nation*, November 22, 1965, with permission of the publisher. Dr. Ryan teaches in the Harvard Medical School Laboratory of Community Psychiatry and is a mental health consultant for the Massachusetts Committee on Children and Youth.

Illegitimacy looms large in the Moynihan Report, in the text and in the illustrations. Only 4 per cent of the relatively dull tables but fully 22 per cent of the large and dramatic charts and graphs concern illegitimacy, which shines through the report as the prime index of "family breakdown." This is one of the main beams in the hypothetical structure being put together. In an oversimplified way, the implicit hypothesis goes like this: the values of Negro culture (produced by centuries of slavery and mistreatment, to be sure) are such that there is little commitment to the main components of family organization—legitimacy, material stability, etc. The implicit point is that Negroes tolerate promiscuity, illegitimacy, one-parent families, welfare dependency, and everything else that is supposed to follow.

The authors of *The Negro Family* take at face value Census Bureau statistics that record illegitimacy rates for whites at about 3 per cent, for Negroes at about 22 per cent. More careful consideration, *in the context of other well-known facts*, would reveal not so much a careless acceptance by Negroes of promiscuity and illegitimacy, as a systematic inequality of access to a variety of services and information.

If we do not attribute the 7-to-1 difference in illegitimacy rates to Negro family instability as a subcultural trait, what does account for these differences? Here, very briefly, are a few pieces of additional data:

Reporting. Illegitimate births are significantly underreported, and are more underreported for whites than for nonwhites. This is true, first, because reporting is dependent upon discriminatory white sources. Second, white illegitimate births occur more often in private hospitals, are attended by sympathetic—and white—doctors, and involve the cooperation of social agencies, all of which work consciously to help the white unmarried mother conceal the fact of illegitimacy.

Shotgun Marriages. A large portion of first-born children are conceived "illegitimately," with the parents marrying before the child's birth. Such marriages are less frequent among Negroes because of the man's financial insecurity.

Abortion. It is estimated that more than 1 million illegal and unreported induced abortions are performed each year. Authorities agree that one-fourth to one-half of these are performed for unmarried women, and that the overwhelming majority of abortion patients are white. Abortions also account for most of the differences in the census illegitimacy figures.

An attempt to calculate the "illegitimate conception" rates—an awkward but interesting term—would probably show that for whites it would be 12–15 percent, for Negroes 25–30 percent. The differences are clearly not so striking: the ratio drops from 7 to 1 to 2 to 1.

Contraception. Access to contraceptive information and services is also unequally distributed in favor of whites. The extent of inequality is not known, but if the differential were as low as 2 to 1 in favor of whites, we would be able to conclude that "illegitimate intercourse"—if we may push the terminology this far—is about the same among Negroes and whites.

In any case, it is not necessary to introduce a complex and highly speculative hypothesis about the malformation of the Negro family by slavery and post-Reconstruction semi-slavery—that is, the sins of our grandfathers. The facts are more easily explained as the results of straightforward discrimination—that is, the sins of ourselves and our contemporaries.

Aid for Dependent Children and Adoption. When they wring their hands about Negro family life, the journalists who have seized on the Moynihan Report are most fascinated with illegitimacy, but their next favorite is its presumed consequence: the number of Negro mothers receiving AFDC support. How, we may ask, does a Negro mother with an illegitimate child "get on" AFDC? First, of course, she must decide to keep the child; how does she make this decision? The answer is remarkably simple: she is rarely called on to make the choice. The services of adoption agencies and maternity homes are mostly for white mothers, who account for about 90 per cent of agency adoptions of illegitimate children, and probably an even higher proportion of independent adoptions. Again to oversimplify: white illegitimate babies get adopted, their Negro counterparts "go on" AFDC. And again we are faced with *contemporary* discrimination—our sins, not the sins of our grandparents.

To summarize, the reported rates of illegitimacy among Negroes and whites tell us nothing at all about differences in family structure, historical forces, instability, or anything else about which the authors speculate. From the known data, we can conclude only that Negro and white girls probably engage in premarital intercourse in about the same proportions, but that the white girl more often takes Enovid or uses a diaphragm; if she gets pregnant, she more often obtains an abortion; if she has the baby, first she is more often able to conceal it and, second, she has an infinitely greater opportunity to give it up for adoption.

The treatment of illegitimacy data in the Moynihan Report is one example of inexpert methodology. A more general defect is the subtly irrational presentation of correlational data to imply a cause-and-effect relationship. The method of argument is, first, to present data about "family breakdown" among Negroes—separation, illegitimacy, broken homes, female household heads, etc.—and then to juxtapose statistics about the "tangle of pathology" among Negroes. In the manner of a propaganda document, the report allows the reader to make the cause-and-effect connection on the basis of his own prejudice. Little or no actual cause-and-effect data is presented.

Of the total of 125 different blocks of information presented—forty-seven tables, eighteen charts and sixty pieces of data in the text—*more than 80 per cent* is purely descriptive , retailing stale and well-known sociological facts. Only nine pieces of information (a scant 7 per cent of the total) relate to the conclusions drawn by the authors. Of these nine, six are reports of studies showing a relationship between broken homes and delinquency, and one is drawn from the 1960 census to show that children with both parents present in the home are—not unsurprisingly—less likely to drop out of school. The final two pieces of evidence show that the tested IQs of children with fathers in the home are higher than those without fathers in the home.

This is the sum total of evidence from which the authors draw such sweeping conclusions as:

At the heart of the deterioration of the fabric of Negro society is the deterioration of the Negro family. It is the fundamental source of weakness of the Negro community at the present time.

Unless this damage (the deterioration of the Negro family) *is repaired, all the effort to end discrimination and poverty and injustice will come to little.*

Three centuries of injustice have brought about deep-seated structural distortions in the life of the Negro American. . . . The cycle can be broken only if these distortions are set right. In a word, a national effort toward the problems of Negro Americans must be directed toward the question of family structure.

Confronted with such enormous conclusions based on such tiny scraps of evidence, an uncharitable response would be "irresponsible nonsense!"; the most charitable possible verdict would be "not proved."

Of the other thirteen pieces of data in which evidence of relationships is presented, two are somewhat tangential, showing that poor people have larger families than rich people, a fact that has not heretofore been very well concealed. The other eleven show relationships between unemployment and broken families, unemployment and illegitimacy, income level and illegitimacy, and unemployment and public assistance under the AFDC program. These, too, are well-known relationships, and anyone with a tolerable command of social statistics could add a whole set of additional correlations: unemployment and infant mortality, income level and dilapidated housing, broken families and number of tuberculosis cases, etc., etc. What these cool correlations mean, when translated from census data to the lives of human beings, is that poor people tend to live in slums, to be oppressed and exploited and mistreated, and to experience enormous amounts of social, economic, mental and physical suffering as a result. A disproportionate share of the poor are Negro and they experience a vastly disproportionate share of this suffering. It would be far more reasonable to conclude not that "family instability" leads to a "tangle of pathology" but that poor Negro families—that is, half of all Negro families— are bitterly discriminated against and exploited, with the result that the individual, the family and the community are all deeply injured.

It is not possible to comment on this smug document without pointing out a few errors of fact. The first—"conditions in Harlem are not worse, they are probably better than in most Negro ghettos"—is followed, predictably, by data about high illegitimacy rates in Harlem to suggest apparently that even in Harlem, the very paradise of ghettos, the Negro family is falling apart.

Another stupefying statement in the report is: "It is probable that, at present, a majority of the crimes against the person, such as rape, murder, and aggravated assault, are committed by Negroes." To support this statement the authors quote *arrest* and *conviction* rates, which are notoriously different from rates of crimes committed. It is well known that Negroes—guilty and innocent alike—are more readily arrested, and convicted, than whites. To conclude from the data offered that Negroes commit the majority of significant crimes is an inept piece of interpretation.

Another fantastic error deserves to be quoted: "The white family has achieved a high degree of stability and is maintaining that stability. By contrast, the family structure of lower class Negroes . . . is approaching complete breakdown." Such a statement reflects a double standard: if we were to use the authors' indices of family stability, principally divorce and illegitimacy, we should have to say that both white and Negro families—American families in general—are "crumbling." White divorce rates have zoomed almost 800 percent in less than 100 years, and white illegitimacy has increased more than 50 per cent in the last twenty-five years—a rate of increase greater than that of Negroes.

What we are confronted with, in fact, is another example of the authors' ineptness—the careless tying together of such vague concepts as "family stability" with a few specific measures of family composition. No sophisticated social scientist would rest a broad concept on such crude and simplistic measures. That the family is an extremely complex institution is almost too well known to require restatement. Its structure and function vary in subtle ways, over time, and from one culture to another. If we were to adopt *The Negro Family's* narrow and wholly inadequate framework for evaluating family stability, we could raise an equally sensational storm about the urban family falling apart when compared with the farm family; or the modern family when compared with the family of our grandfathers' day. Which may suggest why it is unwise to take a few pieces of census data and draw forth portentous conclusions about "the fabric of society" and "family structure" and "structural distortions in the life of the Negro American." It takes more than a desk calculator to make such judgments.

Evidence of improvements in American race relations is to be found all the way from Birmingham lunch counters to national television commercials. As yet, however, the change has had little impact on the life of the average American Negro. He remains badly housed, badly educated, underemployed and underpaid. The terms of the discourse change, but the inequality persists; and we spend more time in explaining this inequality than in doing something about it.

The explanations almost always focus on supposed defects of the Negro victim as if those—and not the racist structure of American society—were the cause of all woes that Negroes suffer. The Moynihan Report, following this line of thinking, singles out the "unstable Negro family" as the cause of

Negro inequality. But the statistics, as has been suggested, reflect current effects of contemporaneous discrimination. They are results, not causes.

The new ideology, accepted now even by some liberals, would make it seem that unemployment, poor education and slum conditions result from family breakdown, "cultural deprivation," and lack of "acculturation" of Southern rural migrants.

To sustain this ideology, it is necessary to engage in the popular new sport of Savage Discovery, and to fit the theory, savages are being discovered in great profusion in the Northern ghetto. The all-time favorite "savage" is the promiscuous mother who produces a litter of illegitimate brats in order to profit from AFDC. Other triumphs of savage discovery are the child who cannot read because, it is said, his parents never talk to him, and the "untenantable" Negro family (apparently a neologism for "unbearable") that is reputed to throw garbage out the window.

If we are to believe the new ideologues, we must conclude that segregation and discrimination are not the terrible villains we thought they were. Rather, we are told the Negro's condition is due to his "pathology," his values, the way he lives, the kind of family life he leads. The major qualification—the bow to egalitarianism—is that these conditions are said to grow out of the Negro's history of being enslaved and oppressed—*generations ago.*

It is all an ingenious way of "copping a plea." As the murderer pleads guilty to manslaughter to avoid a conviction that might lead to his being electrocuted, liberal America today is pleading guilty to the savagery and oppression against the Negro that happened 100 years ago, in order to escape trial for the crimes of today.

The theme is: "The Negro was not initially born inferior, he has been made inferior by generations of harsh treatment." Thus we continue to assert that the Negro is inferior, while chastely maintaining that all men are equal. It is all rather painful, as well as fallacious. For the fact is that the Negro child learns less not because his mother doesn't subscribe to *The Reader's Digest* and doesn't give him colored crayons for his third birthday, but because he is miseducated in segregated slum schools.

The Negro is more often unemployed because he is last hired and first fired—not because his mother preferred a succession of temporary lovers to a permanent husband. Whenever we move toward full employment, the Negro is employed, usually, of course, at the bottom of the status ladder. When workers are needed badly enough, the supposed lack of skills of the Negro suddenly becomes less inhibiting. This was shown during the war, when it was more important to have someone operating the lathe, even if Negro, than it was to preserve the myth of Negro inability.

And the squalor of the Negro family's home in the Northern slum requires no farfetched explanations about Southern rural background. In the first place, most of these families are not recently from the South and few are rural. In the second place, the condition of the housing is more easily explained by the neglect of slum landlords, and the crowding caused by the criminal shortage of decent low-income housing.

It is tempting, when faced with a complex problem, to wallow in the very chaos of complexity rather than to begin the task of unraveling and analyzing and, ultimately, of acting. It is obviously true that the Negro suffers from a never-ending cycle of oppression not only from generation to generation but, in the case of many individuals, from medically uncared-for birth to premature death. Each condition has its labyrinth of causation, and we soon discover that the Negro family of six in the three-room apartment has been placed there not only by the greedy slumlord and the barbarous realtor but also and equally by the venal housing inspector, and even by the noble woman leagued with her sisters in voting for a "progressive" zoning ordinance in her trim suburban town.

But to move from the recognition of infernal complexity to the refuge of damnably inaccurate simplicity is surely heresy. Much has to be done. All of it is difficult, tangled and anxious-making. Still it must be done; there's no escape in the world of sociological fakery.

Time after time, the Negro has had to deny in action the myths and lies that have been constructed to soothe the conscience of his oppressor. He had to deny his supposed docility, first by hopeless revolts against his slave-master, and then by fighting in blue uniforms by the hundreds of thousands; his lack of interest in education by almost magically expanding the few dollars he could lay hands on to send his sons through high school and his granddaughters to graduate school. He had to deny the myth of apathy both by the organized brilliance of a Woodlawn organization in Chicago and the Mississippi Freedom Democratic Party in Mississippi, and by the unorganized bursts of blind energy that we called riots in Los Angeles, Philadelphia, Harlem and Rochester.

If we persist in creating a new set of myths to justify the *status quo;* calling on the sociologists and their friends to give us the ammunition of "family disorganization" and "cultural deprivation," the Negro will doubtless destroy these too. But when we've started to move toward ending the myths that have bound us so long, to end the racism that has truly caused a "breakdown" in our community and our nation, why turn back?

Obviously, if we stop discriminating tomorrow, great damage will remain—damage ranging from miseducation that is at best partly reversible, to hatred and bitterness that may be unalterable. This damage calls for correction and compensation. But we must be clear what we mean by "compensatory programs" and we must face directly what we are compensating for. Compensation should mean that we give back what we took away. For the millions of grown and half-grown Negro Americans who have already been damaged, we must make up for the injury that we did to them. This is what we must compensate for; not for some supposed inherent or acquired inferiority or weakness or instability of the victim whom we injured.

What, then, is to be done? The young Negro man who dropped out of school or, worse, graduated from high school with a seventh-grade education, represents a specific example of damage done—in his lifetime, in our lifetime. The damage must be corrected to the greatest extent possible, by re-education, by training, by any means that become necessary. If a result of the demoralizing experience of growing up Negro is that a man does not in fact have the skills to obtain available work, he cannot be written off and relegated to a life of welfare subsistence. And it is almost as cruel to go through the motions of furnishing him irrelevant skills for imaginary jobs.

But the first order of business remains, now and in the near future, to bring a real end to real discrimination and segregation. These are the major causes of the conditions which the Moynihan Report so easily labels "family instability" and the "tangle of pathology." We must not forget to end discrimination or all our good works will amount to very little.

Laura Carper: The Negro Family and the Moynihan Report

MRS. BOYLE: We'll go. Come, Mary, an' we'll never come back here agen. Let your father furrage for himself now; I've done all I could an' it was all no use—he'll be hopeless till the end of his days. I've got a little room in me sisther's where we'll stop till your throuble is over, an' then we'll work together for the sake of the baby.

MARY: My poor little child that'll have no father!

MRS. BOYLE: It'll have what's far better—it'll have two mothers.

(Juno and the Paycock, Act III, Sean O'Casey)

The culmination of intensive efforts to codify the life of the hapless is a document published by the Department of Labor entitled *The Negro Family: The Case for National Action* and commonly referred to as "The Moynihan Report," after the reputed head of the investigation—the sociologist Daniel Moynihan. With the publication of this document a sociological theory which borders on an ideology has become a political weapon which we are all obliged to examine. In order to understand the theoretical framework within which this document was written, we must take a cursory look at sociological thought in the recent period.

In 1960, Dreger and Miller published in the *Psychological Bulletin* a critical evaluation of the "Comparative Psychological Studies of Negroes and Whites in the United States," which was an examination of the relevant contributions in the field between 1943 and 1958. They concluded that "in the areas of psychological functioning most closely related to the sociological, social class differences show up more clearly as a basis for differentiation between the two groups. Leadership, family life, child rearing practices, fertility and mate selection all seem to conform to social structure rather than to racial lines per se."

Reprinted from *Dissent*, March-April 1966, with permission of the author and publisher. Laura Carper is a freelance writer and is active in social movements in Detroit.

Dreger and Miller's conclusion reflected the intensive efforts of liberal sociological and psychological thought of the period. It was the culmination of a thoroughgoing examination of the corrosive effects of our peculiar social organization and value system on the Negro as compared to the white. They were unable to find a uniquely Negro personality or Negro psychology in any class. Their conclusion became a landmark in the field with which every investigator has been forced to contend.

In April 1964, however, *The Journal of Social Issues* published a collection of studies with an introduction by Thomas Pettigrew and Daniel C. Thompson and a lead article by Thomas Pettigrew which sought to delineate what Dreger and Miller were unable to locate—a Negro personality and a Negro psychology. Frankly admitting that in this effort social psychology was whistling in the dark since the Negro was notorious for his refusal to reveal his inner self to the social investigator and since it was virtually impossible to establish control groups of whites, Pettigrew nevertheless argued that past findings have "underestimated the corrosive effects on young children of impecunious ghetto living." This may indeed be true, but the theoretical basis of the issue is that due to the vicissitudes of his history and the brutality of white society, the Negro has developed a recognizable psychology and a recognizable personality which emerged under slavery, and that this psychology is self-sustaining and transmitted from generation to generation. The studies, together with the introduction, almost seem to argue for the existence of a racial unconscious.

The thinking here represents a powerful tendency in modern sociological thought; and it is this thinking, shorn of its somewhat hesitant and carefully hedged tone, which characterizes the ideological commitment of *The Report on the Negro Family* and the direction its authors feel national action should take.

The thesis of the Report is that the Negro poor "confront the nation with a new kind of problem. Measures that have worked in the past, or would work for most groups in the present will not work here. A national effort is required that will give unity and purpose to the many activities of the Federal government in this area, directed to a new kind of national goal: the establishment of a stable Negro family structure." The presumption is that the Negro poor are no longer merely the victims of white institutional corruption but also, to an undetermined extent, of their corrosive family life; that despite the enactment of the voting rights bill, the creation of the "Manpower Retraining Program, The Job Corps, and Community Action— et al," *fifty percent* of the Negro population is incapable of profiting because of a psychological distemper.

The argument is supported with an array of statistics but without any effort to come to terms with the fact that variations in life style and social adjustment *within* the ghetto and between the Northern and Southern Negro poor are far more varied than between all of them and society at large. Fifty percent of the Negro population is identified as reflecting the "social pathology" these statistics itemize, and the Negro family is recognized as its "source."

On page thirteen of the report there is a graph charting the non-white male unemployment rate and the number of AFDC (Aid to Families with Dependent Children) cases opened each year. This graph is the strongest argument the report offers to substantiate its thesis that the Negro poor have been so crippled by their situation and history that ordinary measures— which I suppose would be full employment, a radical revision of the ghetto school system, integrated education, decent housing, and a rigorously controlled police force—will no longer suffice; that what is now needed is a national effort not to alter our white social institutions but the way the Negro poor relate to each other on the primary personal level—the family.

The graph shows a direct correlation between the non-white male unemployment rate and AFDC cases opened each year between 1948 and 1961. As the unemployment rate drops, AFDC cases drop; as the unemployment rate rises, AFDC cases rise. But in 1962 a negative correlation begins to emerge; in 1963 the lines for each cross; in 1964 AFDC cases continue to rise as the unemployment rate continues to drop. Presumably, the negative correlation after 1962 shows or suggests that giving the Negro male a job will no longer insure or help insure family stability. The conclusion is that something more is needed.

I am not prepared to argue an economic determinist thesis. It is not my contention that the area of full employment is the only front on which we should fight. But I would like to attempt to explain the graph, particularly since the authors of the report direct the reader's attention to the negative correlation and argue that no government program should be instituted which aims at relieving the plight of the Negro poor until the reasons for the reversal are understood.

The first consideration in evaluating statistics is to understand their relevance. *New* AFDC cases must therefore be compared with the unemployment rate of young Negroes. A little investigation shows that the unemployment rate for non-white males as a whole is not reflected in the unemployment rate of non-white youth. Non-white youth, male and female, show a radically different set of statistics; and it is of course the young and not the mature Negro woman who would be a new AFDC case. The unemployment rate for eighteen and nineteen year old non-white men rose from 23.9% in 1961 to 27.4% in 1963, and for eighteen and nineteen year old women who would be obliged to assist in the support of their families from 28.2% to 31.9%. Taken as a whole, the unemployment rate of non-white men between the ages of sixteen and twenty-four during the years in question fluctuates but shows little over-all change. In 1963, the year the lines for AFDC cases and the unemployment rate converge, the rates were especially high. Where the over-all non-white male unemployment rate went down in 1963, the unemployment rate for youth went up and then went down a little in 1964. The picture for young non-white women is comparable. Their rate showed a general tendency to increase.

These figures, although they radically temper the implications of the graph, do not account for the extent of the reversal. A complete explanation must include the famous 1962 change in the social security law. There is a remarkable correlation between AFDC figures and the date of the new law, which authorized greater social and case work service to the poor. In the state of Michigan at least (I choose Michigan arbitrarily, only because I live there and was in a position to discuss the graph with the welfare department), the department has interpreted this law as a directive to alter its standards. Prior to 1962, if an applicant was a poor housekeeper, mentally disturbed, or evidence of a male friend could be found, her application for AFDC was denied; after 1962 she was accepted if she showed need, regardless of her housekeeping practices, her mental health or her social life. Whereas between July 1960 and June 1961 33.4% of the applications were denied, only 28% were denied between July 1963 and June 1964. The strange graph in the Moynihan Report is the result of graphing the wrong things. The negative correlation is due to an inconsistency between youth unemployment rate and the unemployment rate of the non-white male population as a whole and to an important change in policy on the part of the welfare authorities. As a staff member of the department informed me, "it is our policy to give everyone a chance now." The thinking behind the new policy is that by accepting the "undeserving" poor as well as the "deserving" poor, case-work service is made available to those who need it most. It is inevitable that as news of this policy change spreads among the Negro poor and as each of the states slowly alters its policy to conform to this new view, AFDC cases will continue to rise.

The Negro family is not the source of the "tangle of pathology" which the report attributes to the Negro community. It is the pathological relationship between white social institutions and the Negro community which has bred the statistics the report cites—from low scholastic averages to drug addiction to arrest records to illegitimacy to unemployment rates. This is the reason the Black Muslims have chosen to withdraw, and this is the reason the civil rights movement has chosen to confront us.

The statistics I have tried to examine are the supportive evidence the report offers in defense of a social psychological theory. In brief the argument is that American slavery stripped the Negro of his culture and his most minimal human rights; and that the Negro, under continued oppression, developed a matriarchal family organization within which the male played an inadequate role, if any. The argument continues that since American family life is patriarchal, the matriarchal family formulation is pathological and is perpetuating a pathological Negro culture—as the statistics show. But I cannot help wonder with James Tobin, who published an interesting economic study in the Fall 1965 issue of *Daedalus*, why "personal attributes which doom(ed) a man to unemployment in 1932 or even 1954 or 1961 did not handicap him in 1944 or 1951 or 1956." Peter Townsend has pointed out that in 1930 many Englishmen estimated that as many as a million of their fellow-countrymen were unemployable because of their personal problems and only a decade later found that only 100,000 could be characterized in this way. There was a manpower shortage in 1940. What appears to be a social malformation in one period becomes the problem of isolated individuals in another.

The Negro poor are distinguished from the middle class primarily by the fact that they are poor. The father is haphazardly employed and at a very low wage. He is frequently absent from the family scene. He has either deserted or been thrown out by the mother. If he is present and works, he may squander his income. The children are raised by an extended family of adult women. This picture does not focus on fifty percent of the Negro families. But it does include a significant section of the Negro poor. Is it peculiar to them?

"Matriarchy" is a cultural formation common to many oppressed people throughout the history of western civilization—regardless of their own past history and regardless of the values they themselves held. A brilliant and moving characterization of how and why such a family constellation developed among the Irish poor can be found in Sean O'Casey's play *Juno and the Paycock*, from which I took the quotation which precedes this piece. The Irish matriarchal family formation is noteworthy because it existed in conflict with an Irish patriarchal ideal.

Both Patricia Sexton and Oscar Lewis have shown that the poor Puerto Rican family is beginning to move toward the same "pathology" as the Negro: illegitimacy and families with a woman at the helm.

The same can be said of Jewish family life in the *shtetl*. Although illegitimacy was not a problem (partly because divorce merely involved a witnessed statement placed in the hand of the wife; the father was frequently absent, either as a peddler on the road, as an immigrant in America, or as a permanent resident of the house of study who came home only to eat). Newly married couples usually moved into the home of the bride's parents. Among the Hassidic Jews (Hassidism was a movement initiated by the poor), it was common for the father to leave his wife and children without a kopek or a groshen in the house and depart for the Rebbe's court where he would dance and drink and spend all his money. As among the American poor, relations between husband and wife were cold and the roles of each clearly defined. The wife worked and assumed the main burden of supporting the family, and children became adults before they had ever had an opportunity to be children. The man either struggled desperately to make a living with little success or withdrew entirely into a private male society based on discourse or ecstacy and left the family to shift for itself. What the Jewish man succeeded in doing that the Negro man has failed to do is place a positive value on family desertion and personal withdrawal.

Since the Negro man does not rationalize his role as being a desirable religious achievement, it seems to me he would be easier to integrate into the surrounding culture than the Jew. After all, once integration became a viable possibility, even the *shtetl* Jew cast off what no longer served him. And the depth and extent to which oppression and poverty reduced the Jew can be measured by the disintegrative effects of the widespread Messianic movements, two of which emphasized orgiastic sexual practices as a means of insuring the coming of the Messiah.

I have chosen to detail the matriarchal organization of the Jewish family life not because it corresponds to the Negro family but because sociologists look upon Jewish family life as remarkably cohesive. Is the caricature I have drawn of the *shtetl* family accurate? Of course not. I have applied Mr. Moynihan's method of describing the Negro to a description of the Jew. I lumped a few hundred years of history together and failed to distinguish between people. Pathology is in the eye of the beholder. If one eliminates the positive social function of a cultural constellation, if one ignores the meaning personal relations have to the people involved, if one, in short, uses science to depersonalize, what emerges is always pathology. For health involves spontaneous human feelings of affection and tenderness which the Moynihan Report, like my deliberate caricature of Jewish family life, cannot encompass.

Let me also add that I am not trying to draw any direct analogies between the Irish poor, the Jewish poor, or even the Puerto Rican poor, and the Negro poor. I am seeking to show the "matriarchy" within the larger social context of what the report calls "patriarchy" is common to the way of life of poor people. And further, that people living under oppression always develop social formations which appear to the surrounding oppressive culture to be excessive or pathological. The form these so-called excesses take varies from culture to culture and person to person within the culture—but no matter how extreme the nature of the adjustment, once the social pressure which created it is removed, a new adjustment develops. A people is not destroyed by its history. What destroys a people is physical annihilation or assimilation, not its family life.

The question the report raises is the direction a government program would take to insure family stability. What is the quality of the solutions Mr. Moynihan has in mind? The report includes a detailed description of the therapeutic effects of military service. Mr. Moynihan argues that the armed forces are educational and that they "provide the largest single source of employment in the nation." He admits that "for those comparatively few who are killed or wounded in combat, or otherwise, the personal sacrifice is inestimable. But on balance, service in the Armed Forces over the past quarter-century has worked greatly to the advantage of those involved. . . . Service in the United States Armed Forces is the *only* [author's italics] experience open to the Negro-American in which he is truly treated as an equal: not as a Negro equal to any white, but as one man equal to any man in a world where the category 'Negro' and 'white' do not exist." Mr. Moynihan further states that for the Negro "the armed forces are a dramatic and desperately needed change: a world away from women, a world run by strong men of unquestioned authority, where discipline, if harsh, is nonetheless orderly and predictable and where rewards, if limited, are granted on the basis of performance." This view of the desirability of army life is patently absurd. Underlying the Report's understanding of the problems of the Negro family is its author's concept of masculinity. According to the Report "the essence of the male animal, from the bantam rooster to the four-star general, is to strut."

I cannot here counterpose my taste in men or my concept of the good life against Mr. Moynihan's—but it seems clear to me that it is for the Negro male himself to determine his sexual and social style—whether strutting or not.

The challenge to the Negro community is political. It remains to be seen whether we can make room for the poor to acquire social and economic power. This is our social problem—and not the existence of a matriarchal family organization. What is more, Frank Riessman has found that involving emotionally disturbed people among the Negro poor in the civil rights movement can resolve their personal problems. What is destructive to the Negro man and woman is social impotence here and now, and what rehabilitates them is social power and the struggle for it. It is not new for a ruling elite to characterize its poor as incontinent and shiftless. It is the characteristic way in which those on top describe those on the bottom, even when sincerely trying to uplift them. My Negro landlady encountered a helpful woman who tried to tell her that Negro culture was rooted in the life style of slavery and fixed by history. In telling me about the conversation my landlady said, "That woman thinks that if she handed me a bale of cotton, I'd know how to make a dress out of it!" The Negro is not grappling with the social system under which he lived over a hundred years ago, or even with the social system under which he lived ten years ago. He is grappling with the social system under which he lives today.

Part Two

The Dyad

Very little is known about dating and sexual behavior in the Black community. Dating patterns may vary from community to community, region to region, and within and between the social classes in either of those areas. As among whites, dating behavior involves a great deal of deception on the part of both males and females. In general, it is acknowledged that the male attempts to maximize sexual involvement with and minimize commitment to his female date. The reverse is usually true of the female. Success in reaching one goal or the other is often based on the principle of least interest—that is, who is more committed to maintaining the relationship and more likely to give in to the demands of the other partner—for sexual involvement or commitment to a steady relationship or marriage.

It is in the process of trying to achieve conflicting goals that Black dating patterns diverge from white dating behavior.[1] In attempting to elicit commitment from the Black male, the Black female is constantly confronted with the situation of a serious shortage of available Black males. If she does not give in to his demands for premarital sexual relations, there are always other women who will. The competitive nature of the husband market leaves her on the short end of the bargaining process.

---

[1]The observations in this introductory section are based on a preliminary research project on dating and sexual behavior among Blacks in the San Francisco-Oakland area. I am grateful to Ken Melton, Rita Valentine, and Michael Smith for their assistance in this study.

Regardless of this situation, Black women continue to play games within the dating context, especially younger Black women. Because of the strong sexual orientation of many Black males, the Black woman receives many more requests for dates than her white counterpart. For one reason or another, she sometimes agrees to a date and then does not show up or calls at the last minute to cancel it. If she does show, she may avoid sexual relations by stating that she is in the middle of her menstrual cycle or that she has to be home early. The Black female is often reluctant to forthrightly refuse the male's demand for premarital coitus lest it jeopardize her future opportunities for dates.

The Black male sees dating primarily as an opportunity to have sexual relations, although affection may subsequently develop between the dating partners. Among Black males, the principle method for obtaining sexual relations is the "rap." This is an elaborate sexual seduction technique, a conversational art designed to evoke a sexual response in the Black female. Raps consist of telling the female how good she looks, how much pleasure you get from her company, and so on. In reality, this is nothing more than a ritual, since few Black females are persuaded by a "rap" alone. She is usually already attracted to him for other reasons, and the rap becomes the rationale for participating in premarital coitus.

The basis for selecting male dating partners can vary according to the values and needs of the individual female. A male with money—a rarity in the Black community—is much desired by many Black females. The male's personality is very important, but all things being equal, his physique is rapidly becoming the most attractive element for Black women.[2] The process of ranking males by body build can be called the masculinization of female mate selection standards. For years, males have evaluated females in terms of breast size, shapely legs, protruding buttocks and other physical features. Now females are beginning to rank males in terms of their pulchritude. For those of us who are not built like athletes, or are committed to the proposition that individuals should not be ranked by invidious standards, this is a most disheartening trend.

Infidelity, or tipping out, is quite common in the Black community. While the failure to be faithful has always been more or less tolerated in the male, the independence of the Black female leads her to sexual dalliance whenever things do not go right or she feels the desire to "make it" with another male. This practice has become quasi-institutionalized among Blacks and is somewhat accepted in cases where it occurs.[3] Sexual dalliance must, however, be discreet so as not to damage the male ego. It is most common among Black females attending college some miles away from their boyfriends and in the lower class.

---

[2]Many Black females assume that a male with an athletic build possesses large sexual organs, which will guarantee them sexual pleasure. This belief lacks any scientific basis whatsoever.

[3]Although sexual dalliance may be somewhat accepted, many of the conflicts in Black male-female relationships can be traced to this practice.

The first section, "Premarital Dating Patterns," is an excerpt from Hylan Lewis's book *Blackways of Kent*. The subjects of Lewis's study are lower class, rural Blacks. It is important to keep this in mind when reading about the character of dating and sexual relations in that community. Lewis found that Black dating was a casual, catch-as-catch-can matter, a sex game, with clandestine features. Going together, which involved intimacy, was a stable relationship and likely to lead to marriage. Courtship was not as fixed or stable a pattern of wooing as going together.

The next selection, excerpted from David Schulz's book *Coming Up Black*, also deals with courtship in a lower class setting. He attempts to elaborate on, and more fully document, Lewis's suggestion that gifts and economic support play an important role in Black dating relationships. In this regard, he develops a typology of boyfriends based upon the longevity of their liaisons and the extent of their economic support of the female partner. One can discern a dichotomy of economic relationships here; either the male is contributing to the economic maintenance of the female partner, or he is attempting to exploit her for financial gain.

Black men who prefer to exploit women are in reality enhancing their masculine image. Not only must they extract money or gifts from their female partners but must view doing so as exploitation. According to Liebow, the men prefer to see themselves as exploiters, women as the exploited. A woman's desirability is assessed in terms of her wealth or earning power. As one lower class subject, who had pimping intentions, revealed to Liebow about his female companion, "She's not pretty but she's got a beautiful job."[4]

The exploitative ethic of the Black male must be reconciled with other impulses, especially the desire to love and take care of a "nice" woman in his life. Indeed many Black males are exploited for economic gain by Black women. As Liebow found, however,

This is not to suggest, however, that one must wholly discount men's view of themselves as exploiters and users of women. A poor man who can get hold of some money is that much less poor for the moment he has it. And in a world where sexual conquest is one of the few ways in which one can prove one's masculinity, the man who does not make capital of his relationship with a woman is that much less a man.[5]

One empirical study of lower class Black dating patterns was conducted by Carlfred Broderick. Some of his general findings were that dating began earlier for Black females, going steady was the prevalent mode of dating when the Black female reached sixteen years of age, and Black girls were more desirous of getting married someday than Black males.

[4]Elliot Liebow, *Tally's Corner* (Boston: Little, Brown and Company, 1967), p. 138.
[5]*Ibid.*, p. 150.

The last finding is especially significant, considering the shortage of Black males. By the age of fourteen, most Black girls (90 percent) expressed hope that they would marry someday. By the age of sixteen, less than 75 percent of the Black males said they ever wanted to get married. One can easily understand the tendency toward steady dating, considering the competitive nature of male selection. Once a Black woman has a man, she tries to hold on to him.

Sex attitudes and behavior take on a special significance in the comparative analysis of Black and white family behavior. American folklore and slave myth have accorded a special role to Blacks—that of a peculiarly desirable or essentially different sexual object. Regardless of the validity of stereotypes about the sexual prowess of Black people, it is generally conceded that more permissive sex codes and behavior exist in the Black community.

The reasons for the difference between Black and white sexual behavior are not clearly known, but it is generally assumed that the greater sexual permissiveness of Blacks can be traced to the historical experience of slavery. During the era of Black enslavement, the sexual impulse was released from the constraints imposed by tribal units in Africa. Black slaves were mated like animals to breed future slaves. The Black slave woman was forcibly subjected to carnal attacks by her master, overseer, or other slaves. As a result, the nexus between sex and marriage was a tenuous one.

Permissive sexual behavior continued after the demise of slavery, and the lack of a puritanical tradition among Blacks in this country was one of the reasons. Unlike the role of religion for most white Americans, Blacks were oriented toward emotional release rather than setting high moral standards. Premarital and extra-marital sexual behavior has never been countenanced by the Black church, but for the most part the violation of America's moral code has not received much attention from Black ministers or their parishioners. (There are, of course, exceptions to the practice of ignoring illicit sexual practices, especially among the Black bourgeoisie and the religious fundamentalists.)

There is very little empirical research comparing Black and white sexual behavior. This is especially true of studies using experimental controls, random sampling, and other rigorous scientific measures. Most data on Black sexual behavior have come from studies dealing with aspects of Black life other than sexual behavior.

In fact, only one major study has presented data on Black sexual behavior as of this writing. The Kinsey researchers gathered data on Black sexual behavior in their monumental study but did not include their findings in the first two volumes. The results were released later in a book by Kinsey's associates on the research project.[6] What they found confirmed the views of other authorities on Black family life—that Blacks were more permissive in

---

[6]Paul Gebhard et al., *Pregnancy, Birth, and Abortion* (New York: Harper & Row, 1958), pp. 155–158.

their sexual behavior than whites. Their study revealed that for Black females, by age 20, the rates for premarital sex behavior, by educational level, are these: 0 to 8 years of schooling, 82 percent; 9 to 12 years, 82 percent; and 13 or more years, 49 percent. In general, Black females have higher rates of premarital coitus and premarital pregancy than do whites. But the rates are significantly affected by social class membership if we accept the educational levels as measurements of class differences within the Black group.[7]

While the influence of social class appears to be the same for both Blacks and whites, in the teenage years the level of exposure to premarital sexual relations is about three to four times higher for Black females than white females. Therefore, while at age 20 only 16 percent of white grammar-school-educated girls have had premarital sexual relations, over 80 percent of comparable Black females have. In fact, at the age of fifteen, more grammar-school-educated Black females have experienced coitus than white males of the same age.[8]

The Kinsey research reported on only Black females. There is no systematically conducted study, to my knowledge, on the premarital sexual behavior of Black males. One team of researchers, Homan and Schaffner,[9] did report that among a large sample of army inductees a great majority of whites, but nearly all of the Black males, had experienced premarital sexual relations. This writer's own research into the premarital sexual behavior of Black males uncovered almost no Black males who would admit to nonparticipation in premarital sexual activities.[10]

In essence, we might say that differences in the sexual behavior of Blacks and whites are very similar to the same differences between males and females. However, socialization by the parents appears to be more directly responsible for sex role differences, while cultural factors are more influential in racial differences. Although the family is usually the primary mediator of cultural values, there seems to be more peer group socialization among Blacks and lower class whites. This is confirmed by Hammond and Ladner, who report that:

It appears that among adolescents the most important socializing influences are conversations of peers and adults; observations of these groups; and actual participation in or imitation of the acts themselves. There is no sequential ordering of these influences. The child may observe a sexual act, engage in it, and later hear a conversation about it. What may at first have been imitative play then comes to have a new conceptual meaning for him. The point should be stressed, however, that most

---

[7] *Ibid.*

[8] *Ibid.*

[9] Lewis Homan and Bernard Schaffner, "The Sex Lives of Unmarried Men," *American Journal of Sociology,* 52 (1947), 501:507.

[10] Robert Staples, *Sex and Games in the Black Community* (unpublished manuscript, 1969).

of these children are exposed to sex at such an early age that they have not had the opportunity to formulate convictions which would sustain them against sexual involvement.[11]

In this section on sexual behavior, Frazier offers excellent insights into the patterns of African sexual behavior and the ways in which they were modified under the institution of slavery. This work is one of the most important treatises on Black sexual behavior and the historical forces that shaped its present-day manifestations.

The article by Staples further explores the psychosocial aspects of Black sex behavior and adds a new dimension by consciously legitimating Black sexual patterns as suiting the needs of the Black community. While some Blacks will take exception to his view of the permissive character of Black sexual relations, he indicates the therapeutic value of a permissive sex code for Blacks, especially females.

Kenneth Clark's discussion of Black sexual behavior, on the other hand, deals with its negative aspects. His attempts to dichotomize class differences in Black sexual behavior might be questioned: middle class Blacks also have a permissive code relating to sexual behavior. While frigidity and guilt in sexual relations may be more common among middle class Blacks, the lower class origin of many members of the Black bourgeoisie leaves their permissive sexual values intact.

The last article in this section, by Reiss, is an important study of premarital sexual standards among a school and adult sample of Blacks and whites. In this attempt to ascertain how such factors as social class, religion, and concept of romantic love affect premarital sexual standards, he found that, in general, Black males are the most permissive race-sex group, while white females are the most restrictive. Among women and whites, sexual permissiveness is more likely to be influenced by such social forces as church attendance and belief in romantic love. Among men and Blacks, such influences are not so great. The white woman's permissiveness is affected by all the variables investigated; that of Blacks is affected by none of them. Also, even with social class eliminated as a possible factor, Blacks still had more permissive premarital sexual standards than whites.

Sex role behavior in the Black family differs considerably from the prototypical white model. Once again, we must look to the past for at least a partial explanation of these differences. One of the most important influences of slavery was the attempt to socially castrate the Black male. His role was primarily as a breeder of children who would serve as part of the organic capital of the slaveowning class. The normal masculine functions such as economic support, socialization, and physical and psychological

[11] Boone Hammond and Joyce Ladner, "Socialization into Sexual Behavior in a Negro Slum Ghetto" in *The Individual, Sex, and Society,* edited by Carlfred Broderick and Jessie Bernard (Baltimore: Johns Hopkins Press, 1969), pp. 41–51.

protection were denied him by virtue of his slave status.[12] Masculinity, for him, was defined in terms of his sexual and procreative ability.

The end of slavery still found him unable to exercise normal male prerogatives. Lacking the institutionalized means for goal achievement in American society, he found ego gratification and social approval by continuing to carry out the role of a super-stud. His self-concept as a sexual being stemmed from the lack of alternative sources of status in a society bent on depriving him of his manhood. Sex became, then, not only a source of physical pleasure but a means of status acquisition within the context of the Black community.

Most discussions of the Black male revolve around his lack of masculinity, not the esoteric way in which it is manifested. The most common theme of such discussions is that Black males reared in female-dominated homes are likely to acquire feminine characteristics, which they attempt to disguise by an exaggeration of "normal" masculine behavior. Because of the large number of female-headed households among Blacks, a significant portion of Black males are reared in predominantly female households. Consequently, many Black males lack a consistently present male figure with whom to identify and from whom to learn essential components of a male role.

One conclusion that ensues from this analysis is that many Black males are latent homosexuals. Frazier believed that since it was generally the father who was absent from the broken Black family, the boys especially suffer because there is no adult to provide the model or image of the values which should shape their personalitites. Moreover, since white America would not allow Black men to play the socially defined masculine role, middle class Black males have tended to cultivate their personalities as a compensation for their lack of masculinity. Thus, Frazier concluded that we cannot determine to what extent homosexuality among Black males is due to a broken home and an inability to play a masculine role.[13]

Another indicator of the social castration of the Black male is research findings that Black males score higher than white males on a measure of femininity.[14] These studies used the Minnesota Multiphasic Inventory (MMPI), a psychological instrument that asks the subject the applicability to himself of over 500 simple statements. As a measure of femininity, Black males in this study agreed more often than white males with such feminine choices as "I would like to be a singer" and " I think I feel more intensely than most people do."[15]

[12] Cf. Maurice Davie, *Negroes in American Society* (New York: McGraw-Hill Book Company, 1949).

[13] E. Franklin Frazier, "Problems and Needs of Negro Children and Youth Resulting from Family Disorganization," *The Journal of Negro Education*, 19 (1950), pp. 269–277.

[13] M. G. Caldwell, "Personality Trends in the Youthful Male Offender," *Journal of Criminal Law, Criminology, and Police Science* (1959), pp. 405–416; J. E. Hokanson and G. Calden, "Negro-White Differences on the MMPI," *Journal of Clinical Psychology* (1960), pp. 32–33.

[15] Cf. Thomas Pettigrew, *A Profile of the Negro American* (Princeton, N.J.: D. Van Nostrand Company, 1964), pp. 17–22.

After reviewing the above evidence, one might safely assume that Black males definitely have some sex-role identity problems. However, another view can be taken of the Black male and his masculinity complex. First, the number of overt homosexuals among Blacks is very small compared to that of white homosexuals.[16] And speculating about latent homosexuality is risky when one considers that it is almost impossible to verify the existence of latent homosexual tendencies in an individual by any objective scientific measures now available to us.

The fallacy of such measures as the MMPI is reflected by the definition of Black males as feminine because of their aspirations to be a singer. This reveals how white standards cannot always be used in evaluating Black behavior. Blacks live in a subcultural world with ways of acting, thinking, and believing different from those in the white middle class world. A singer such as James Brown occupies the same status and commands the same prestige in the Black community as the President of the United States does in the white community. An entertainer is an eminently sucessful role model for Black youth; many aspire to be entertainers since this appears to be an observable means for achieving success in American society, not because Black males are more feminine than white males.

We might also question how much of a problem males do have in learning their sex role identity in father-absent homes.

First of all, a female-headed household without an adult male in residence but where young children are growing up—and where, therefore, it is likely that the mother is still young—is seldom one where adult males are totally absent. More or less steady boyfriends (sometimes including the separated father) go in and out. Even if these men do not assume a central household role, the boys can obviously use them as source material for the identification of male behavior. To be sure, the model is not a conventional middle-class one, but it still shows what males are like.[17]

Moreover, men are not the only ones who teach boys about masculinity. Sex roles can also be learned by learning the culturally determined expectations of these roles. According to Lynn:

Despite the shortage of male models, a somewhat sterotyped and conventional masculine role is nonetheless spelled out for the boy, often by his mother and women teachers in the absence of his father and male models. Through the reinforcement of the culture's highly developed system of rewards for typical masculine role behavior and punishment for signs of femininity, the boy's early learned identification with

---

[16]Robert Staples, "The Sex Behavior of Low-Income Negroes," *Sexology*, 34 (October 1967), pp. 152–156.

[17]Ulf Hannerz, "The Roots of Black Manhood," *Transaction*, 6 (October 1969), p. 16.

the mother weakens. Upon this weakened mother identification is welded the later learned identification with a culturally defined, stereotyped role.[18]

Finally, it should be remembered that if men define something as masculine, then for all practical purposes it becomes masculine to them.[19] For Black males, masculinity is the way they act. Another culture's definition of masculinity is of little significance to them. Certain manifestations of masculinity have been historically denied them. They have been unable to provide for their families or give them protection from white invaders. But this is related to broad social and economic factors, and we should address ourselves to eliminating those elements in American society that prevent Black males from carrying out these functions.

In the section on the male sex role, the article by Nathan Hare describes some of the sex role problems faced by Black males in this society. According to Hare, the Black male has been deprived of his masculinity by white America and adopts a number of traits in order to accentuate his maleness and distinguish himself from females. Hare makes the important point that one function of the myth about the Black male's sexual prowess is to mitigate the guilt of white men over their easier access to Black women in the Deep South.

In a similar vein, Fanon discusses the anxieties created in white men by the alleged sexual potency of the Black male. The Black male is seen as a biological threat, one who can unleash all the destructive urges of the sexual impulse upon white womanhood. From the sensual pleasures received from such sexual unions, white women may be attracted to Black men in massive numbers. Such are the unconscious fears of white males who reify the cultural myth of the sexually virile Black male.

Bond and Peery attempt to refute the notion that the Black male has been emasculated. They deny the absence of virility and the presence of effeminacy in the Black male. In their opinion, such beliefs that Black women are responsible for the castration of Black men are devices to turn Blacks' attention away from racism and place the blame for their oppression on one another. Black men, they say, have demonstrated their manhood in their past resistance to oppression, and whites are keenly aware that Black men now leading the Black liberation struggle are "men" in every sense of the word.

If the Black male has been culturally slandered by calling him emasculated, then the Black woman has been even more maligned by the stereotype of her role as an overbearing matriarch controlling everything that happens

---

[18]David Lynn, "The Process of Learning Parental and Sex Role Identification," *Marriage and Family Living*, 28 (November 1966), pp. 466-470.

[19]A basic tenet of social psychology is that if men define situations as real, then they are real in their consequences. Cf. W. I. Thomas and Florian Znaniecki, *The Polish Peasant in Europe and America* (New York: Alfred A. Knopf, 1927).

in the Black family. Instead of having all sorts of rights and powers denied to white women, she can aptly be described as a slave of a slave.[20] When white America ripped away the Black male's normal functions, it left the Black woman defenseless against all the destructive forces of a racist society. To add insult to injury, she was used—and is still being used, in some cases— as the scapegoat for all the evils that the colossus of American racism has perpetrated on Black men.

Many Black women are forced to work to help house, clothe, and feed their families. While Black women constitute a substantial proportion of the Black labor force, they are systematically exploited by being paid less for doing the same work that men do or by being relegated to low-paying "female" jobs in which there is no possibility for advancement. In terms of incomes, the Black woman is at the bottom of the ladder. The median family income for Black families headed by a woman today is $3,270 a year, less than half the $6,778 income for Black families headed by a male. The jobless rate for Black women is 6.7 percent, as against 4.2 percent for Black men, 3.6 for white women, and 2 percent for white men. Where Black families are headed by women, the chances are that the family will be living in poverty. In the under $2,000–$4,000 range, women head more that half these households.[21]

In the section on the female sex role, Barbara Rhodes' article spells out some new directions for the Black woman. She not only must carry out the maternal and spousal roles in the family but must concern herself with the political struggle of her people. In the process of changing her role, she must create a new self-definition which is related to the Black experience and break away from the definitions of her role imposed upon her by white America. Not only must she redefine her role in terms of the Black reality but must mediate the Black experience to her children so that they too can become healthy beings, with personalities undistorted by the dynamics of a racist system, and can participate in the Black movement toward self-determination.

The article by Staples attempts to debunk the cultural myth of the matriarchal character of Black society. By examining the dynamics of power in human society, he shows how Black women are far from having the power to control the Black community or even the Black family. What authority she does have she received by the default of the Black male. His failure to act can, in turn, be traced to the shackles placed on him by white America. The *raison d'être* of this matriarchal myth is discussed and its implications for the future of the Black liberation struggle delineated.

Gail Stokes makes a plea for the Black male to respect her Black womanhood. Her statements illustrate how the exploitation of the Black male in this country leads to his oppression of the Black woman. Her article reflects some of the conflicts in lower class Black families that result from their abject poverty.

---

[20] Frances M. Beal, "Double Jeopardy: To Be Black and Female," *New Generation*, Fall 1969.

[21] Sylvia Porter, "Negro Women and Poverty," *San Francisco Chronicle*, August 5, 1969, p. 48.

From an objective look at the Black husband-wife relationship, one must unfortunately conclude that it is characterized by conflict and hostility. It makes little sense to create a myth about the happiness or stability of Black marriages. The high rate of divorce, desertion, and separation reveal that all is not well in the Black conjugal relationship. Therefore, we would do better to concentrate on the institution of marriage itself and the factors in the social structure which make marriage such a risky affair.

While it may be considered heresy to challenge the viability of such a sacrosanct institution as marriage, a growing segment of family sociologists are beginning to question whether marriage is the best state for all adults in this society. In fact, the theme of the 1969 National Council on Family Relations Meeting was "Beyond the Anti-Family Society"; and its purpose was to discuss whether the future would see the family surviving as an important institution in our lives. One sociologist has stated that most people achieve at best a life of quiet desperation in their family relations.[22]

In explaining the preponderance of dissolved marriages among Blacks, a multi-factorial approach is necessary. Frazier believed, for instance, that the indiscriminate mating of Blacks, the lack of a legal basis for marriage, meant that marriage failed to become an institution deeply rooted in the mores and folkways of Black people.[23]

Not only was there an absence of traditional mores concerning marriage but Blacks lacked the economic underpinnings that made white marriages much more stable. A very important element in the past that contributed to the stability of the white family was its patriarchal character. The patriarchal white family was based upon the economic hegemony of the white male. The only income and property rights enjoyed by a woman were those her husband gave her. In other words, the stability of the white family was, in large part, dependent on the subordination of white women. Once they entered the labor force in large numbers and developed some sort of economic independence, the divorce rate in this country more than doubled.[24]

In comparision, the Black woman has long been economically independent. In cases where she has been dependent on the male for economic support, the marriages have been more stable. One reason for the high divorce rate in the Black middle class may be the higher educational rank of Black college women, almost half of whom have more education than their husbands.[25] In general, marriages in which the wife has a higher socioeconomic status than the husband are less stable than marriages in which the husband is of an equal or higher socioeconomic level.

In cases where the economic and educational factors are not influential, the more independent and nonconforming nature of the Black female can create conflict in the marriage. Whereas white women are sometimes intimi-

---

[22]William Goode, *World Revolution and Family Patterns* (New York: Free Press, 1963), p. 38.

[23]E. Franklin Frazier, *The Negro Family in the United States* (Chicago: University of Chicago Press, 1939).

[24]The divorce rate has actually increased 800 percent in the past 100 years.

[25]Jean Noble, *The Negro Woman College Graduate* (New York: Columbia University Press, 1956).

dated by their husbands, Black wives are more likely to give as good as they get. If her husband yells at her, she yells back. If he fools around with other women, she makes it with other men. The double standard of male prerogatives does not apply in marriage any more than it does in premarital sexual relations. For some Black women, losing their husband is of negligible consequence. The important thing is that she was married at one time.

Furthermore, the idea of a happy marriage may be more fantasy than fact for most of the white population. One expert on the subject, Clifford Adams, remarked, "Odds on any marriage being a success are shorter than those of hitting the jackpot on a pinball machine in Las Vegas." He goes on to say that sex is one of the most important subconscious factors influencing the male in mate selection, while love is the first thing the woman seeks; sex is ranked only sixth in her desires. Under these circumstances how can marriages last? Consequently, government statistics showing that only 28 percent of all marriages end in divorce are misleading. If you take into account annulments and desertions, which are not included, the figure would be nearer 40 percent. Adding to this what Adams calls "the morbidity marriage," in which a man and woman continue living together just for appearances or convenience while actually hating each other, we find that only about 25 percent of marriages are really happy.[26]

In the last section, "Husbands and Wives," an excerpt from Lee Rainwater's renowned study "The Crucible of Identity: The Negro Lower-Class Family" explores some of the dynamics of married life among lower class Blacks. In his analysis, he focuses on how economic problems generate tension in the husband-wife relationship. When the Black male ceases to provide for his family, his wife may take the attitude that she is just as well off without him as with him. The failure of Black men to secure regular employment due to America's job ceiling for Blacks consequently impairs their chances for marital success.

Staples' article reviews some of the problems besieging Black marriages and states that a recapitulation of the African past would help stabilize Black marriages. He also suggests that one way to reduce marital conflict would be to prepare Black males in advance for their marital roles. This premarital preparation program would be Black-oriented, and the educators would be male members of the Black community.

Blood and Wolfe's representative sample of Black and white blue-collar marriages in the Detroit metropolitan area shows differences in marriage patterns even when comparisons are limited to low blue-collar or high blue-collar marriages only. They found that Black families are more often wife-dominant at the expense of equalitarianism in making major family decisions. The division of labor in Black homes involves less sharing and flexibility, despite a slightly higher proportion of working wives. Black wives are more self-reliant in coping with their own emotional problems and emphasize their own contributions to the family welfare, rather than the husband's

---

[26]Clifford Adams quoted in the *San Francisco Chronicle*, July 7, 1969, p. 2.

occupational prospects. Black men are less companionable to their wives and are generally evaluated less favorable as marriage partners than are white husbands of the same occupational level.

The excerpt from Frazier's polemical work *The Black Bourgeoisie* examines marriage patterns in the middle class strata. Although the economic variable is not as salient a factor, the Black middle class marriage is also riddled with frustrations and conflict. Frazier's analysis indicates that the problems in Black middle class marriages stem from the make-believe world of the Black bourgeoisie, whereby they lack the economic basis and "genuine" values of the white middle class.

3

Premarital Dating Patterns

Hylan Lewis: Courtship, Marriage, and the Family

The general interest, values, and behavior in the sex area are somewhat similar to—and in fact are related to—the whiskey drinking patterns [in the Black community]. Unconcealed sex interest and activity are widespread. Among nonrespectable persons this behavior tends to be more frank, unashamed, and public—sex and the values related to it are a prominent feature of the life-way of this category. Sex and sex experiences are important parts of anecdotes, banter, jokes, and boasts. In general, the behavior of respectables tends to be more discreet; however, in a community where one basis of fixing status or typing is the current sex liaison or the recognized propensity or disposition for sex dalliance, references to upper status men such as the following are not uncommon: "He'll play too, if he gets a chance or you let him." Sex dalliance is taken for granted, and there is an enduring interest in the sex status and behavior of others.

Lower status females show a great deal of sex initiative and independence: "I don't have to worry about no one man"; "Anything he can do, I can do." There are some women in all levels of the population who are

Reprinted from *Blackways of Kent* by Hylan Lewis (Chapel Hill: University of North Carolina Press, 1955), pp. 82–93. By permission of the University of North Carolina Press. Hylan Lewis is Professor of Sociology at Brooklyn College.

known as "women who have always done what they want to do." Involved in such behavior or attitudes are the general tendency to take sex and sex experience for granted—as normal and desirable goals; the female assumption—often explicit—that the male is promiscuous; and a rather strong feeling about established claims on the male. Particularly among the nonrespectables, the relative independence and lack of sex passivity on the part of the female, plus the dalliance tendencies of the male, add up to a considerable amount of tension that seems to underlie many liaisons and marriages. This situation plays a great part in much of the husband-wife bickering and violence that is fairly common and which in many cases is predictable and anticipated with some humor by neighbors.

Gifts or some degree of support from the male are a constant in nonmarital liaisons; they are taken for granted and freely discussed. There is some informal ranking of men on a basis of the regularity and amount of gifts or support. A woman who "runs out" on a man who has "been good to her" runs the risk of violent retaliation; she is likely also to be condemned by other women for committing something of an ethical breach. In the same vein, a woman who has a man who is especially "good to her" is considered fortunate and often receives advice to "hold what you got."

In a culture where the sex interest is an important one and has major functions aside from reproduction and the husband-wife relationship, there is a question as to how long sex interest and activity continue. Certainly the evidence indicates that the interest, at any rate, persists throughout the upper age groups in both men and women. There are even a few documented instances of significant activity in the upper age groups as well. The evidence for the interest appears in the conversation of widows and widowers about marriages and marriage possibilities; in the good humored mutual joshing and joking among older people; in the sexual content of reminiscences and jokes; in allusions to current or recent liaisons of older people; and in the exchange of gossip and news about the affairs of younger people. The older men might joke about their current inactivity, pointing out that it is "all in the mind now"; the older women never do, although they may point out that they, in effect, have retired from sex activity. With women, there is always implicit the idea that they could if they wanted to—and that they are in fact desirable to some man or men now.

The following documentary material suggests the prevalence of the interest and something of the flavor and range of nonmarital sex activity, particularly among the lower status category.

On the activity of younger girls:

These young girls gets out sooner and does more than we use to do. We never drank whisky and went out with mens that young.... Some of these girls ain't nothing but babies; they starts when they's twelve and thirteen years old and before you can turn around they's having babies by some of these old men and having to stop school.... I done plenty myself when I used to get around but my mother would have killed me if I had a done what these babies is doing. M—— ain't but about fifteen or sixteen years old and she done had practically all these men around here; she "burned" K—— and M—— and they had to take her down to the State Hospital for treatment; I reckon the nurse still goes over there.

High school boy's banter, illustrating social pressures:

Old N—— ain't never had none; the girls say he won't do it. Somebody ought to take him out and make him git some; but he wouldn't know what to do if he got it.

Here it is winter coming on and boy, you ain't got no place to go and nobody to keep you warm. . . . I got somebody to keep me warm; you'd better get somebody yourself.

High school girl on personal preferences:

I'd rather fool around with older men and married men than these young boys; they ain't got nothing and they worry you to death.

On female sex aggression and single standard, from a lower status woman:

Why don't he say something to me—he's human, ain't he? Of course, I'm married but my husband do what he want to do and I do what I want to do. . . . Do I have a chance still?

On female sex aggression, from an upper status woman:

I told him: "You come around and pick me up and we'll go and what we do ain't nobody's business but ours. Let me worry about my husband."

An approach by a male:

When can we get together? You just got me so that I don't think about nothing but you. . . . Just about how much would it cost and take for all the arrangements?

On sex jealousy:

He's a fool. He married that woman when she already had three children by other men. Now, he don't allow nobody else to hardly look at her; he'll near kill her if he catch her talking to a man.

On typing and placing:

She's a good girl, but she just can't say no. She just don't know how to say no.
That man there, he got a woman down the street.
He's a good, honest straight man; you don't never hear nobody say nothing about him and no womens. That's hard here in Kent because the womens treats the men nice; but it's a small town and the folks likes to talk. . . . I reckon he must go out of town because all you mens is devils.

On the interest and activity of the aged; a woman in her seventies:

A woman ain't never too old to have a boy friend. . . . I tell you the truth, I wants one to come and see me about once a week and pep me up and unruffle me. That's what God made the men for.

Among the differentiated, or respectable and more stable families, sex behavior lacks the frank, open, and, to some extent, promiscuous character of the relations among their opposites. Public behavior with respect to sex and whisky go far to define respectability. Since pride, respectability and the approach to conventional morals tend to be earmarks of the respectable family, this group tends to frown upon, is ashamed of, and seeks to dissociate itself from "lower class" behavior. The fear of "contamination" of children is not groundless; this is probably the chief parental fear from the "lower class." These respectable parents seek to offset the threat by rigid discipline and supervision as well as by "getting the children out of the situation," if possible, by sending them away. Some of the respectable families have not escaped what for them is the acute shame of illegitimacy.

E. Franklin Frazier points out that the social significance of illegitimacy among Negroes becomes apparent only when we view it in relation to the organization of Negro life in the South. In many areas "Negro life follows the folkways that emancipation modified but did not destroy."[1] In Kent as elsewhere in the South, "in some cases the illegitimacy has taken place during the disorganization following emancipation."[2] More recently, it is related to movement, change, and contact with different ways of life that have resulted in general disorganization of family life. A good portion of Kent's Negroes are marginally rural people in the process of adapting to the demands of a modern culture that has a significant urban and industrial content.

The rate of illegitimacy among Kent Negroes is high;[3] how high is difficult to say with accuracy because much depends on definition, and records are incomplete and unreliable in many instances. Statistics as to illegitimacy make no subtle distinctions, but community gossip and hearsay

---

[1] E. Franklin Frazier, *The Negro Family in the United States* (Chicago: University of Chicago Press, 1939), p. 110.

[2] *Ibid.*, p. 113.

[3] School records indicate that the rate is around twenty percent.

do. These types of situations are locally recognized and described: (1) conception out of wedlock but marriage before birth of child; (2) conception out of wedlock with no marriage to father of child—although marriage may take place before or after birth to another man; (3) conception out of wedlock with eventual abortion, miscarriage, or stillbirth; (4) birth of child to a married woman with the imputed father other than the husband; (5) the offspring of marriages that are in fact bigamous (divorce has been impossible, yet there are several instances of "divorced" people remarrying and raising a second family).

Given the fact that practically everyone knows everyone else, instances of illegitimacy and alleged illegitimacy are generally known and talked about freely. In most cases, the father or alleged father is identified. Many men admit such facts and openly or tacitly recognize their issue; there is a tendency among some men to boast about the number of children they have "out in the bushes." The mothers of illegitimate children (except those who are married to men other than the father) tend to be frank, almost casual, in their references to the fact—and even to the circumstances of "getting caught." The remarks of Frazier with respect to comparable situations are pertinent for many local women:

The attitude of these women indicates that they regard sex relations as normal behavior during a courtship which may or may not lead to marriage. When it results in the birth of a child, certain obligations are thereby imposed upon the mother. These obligations are the obligations which every mother should feel toward her offspring.[4]

However, there are many girls and many parents whose views are more conventional; once pregnancy ensues—barring abortion or miscarriage—individual, family, and community pressures begin to operate. It is considered the right thing for the man to marry the girl, and if he does, he is commended. The chances of the man marrying her are high if she has not been promiscuous.

In general, the fact that a girl or a woman has had an illegitimate child does not materially affect her marriage chances. A father in telling a group of men that his son had recently married said: "She's a nice girl, nice family and all—of course, she done had a baby, but that ain't nothing."

The community attitudes toward the illegitimate child are not harsh. It is better, of course, to have been born in wedlock, but the stigma for child and mother, unless they belong to the more stable families, is not great. The sanctions are few, other than mild gossip, which is certain, and possible "churching," i.e., being called before the church and having to express contriteness and to ask forgiveness. In the local Baptist church, when a member has an illegitimate child, the established procedure is for the members of the Deaconess Board or some representative to call on the person and

[4]Frazier, *op. cit.*, p. 115.

ascertain "if they are sorry and if they will do it again." The emissaries report to the full church, and usually the person who is contrite and asks forgiveness is forgiven and welcomed back into the fellowship of the church. In the last few years this has occurred three times.

There is hardly a family in the community that doesn't have some member or members—in this or the previous generation—who have been touched or are alleged to have been touched by illegitimacy. In some cases where members of the present generation have had a common father but have had different mothers without the father having been married to both, kinship ties are openly recognized.

Indeed, some individuals in the community are known interchangeably by two surnames: by the name of the mother who was unmarried when the individual was born and by the name of the father, or of the mother's husband, or of the family that raised him, or even by some name that is chosen personally. Adoption is likewise a fairly frequent phenomenon; it is usually taken for granted that the adopted person is the illegitimate offspring of relatives or friends.

There was not a single male in Kent who by manner or reputation would fit the stereotype "sissy," nor were specific references made to individuals in this community as sex deviates, even in jest. Informants can remember but two instances in recent times of males who were suspect because of their effeminate manner. However, aberrant sex behavior and types are not wholly unfamiliar. Younger men, who have been in the army or to urban centers, in recounting experiences often make reference to that type of behavior. A suggestion of latent perversion is seen in the fondling behavior of some men when drunk; there are one or two who are known as biters and pinchers when they get drunk.

There was one female nonrespectable, a migrant to the community from a nearby urban center, who was variously referred to as a "woman-lover," "morphodite," "mermaid." An elderly woman, who is herself viewed as eccentric, reported rebuffing this person's advances. This one instance was widely circulated and laughed about, but mixed with the humor there was considerable indignation and rejection of the deviate. In general, sex orthodoxy and competence are taken for granted and are central in the typical personality structure as it is manifested in public behavior and verbalizations.

It is difficult to gauge the frequency of abortions. Infrequent references are made to persons who "got rid of it" or to the individual who "has had five or six abortions." For the most part, the persons indicated are persons of some sophistication or status and means. These factors in the general situation must be considered: the social sanctions against bearing an illegitimate child are apparently not severe except among the differentiated, respectable families having significant pride and stability. Thus, in general, the pressure to abort is less, the support of the extended family eliminates much of the economic pressure and also gives some psychological security, the knowledge of efficient methods or techniques is not widespread, there are no generally known specialists in the local community, and the emphasis in the religion upon forgiveness and salvation dwarfs the notion of terrific punishment for transgression.

Older informants in speaking about folk methods and beliefs mention such concoctions as a brew from an unknown root gotten from the woods, brew from the roots of a cotton plant, and a brew from green coffee. One person recalled a woman who was supposed to have used the handle of an umbrella for purposes of opening the womb. They point out that "nowadays these girls when they gets caught sometimes tries to get something from the drugstore." There is a belief in some quarters that it is harder to abort a boy baby than a girl baby.

Older people knew nothing of condoms in their youth. Older women report the use of cotton wadding sprinkled with soda as a contraceptive device. Among the reasons still given in some quarters for eating starch or clay[5] is the belief that menstruation will be assured or eased. Among the younger people, the most common contraceptive devices are the condom and the vaginal douche. Among the unmarried males there appears to be more anxiety about contracting a venereal disease than about conception.

Courtship is referred to as "going together" or "courting"; the former expression is heard more frequently and has a slightly different connotation from "courting" or "courting strong," as the expression often goes. "Going together" implies a mutually agreeable stable relationship that will likely lead to marriage and it is tacitly recognized in most instances that intimacy is involved. "Courting" suggests a wooing relationship that is not as fixed or stable as "going together." "Going out" or dating is more casual and catch-as-catch-can; it is a kind of sex game that usually has clandestine or illicit features. An oblique recognition and temporary rejection of some of the accepted values in courtship are seen in the statement of a young man:

I used to go with her. And I was treating her real nice because I wanted to marry her. I was acting like white folks and never tried to "date" her or nothing—I wanted her for my wife. I used to take her to the movies and places and take her right back straight home. But I reckon that wasn't what she wanted; I was too slow and treated her too nice because this other guy came along. . . .

"Acting like white folks" doesn't necessarily mean aping the whites as such; rather it is a recognition that the whites know and are sophisticated about proper conduct. It is a design for proper and conventional conduct rather than the disposition to ape or imitate what are considered *per se* superior ways. The same person who made the above statement in another

[5]Starch eating is more prevalent than clay eating among women. These, plus the smaller amount of soot eating reported, are sex-linked behavior, although young men report having eaten starch as youths. All seem to be related in some way to beliefs about the sex physiology of the female. Random questioning among women indicated that about two-thirds have been or are now starch eaters.

context referred to whites as being "dirtier" than Negroes in the area of sex morality.

The great bulk of courtship behavior among the young people takes place outside the home: through the movies, automobile rides, and, to a lesser extent, the taverns and the churches. Occasional trips to out-of-town entertainment spots are a part of the pattern. In season, rural lanes, the woods and the fields ("Green's Hotel") are popular. The lack of "nice places to go" is a matter of frustration among some of the younger people. For example: "There ain't no decent place to take a girl in this town. All you can do is take her to the movies, and you gets tired of that. If you ain't got a car, you just ain't nowhere."

The marriage ceremony tends to be a "private affair." The vast majority of the marriages are civil affairs performed by the local probate judge. In general, the couple about to be married take few persons into their confidence; they secure the license with a minimum of publicity, and at a later date—always at night—"slip up to Judge Priest's." After the marriage the news is spread rapidly by word of mouth. Usually they take up residence with one of the parents or some relative.

During this study eight marriages were performed locally in which the principals were local residents; in only three instances were ministers' services used. One was the holiday marriage of the only child of one of the differentiated families to a fiancé of college days; one was the marriage of an elderly deacon to a relative of a minister. Within the past ten years there has been but one full scale wedding. For most persons in Kent, marriage is a matter of "going to the judge's tonight."

David A. Schulz: The Role of the Boyfriend

The importance of the boyfriend's role becomes apparent when one realizes that four of the five women in this group who are now heading households receive support from boyfriends. The amount of support and the type of relationship that exists vary considerably and suggest a typology consisting of four different roles which a boyfriend may play and for which there is some support from segments of this population. These types are: the quasi-father, the supportive biological father, the supportive companion, and the pimp. The image of the pimp has dominated the literature thus far. In this relationship the male is largely exploitive.

However, there is also in the literature some evidence that these nonmarital liaisons between men and women of the Negro lower class are more stable than is commonly acknowledged. In *Blackways of Kent*, Lewis men-

From David A. Schulz, *Coming Up Black: Patterns of Ghetto Socialization*, pp. 136–144. © 1969. Reprinted by permission of Prentice-Hall, Inc., Englewood Cliffs, New Jersey. Dr. Schulz is Assistant Professor of Sociology at The Pennsylvania State University.

tions in passing that "gifts and some degree of support from the male are taken for granted and freely discussed. There is some informal ranking of men on a basis of the regularity and amount of gifts or support."[1] In this section fuller documentation of this support in nonmarital liaisons will be presented. In so doing, we hope to make it apparent that the lower-class Negro man contributes to the welfare of his woman more than is commonly acknowledged, and plays an important role of surrogate father to her children.

The Quasi-Father

The distinguishing marks of the quasi-father are that (1) he supports the family regularly over long periods of time (eleven years is the longest known, though this was interrupted by a short marriage; five years is the longest consecutive time known at present). Often he will go with his woman to the store and buy her week's food. (2) His concern extends directly to her children as well. He will give them allowances or spending money, attempt more or less successfully to discipline them, and will take them out to the park, to the movies, or to other places for entertainment. (3) He frequently visits the family during the week, and may or may not reside with them in the project—usually not. The relationship is not ordinarily conducted clandestinely, but in full knowledge of kin on both sides—particularly the parents, if they reside in the same city with the couple. In return for this he receives (1) his meals (some or all if residing with the family); (2) washing and ironing; (3) sexual satisfaction, and (4) *familial companionship*. In short, he seems to be bargaining for more than just a woman in seeking intimacy in the context of a family. To illustrate let us take the example of Jay and Ethyl.

Ethyl Perry (thirty-three) went with Jay (twenty-four) for over five years. During that time he took her out, bought her the majority of her furniture, and supplied her with fifteen to twenty dollars per week, usually by means of buying her week's food. In addition his family contributed several pieces of furniture and invited Ethyl over for meals on occasion. None of her six children is his. Ethyl describes Jay as a "nice person . . . kind-hearted" and by this she means that ". . . he believes in survival for me and my family, me and my kids. He don't mind sharing with my youngsters. If I ask him for a helping hand, he don't seem to mind that. The only part of it is that I dislike his drinking." It's not the drinking as such that Ethyl dislikes, but the man Jay becomes when he drinks. He becomes angry and quick tempered, but has yet to beat Ethyl when in such a state.

Jay's concern for Ethyl's children is expressed in various ways. As Dovie, Ethyl's fifteen-year-old daughter, sees Jay, he tends to be bossy. "He be all right sometimes but he drinks and that's the reason I don't like him. . . . He tries to boss people. Like if my boyfriends come over here he be saying I

---

[1] Hylan Lewis. *Blackways of Kent* (Chapel Hill: University of North Carolina Press, 1961), p. 84. See also E. Franklin Frazier, *op. cit.*, p. 215, and Drake and Cayton, *loc. cit.*

can't have no company." But Mary, her eighteen-year-old daughter, revealed that Jay gave her a small washing machine for her baby's diapers. She said, "My mother's *boyfriend* bought it. . . . It was about three days after my baby was born."

Jay's concern is expressed in other ways as well. He took the children to the movies, to the park, gave them a small allowance as spending money each week when he bought the groceries, and once, when Ethyl was sick, he took care of the youngest two for nearly a month while she was in the hospital. During the years that they were going together Jay visited the family several times a week, most frequently spending the weekend with them. He continually asked Ethyl to marry him, though Ethyl felt he was only half serious. Jay was asked why he bothered to take care of Ethyl and he replied, "That's a personal question. . . . Well, first of all I help her because I love her and we're going to get married sometime, but not just now because we can't afford it."

A second example is that of Tilly (thirty-three) and Sam (thirty-four—looks twenty-five). Tilly has been going with Sam for over eleven years—even while married to her second husband, whom she finally left for Sam. He helps the budget regularly out of his pay as a dock worker in a river barge yard. Tilly says, "Sam gives me thirty dollars a week." He has also bought several small pieces of furniture and takes her out almost every weekend. He lives just around the corner with his cousin, visits the family almost every night, and sometimes spends the night, though he usually sleeps with his cousin.

Tilly feels that Sam "treats her kids better than their daddy do. He buys them certain things [such as] clothes. He spanks them. . . . He takes them different places." She further feels that it is very important that a man treat her kids right. "If they don't care for the kids or anything then that's a bad man. . . . First he's got to love your kids before he loves you."

Her sons Richard (ten) and William (seventeen) confirm the fact that Sam is concerned about the children. Richard says, "He takes up for us when we get a whipping. . . . He tells her not to whip us this time." When asked, "Does he have pretty good control over the kids?" William replied, "They do what he say most of the time. Irvin [eighteen] don't, but the rest of them will."

They are still going together and Sam proposes marriage with some regularity, but Tilly shies away. "I think I'm better off just not having a husband. . . . I wouldn't definitely say I would get a good one. I might get a bad one. I don't want to take a chance." Even though she has known Sam since childhood, she is not certain about him. He drinks a lot but is not to her knowledge the violent type—at least he is not as a single man. Her fear is that when he "has papers on her" he might change. Her experience with her second husband taught her how quickly a man could change on her.

And so Ethyl broke up with Jay, never having seriously considered marriage while going with him, and Tilly says that *maybe* in three of four years she will be ready for marriage to Sam. Marriage has not yet resulted because in both instances the family is doing better under the combined resources of welfare and the boyfriend's assistance than they could do under his wages alone, and in both instances the woman is afraid of the man's drinking behavior. In both instances the boyfriends are well known by the women's families and visit frequently with them.

Since breaking with Jay, Ethyl has been living with a new boyfriend, Raymond (twenty-nine), and says that she is seriously considering marriage to him—at least to the extent that she has decided to get a divorce. Thus, marriage may or may not be a result of a quasi-father relationship, but it does provide the context in which a woman with children is likely to make up her mind one way or another about a man. It is interesting to remember here that three of the five women [in the study] still living with their husbands began their relationship "common law." Only one of the quasi-fathers at present lives with his woman.

The Supportive Biological Father

A second type of boyfriend is the supportive biological father. Here the concern of the man—and largely that of the woman also—is to support the children that they have brought into the world without seriously considering marriage to one another. In some instances the man or woman may well be married to someone else. The man's support may be voluntary, as in the case of Edward Patterson, or it may be as the result of a voluntarily signed acknowledgment that the children are his.

In the case of Leona Wards (fifty) and Larry (forty-nine), Leona was married once and had four children by her first husband. His "cutting out" and drinking led to a separation and Leona took up with Larry, who gave her three children, in ages now from eighteen to thirteen, before he married another woman a couple of years ago. He played the role of supportive biological father before he married. They had been going together for nearly *sixteen* years, though only Leona was true to the relationship. She has never remarried and claims that even now she has no boyfriend because they are too much trouble at her age, although she admits that she would enjoy a companion in her declining years.

Larry has taken the children on long trips, such as the one to Arizona in 1963, he has bought them clothes, especially at Christmas time, and has paid regularly the amount of fifteen to twenty dollars a week for their support since 1954. At that time he acknowledged that the children are his and the court fixed the amount for their support.

Leona's being true to Larry is a part of her rearing as she sees it. Her mother died in 1927 and "daddy went haywire," so she went to live with her maternal aunt and her husband, Uncle Paul—"gentle Paul"—who was a Baptist minister. Her aunt was a very strict woman and quite respectable.

Leona's marriage lasted fourteen years, and at the end she left her husband because he was undependable in his support of her and the children. While separated she met Larry, her boyfriend:

At the time I met Larry, my first husband and I wasn't together. I met Larry through the [same] church. He asked me [to marry] and I told him not until my husband's children got off my hands and out of the way. I never wanted a stepfather over my children . . . it was something that Lewis and I have always said.

Her main departure from her rearing was having children out of wedlock, and while she loves the children, she regrets the departure:

That's the only thing in life I didn't want—to have children without being married. I just wasn't reared like that. But *they are all by one man.* They're not by this, that one, nor the other one. They're all by one man.

Leona is proud to be able to say, "I have been by Larry as if he and I were married." But he was not true to her. She broke off their relationship by cutting him with a knife.

While it is true that Larry is legally obligated to care for his children, it is noteworthy that he claimed them as his in the first place and that he supports them in gifts over and above his legal obligations. His inability to believe that Leona was true to him, plus her reluctance to have a stepfather over her husband's children, at least one of whom has not yet left home, contributed to the factors other than economic that mitigated against their marriage— but did not prevent them from courting for sixteen years.

Most of the care that fathers give to their outside children seems to be much less regular than Larry's, but is, nevertheless, largely voluntary. Edward Patterson, for example, has three by two different women. His outside children live with their mothers, and when he gets tired of his wife he moves out and lives with Leddie B., by whom he has had two children. His legitimate children complain that when he goes to visit one of the outsiders, he gives her and her siblings more money for spending than he gives his legitimate children. His wife protests that he stole their TV set and gave it to the mother of one of these children, and his son claims that when he returned to his home in the country recently, he bought several dresses for his outside child living there. Mr. Patterson will not speak of these outsiders and keeps his money matters to himself. His wife has opened letters from the mothers of these children requesting regular support, but does not know if he is giving only to them. She believes that he spends most of the $406 a month take-home pay he earns from his job on these women and their children.

The Supportive Companion

A less durable relationship exists in the case of the "supportive companion" who "keeps a woman." Here the concern of the male is mainly to have a good time with a clean woman. The concern of the woman is for support and companionship. Such a relationship is not to be confused with prostitution, for it is not a mere matter of a business transaction but a search for intimacy on both parts, a search conducted in the context of severe economic and emotional handicaps. In this community such a relationship is likely to occur between an older man (late twenties, early thirties) and a younger woman (early twenties, teens) who has had children outside of wedlock.

In such a relationship, the man rarely keeps the woman in her own apartment, as would be the case in more solvent circumstances, where the woman is usually single and without children. Rather, he provides a regular "weekend away" at his apartment or other suitable place where they can be together away from the children. He takes her out, provides her with spending money and a good time. Should she conceive a child, he is least likely of all types to want to assume support of the child. Responsibility is what he is trying to avoid.

The example of Madeline (sixteen) and Jerry (twenty-three) is a case in point. They knew each other about a year during 1959–1960. Madeline had already had two children by two other men. Jerry came by for dinner occasionally, but usually he made the weekend scene at a motel apartment he rented for the occasion. When Friday came round, he would give Madeline money which she often turned into dresses or other items to enhance her appearance. Madeline says, "Jerry's not like a lot of men that you find. A lot of men, if they do something for you they feel they own you." Jerry gave her "fifteen or twenty dollars, sometimes more" each week and had keys to a two-room kitchenette for the weekend. Madeline says, "We were always together [on the weekend]. Where I went he usually went, where he went I went. We'd go to the apartment and everything. But lots of times we would go and just watch TV or sit and talk or have a drink or something. Then we would go—especially in the summertime—we'd go there because they had air conditioning."

The Pimp

. . . The pimp is characteristic of the young man of the street who lives off the labors of prostitutes or off women who are able to earn their own way through wages or welfare. He is kept by his woman and dresses like a dandy. None of the women living in broken homes has had a pimp, but Andrew Buchanan claims he was one as a youth. The pimp relationship may be, for the man at least, quite often a *pre*marital experience. . . .

Speculation on Extensiveness and Relationship in Time

While there is no accurate measure of the prevalence of these four types of boyfriends, the data are suggestive. The pimp is the most talked about male-female nonmarital relationship in the literature. These data, however, suggest that it is not as prevalent in the project as is commonly assumed. It is possible that pimping may be more or less restricted to the younger men and may phase out into less exploitive relationships with females as the men grow older. Therefore, the frequency of the pimping relationship may well be exaggerated, since the younger men tend to be more vocal about their exploits, and the older men who now view such activity with a certain resentment may bewail the fact that "things used to be much better."

A man may play one or more boyfriend roles in his life. We can thus see these types as phases in a developmental sequence. The pimp is an early role of the young man of the street who would rather "live sweet" than work, or who has found that his value on the love market is greater than it is on the labor market. The data suggest that such a relationship is quite likely to terminate when the man reaches his mid-thirties. He may then decide to marry the woman he has pimped off because by then he has had one or more children by her, or because he is, after having sown his wild oats, seeking now a more intimate and lasting relationship. If he does marry her, then he comes under the norm that it is "unfair" to pimp off a woman you are married to.

No one, however, has gone from a pimping relationship directly to marriage with the same woman. In the case of Edward Patterson, who pimped off several women for several years before marriage, a quasi-father relationship was entered into with another woman for four or five years before he married her as the result of an unwanted pregnancy. This marriage has lasted nineteen years.

The quasi-fathers are in their late twenties or early thirties, and in one of the three instances, marriage is actively sought by the woman. In the other two the males are still being tested. This opportunity to get to know a man under near familial situations is a boon to these women, who have been disappointed in marriage one or more times. He can prove that he is a good provider and a gentle, "good" man. Not all quasi-father relationships terminate in marriage.

The supportive companion is, if the data from these inferences are correct, more likely to be the relationship that exists between an older man (late twenties or early thirties) and a younger woman (late teens, early twenties). It may be an alternative for a rejected quasi-father, who sought but could not obtain marriage, and whose income is stable enough to permit such indulgence. Finally, most men can play, if they so desire, the role of supportive biological father throughout most of their lives, since almost every male has had at least one child outside of wedlock. For some who never marry, this may be the extent to which their craving for familial companionship is expressed—the occasional gift to an illegitimate child.

Carlfred B. Broderick: Social Heterosexual Development Among Urban Negroes and Whites

Most research on the development of heterosexuality is concerned either with the earliest or the latest stages in the process. The focus is either on the problem of sex role learning and identification among young children, or on the sexual and social dilemmas of later adolescence and early adulthood. The purpose of this paper is to compare patterns of social heterosexuality of Negroes and whites during the relatively uncharted middle period from ten through 17 years of age.

In the larger study from which these data were drawn, four major components of social heterosexual development have emerged. The first component of heterosexual orientation is a positive attitude toward the general subject of romantic interaction with the opposite sex. This diffuse approval is reflected, for example, in one's enjoyment of romantic movies or in one's positive attitude toward marriage. The second component builds upon the first and involves an emotional attachment to some particular member of the opposite sex. Items on whether a boy has a girlfriend or has been in love get at this factor. At the earlier ages, these items most often index emotional rather than social involvement, since the level of reciprocation is typically very low. At the later ages, they more often are associated with reciprocal social behavior as well as feelings. The third component might be negatively defined as the absence of social prejudice toward the opposite sex as a class of persons. This social openness is expressed primarily in sociometric items, although items on playing kissing games at parties also bear on it since this would necessarily involve mixed parties. The fourth and most advanced component of social heterosexuality during this age span involves actual social interaction on a romantic pair basis. This component of heterosexuality is tapped by questions on such interactions as serious kissing, dating, and going steady.

For the purpose of comparing the two racial groups, a simple index of social heterosexuality was developed from the nine questionnaire items used as examples above. These nine were chosen from a much larger number of items on a self-administered questionnaire to represent all of the four basic components of heterosexuality and to show evidence of construct validity; that is, each item differentiated between the sexes or among ages or communities in a meaningful way and related consistently to other variables. The exact wording and derivation of each item is given in Table 1.

Based on his responses to these items, each individual was assigned a social heterosexuality score. These scores ranged from zero to nine depending on how many of his responses were positive (heterosexual). A score of

Reprinted from *Journal of Marriage and the Family*, 27 (May 1965), pp. 200-203, by permission of the National Council on Family Relations and the author. Dr. Carlfred B. Broderick is Associate Professor of Family Relationships, The Pennsylvania State University.

Table 1. Nine Items Contributing to the Social Heterosexuality Score

1. "Would you like to get married someday?" *Yes* response was scored as positive, *No* and *Don't Know* were scored as negative.
2. Under a cartoon showing a group of boys and girls watching a love scene (a couple embracing) on the screen of a movie theater, the questions: "How do the boys feel about what they are seeing?" and "How do the girls feel about what they are seeing?" The responses concerning one's own sex group were considered a measure of one's own attitude. They were coded as *positive* (they enjoy it; they wish they were doing that) or *other*, which included a range of negative, neutral, and conditional responses.
3. "Do you have a girlfriend now?" (Or "Do you have a boyfriend now?" for the girls.) *Yes* or *No.*
4. "Have you even been in love?" *Yes* or *No.*
5. "Name your best friend" and "List any others you like almost as well." (Five spaces were provided in all.) This item was scored positively if one or more members of the opposite sex were listed among the friends.
6. "Sometimes people play kissing games at some of their parties. Have you ever played kissing games?" *Yes* or *No.*
7. "Kissing in kissing games is usually just for fun. At other times a kiss may mean something special. Have you ever seriously kissed a girl?" ("A boy," if the respondent was a girl.) *Yes* or *No.*
8. "Have you ever had a date?" *Yes* or *No.*
9. "How many times have you gone steady?" Once or more often were counted as positive responses.

nine would indicate that the individual definitely wanted to get married someday, he liked the love scenes in movies, he had a girlfriend, he had been in love, he had named at least one member of the opposite sex among his five closest friends, he had played kissing games at parties, he had seriously kissed a girl on his own initiative, he had begun to date, and he had gone steady at least once. Someone with a score of zero, on the other hand, would have felt or experienced none of these things.

Sample

The sample consisted of 1,262 young people. It included all the fifth through twelfth graders attending school within the district on the day the study was made. The area in which these young people live is part of the industrial complex of a middle-sized Pennsylvania city. Its economy is dominated by heavy industry and by a nearby military installation of some size.

Just over one quarter of the sample were Negroes. The primary ethnic origins of the white families were Eastern European. Although they lived in the same community, sent their children to the same schools, and derived thier income from the same employers, there were several important differences between the circumstances of the Negro and white families in the sample.

Most fathers of both races were blue-collar workers, and although there were members of both races in each occupational category, Negroes were under-represented among the foremen, skilled, and semi-skilled and over-represented among the unskilled. The difference in occupational distribution of the two groups was significant at the .001 level.

In addition to these occupational differences, there were important differences in the family composition of Negroes and whites in the sample. Thirty-five percent of the Negro families had been broken by either death, divorce, or separation, whereas only 13 percent of the white families had been disrupted (the difference is significant at the .001 level). The sibling constellations of the two groups were also quite different. The proportion of only children among the white subjects was almost twice as great as among the Negro subjects (17 percent compared to nine percent). On the other hand, nearly twice as many Negro as white subjects reported having both brothers and sisters (60 percent compared to 36 percent). These figures indicated that the Negro subjects came from large families far more often than the white subjects.

Since there were these substantial socio-economic and familial in addition to racial differences between the two groups to be compared, it might be argued that any difference in the pattern of social heterosexual development of Negroes and whites might be explained solely on the basis of these uncontrolled background factors. Unfortunately, with the present sample it was not possible to control on these factors (occupation, family stability, and family size) because the numbers in some cells would have become too small. It was possible, however, to test for the independent influence of these factors within one race (the white race) by examining the relationship of each background variable to each of the nine items of the social heterosexuality score. Only one item, attitude toward marriage, was significantly related to these background factors. Children from white-collar homes and from stable families were significantly more positive in their attitudes toward marriage than were children from blue-collar or broken homes.This relationship probably helps to explain why Negroes had a substantially lower percentage of positive responses than whites on this item and on no other item. This cannot, however, account for the results reported below since its effect is to reduce rather than to exaggerate the overall relationship between race and heterosexuality reported in this paper.

For purposes of comparison, each of the races was subdivided by age groupings (10–11, 12–13, 14–15, and 16–17-year-olds) and by sex. Table 2 indicates the manner in which the 1,262 subjects were distributed among the

Table 2. Total Number in Each Analytical Cell

Age	White		Negro	
	Boys	Girls	Boys	Girls
10–11	79	77	25	37
12–13	143	104	49	47
14–15	166	154	52	50
16–17	100	98	46	35
Total	488	433	172	169

resulting 16 groups. Ten-year-olds were under-represented since any below
the fifth grade level were not included in the sample. Sixteen- and 17-year-
olds were also under-represented due to substantial school dropouts at these
ages.

All significant statements for the remainder of the paper are based on
simple t-tests or Chi-square tests, whichever is appropriate. The .05 level of
significance is accepted throughout.

Findings

The mean social heterosexuality scores for each of the 16 groups described above are presented graphically in Figure 1. It can be seen that
among the whites, girls were significantly more heterosexual in their social
orientation than boys at every age. In fact, at every age the mean score for
white girls is higher than the mean score for boys two years older than
themselves. An analysis of the particular items which contribute to this

Figure 1. **Mean Social Heterosexual Scores of Negroes and Whites by Sex and Age**

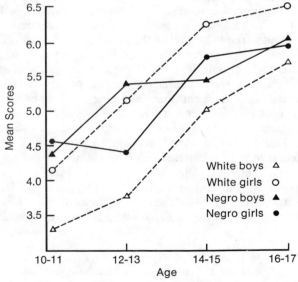

Differences between means are significant at or beyond the .05 level as follows: (a) between white boys and white
girls at every age, (b) between Negro boys and Negro girls at ages 12–13, and (c) between Negro boys and white boys
at age 12–13.

Table 3. Percent of Positive Responses to Each Item by Age, Sex, and Race

Item—Age	White		Negro	
	Boys	Girls	Boys	Girls
1. Marriage				
10–11	57	87*	71	76
12–13	63	89*	60	74
14–15	61	90*	67	85
16–17	77†‡	90*	58	84*
2. Romantic movie				
10–11	45	80*	68†	70
12–13	53	82*	75†	73
14–15	62	83*	83†	78
16–17	62	88*	62	79
3. Girlfriend/boyfriend				
10–11	49	68*	65	64
12–13	49	66*	71*†	51
14–15	45	76*	58	72‡
16–17	46	78*	62†	71
4. Love				
10–11	39	60*	46	57
12–13	47	62*	60	48
14–15	60‡	72†	57	67
16–17	61	69	67	67
5. Cross-sex friend				
10–11	31	29	52	54†
12–13	30	38	48†	45
14–15	54†	59†	49	58
16–17	60	71	81†‡	75
6. Kissing games				
10–11	49	53	68	62
12–13	61‡	81*‡	92†‡	72
14–15	80†	83	87	84
16–17	83	78	85	86
7. Serious kiss				
10–11	22	21	38	39†
12–13	28	41*‡	51†	48
14–15	50‡	62*	62	65
16–17	72‡	73	79*	59
8. Date				
10–11	20	18	16	20
12–13	30	29	49*†‡	21
14–15	69‡	70†‡	69*‡	48‡
16–17	89‡	82‡	93‡	88‡
9. Steady				
10–11	27	17	40	27
12–13	34	46*‡	59*†	34
14–15	49‡	57	58	44
16–17	59	66	63	51

*Significant difference between the sexes (p < .05).
†Significant difference between the races (p < .05).
‡Significant difference from previous age (p < .05).

overall sex difference (Table 3) shows that girls gave more heterosexual responses than boys on wanting to get married (significant at every age), claiming a boyfriend/girlfriend (significant at every age), having been in love (significant at 10–11 and 12–13), and having kissed "when it meant something special" (significant at 12–13 and 14–15). Except for the kissing item, these items all involve romantic attitudes rather than social behavior; and it is worth noting that despite the striking sex differences on these items, there were no corresponding differences on involvement in kissing games, cross-sex friends, dating, or going steady.

This same sex differential was observed among Pennsylvania rural and suburban white youth involved in other phases of the larger project, and was observed also in a middle-class white Southern sample reported earlier.[1] As can be seen in Figure 1, however, urban Negro subjects did not conform to the usual pattern. Negro boys did not trail Negro girls in their heterosexual orientation or involvement. In fact, the only significant difference between the sexes was at 12–13, when the boys' mean score exceeded the girls'. At that age, the Negro boys, significantly more often than the girls, reported having a girlfriend/boyfriend, having begun to date, and having gone steady (Table 3). The latter two in particular involve heterosexual social interaction rather than romantic fantasy. The Negro boys also are significantly more heterosexually oriented than white boys at ages 12–13. (The difference approaches significance at ages 10–11 also.) The items differentiating them are the same as those setting the Negro boys apart from the Negro girls at that age, with the addition of the romantic movie, cross-sex friends, and the two kissing items. These differences may reflect the fact that Negro boys tend to be sexually involved at an earlier age than white boys. The difference effectively disappears at ages 14–15, by which age it may be assumed that the white boy has caught up with his Negro counterpart.

One additional observation might be made about the item on attitude toward marriage. It was mentioned earlier that lower-class status and unstable home life tended to be associated with negative feelings about the desirability of marriage. This pattern held not only in this community, but in all of the other communities studied in the larger project. It held for the Negro girls in the present sample. Among the Negro boys, however, the reverse held true. As can be seen in Table 3, at 10–11, 71 percent of these boys felt sure that they wanted to get married some day; at 12–13, the percentage had dropped to 60 percent; and, after a brief rally at 14–15 (back to 67 percent), it dropped finally to 58 percent at 16–17. This suggests a process of progressive disillusionment with marriage among teen-age Negro boys in this community. It seems probable that high levels of unemployment among Negro males help to make the acceptance of family responsibility unattractive. The prominence of matrifocal family patterns among lower-class Negro families might also contribute to the negative

---

[1] C. B. Broderick and S. E. Fowler, "New Patterns of Relationships between the Sexes among Preadolescents," *Marriage and Family Living*, 23 (February 1961), pp. 27–30. See also C. B. Broderick, "Socio-sexual Development in a Suburban Community," *Journal of Sex Research (in press)*.

attitude toward marriage which these data reveal. If longitudinal research confirms the reality and universality of this progressive disillusionment, it may help to clarify the dynamics of marital instability among Negroes.

Summary and Conclusions

Questionnaire data were collected from 341 Negro and 921 white 10–17-year-olds living in the same urban industrial community. An index of social heterosexuality was developed which permitted interracial comparisons by sex and by age. The most striking difference between the races occurred during the pre-adolescent and pubescent ages of 10–13 years. At these ages, the white children showed the traditional pattern, with girls far more romantically oriented than boys although at about the same level in terms of actual heterosexual interaction. Negro boys, however, showed none of the heterosexual reserve of the white boys. They did not trail the Negro girls on any item except attitude toward marriage and, in fact, showed a higher level of heterosexual interaction at 12–13 than the girls did. This high level of preadolescent heterosexual interest and involvement among Negro boys, together with an apparent progressive disenchantment with marriage, suggests that the pattern of socio-sexual development in the Negro subculture may differ markedly from that of the dominant culture.

The present study, depending on cross-section analysis and self-administered questionnaires, has been able to indicate only the broad outline of developmental patterns in the two races over the span of the important "middle" years. Further explication of the process must await longitudinal data and depth interviews.

4

Sexual Behavior

E. Franklin Frazier: Sex Life of the African and American Negro

The sexual behavior of Negroes, like the sexual behavior of peoples all over the world, can only be understood when it is studied in relation to the social and cultural context in which attitudes and patterns of behavior in regard to sex are formed.

In all of Africa, sexual behavior is rigorously regulated by the customs or the mores of the different African societies. Although the sexual behavior of Africans may strike Westerners as "immoral" or bizarre, this does not indicate licentiousness on the part of Africans. As the result of European contacts, however, social disorganization has resulted, involving unregulated sex relations and what might be regarded as immoral conduct. However, such conduct is immoral only from the standpoint of the traditional African norms governing sexual behavior.

The sexual behavior of the American Negro presents a different problem because here we are dealing with a people who have been stripped of their traditional social and cultural heritage and have been in the process of assimilating European culture over a period of three centuries or more.

Africa

The diversity of peoples and cultures in Black Africa, or Africa south of the Sahara, makes it difficult to generalize about the sex life of Negroes. Nevertheless, there are certain basic features regarding the social organization and the mode of making a living in the area that make it possible to note the important determinants and elements in the sex life of the people.

The Family

The most important feature in regard to the social organization of the people of this area is the primary role of the family and the obligations of kinship. Although the ideal African family is polygamous, because of the sex ratio and differences in wealth, the number of men with more than one wife is limited. The polygamous families consist of one man with several wives and several sets of children, forming a joint family; since these joint families include several generations, they form what are known as extended families. These joint or extended families are a part of a larger kinship group or lineage. The sex life of the African can only be understood in relation to these lineage groups, which provide the basis of social obligations of people who are engaged in making a living and reproducing themselves.

Religion

The first fact of importance in understanding the sex behavior of Africans is that it is determined largely by their religious attitudes, which are associated with procreation. It is necessary to emphasize this basic fact because what follows in regards to the sex behavior of Africans is a logical consequence. To the African, the values associated with sex are a part of the religious values associated with reproduction and not with sex itself, which, in the Western mind, has become largely divorced from procreation. For example, Africans do not believe that female chastity is a virtue, except within the restraints imposed by the society. In many African tribes or societies, sexual relations between unmarried persons are permitted, and under certain circumstances unmarried men are permitted to have sexual relations with married women. Then there are societies that regard conception before the puberty ceremonies, which involve religious rites, with greater disapproval than conception before marriage. Moreover, the idea of sexual exclusiveness in marriage ceases to have meaning where there is childlessness, and a sister may substitute for a barren wife or men may father children of their dead kinsmen.

Premarital and Extramarital Relations

Let us consider more specifically the attitudes of certain tribes towards premarital sexual relations. Among the Mohammedans in the Nupe kingdom in northern Nigeria, there is a deeply rooted traditional respect for chastity and the sanctity of matrimonial ties. But because of a system of class polygamy that permits men of the privileged stratum to enjoy women of a certain stratum, there is much extramarital sexual relations on the part of sex-starved women who are cast aside when their husbands take other wives.

This is not representative, however, of West Africa. Among the Hausa, unmarried boys and girls sleep together with the connivance of their parents. In northern Dahomey, among the Somba, if a girl is betrothed as a child she may take a lover other than her future husband. The children she may have by the lover will be counted as her husband's children. Among the Dogon the period of sexual freedom begins as soon as sexual relations are permitted between a betrothed couple. Each takes a lover and their relations with the lovers are controlled by certain rules. For example, when the girl becomes pregnant, the relationship with her lover ceases. In other parts of West Africa premarital sex relations may occur but often on the condition that conception does not occur before the puberty rites. Among some of the peoples of West Africa, a bride's virginity is tested and a Hausa husband may publicize her failure by breaking a pot outside her house. Sometimes when the girl is found not to be a virgin the bride-price is reduced.

In East Africa among the warrior people, such as the Masai, premarital sex relations are institutionalized. The young warriors, who are organized to defend the cattle, carry on sex relations with girls who form a part of the village especially organized for that purpose. However, if a girl becomes pregnant, the man is required to pay for her initiation ceremonies. Among the Nuer, sex relations are regarded as a phase of the courtship behavior. But among another tribal group, the Luhya, when a man intends to marry a girl he makes no sexual advances, but behaves in a formal manner. Among the Hima, who have no institutionalized premarital sex relations, a married man is expected to let his brothers have sex relations with his wife. Among the peoples of Central Africa, many of whom trace their descent through their mothers rather than through their fathers, much emphasis is placed upon the puberty rites. This involves close supervision of the girls in their relations with males, and great emphasis is placed upon seeing that the girl does not become pregnant before initiation, which involves much instruction concerning sex. Among the Yao, for example, the initiation of girls is concluded with defloration. Among some of the peoples of this area, there was once a test of virginity at initiation. Some of the patrilineal tribes in Central Africa once attempted to supervise the girls before initiation, but it does not appear that much importance was attached to premarital virginity.

Turning to South Africa, one finds that among most of the peoples in this area sexual relations between boys and girls have been permitted. The warlike Zulus allowed freedom of sexual intercourse to couples who were planning to marry. But among other tribes there were various restrictions upon premarital sexual relations. For example, the Kgatla in the Bechuanaland Protectorate severely condemned prenuptial sex relations and if an unmarried girl became pregnant she was humiliated and publicly mocked and her child was generally killed.

It has already been noted that among the Mohammedanized peoples in the urban areas of Nupe the system of class polygamy has resulted in extramarital sex relations on the part of women. Here we are especially concerned with the general phenomenon of extramarital relations that occur in many parts of Africa. Among the Hausa people in Nigeria, where the women are subject to the Mohammedan rule of seclusion of wives, prostitution has been a long-established means by which women escape from marriages entered into against their will. Similarly, among many African peoples extramarital sex relations are permitted when the husband is impotent. There are tribes in Nigeria in which married women who have not borne children may have sex relations with other men because it is believed they may thus increase their chances of pregnancy.

But it should be emphasized that the freedom permitted in regard to premarital and extramarital relations does not mean that there are promiscuous sex relations. Where either occurs it is carried on according to established customary practices. Moreover, the general disapproval of sexual promiscuity in every part of Africa is indicated by the inability of promiscuous women to enter into marriage relations. Among the Luhya, to whom reference has been made, a girl who has had more than two or three love affairs will have little chance of marriage. Among the Nuer in the Sudan, a woman of easy virtue will have lovers but no offers of marriage, and if she has borne a child she will most likely become a prostitute. Once more it must be pointed out that, since sex is regarded as fundamental to procreation, the crucial factor in most parts of Africa is whether a girl has had sex relations before or after initiation.

Impact of Western Civilization

Important changes have occurred in Africa as the result of the impact of Western or European civilization, and it is necessary to indicate the nature of these changes in the sex behavior of Africans. The introduction of commercial crops has not only affected the system of subsistence agriculture but has also tended to uproot the basis of the traditional social life. By drawing males into the market economy it has created an imbalance in the sex ratio in rural communities. Men leave their wives and children and unmarried men no longer grow up under the supervision of their fathers. As a result, the women are left to seek new sexual companions. Since the woman's economic function is disrupted or lost, she begins to regard sex as a personal pleasurable experience no longer associated with procreation.

Perhaps the most important direct effect of Western contacts upon sex behavior is due to the influence of Christianity. The Christian missionaries have generally regarded with disapproval the initiation rites and ceremonies, which in their eyes were immoral. A more objective view reveals that these rites were the means by which sex was socialized in that it was surrounded by religious attitudes that formed the basis of human solidarity. When these traditional sex behaviors were frowned upon or disallowed, the African girl and the boy grew up without any moralizing influence. The sex impulse became an individual biological matter to be satisfied in an adventitious manner.

The "freeing" of the sex impulse from the social control and moralizing influences of traditional African culture reached its extreme form in the towns and cities in Africa, which owe their existence to European industry and commerce. In the cities that had existed before European contacts, kinship had continued to form the basis of social life; in the new cities the old kinship basis has been undermined or destroyed. In its place has come, as in the West, a type of social existence that is based on a market economy, with money and wages. Social relations have thus become secularized. The traditional marriage payment, which often included cattle that had been carefully reared by the boy with a view to his betrothal and marriage, has become a simple financial transaction devoid of the sentiment and religious feeling that had bound the two families in the marriage payment or brideprice. With the migration of women, who have lost their traditional economic function, to towns and cities, illegitimacy and prostitution have become problems in the new cities of Africa. Sex is no longer associated with procreation and has lost its moral or religious significance. The purely hedonistic aspect of sex has become the chief value. It is in the new cities, with uprooted men and women, that sexual promiscuity flourishes.

In the modern cities, not only has social disorganization taken place, but life has been reorganized on a new basis, according to novel patterns and standards of behavior. New classes are coming into existence as the result of changed social distinctions and different sources of income and wealth. In the cities, where the most Westernized elements form the upper social strata, many have adopted the sex attitudes and patterns of behavior of their Christian teachers. Unfortunately, very often the so-called public sex morality of the West is not a true indication of their real sex behavior. Among the more sophisticated Westernized men and women are many who live according to what they find the most desirable in the sex attitudes of both Africans and Christians.

United States

What has been pointed out in regard to the sex life of the Negro in the new cities of Africa provides a convenient transition to a discussion of the sex life of the Negro in the United States.

Plantation Life

The Negroes who were brought to the English colonies and the United States were stripped almost completely of their cultural heritage. This was the result of the manner in which the Negro slaves were captured and sold on African slave markets, not to mention the manner in which they were "broken into" the plantations in the West Indies and in the United States. During the intertribal wars and the slave raids in Africa, the victims of the slave trade were torn from family and friends, and clan ties were broken. They were herded in barracoons or "concentration camps" on the coasts of Africa to await the slave ships that would transport them to the New World. In the New World, no respect was shown for kinship and other ties or for the African concept of what was normal or what was expected in sex behavior. The African Negro's sex appetite was not extinguished during this process. There are records of slaves in Louisiana who, being unable to find mates among the female Negro population, went into the woods and mated with Indian women. This is indicative of an important fact, that the plantations demanded predominantly male Negroes and that it was not until 1840 that there were as many female Negroes as male Negroes in the United States.

Therefore, in considering the sex life of the American Negro, one must begin with the fundamental fact that at the beginning of his history in the United States his sexual behavior was determined by raw sex impulses and that these impulses were restrained by the discipline of the plantation regime. It was only gradually that the Negro's sexual behavior was socially and institutionally regularized, resulting from his acculturation and the development of the Negro community.

Under the plantation regime there was considerable variation in the sex behavior of Negroes. These variations were related to the extent to which the discipline of the plantation, and the consequent relations between Negroes and whites, enabled the Negroes to acquire the habits, attitudes, and sentiments of the whites. Under the most favorable conditions, the slaves acquired, through close association with whites, their ideas and attitudes concerning sex. This was achieved largely through moral and religious instruction, during which the slaves became a part of the white family group and participated in their religious life. This moral and religious discipline in sexual behavior was given a substantial basis in the opportunity to be "married," although not legally, according to some form, and to maintain a "conventional married" life. Such favorable conditions were the lot of a relatively small number of slaves: the house servants and the skilled mechanics. For the great body of slaves, the field hands, sexual relations between men and women were more or less casual and could be broken off at will or ended when the master sold his slaves or decided to break up sexual unions that displeased him.

Amalgamation of Races

An important aspect of the sex life of the Negroes during slavery and even since their emancipation has been the amalgamation of the races. From the beginning of the enslavement of Negroes there has been racial mixture, almost all of which has been outside of marriage or law. About one-twelfth of the slave population was comprised of mulattoes or mixed bloods, and three-eighths of the Negroes who were free before Emancipation were of racially mixed ancestry.

The conditions under which this racial mixture occurred have had a profound effect upon the attitudes of the Negro woman—but more especially of the mulatto woman—toward sex. The sexually seductive Negro or mulatto woman has been romanticized and all sorts of beliefs have grown up about the peculiar sexual attributes of the Negro, but more especially the mulatto, woman.

There has been, in addition, the influence of a racially mixed group who made up the backbone of the free Negro population because of their superior cultural and economic status. It was from this group that an intermediate caste was formed in some southern cities, such as in New Orleans. Institutional family life took root among these Negroes, and Western patterns of sex behavior and sex attitudes became a part of their traditions. These sex attitudes and patterns of behavior of the well-to-do free Negroes were practically the same as those of the slave-holding and propertied whites in the South, just as the sex life of the poor elements among the free Negroes did not differ from the free-and-easy sex behavior of the "poor whites."

Influence of Emancipation

The Civil War and Emancipation not only removed the discipline that the slave-holders had exercised over the sex life of the slaves but also tended to uproot their customary ways in sex relations. Thousands of Negroes became foot-loose and, wandering about the country, attempted to satisfy their sexual impulses whenever they had the opportunity. Many of them were especially attracted to the cities, where disorganization of Negro family life and sexual promiscuity have had a long history. Moreover, it was during this period that venereal diseases began to spread among the poor and illiterate Negroes.

After a period of much social disorganization the great mass of the Negro population in the South settled down to a way of life based on a modified form of the plantation system. It was among the rural Negro people that certain modes of sex behavior developed which may be fairly adequately described in a general way. Among the people the sexual impulse was regarded as a natural or human impulse that required satisfaction. There was no feeling of guilt about the desire to seek sexual satisfaction, except in those areas where the Protestant churches had introduced a puritanical attitude toward sex. Even in these circumstances they rationalized between the "natural" impulse to seek sexual satisfaction outside of marriage and the teachings of the Church. For example, following the Civil War in a number of localities in the South, there sprang up the quasi-theological doctrine that "two clean sheets cannot soil each other." According to this doctrine, premarital or even extramarital sexual intercourse between two Christians was not sinful, but such a relationship on the part of a Christian with a "sinner," or with a person who had not been converted, was sinful. It should not be inferred from this, however, that sex had only a hedonistic value. Although sex was natural and pleasurable for the masses of Negro folk, sexual free-dom was a male prerogative; for women it was not so much a pleasurable experience as the means to reproduction, the means by which she fulfilled her destiny.

In the isolated rural areas of the plantation South where the Negroes were only slightly influenced by European ideas and sentiments regarding sex, there was considerable indulgence towards adolescents in their sexual con-tacts. When these sexual relations resulted in children, the children generally became members of the girl's family, even when the boy wanted to marry the girl, because her parents thought that she was too inexperienced to assume the responsibilities of motherhood or that the boy did not have sufficient economic means to support a family. Consequently, a Negro girl during a series of sexual contacts might have had three or four children by the time she was old enough or mature enough to marry. Her husband would accept her children as a part of the family, to which he might bring his children by other contacts and add children by his wife. Often, because of the mobility of males, one could come across Negro families with only females representing two or even three generations.

Such sexual behavior on the part of rural Negroes cannot be regarded as typical of all Negroes. It reflects a number of economic and more especially of social and cultural factors that have influenced the sex behavior of Negroes in the plantation South. In the areas outside of the cotton planta-tion areas, where Negroes have assimilated more of European sexual mores and have developed a community life based on land ownership, their sexual behavior approximates that of the whites. For example, the Negro church has exercised an effective control over premarital and extramarital sexual relations. It is regarded as a serious sin or social offense in some communi-ties for a girl to become pregnant. In the areas in the upper South, especially among the Negro land-owners who take pride in their social position and "purity of morals," for a girl to become pregnant before marriage has resulted in disgrace and expulsion from the community.

Urban and Northern Migration

The influence of these social and cultural factors upon the sexual behavior of Negroes has been greatly affected by the migration of Negroes to the cities, especially to the cities of the North. Rural folk who had maintained a relatively stable family life based upon habit and sentiments developed in the same household were unable to withstand the disintegrating effects of the urban environment.

All forms of social disorganization resulted from city life, and the most striking effects of this were on family life and the control of sex behavior. The most important effect upon sex life was the change in the attitudes of women. The males continued to seek sexual satisfaction wherever they could find it, and this continues to be reflected in the high illegitimacy rates among Negroes in cities. But the attitude of the urban Negro woman changed, sex became divorced from procreation and its pleasurable aspect was enhanced. The rural Negro woman might enjoy sex, but it was devoid of the romantic element that it acquired in the urban environment. Romanticization and even glorification of sex were stimulated by the songs and movies that are a part of the social world of Negroes in the slum areas of American cities.

Negro Middle Class

In the cities of the South as well as in the cities of the North, although more especially of the North, a new social stratification among Negroes resulted in a sharp differentiation of their sex behavior. In the older stratification of Negro society there was an upper class that formed what resembled a superior caste. It was differentiated from the great mass of the Negro population by lighter skin color, more education, and better income, although not entirely by occupation. In addition to their white ancestry, the most important factor was their standard of civilized behavior—which meant primarily that they maintained a conventional or puritanical code of sexual ethics. In the newer class structure that has emerged as the result of urbanization, the old puritanical sexual ethics have been lost, although they continue to influence the thinking and behavior of the new middle class which has become dominant in the Negro community.

The new middle class rejects anything associated with the Negro folk, and the free-and-easy sex life of the Negro folk is regarded as the most distinguishing characteristic of this class. But this respectable middle class, which represents on the one hand a pseudosophistication and on the other hand an absence of deeply rooted institutional controls of sex, cannot escape from its social origins; consequently, there is much hypocrisy about sex and much sexual irregularity. The importance of sex to this class is indicated by their extreme sensitivity to any charge that Negroes are freer or more easy in their sex behavior than whites. There is an element among this class whose behavior is more influenced by the churches and who inculcate in their children and maintain sexual conducts according to the accepted American standards. Among this stratum of the Negro middle class the tension between the sexual urge for gratification and the conventional standards is reduced to a minimum.

Psychosocial Aspects of Negro Sex Behavior

Here one should consider some of the psycho-social aspects of the sexual behavior of Negroes, which are closely related to their inferior status in American society. First, it should be noted that the Negro male has never been permitted to play the male role as defined by American culture. Second, white women have been taboo so far as Negro males are concerned. Third, the Negro woman has been defined mainly as a sexual object. All three of these facts have influenced the sex behavior of Negroes in the United States.

For the Negro male, sex has often been the means by which he has asserted and attained his masculinity. Much of the sexual promiscuity of Negro males has been due to this rather than to any great sexual energy or powers that overrode social controls. Their sexual prowess has been a means of overcoming their inferior status not only in family relations but in relation to the white world. It is not without significance that the nicknames of some prominent Negroes indicate sexual prowess.

When the Negro male cannot attain his maleness through normal sex outlets, there is always the female role open to him. After all, the Negro woman was able to adjust to American society in a way that the Negro male could not do normally. Not only does the color line tend to disappear among homosexuals, but in the female role the Negro male no longer offers a challenge to white male dominance. Perhaps, and this is speculation, the Negro male homosexuals who publicly exhibit their deviation may represent the sexual adjustment of the Negro male to American society. Since the Negro woman's role has been defined largely as sexual, her emphasis of sex conforms to her position in American society.

The policy of the United States toward Negroes has only recently changed from one of separate development to one of integration. One can only speculate therefore upon the future sex behavior of the Negro. The lower classes in the Negro community will probably continue to lead a more or less free sex life. But as larger numbers rise to middle-class status they will adopt the conventional sexual patterns of Americans.

Whatever influence the Negro may have had on the sexual behavior of Americans has been through the subtle means of music rather than through any consciously formulated philosophy in regard to sex.

References

Ashton, Hugh, *The Basuto*. London: Oxford University Press, 1952.

Busia, K. A., *Report on a Social Survey of Sekondi-Takoradi*. London: Crown Agent for the Colonies, 1950.

Dollard, John, *Caste and Class in a Southern Town*. New Haven: Yale University Press, 1937.

Duvallon, Berquin, "Travels in Louisiana and the Floridas in the Year 1802." *J. Negro Hist. 2*; 172–181, 1917.

Evans-Pritchard, E. E., *The Nuer*. London: The Clarendon Press, 1941.

Frazier, E. Franklin, *The Negro Family in the United States*. Chicago: University of Chicago Press, 1939.

Herskovits, Melville, *The American Negro: A Study in Racial Crossing*. New York: Alfred A. Knopf, Inc., 1928.

Hollman, Ellen, *Rooiyard*. Capetown: Oxford University Press, 1949.

Kardiner, Abram, and Lionel Oversey, *The Mark of Oppression*. New York: W. W. Norton & Co., Inc., 1951.

Labouret, Henri, *Les paysans d'Afrique occidentale*. Paris: Gallimard, 1941.

Nadel, S. F., *A Black Byzantium*. London: Oxford University Press, 1942.

Park, Robert E., "Negro Home Life and Standards of Living." *Ann. Am. Acad. Polit. Soc. Sci. 49*; 149–163, 1913.

Phillips, Arthur (ed.), *Survey of African Marriage and Family Life*. London: Oxford University Press, 1953.

Powdermaker, Hortense, *After Freedom: A Cultural Study in the Deep South*. New York: The Viking Press, Inc., 1939.

Radcliffe-Brown, A. R., and Daryl Forde (eds.), *African Systems of Kinship and Marriage*. London: Oxford University Press, 1950.

Reuter, Edward Byron, *The Mulatto in the United States*. Boston: Badger, 1918.

Schapera, I. (ed.), *Western Civilization and the Natives of South Africa*. London: Routledge, 1934.

Robert Staples: Mystique of Black Sexuality

Black sexuality has always held a certain mystique for white Americans, and one can only wonder why, since both the positive and negative aspects of Black sexual behavior are results of white racism. A look at history demonstrates that the sexual behavior of Black Africans was strictly regulated by the customs of the different African societies until their brutal transplantation to the new world. Unlike the Victorian code of sexual behavior so endemic to whites, Africans saw sex as a matter between individuals and not determined by God.

The women of Africa were brought to this country to service the lust of the white master class. Although Black women had other functions in the domestic and labor realm, their major task was to bear the brunt of the double standard. The double standard, which is still very common among whites, allowed premarital and extramarital sexual expression for men and denied it to women. But some women had to serve as the sexual objects for the liberated white male, and Black women were forced to take this role.

For years the sexual subjugation of Black women has allowed the white woman to remain 'pure.' During slavery the Black woman was a captive source for the carnal desires of lustful white men. After slavery Black women remained the sexual prey for the white man; for, what he had forcefully taken during the ante-bellum period, he continued to take, appropriate and buy in the post-bellum era.

"Mystique of Black Sexuality," by Robert E. Staples. *Liberator*, Vol. 7, No. 3 (March 1967), pp. 8–10. Copyright © 1967 by *Liberator* magazine. Robert Staples is a member of the Department of Sociology and the program in Comparative Culture at the University of California, Irvine. Previously he taught at California State College, Hayward, and at Fisk University. He is a specialist in Family Studies and has been a student of Black family life for over ten years.

The sexual exploitation of Black women took place in several ways. As usual the economic factor was a key one. In the book *Caste and Class in a Southern Town*, the author John Dollard writes:

An informant pointed out what it means to the Negro woman who gets two to four dollars a week as a cook to have the man of the house offer her five dollars for sexual intercourse. She probably has a family to support, certainly has bills to pay and needs the money.

In this same book, Dollard leaves no doubt that Black women were the victims of the double standard. He points out:

Testimony seems to be quite widespread to the fact that many, if not most, Southern boys begin their sexual experience with Negro girls, usually around the ages of fifteen or sixteen. It was said further that many white men do not have experiences with white women until they marry.

The flagrant violation of the Black woman's body served to devalue the worth of virginity to her. What good was it to value something one was not allowed to have? As a consequence the deeply rooted feelings of guilt about sex never became entrenched in the psyche of Black women as they did in her white counterpart. Although the premarital sexual behavior of white women closely approximates that of Black women, the vicissitudes of the past have ironically allowed Black women to experience sexual relations without the crippling feelings of guilt and fear so characteristic of the white female.

What is frequently seen as the sexual laxity of Black people is actually their guilt-free attitude towards the sex act. Black men and Black women frequently mate as equals, in a relationship that has a meaning for both. Sociological studies reveal that Black women receive more sexual satisfaction in marriage and are more aggressive partners during coitus than white women.

In one such study, sociologist Lee Rainwater reported that:

Negro women communicated a sense of the acceptability of a woman's interest in sex that is different from the way white wives speak of their sexual roles. They communicate a sense of wanting to enjoy sexual relations.

The main difference between Negroes and whites is that among Negroes, rejecting attitudes toward sexual relations are somewhat less frequent. . . . Negro women are more interested in sexuality than their white counterparts. . . . Negro husbands do not as often moderate their enthusiasm for sexual relations as white husbands.

These same sociological studies also claim that Negro marriages are love-less and that Black women decry the lack of affection from their husbands. This brings up several interesting questions. Are white marriages so replete with love? Can a group of people with the racist attitudes of American whites love anyone while hating and oppressing Black people? As the psychologist Erich Fromm has stated: "If a person loves only one other person and is indifferent to the rest of his fellow men, his love is not love but a symbiotic attachment, or an enlarged egotism."

Afro-American marriages are sometimes tension-ridden and loveless because of the conditions under which Black Americans are forced to live. They cannot take the same things for granted as whites due to their marginal position in the social and economic constellation of American society. The constant assaults on their dignity and pride as human beings by white racism has its repercussions in their home life. Often their bitterness toward the racist society is deflected onto their mate. This is what Stokely Carmichael means when he says Blacks have got to create a spirit of love in their community and let the hate return to its source, white racism.

The truth is that a great number of white women are not finding much love in their marriages. One should be able to find sexual satisfaction in a love relationship, but over half of American white women fail to achieve sexual gratification before or after marriage. In contrast, Black women get something out of marriage other than economic security or the status of housewife. For what is often denied their white counterparts, sexual satisfaction, is often taken for granted by Black women. Whether their marriages contain the illusory concept of love or not, Black women at least salvage the spirit of eros for their own.

One can understand the implications of the differences in white and Black sexual behavior if it is viewed in the perspective of American (white) values. In this country everything is sold for a profit, exploited for some value within the context of supply and demand. Few things are valued for their intrinsic worth or what it means to other people but for what it means to the individual's ego.

Girls are brought up to believe their ultimate goal is marriage. At the same time they are implicitly or explicitly taught that all boys want from them is sex. If a girl wants to achieve her goal of marriage, she must make the boy marry her first if he wants the sexual gratification, or else she will be denied the opportunity for the marital state. While this ideal of premarital chastity is presently being violated, the exploitative character is still very much present, and the girls continue to have guilt feelings about participating in sex relations.

It is in the premarital stage that we see the greatest difference in Black and white sexual behavior. The biggest difference is that few Black males have a double standard of sexual behavior. The nonvirginal Black female is not excluded as a future prospect for marriage. In fact the girl who tries to use her sexual favors as an inducement for marriage is often looked down on by Black males. Few Black men will marry a woman just for sex relations. The marriage must have a more profound base than the enticement of sexual relations.

Unlike white males, Black men are seldom known to purchase sex from a prostitute. If Black prostitutes did not have the business of white males, they would soon starve. Black men expect sexual intimacy with Black women as a natural aspect of any profound human relationship. To this extent, Black men and women need not see each other as enemies, one wanting sex and the other marriage, competing for conflicting goals. They enter the marital state for reasons other than one winning a victory over the other.

In recent years, the liberalization of American sexual attitudes has led to increased premarital sexual experimentation on the part of white females. But they are not easily freed from their Victorian past. If they should become illegitimately pregnant, the greater sex guilt of the white woman drives her to undergo an abortion (which many consider to be a greater sin than an illegitimate birth) rather than face the consequences of an irrefutable proof of her illicit act.

The illegitimacy rate of whites is also distorted by forced marriages. Over 25 percent of white brides are pregnant at the time of marriage. Marriages initiated for this reason are notable for their high rate of failure. Black people seldom feel compelled to avoid the stigma of illegitimacy by this method.

One frequently hears the question: are Black people sexually superior? The answer depends on the meaning of the question. Sexual superiority cannot be judged by the size of a man's penis or the rhythmic movement of Black females. But, if sexual superiority means to enjoy the pleasures of sexual congress without feelings of guilt and fear, freed from the restraints of white puritanism, then the answer must be in the affirmative.

Kenneth B. Clark: Sex and Status

In Negro adults the sense of inadequate self-worth shows up in lack of motivation to rise in their jobs or fear of competition with whites; in a sense of impotence in civic affairs demonstrated in lethargy toward voting, or community participation, or responsibility for others; in family instability and the irresponsibility rooted in hopelessness.

But, because, in American life, sex is, like business advancement, a prime criterion of success and hence of personal worth, it is in sexual behavior that the damage to Negro adults shows up in especially poignant and tragic clarity. The inconsistency between the white society's view of the Negro as inferior and its sexual exploitation of Negroes has seemed to its victims a degrading hypocrisy. Negroes observe that ever since slavery white men

Abridged from pp. 67-74 in *Dark Ghetto*, by Kenneth B. Clark. Copyright © 1965 by Kenneth B. Clark. Reprinted by permission of Harper & Row, Publishers. Dr. Clark is Director of the Social Dynamics Research Institute of the City College of the City University of New York.

have regarded Negroes as inferior and have condemned interracial marriage while considering illicit sexual relationships with Negro women appropriate to their own higher status. The white man in America has, historically, arranged to have both white and Negro women available to him; he has claimed sexual priority with both and, in the process, he has sought to emasculate Negro men. Negro males could not hold their women, nor could they defend them. The white male tried to justify this restriction of meaningful competition with the paradoxical claim that Negro males were animal-like and brutish in their appetites and hence to be feared and shunned by white women. The ironic fact has been that, given the inferiority of their racial status, Negro males have had to struggle simply to believe themselves men. It has long been an "inside" bit of bitter humor among Negroes to say that Negro men should bribe their wives to silence.

Certain Negro women of status who have married white men report that their choice was related to their discovery that the Negro men they knew were inferior in status, interests, and sophistication and hence unsuitable as partners. Many problems of race and sex seem to follow this principle of the self-fulfilling prophecy. The Negro woman of status may see the Negro male as undesirable as a sexual partner precisely because of his low status in the eyes of whites. Unlike a white female who may reassure herself that the lower the status of the male, the more satisfying he is as a sexual partner, the upper-class Negro female tends to tie sexual desirability to status and exclude many Negro males as undesirable just because their status is inferior. It is a real question whether this "discovery" is based on fact or whether these women are not accepting the white society's assumption of the low status of Negro men and therefore expecting them to be weak. On the other hand, frustrated, thrill-seeking white males or females who have been told all their lives that Negroes are primitive and uninhibited may seek and find sexual fulfillment among the same Negroes who are cool, distant, or hostile in their relationship to other Negroes. In sexual matters it appears that those who expect weakness or gratification often find what they expect. . . .

White men were accustomed to possessing Negro women without marriage, but today the fact that a number of white men are married to Negro women of status, particularly those who are well known in the theatrical world, indicates that Negro women are placing higher value upon their own dignity than many other Negro women were permitted to in the past—and so are the white men who marry them. But, though a Negro woman may gain status by marrying into the white community, Negro men, even in the North, remain vulnerable if they seek to cross racial lines and to break this most fearsome of social taboos. When they have done so they have paid a tremendous price—lynching, murder, or a prison sentence in the South, social condemnation in the North—but, above all, the price of their own self-doubt and anxiety. The full complexity of social disapproval and personal doubt is difficult to resist psychologically even when the law allows and protects such nonconformist behavior.

The emerging, more affirmative sexual pride among Negro males may have as one of its consequences an increasing trend toward more open competition between white and Negro males for both white and Negro females. One of the further consequences would probably be an intensification of hostility of white males toward interracial couples and toward the white female participants, reflecting the desire on the part of the white male to preserve his own competitive advantage. One would expect him then to employ his economic and political power—without suspecting the fundamental basis of his antagonism—to maintain the inferior status of the Negro male for as long as possible. An important level of racial progress will have been reached when Negro and white men and women may marry anyone they choose, without punishment, ostracism, ridicule, or guilt.

The Negro Matriarchy and the Distorted Masculine Image

Sexual hierarchy has played a crucial role in the structure and pathology of the Negro family. Because of the system of slavery in which the Negro male was systematically used as a stud and the Negro female used primarily for purposes of breeding or for the gratification of the white male, the only source of family continuity was through the female, the dependence of the child on his mother. This pattern, together with the continued post-slavery relegation of the Negro male to menial and subservient status, has made the female the dominant person in the Negro family. Psychologically, the Negro male could not support his normal desire for dominance. For the most part he was not allowed to be a consistent wage earner; he could not present himself to his wife and children as a person who had the opportunity or the ability to compete successfully in politics, business, and industry. His doubts concerning his personal adequacy were therefore reinforced. He was compelled to base his self-esteem instead on a kind of behavior that tended to support a stereotyped picture of the Negro male—sexual impulsiveness, irresponsibility, verbal bombast, posturing, and compensatory achievement in entertainment and athletics, particularly in sports like boxing in which athletic prowess could be exploited for the gain of others. The Negro male was, therefore, driven to seek status in ways which seemed either antisocial, escapist, socially irresponsible. The pressure to find relief from his intolerable psychological position seems directly related to the continued high incidence of desertions and broken homes in Negro ghettos.

The Negro woman has, in turn, been required to hold the family together; to set the goals, to stimulate, encourage, and to protect both boys and girls. Her compensatory strength tended to perpetuate the weaker role of the Negro male. Negro boys had the additional problem of finding no strong male father figure upon which to model their own behavior, perhaps one of the reasons for the prevalent idea among marginal Negroes that it is not masculine to sustain a stable father or husband relationship with a woman. Many young men establish temporary liaisons with a number of different women with no responsibility toward any. Among Negro teen-agers the cult of going steady has never had the vogue it seems to have among white teen-agers; security for Negroes is found not in a relationship modeled after a stable family—for they have seen little of this in their own lives—but upon the relationship they observed in their own home: unstable and temporary liaisons. The marginal young Negro male tends to identify his masculinity with the number of girls he can attract. The high incidence of illegitimacy among Negro young people reflects this pervasive fact. In this compensatory distortion of the male image, masculinity is, therefore, equated with alleged sexual prowess.

The middle-class white and Negro male often separates women into two categories, good women with whom he will go steady and marry, and others with whom he has and will continue to have sexual relations alone. The lower-class Negro is, in a way, more sophisticated than either in his refusal to make undemocratic distinctions between "good girls" and "others." The consistently higher illegitimacy rate among Negroes is not a reflection of less virtue or greater promiscuity, but rather of the fact that the middle-class teen-agers are taught the use of contraceptives and learn how to protect themselves from the hazards of premarital and illicit sexual contacts. The middle-class girl is able to resort to abortions, or she gives birth secretly, surrendering the child for adoption. In the case of marginal young people, or the upwardly mobile Negro, what contraceptive ideas he has are unreliable; and rarely does the girl participate in protection, in part because it is taken as a sign of masculinity for the male to supervise such matters. Illegitimacy among these groups, therefore, is a consequence, in large part, of poverty and ignorance.

Among Negro middle-class families the attitude toward sex is vastly different from that among marginal and lower-class Negro groups. The middle-class Negro fears he will be identified with the Negro masses from whom he has escaped or tried to escape, and sex is a focal point of anxiety. The middle-class girl is often so rigidly protected that normal sexual behavior is inhibited, or she learns to be sophisticated about the use of contraceptives. For her, as for white middle-class girls, sex is tied to status and aspirations. She wants to make a good marriage—marriage to a white man might even be available—and the motivation to avoid illegitimate pregnancy is great.

The marginal young people in the ghetto, through their tentative and sporadic relationships, are seeking love, affection, and acceptance perhaps more desperately than young people elsewhere. Person-to-person relationships are, for many, a compensation for society's rejection. They are, in a sense, forced to be quite elemental in their demands, and sex becomes more important for them than even they realize. They act in a cavalier fashion about their affairs, trying to seem casual and cool, but it is clear nonetheless that they are dominated by the complexity of their needs.

The girl, like the boy, has no illusions. Unlike the middle-class girl who believes—or demands—that each relationship should be forever, and who tries to hold on to the boy, the marginal Negro lower-class girl is realistic about the facts of the situation. Nor does she expect to hold the boy. Sex is important to her, but it is not, as in middle-class society, a symbol of status, to be used to rise into a better family or a higher income bracket. The marginal Negro female uses her sex, instead, to gain personal affirmation. She is desired, and that is almost enough. The relationship, whatever its social and psychological limitations, is pure in the same sense as innocence— that is, it is not contaminated by other goals. For her and for the boy, sex is time-contained, with its own intrinsic worth and value, not animal in its expression, but related to the urgent human need for acceptance; it is sophisticated, not primitive.

This innocent sophistication includes the total acceptance of the child if a child comes. In the ghetto, the meaning of the illegitimate child is not ultimate disgrace. There is not the demand for abortion or for surrender of the child that one finds in more privileged communities. In the middle class, the disgrace of illegitimacy is tied to personal and family aspirations. In lower-class families, on the other hand, the girl loses only some of her already limited options by having an illegitimate child; she is not going to make a "better marriage" or improve her economic and social status either way. On the contrary, a child is a symbol of the fact that she is a woman, and she may gain from having something of her own. Nor is the boy who fathers an illegitimate child going to lose, for where is he going? The path to any higher status seems closed to him in any case.

Illegitimacy in the ghetto cannot be understood or dealt with in terms of punitive hostility, as in the suggestion that unwed mothers be denied welfare if illegitimacy is repeated. Such approaches obscure, with empty and at times hypocritical moralizing, the desperate yearning of the young for acceptance and identity, the need to be meaningful to some one else even for a moment without implication of a pledge of undying fealty and foreverness. If, when the girl becomes pregnant, the boy deserts or refuses to marry her, it is often because neither can sustain an intimate relationship; both seem incapable of the tenderness that continues beyond immediate gratification. Both may have a realistic, if unconscious, acceptance of the fact that nothing else is possible; to expect—to ask—for more would be to open oneself to the inevitable rejections, hurts, and frustrations. The persistent experience of rejection spills over into the anticipation and acceptance of rejection in a love relationship. This lack of illusion stems from the fact that there can be no illusion in any other area of life. To expose oneself further to the chances of failure in a sustained and faithful relationship is too large to risk. The intrinsic value of the relationship is the only value because there can be no other.

Among most lower-class Negroes, competition in sex is predominantly heterosexual and free. In the Negro middle class sexual freedom and expression are often identified with lower-class status, and many men and women are therefore governed chiefly by their inhibitions and cannot act freely in matters of sex. The men may be impotent, the women frigid, and both afflicted with guilt. Some compensate for the restraints on sexual adequacy and fulfillment through fantasies and boasting about a false prowess. Other middle-class Negro men retreat into noncommittal peripheral relationships with women, avoiding all alternatives—homosexuality, heterosexuality, or verbal bombasts—as risks requiring more ego strength than their resources permit. Instead, a blank and apathetic sexlessness dominates their lives. They withdraw from all commitment to another person seeking refuge from the dangers of personal vulnerability.

Considering the depth and the complexity of the need, aggressive sexual behavior may, for many of the racially damaged, make the difference between personal stability and instability. Until the lower-class Negro is free to compete for and to win the socially acceptable rewards of middle-class society, the ghetto's pattern of venereal disease, illegitimacy, and family instability will remain unbroken. But when that time comes, no one can expect destructive sexual activity to cease abruptly. What is more likely is a shift to another, some would say "higher," level of behavior; then the Negro's sexual "misbehavior" will be indistinguishable in all respects from that of the respectables—with full participation in divorce, abortions, adultery, and the various forms of jaded and fashionable middle- and upper-class sexual explorations. There might even be the possibility of sexual fulfillment and health.

Ira L. Reiss: Premarital Sexual Permissiveness among Negroes and Whites

Many studies of the American Negro have something to say about Negro sexual behavior and beliefs, but assertions made in this area are most likely to be over-all impressions gained through participant observation or intensive interviews with a few individuals. More precise empirical investigations of Negro sexual behavior and beliefs have also been done. In all of these reports, the consensus is that Negroes' sexual attitudes are more permissive than whites'. Case studies elaborate the meaning of this greater permissiveness, and historical analysis helps explain it. But the connection between sexual permissiveness and religion, love beliefs, and courtship activities, has not been empirically explored. This paper reports a current investigation of the factors related to pre-marital sexual permissiveness in a bi-racial sample of students and adults.

The Study

The two major samples utilized in this study were: (1) an adult sample of 1515 individuals aged 21 and older drawn randomly from across the nation; (2) a high school and college student probability sample of 903 stu-

Reprinted from *American Sociological Review*, 29 (October 1964), pp. 688-689, 696-698. By permission of the author. Footnotes have been renumbered. Ira L. Reiss is Professor of Sociology and Director of the Family Study Center, University of Minnesota.

dents ages 16–22, drawn from two high schools and two colleges in Virginia and one college in New York state. One of the high schools and one of the Virginia colleges were all Negro; the other three schools were all white. Only juniors and seniors were used in the high schools. These five schools were chosen because they represented a wide range along the conservative-liberal dimension of permissive attitudes toward premarital sexual relations.

Approximately 30 percent of the student sample were Negroes; 70 percent were white. All students were single. The national sample was compared with 1960 census data and is representative in most respects. Slightly more than 10 percent of this sample were Negroes. About 80 percent of the total sample were married. Less than 3 percent of both samples refused to respond.

A questionnaire was administered to the student sample in 1959 and to the adult sample in 1963. The questionnaire contained Guttman scale questions to measure attitudes toward premarital sexual permissiveness. . . . Each question refers to a particular type of sexual behavior under a particular condition of affection, that is, each asks the respondent his views on the acceptability of kissing, petting and coitus under conditions of engagement, love, strong affection, and no affection. In American culture, the meaning of the physical behavior depends on the type of affectional relationship involved.

These 12-item scales met all criteria for a Guttman scale in the five-school sample and in the national adult sample, without dropping any of the questions. These scales have been, I believe, more rigorously tested and verified than any others in the area of premarital sexual permissiveness. . . .

Summary and Conclusions

Examination of data bearing on four hypotheses concerning premarital sexual permissiveness shows some rather important differences between whites and Negroes in social and attitudinal correlates of permissiveness. Many of these differences can be at least partially explained by the Negro historical experience with slavery and its effects on contemporary family life among Negroes. Indeed, the long standing tradition of permissiveness in the Negro-American sub-culture is in my opinion a key explanatory factor. . . .

The analysis reported here indicates that Negroes are generally more inclined to accept premarital sexual permissiveness but that permissiveness has different sources and implications in the Negro group than it does in the white group. For example, students in the New York white college are as permissive as those in the Negro schools, but the vast majority of these white students are low on church attendance and low on romantic love beliefs. The Negro students are higher on both these variables. Thus, a liberal or permissive attitude toward premarital sexual behavior can be generated and maintained in two quite different cultural milieus.

In investigating these Negro-white differences I found that the differences between men and women *within* both racial groups were similar to the differences between Negroes and whites generally. Men are significantly more permissive than women; romantic love doesn't affect men as much as it does women, and among white students church attendance and the number of times in love affects female more than male permissiveness. These differences tend to support the analogous differences between races; perhaps they reflect a general difference between more and less permissive sub-cultures in our society. The fact that the social factors we examined affected white more than Negro and female more than male permissiveness suggests that an inverse relation exists between the sub-cultural level of permissiveness to social factors. The theoretical statement that would subsume as special cases these sex and race differences is: *The lower the traditional level of sexual permissiveness in a group, the greater likelihood that social factors will alter individual levels of sexual permissiveness.*

Let us review the findings with this proposed theory in mind. Church attendance was not significantly associated with permissiveness for Negroes generally, but church attendance conditions the relation of romantic love to permissiveness for Negro women. Perhaps the emotional quality of Negro religion accentuates a somewhat similar emotional belief in romantic love. Studies of the Negro church indicate that it is a source of emotional satisfaction rather than an inhibitory influence on sexual behavior. This emotional quality, however, is probably less characteristic of middle- and upper-class Negro churches. The Negro churches in general may in fact strive to reduce sexual permissiveness, but the strong tradition of sexual permissiveness among Negroes may counteract this effort, whereas the less permissive white customs would not have this effect. Church attendance has a more potent effect on permissiveness among white women than among white men: again, a stronger tradition of sexual permissiveness for men may cancel religious efforts to control sexual behavior.

Romantic love is susceptible to a similar interpretation. The positive association between romantic love and permissiveness among Negro women suggests that they have a more emotional and sexual interpretation of romantic love than 'white women do. White women seem more inclined to stress the idealistic aspects and the less sensual overtones of romantic love. Additional evidence on this point is that Negro women in the student sample who are high on romantic love are most likely to accept "permissiveness with affection," or coitus for both men and women when they are involved in some form of stable affectionate relationship. In contrast, white women who are high on romantic love are most likely to accept abstinence.[1] Again, the stronger tradition of sexual permissiveness among Negro women colors differently their view of romantic love. Similarly, the fact that romantic love does not affect permissiveness among men of either race may reflect other traditional motivations to sexual behavior that are relatively independent of factors like romantic love.

---

[1] Although they are relatively permissive, Negroes in our sample are not generally promiscuous. . . . They tend to require affectionate relations as a basis for sexual behavior. . . . Negroes were less inclined than whites to accept affectionless kissing and petting.

The relation between number of times in love and permissiveness is affected by the same racial and sexual differences. This relationship held only for white students. Here too I would argue that as a consequence of their traditional acceptance of sexual permissiveness, Negroes do not "need" to fall in love to promote permissive sexual behavior. The analogous sex difference explains why this relation is stronger for white women than for white men, and why the men among whom the relationship is strongest are a small group high on romantic love and somewhat low in permissiveness.

Thus, within traditionally less permissive groups—women and whites—individual permissiveness is more likely to be affected by such social factors as church attendance, belief in romantic love, and falling in love. In the highly permissive groups—men and Negroes—individuals find support and justification for liberal sexual attitudes: their permissiveness is therefore less subject to alternation by social factors. Highly permissive individuals in less permissive social categories are permissive *not* because they have long-standing traditions to support it but because they are located in the social structure in such a way as to avoid inhibitory forces (e.g., church attendance and the idealistic version of romantic love) and to maximize experiences that promote permissiveness (e.g., falling in love). The highly permissive white college students are low on church attendance, tend not to believe in romantic love and report falling in love relatively often. The equally permissive Negro students lack these characteristics; their permissiveness seems to be a consequence of a long-standing supporting tradition. This interpretation of the distinction between more and less permissive sub-cultures is further supported by the contrast between the two extreme groups—Negro men and white women. White women's permissiveness is affected by *all* the variables investigated; that of Negro men is affected by *none* of them.[2]

The theory I have suggested implies that to understand social changes in sexual permissiveness we should study the less permissive groups, for they are most likely to change. To evaluate the efficacy of any variable in affecting sexual permissiveness, one must know the level of permissiveness in the group sampled. Finally, the theory suggests that differences in the area of sexual permissiveness between races are analogous to the differences between sexes; studying one set may well be essential to understanding the other.

[2]In this paper I have not gone into the social basis for different traditions regarding premarital sexual permissiveness. Perhaps the traditionally permissive groups have less to "lose" by being highly permissive. Men cannot become pregnant and Negroes have less social standing to lose. Negro marital institutions have high divorce, desertion, and separation rates which tend to reduce the attractiveness of a marital as compared with a non-marital relationship. Among both Negroes and whites, the male role in the family institution is socially somewhat less emphasized than the female role, and this may encourage a preference for the unmarried state and its benefits. Perhaps we are developing a more permissive or "Scandinavian" type of culture in America, integrated with a stable family system and enhanced by relatively widespread access to the means to control pregnancy. This sort of culture seems to be evolving in parts of our middle and upper classes, as evidenced by their acceptance of "permissiveness with affection.". . .

5

Male Sex Roles

Nathan Hare: The Frustrated Masculinity of the Negro Male

There is a saying that "the only people free in America are the white man and the Negro woman." While this is true only in a special sense, it does point to the simple fact that Negro men are extremely frustrated in playing the masculine role. This leads to a psychological effort to compensate for feelings of inadequacy by way of a struggle for conspicuous masculinity. Many cloak their deepseated feelings of inadequacy in boldly masculine garb and mannerisms. . . .

The bouncing jitterbug walk and the bluffing demeanor of Negro males is still another aspect of the quest for conspicuous masculinity. While white men think nothing of crossing their arms or legs as a gesture of refinement, Negroes typically spread their legs and lean forward ever so slightly to achieve an effect not open to women wearing dresses and skirts.

Then, there are the masculine epithets such as "man," "stud" (a stallion), "Jack" (a male mule), "cat" (lion or panther) and the like to suggest a masculine ferocity they long for but do not have. Women are accordingly given less ferocious labels such as "babe" and "chick." (This does not

Reprinted from *Negro Digest*, August 1964, pp. 5-9. Copyright August 1964 by Negro Digest. Reprinted with permission of the author and publisher. Nathan Hare is former chairman of the Black Studies Department at San Francisco State College. He is currently the publisher of the journal *The Black Scholar*.

include "broad," which apparently has come down from slavery days meaning a Negro slave's wife owned by the master of another plantation and called an "abroad" wife.)

The frustrated masculinity of the Negro male also is apparent in the extreme suspicion of homosexuality among even the most normal of men. Thus, the Negro man who plays the classical piano or dances the ballet is likely to be called homosexual much more so than in the case of white men. A Negro man with the refined bearing of Rock Hudson would be viewed with suspicion or regarded as "queer." Much of this is realistic anxiety, for it is true that Negro males are frustrated in the effort to play a male role.

Before the coming of nonviolence in racial discord, with its relative safeguards against resisting white mobs, Negro women and children were typically sent in. Men hung back, apparently, then rushed in after the situation was underway. Witness Rosa Parks, who sparked the passive resistance movement; Autherine Lucy, first Negro to enter the University of Alabama; Ada Lois Sipuel-Fisher, first Negro to enter the University of Oklahoma in a non-segregated capacity; and Daisy Bates, who stood up to Faubus along with the Little Rock Nine. Now that the pattern has been set and the Ku Klux Klan tamed, Negro males have become more reckless, although one wonders what they would do without Constance Baker Motley of the NAACP legal staff and Gloria Richardson, militant leader of the Cambridge, Maryland, protest.

This is in contrast to the cultural expectation that men should be the aggressive guardians of their women and children. Yet, in some Deep South communities, Negro males cannot even preserve the sanctity of their homes from invading white suitors. The fact that the Negro man cannot protect his family presents a special problem to the Negro male psychology. Negro women can, and often do, rationalize: "We'd get our rights if our men would face up to the white man." Negro males, on the other hand, have no one on whom to project the blame. Rather they are likely to internalize the contempt held by their women, who have two national organizations—the National Council of Negro Women and the National Association of Colored Women's Clubs—while Negro men have none as such.

Witness the incident in Chicago during the summer of 1957 when a group of 100 Negroes (having obtained official permission to use Calumet Park which then was regarded as "white") were stoned by 150 white teenage boys. Most of the men present ran off leaving four teenage boys and the women and children to fend for themselves. On an individual level, one irate woman complained that her husband pretends to snore whenever she must arouse him from bed to check some mysterious noise downstairs, say, in the kitchen.

Similarly, Negro males are frustrated in the effort to play the role of provider. This is illustrated in the fact that a major tenet of the Black Muslim movement is to restore the male to a respectable position in their families. Women are expected to obey their husbands and relinquish some of their power in the family group. Men are bound, in turn, to a struggle to provide for and protect their families. While there is some doubt that the

Muslims are successful in accomplishing these goals, it is true that in Muslim services, unlike many Christian churches which are disproportionately filled by women and children, men do dominate the conduct of church affairs.

But the fact remains that Negro men in general are impeded in the role of "provider." They are more likely to have their salaries outstripped by their women. Census figures for 1960 show that considerably more white males than females are enrolled in college (8.9 percent to 5.3 percent). This is not true for Negroes, where 3.7 percent of the males were enrolled in college against 3.3 per cent of the females. Even if a Negro male does go to college, he is more likely to wind up in a non-professional occupation. While considerably more white males than females are professional, the reverse is true for Negroes. Needless to say, there is often a strain between the non-professional Negro male and his professional wife. He may resent her professional associates while she may reject his non-professional friends. The non-professional husband may feel sensitive to the professional status of his wife in contrast to his own, and she may feel the need to apologize for him before her professional friends.

Even those Negro males who go to college and work in professional capacities are most often pushed into the traditionally feminine occupations of school teacher and social worker. Beneath the college rank, high school women graduates may get clerical jobs in the "white collar" category and feel a prestige not accruing to their blue collar mates.

Thus, many Negro women express the belief that a Negro man "can't do nothing for you (financially)" or "don't know how to treat a woman." Such women pride themselves on the possession of white "sponsors" who pay their clothing bill or the rent. The Negro male—they feel—is minus the masculine prestige contingent on the ability to provide luxuries and satisfaction for females. The paramount importance of the occupation to the male's self-respect has been pointed out by Harold Finestone (see "Cat, Kicks, and Color," in *Identity and Anxiety*, ed. by Maurice Stein and Arthur Vidich). Thus some reject work altogether and turn to pimping as a compensatory exploitation of the female. But this is counter to a culture which expects the contrary only.

Many persons mistakenly point to the Negro male's success in sports as an indication that Negro males possess superior masculinity. But this is not necessarily so. Such theorists may be overlooking the fact that the athletic field may be especially attractive to individuals who have a need to spotlight or show off a conspicuous masculinity. Professor Kirson Weinberg, of Chicago's Roosevelt University, made a study of professional boxers, for instance (see "The Occupational Culture of Boxers," *American Journal of Sociology*, 1950), and found among them young men who were called "sissie" in childhood or who originally had feminine-sounding names. One individual decided to learn boxing because his sister had grown tired of taking up for him. Much of the viciousness of welterweight champion Emil Griffith's fatal fight with Benny Kid Paret was said to be the result of hostility generated at the weigh-in when Paret patted Griffith (who also is a designer of women's hats) on the buttocks and called him a woman in Spanish.

The lynch mob also has helped to exaggerate and spread the myth of the Negro's superior masculinity. Yet only one out of six lynch victims were even accused, initially, of rape (see Arthur Raper, *The Tragedy of Lynching*). Sex was merely used as a pretext by angry white mobs. Even so, there is an old theory that many Negro sex offenders are "acting out" their frustrations; especially when the victim is white. One Negro simply walked up to a strange white woman in a Chicago elevator and hit her in the mouth. He explained that he simply had an irresistible impulse to bop her, not to rape her, and did not molest her sexually. Although many a man has shared this urge toward women of both races, the point is still conceivable. Another who raped a Negro girl said that he had always been too shy or meek to approach a woman in the usual manner.

But this has not offset the myths and jokes among whites regarding extreme or animalistic sexual prowess and equipment attributed to Negro males. It has helped to make the Negro male an object of curiosity to more than a few white women, but in turn has been utilized by white supremacists to salve their guilt regarding their easier access to Negro women in the Deep South (see John Dollard, *Caste and Class in a Southern Town*). At the same time, the white supremacists develop fears that their own weird tales may contain some element of truth. The next step naturally is to try to stifle or minimize the masculinity of the Negro male in actuality, sometimes even by outright castration.

John O. Killens, author of a novel about Negro men at war (*And Then We Heard the Thunder*) was no doubt aware of this when he had a woman character tell the hero, Solly: "The one thing they will not stand for is for a black man to be a man. And everything else is worthless if a man can't be a man."

Frantz Fanon: Black Skin, White Masks

If one wants to understand the racial situation psychoanalytically, not from a universal viewpoint but as it is experienced by individual consciousnesses, considerable importance must be given to sexual phenomena. In the case of the Jew, one thinks of money and its cognates. In that of the Negro, one thinks of sex. Anti-Semitism can be rationalized on a basic level. It is because he takes over the country that the Jew is a danger. An acquaintance told me recently that although he was not an anti-Semite he had been

From *Black Skin, White Masks*, by Frantz Fanon (New York: Grove Press, 1967), translated by Charles Lam Markmann, pp. 160-172. Reprinted by permission of Grove Press, Inc. Copyright © 1967 by Grove Press, Inc. The late Frantz Fanon was a psychiatrist in Algeria and a leading theoretician on Third World revolutionary movements.

constrained to admit that the majority of Jews whom he had known during the war had behaved very badly. I tried in vain to get him to concede that such a statement was the fruit of a determined desire to find the essence of the Jew wherever it might exist.

On a clinical level, I am reminded of the story of the young woman who suffered from a kind of tactile delirium, constantly washing her hands and arms ever since the day a Jew had been introduced to her.

Jean-Paul Sartre has made a masterful study of the problem of anti-Semitism; let us try to determine what are the constituents of Negrophobia. This phobia is to be found on an instinctual, biological level. At the extreme, I should say that the Negro, because of his body, impedes the closing of the postural schema of the white man—at the point, naturally, at which the black man makes his entry into the phenomenal world of the white man. This is not the place in which to state the conclusions I drew from studying the influence exerted on the body by the appearance of another body. (Let us assume, for example, that four fifteen-year-old boys, all more or less athletic, are doing the high jump. One of them wins by jumping four feet ten inches. Then a fifth boy arrives and tops the mark by a half-inch. The four other bodies experience a destructuration.) What is important to us here is to show that with the Negro the cycle of the *biological* begins.

No anti-Semite, for example, would ever conceive of the idea of castrating the Jew. He is killed or sterilized. But the Negro is castrated. The penis, the symbol of manhood, is annihilated, which is to say that it is denied. The difference between the two attitudes is apparent. The Jew is attacked in his religious identity, in his history, in his race, in his relations with his ancestors and with his posterity; when one sterilizes a Jew, one cuts off the source; every time that a Jew is persecuted, it is the whole race that is persecuted in his person. But it is in his corporeality that the Negro is attacked. It is as a concrete personality that he is lynched. It is as an actual being that he is a threat. The Jewish menace is replaced by the fear of the sexual potency of the Negro. O. Mannoni said:

An argument widely used by racialists against those who do not share their convictions is worthy of mention for its revealing character. "What," they say, "if you had a daughter, do you mean to say that you would marry her to a Negro?" I have seen people who appeared to have no racialist bias lose all critical sense when confronted with this kind of question. The reason is that such an argument disturbs certain uneasy feelings in them (more exactly, *incestuous* feelings) and they turn to racialism as a defense reaction.[1]

Before we go further, it seems important to make this point: Granted that unconscious tendencies toward incest exist, why should these tendencies

---

[1] [Dominique] O. Mannoni, *Prospero and Caliban: The Psychology of Colonization* (New York, Praeger, 1964), p. 111, note 1.

emerge more particularly with respect to the Negro? In what way, taken as an absolute, does a black son-in-law differ from a white son-in-law? Is there not a reaction of unconscious tendencies in both cases? Why not, for instance, conclude that the father revolts because in his opinion the Negro will introduce his daughter into a sexual universe for which the father does not have the key, the weapons, or the attributes?

Every intellectual gain requires a loss in sexual potential. The civilized white man retains an irrational longing for unusual eras of sexual license, of orgiastic scenes, of unpunished rapes, of unrepressed incest. In one way these fantasies respond to Freud's life instinct. Projecting his own desires onto the Negro, the white man behaves "as if" the Negro really had them. When it is a question of the Jew, the problem is clear: He is suspect because he wants to own the wealth or take over the positions of power. But the Negro is fixated at the genital; or at any rate he has been fixated there. Two realms: the intellectual and the sexual. An erection on Rodin's *Thinker* is a shocking thought. One cannot decently "have a hard on" everywhere. The Negro symbolizes the biological danger; the Jew, the intellectual danger.

To suffer from a phobia of Negroes is to be afraid of the biological. For the Negro is only biological. The Negroes are animals. They go about naked. And God alone knows. . . . Mannoni said further: "In his urge to identify the anthropoid apes, Caliban, the Negroes, even the Jews with the mythological figures of the satyrs, man reveals that there are sensitive spots in the human soul at a level where thought becomes confused and where sexual excitement is strangely linked with violence and aggressiveness." Mannoni includes the Jew in his scale. I see nothing inappropriate there. But here the Negro is the master. He is the specialist of this matter: Whoever says *rape* says *Negro*.

Over three or four years I questioned some 500 members of the white race—French, German, English, Italian. I took advantage of a certain air of trust, of relaxation; in each instance I waited until my subject no longer hesitated to talk to me quite openly—that is, until he was sure that he would not offend me. Or else, in the midst of associational tests, I inserted the word *Negro* among some twenty others. Almost 60 percent of the replies took this form:

Negro brought forth biology, penis, strong, athletic, potent, boxer, Joe Louis, Jesse Owens, Senegalese troops, savage, animal, devil, sin.

Senegalese soldier, used as the stimulus, evoked dreadful, bloody, tough, strong.

It is interesting to note that one in fifty reacted to the word *Negro* with *Nazi* or *SS*; when one knows the emotional meaning of the SS image, one recognizes that the difference from the other answers is negligible. Let me add that some Europeans helped me by giving the test to their acquaintances: In such cases the proportion went up notably. From this result one must acknowledge the effect of my being a Negro: Unconsciously there was a certain reticence.

The Negro symbolizes the biological. First of all, he enters puberty at the age of nine and is a father at the age of ten; he is hot-blooded, and his blood is strong; he is tough. As a white man remarked to me not long ago, with a certain bitterness: "You all have strong constitutions." What a beautiful race—look at the Senegalese. . . . Weren't they called *our Black Devils* during the war? . . . But they must be brutal . . . I just can't see them putting those big hands of theirs on my shoulder. I shudder at the mere thought of it. . . . Well aware that in certain cases one must interpret by opposites, I understand this extra-fragile woman: At bottom what she wants most is to have the powerful Negro bruise her frail shoulders. Sartre says that when one speaks the phrase "a young Jewess," there is an imaginary reek of rape and pillage. . . . Conversely, we might say that the expression "a handsome Negro" contains a "possible" allusion to similar phenomena. I have always been struck by the speed with which "handsome young Negro" turns into "young colt" or "stallion." In the film *Mourning Becomes Electra*, a good part of the plot is based on sexual rivalry. Orin rebukes his sister, Vinnie, because she admired the splendid naked natives of the South Seas. He cannot forgive her for it.

Analysis of the real is always difficult. An investigator can choose between two attitudes toward his subject. First, he can be satisfied only to describe, in the manner of those anatomists who are all surprised when, in the midst of a description of the tibia, they are asked how many tibular depressions *they* have. That is because in their researches there is never a question of themselves but of others. In the beginning of my medical studies, after several nauseating sessions in the dissection room, I asked an older hand how I could prevent such reactions. "My friend, pretend you're dissecting a cat, and everything will be all right . . . ." Second, once he has described reality, the investigator can make up his mind to change it. In principle, however, the decision to describe seems naturally to imply a critical approach and therefore a need to go farther toward some solution. Both authorized and anecdotal literature have created too many stories about Negroes to be suppressed. But putting them all together does not help us in our real task, which is to disclose their mechanics. What matters for us is not to collect facts and behavior, but to find their meaning. Here we can refer to Jaspers, when he wrote: "Comprehension in depth of a single instance will often enable us, phenomenologically, to apply this understanding in general to innumerable cases. Often what one has once grasped is soon met again. What is important in phenomenology is less the study of a large number of instances than the intuitive and deep understanding of a few individual cases."[2] The question that arises is this: Can the white man behave healthily toward the black man and can the black man behave healthily toward the white man?

A pseudo-question, some will say. But when we assert that European culture has an *imago* of the Negro which is responsible for all the conflicts that may arise, we do not go beyond reality. . . . On the screen the Negro faithfully reproduces that *imago*. Even serious writers have made themselves its spokesmen. So it was that Michel Cournot could write:

[2]Karl Jaspers, *Psychopathologie generale*, translation by Kastler and Mendousse, p. 49.

The black man's sword is a sword. When he has thrust it into your wife, she has really felt something. It is a revelation. In the chasm that it has left, your little toy is lost. Pump away until the room is awash with your sweat, you might as well just be singing. This is *good-by.* . . .Four Negroes with their penises exposed would fill a cathedral. They would be unable to leave the building until their erections had subsided; and in such close quarters that would not be a simple matter.

To be comfortable without problems, they always have the open air. But then they are faced with a constant insult: the palm tree, the breadfruit tree, and so many other proud growths that would not slacken for an empire, erect as they are for all eternity, and piercing heights that are not easily reached at any price.[3]

When one reads this passage a dozen times and lets oneself go—that is, when one abandons oneself to the movement of its images—one is no longer aware of the Negro but only of a penis; the Negro is eclipsed. He is turned into a penis. He *is* a penis. It is easy to imagine what such descriptions can stimulate in a young girl in Lyon. Horror? Lust? Not indifference, in any case. Now, what is the truth? The average length of the penis among the black men of Africa, Dr. Pales says, rarely exceeds 120 millimeters (4.6244 inches). Testut, in his *Traité d'anatomie humaine,* offers the same figure for the European. But these are facts that persuade no one. The white man is convinced that the Negro is a beast; if it is not the length of the penis, then it is the sexual potency that impresses him. Face to face with this man who is "different from himself," he needs to defend himself. In other words, to personify The Other. The Other will become the mainstay of his preoccupations and his desires.[4] The prostitute whom I mentioned earlier told me that her hunt for Negroes dated from the time when she had been told this story: One night a woman who was in bed with a Negro went mad; she remained insane for two years, but then when she had been cured refused to go to bed with anyone else. The prostitute did not know what had driven the other woman mad. But she sought furiously to reproduce the same situation, to discover this secret which was part of the ineffable. One must recognize that

---

[3] *Martinique* (Paris, Collection Metamorphoses, Gallimard, 1948), pp. 13–14.

[4] Some writers have tried, thus accepting prejudices (in the etymological sense of the word), to show why the white man does not understand the sexual life of the Negro. Thus one can find in De Pedrals this passage, which, while it does nevertheless convey the truth, still leaves aside the deep causes of white "opinion":

The Negro child feels neither surprise nor shame at the facts of reproduction, because he is told whatever he wants to know. It is quite obvious, without having to fall back on the subtleties of psychoanalysis, that this difference cannot help having an effect on his way of thinking and hence on his way of acting. Since the sexual act is presented to him as the most natural, indeed the most commendable thing in view of the end that it pursues—impregnation—the African will retain this outlook as long as he lives; while the European, as long as he lives, will always unconsciously keep alive a guilt complex that neither reason nor experience will ever succeed in altogether dissipating. In this way the African is inclined to view his sexual life as only a part of his physiological life, just like eating, drinking, and sleeping. . . . A conception of this kind, one would suppose, precludes the distortions into which the European is led in order to reconcile the conflicts of a tortured conscience, a vacillating intellect, and a frustrated instinct. Hence the fundamental difference is not at all of natures, or of constitutions, but of conceptions; hence too the fact that the reproductive instinct, stripped of the halo with which the monuments of our literature have adorned it, is not at all the dominant element in the life of the African as it is in our own, in spite of the statements of *too many students inclined to explain what they have seen by the sole method of analyzing themselves.* (Denis Pierre de Pedrals, *La vie sexuelle en Afrique noire,* Paris, Payot, 1950, pp. 28–29.) My italics—F. F.

what she wanted was the destruction, the dissolution, of her being on a sexual level. Every experiment that she made with a Negro reinforced her limitations. This delirium of orgasm was unattainable. She could not experience it, so she avenged herself by losing herself in speculation.

One thing must be mentioned in this connection: A white woman who has had a Negro lover finds it difficult to return to white men. Or so at least it is believed, particularly by white men: "Who knows what 'they' can give a woman?" Who indeed does know? Certainly "they" do not. On this subject I cannot overlook this comment by Etiemble:

Racial jealousy produces the crimes of racism: To many white men, the black is simply that marvelous sword which, once it has transfixed their wives, leaves them forever transfigured. My statistical sources have been able to provide me with no documentation on this point. I have, however, known some Negroes; some white women who have had Negroes; and, finally, some Negro women who have had white lovers. I have heard enough confidences from all of them to be able to deplore the fact that M. Cournot applies his talents to the rejuvenation of a fable in which the white man will always be able to find a specious argument: shameful, dubious, and thus doubly effective.[5]

An endless task, the cataloguing of reality. We accumulate facts, we discuss them, but with every line that is written, with every statement that is made, one has the feeling of incompleteness. Attacking J. P. Sartre, Gabriel d'Arbousier wrote:

This anthology, which puts Antilleans, Guianans, Senegalese, and Malagasies on the same footing, creates a deplorable confusion. In this way it states the cultural problem of the overseas countries by detaching it from the historical and social reality of each of them, from the national characteristics and the varying conditions imposed on each of them by imperialist exploitation and oppression. Thus, when Sartre wrote, "Simply by plunging into the depths of his memory as a former slave, the black man asserts that suffering is the lot of man and that it is no less undeserved on that account," did he take into consideration what that might mean for a Hova, a Moor, a Touareg, a Peul, or a Bantu of the Congo or the Ivory Coast?[6]

The objection is valid. It applies to me as well. In the beginning I wanted to confine myself to the Antilles. But, regardless of consequences, dialectic took the upper hand and I was compelled to *see* that the Antillean is first of all a Negro. Nevertheless, it would be impossible to overlook the fact that there are Negroes whose nationality is Belgian, French, English; there are also Negro republics. How can one claim to have got hold of an essential

[5] "Sur le *Martinique* de M. Michel Cournot," *Les Temps Modernes*, February, 1950, p. 1505.

[6] "Une dangereuse mystification: la theorie de la negritude," *La Nouvelle Revue Critique*, June, 1949.

when such facts as these demand one's recognition? The truth is that the Negro race has been scattered, that it can no longer claim unity. When Il Duce's troops invaded Ethiopia, a movement of solidarity arose among men of color. But, though one or two airplanes were sent from America to the invaded country, not a single black man made any practical move. The Negro has a country, he takes his place in a Union or a Commonwealth. Every description should be put on the level of the discrete phenomenon, but here again we are driven out to infinite perspectives. In the universal situation of the Negro there is an ambiguity, which is, however, resolved in his concrete existence. This in a way places him beside the Jew. Against all the arguments I have just cited, I come back to one fact: *Wherever he goes, the Negro remains a Negro.*

Jean Carey Bond and Pat Peery: Has the Black Man Been Castrated?

In Black communities all over the country today, intelligent and imaginative people are discussing the political, economic and cultural aspects of the Black liberation struggle. Viable approaches for changing the Afro-American's condition in America are beginning to emerge. Almost without notice, an issue slipped in the back door of these discussions and then assumed controversial proportions as soon as its presence was acknowledged. We refer to what has become a burning question in our community, and rightly so: What should be the role of women in the movement? Subdivisions of this lead question are: What have been the traditional relations between Black men and women? What are the factors that have defined or determined those relations?

Despite the obvious interest of both men and women in this issue, and despite the inclination of both to comment at length and take rigid positions, we are appalled at a reigning lack of seriousness and sobriety in the debate. Black publications are full of, on the one hand, hysterical and bitter indictments of the past and present conduct of Black men from the bruised and now twisted consciousnesses of sisters who have been driven to irrational extremes by the conditions of a world they never made. On the other hand, we find the equally neurotic but voguish creed that women must abandon their "matriarchal" behavior, learn to speak only when they are spoken to and take up positions three paces (or is it ten?) behind their men.[1]

Reprinted from *Liberator*, Vol. 9, No. 5 (May 1969), pp. 4–8. By permission of the publisher. Copyright © 1969 by *Liberator*. Jean Carey Bond is a freelance writer. Pat Peery is a city planner.

[1] It seems to us that many Black women who give lip service to the latter, male-inspired philosophy have played an interesting psychological trick on themselves. Feeling both guilty and resentful in their relations with Black men, they merely alter the mode of attack to fit the new Black party line. Their aggression now

As far as we know, the question as to whether her place is not properly beside, rather than in front of or behind, the Black man, has yet to be raised.

For their part, many Black men berate Black women for their faults— faults so numerous and so pronounced that one is hard-put to discern in their tirades any ground, short of invisibility, on which Black womanhood might redeem itself. They do this, blind to the age-old implications of such a vociferous rejection of a part of themselves. Others run on about the necessity of subordinating women to their superior and manly will in the planning and execution of revolution with a monumental indisposition to examine their motives for advancing this precept.

We view these superficial and unbalanced attitudes as being predicated on a popular and dangerous fiction: the myth of Black male emasculation, and its descendent concept, the myth of the Black female matriarchy. These companion myths are not recent in their origin; however, they have most recently been popularized through the highly publicized and highly touted work, *The Negro Family: The Case for National Action* by Daniel Patrick Moynihan—so successfully popularized that even Blacks have swallowed his assumptions and conclusions hook, line and sinker. It is ironic that, at a time when Blacks are newly perceiving and denouncing the shallowness of white analyses of the Black experience, many members of the avant-garde are still capable of being mesmerized by racist social scientific thought which has utterly failed to produce in-depth studies of the Afro-American social structure.

The emasculation theory, as interpreted by Blacks, is two-pronged, one version being primarily followed by women, the other commanding the allegiance of both men and women. Version Number One alleges that Black men have failed throughout our history to shield their women and families from the scourge of American racism and have failed to produce a foolproof strategy for liberating Black people. It is therefore concluded that Black men are weak, despicable "niggers" who must be brushed aside and overcome by women in the big push toward freedom. Version Number Two also arrives at the point that Black men are weak via the route that Black women castrated them by, among other things, playing their economic ace-in-the-hole. (Moynihan's Black matriarchy proposition is based, incredibly, on the statistic that one quarter—only one quarter—of all Black families are headed by women.) Also linked to this thesis is the woefully misbegotten notion that Black women complied with their rapists and used their bodies to rise on the socio-economic ladder, leaving Black men behind.

What this all adds up to is that Black men and women are placing ultimate blame for their subjugation on each other, a propensity which fairly reeks of self-hatred. In other words, Blacks are still crippled by self-doubt and, even

takes the form of patronizing, "understanding" pronouncements about the Black male's so-called inadequacies. Dripping with self-admonition and promises to act right in the by-and-by, they neatly assuage the guilt but not the resentment, which to be sure will rear its ugly head in the near future, as troublesome as ever, never having been honestly confronted by either women or men. In the case of some unmarried sisters, we suspect that sheer opportunism motivates their public approval of this idea. What better way to get a man, they reason, than to proclaim your willingness to be his slave?

in 1969, lean painfully towards the view that Europeans could never have kept us in this bind for so long were it not for our own weakness, i.e., inferiority. It is not difficult to understand why we are unable to see the forest for the trees. After all, the cat who sponges off of you, knocks you around every now and then and maybe leaves you, is Black not white. And by the same token, the chick who tells you this is her money, she made it, and you can just get-the-hell-out, is Black not white. But we are, in fact, focusing only on the trees when we expend time and energy in this senseless and debilitating family squabble while the real culprits stand laughing in the wings.

What is emasculation? In the broad sense, an emasculated people (cultural group) are a broken people, a people whose spirit, strength and vigor have been destroyed, who have been reduced to a state of almost total ineffectuality. Specifically applied to a male, emasculation connotes the absence of virility and can mean, though not necessarily, effeminacy. Notwithstanding the colossal suffering which has befallen Black people here and abroad as a result of their colonization by Europeans, with its numerous deleterious effects on the Black psyche, do our people truly fit the description given above? And notwithstanding the often literal, but more often, symbolic castration of hundreds of thousands of Black individuals throughout our sojourn in the wilderness, have Black men really been stripped of their virility? We contend that as a whole people Afro-Americans lack neither spirit nor strength nor vigor, for it is they who have given to this nation the only culture it has, the only humanity it has.

As for Black men, we must ask the question: If the Black male's castration is a *fait accompli* of long standing, why the frantic need on the part of whites to replay the ritual of castration over and over again in a hundred different ways? The answer is simple: The enduring manhood/humanity of Blacks, burning bright despite all efforts to extinguish it, is the nemesis of Western civilization. Nowhere do we find this point more beautifully made than in Ron Milner's brilliant play, *Who's Got His Own*. The memorable character of S—house Tim embodies the compelling thesis that no matter what level of degradation a Black man might be reduced to, within the solitary confinement of his soul his manhood crackles white hot, so potent that even from its grotesque cocoon it sends out vibrations to the next generation. From whence comes the militant fury of Tim Jr., which explodes in a near-fatal assault on his white "buddy," if not from the heart and mind of that tomming, wife-beating, evil-tongued, indomitable S—house Tim?

Moynihan and his gang postulate that Black society is matriarchal, and that Black women have been the primary castrating force in the demise of Black manhood. The casting of this image of the Black female in sociological bold relief is both consistent and logical in racist terms, for the so-called Black matriarch is a kind of folk character, *largely fashioned by whites* out of half-truths and lies about the involuntary condition of black women. The matriarchal fairy tale is part of a perennial tendency among whites to employ every available device in *their* on-going effort to demasculinize the Black male. Movies and radio shows of the 1930's and 1940's invariably peddled the Sapphire image of the Black woman: She is depicted as iron-willed, effectual, treacherous towards and contemptuous of Black men, the latter being portrayed as simpering, ineffectual whipping boys. Certainly, most of us have encountered domineering Black females (and white ones too). Many of them have been unlucky in life and love and seek a bitter haven from their disappointments in fanatical self-sufficiency. Others, out of a tragic fear, brutalize their sons in the child-rearing process, hoping to destroy in them aggressive tendencies which might eventually erupt in assaults against white men and the white system. But it must be emphasized that the white man's Sapphire caricature does not closely resemble the real domineering Black female, much less the majority of her sisters who do not share that classification.

We submit that in reality Black women, domineering or no, have not had the power in this male-dominated culture to effect a coup against anyone's manhood—in spite of her oft-cited economic "advantage" over the Black man. A matriarchal system is one in which power rests firmly in the hands of women. Whatever economic power may accrue to Black women by way of the few employment escape valves permitted them by the oppressing group for their own insidious reasons, this power is really illusory and should not be taken at face value. American society is patriarchal—white women suffer the slings and arrows of that system, in the first instance. Black women are victimized on two counts: they are women and they are Black, a clear case of double indemnity. For the duration of their lives, many Black women must bear a heavy burden of male frustration and rage through physical abuse, desertions, rejection of their femininity and general appearance. Having a job provides relief for her stomach but not for her soul, for a Black woman's successful coping with the economic problem (and we might throw in the education problem) enhances her rejection by Black men, or else invites acceptance in the form of exploitation. Stymied in his attempt to protect and free the Black woman (and himself), the Black man further degrades her. She, doubly powerless and vengeful, insults his manhood by whatever means at her disposal. Thus are many Black men and women hateful partners in a harrowing dance.

These points have never been lost on white folks, and they continue to bend them to their design of divide and rule. Their past and current success is insured by the persistent adherence of many Blacks—including most would-be revolutionaries—to the basic premises of the American value system, from whence all definitions of masculinity, femininity, right and wrong proceed. It is the transference of values, which work for the oppressor in the capitalist context, to the milieu of the oppressed, where they are dysfunctional, that has pitted Black man against Black woman and vice versa—a situation which, needless to say, is anathema to the pursuit of self-determination.

The salient point, though, in our effort to debunk the castration theory is that although whites falsify the image of Black women and use the distortion as one of several castrating tools, their attempt is ultimately abortive. For while Mr. Charlie does set Black manhood on the run, it always escapes the pursuer's final lurch and turns up, shaken but together, at the wheel of an Eldorado, in a smoke-filled poker den, in a Black woman's bed or on the side of her jaw. More importantly, it has turned up throughout our history in the form of resistance to oppression. Sojourner Truth and Harriet Tubman notwithstanding, Black men hold the majority among our political (and cultural) heroes: Frederick Douglass, W. E. B. Du Bois, Marcus Garvey, Malcolm X, etc. Indeed, the Black man always surfaces with his manhood not only intact, but much more intact than that of his oppressor, which brings us to the question: Just who is the emasculated person in this society? Surely it is the white man whose dazzling symbols of power—his goods, his technology—have all but consumed his human essence. Yes, he is effective because his power enables him to rule; but he is emasculated in that he has become a mere extension of the things he produces. The contrary is true of Blacks. Do any of us doubt that Muhammed Ali is the heavyweight champion of the world? What does it matter that whitey took his jewel-encrusted belt away?

If we accept the emasculation theory, we must accept a host of outrageous misrepresentations of the Black personality. We must accept the quaint Southern myth that most slaves were "good niggers" who passively accepted their lot, the companion theory being that slavery was not really so bad. We must accept most of the stereotypes that have been paraded before us down through the ages, as, for example, William Styron's Nat Turner, because any fool knows that eunuchs, figurative or actual, do not lead slave revolts. Eunuchs do not write plays that pulverize the very foundations of American theater. Eunuchs do not refuse to fight in unholy wars, thumbing their noses at such things as trophies and fame, things which some men sell their souls to achieve. Eunuchs only do the bidding of the king. Such acts of defiance as these are wrought by *men* in the name of all Black people.

6

Female Sex Roles

Barbara Rhodes: The Changing Role of the Black Woman

In Nkhrumah's *Handbook of Revolutionary Warfare for Freedom Fighters in Africa*, he says, "The degree of a country's revolutionary awareness is measured by the political maturity of its women." This statement should provoke serious thought in America because of the Black people's intense struggle for liberation and the growing revolutionary spirit. Several years ago the prevalent philosophy toward Black women expressed by a militant Black organization was that the only position of the Black woman in the revolution was prone. That Black people have developed in terms of their revolutionary consciousness is evidenced by the fact that they have now reached the point of concern with the position of the Black woman in a revolution.

We are not now involved in a revolution. We are, however, involved in the building of a revolutionary consciousness. As a Black woman living in the United States today, I strongly feel that the necessity for a political maturity of Black women must be recognized. It must be recognized by Black men, and most importantly, by Black women themselves. Black women must examine the role that has been defined for them by this white society, a role that society has systematically used to elevate them above their Black men. The white society calls it the "matriarchy." That role shows the Black woman's adaptability to conditions imposed upon her Black man and upon her in this country. But when the white society defines the role of the Black woman as a matriarch, it is done in a negative way. It is not that a matriarch is to be criticized; many societies function very effectively under a matriarchal system. However, American society is traditionally patriarchal, and so the women's assumption of head of the household becomes a point from which to attack the male, who is not fulfilling his function in terms of this society's expectations.

The Black woman has often allowed herself to be confused because of the role which white society says she should play as a woman and the role they force her to play as a Black woman. In this confusion, Black women have attempted to act like white women. This is neither possible nor desirable. The white reality is not the Black reality. The role the white woman plays in this white world the Black woman cannot play. And she must not try. The Black woman must be involved in the struggle for the liberation of her people.

How is the Black woman to be involved? Many Black women in their new-found Black consciousness feel that they must look to the Black man to define their role, as they once accepted the role defined for women by the white man. But this is not necessary. There is no role for the Black woman that can be outlined and handed to her by someone else. Defining roles is expedient, but it is not always effective. Take the role historically assigned to Black women as a matriarch. This role defining allows for value judgments, judgments that elevate the Black woman 'at the expense of the Black man. The Black man cannot perform in the role assigned to man by white society because it is a role defined for white men. But the white man, he who stops the Black man from assuming this role, attacks the Black man on the basis of his not functioning in this role. Because the role is defined, if one does not carry out its definition, one can be attacked. This is expediency. An effective relationship in terms of the functions of Black men and women would be that distribution of functions which best relates to their Black reality. This is not expedient. But it is functional, and we as Black people are concerned with survival. It is the white man who is concerned with expediency. When it comes to Blacks, the white man's expediency keeps him on top.

The Black woman must act from a base of political awareness. This is the guiding principle in terms of her functioning. Then, as a mother, teacher, neighbor, or organization member, she is functioning in the building of the revolutionary consciousness of Black people.

How does a Black woman become politically aware? First, she must discard the myth of femininity that would effectively halt her progress. By femininity, I do not mean such superficial feminine traits as tone of voice and language. I am talking about the femininity that would prevent the Black woman from dealing seriously with ideas. The Black woman must free her mind from these restraints. She must open her mind to the ideologies of the Black struggle and allow it to consider total involvement in the effort to liberate Black people.

Black women must open their minds to all ideas that involve their survival. This is the education they must pass on to their Black children. They must continue to be effective counterparts of their Black men. The relationship between man and woman and the relationship between mother and child are extremely important for Black people. Black children must not be allowed to be conditioned by a white society, unaware of their Black reality. They must be conditioned by a Black mother, to the realities of this society and the realities of involvement in a Black liberation struggle.

No more will Black men submit to the emasculation inherent in the calling of their Black women matriarchs. They are determined to claim the total dignity of manhood at whatever cost. The role of the Black woman as it relates to that will be crucial. What is this role? Black women must supply the answers for themselves. Only they can determine how they will relate to these changing times. The suggestions that follow reflect the thoughts of one Black woman.

More than Empty Rhetoric for the Child

When the Black woman is faced with the multiple problems of raising a Black child in a white society, is it enough for her to say to the child, "Listen, my child, Black is beautiful"? Does the child understand what the mother is saying? Does this enable him to deal with the white environment as a proud, assured Black person? I say a resounding no! A child can understand when he is told, "You are beautiful." A child cannot understand when he is told, "Black is beautiful; you are Black and you are beautiful." The child does not understand the suffering and pain that has given significance to the phrase "Black is beautiful." The child does not understand the depths of darkness from which Black people have ascended, proudly lifting the darkness with them, glorifying in this darkness that is their Black selves, and proclaiming its beauty as innate and proud that it is manifest without. How can the child know all this? To the child, this phrase is empty rhetoric. As surely as he knows that darkness follows light in the passing of the days, he will come to know this. When he comes to this knowledge of his Blackness, he will willingly embrace it if he has been truly made to believe in his beauty as a person. "Child, you are beautiful. You are truly beautiful." This is what Black mothers must tell their children. In word and in deed, the Black mother must affirm all those qualities that make a person a total and beautiful person. She must affirm them from a conviction that she is beautiful. She must have no questions, no doubts. "Listen, my child, this fact let no one question; from it flows the strength of your existence. You are a beautiful person."

Not only must the Black mother affirm the beauty of her child, she must nurture it. It lies in the child like the seed of an oak tree with potential to develop into strength and endurance. But it must be nurtured. It must be cultivated carefully, for a seed has not yet taken root and lies vulnerable. Cultivate it; let its roots sink into the soil that is the child's very being, and it cannot be destroyed.

The child must be taught that there are those who would rob him of his beauty, that there are those who would deny its existence. The child must be taught that those who would so approach him are his enemies. He must be taught to identify his enemies. He must be taught to defend the beauty that is the wellspring of his being. This belief in his beauty is the foundation of his belief in all other things that make him a total person. From it flows the confidence that nurtures growth of intellect. From it flows the faith in self that nurtures courage to act. It is the very foundation from which springs courage to act. It is the very foundation from which springs the child's power to assert self. Love of self is a powerful weapon. It is man's best weapon in the war of survival. Black mothers must arm their every child with this weapon. When man loves self, he would rather be destroyed attempting to save self than let another destroy him. He will take whatever means necessary to assure the survival of the self he loves. Whatever means necessary. . . .

How is the Black mother to teach her child to identify his enemies? Who are those who would deny the beauty of the Black child, and why do they proceed systematically to do so? The answer to these questions is contained in the history of America. It is contained in a history based in large part on the denial of the beauty of the Black man and woman. This denial has robbed the Black man of one of his most essential weapons in the war of survival, love of self. By so robbing the Black man in America, this country has been able to keep him subjugated, to heap its frustrations upon him, and to use him to sustain the myth of white superiority.

The Black mother must open her mind to the facts of history, for these facts attest to the creation of the myth of white superiority largely at the expense of Black human beings. In its most recent pages, history attests to outrage after outrage being perpetrated on Black people because of the necessity of sustaining this myth. The outrage of little girls being bombed in a church in Alabama in 1964, of Black leaders being assassinated, Evers in Mississippi and King in Tennessee. Incident after incident of physical atrocities have been enacted against Black people. As many atrocities are being committed today as 150 years ago.

However, the Black mother must look further than a review of the physical imhumanity of white America to the Black man. She must look closely at the psychological atrocities perpetrated against Black human beings. These psychological atrocities had their birth during slavery and have survived to this very day, attaining, as they age, a higher degree of sophistication. It is these psychological atrocities that must be combatted because they work to destroy the Black man's love of self. These psychological atrocities have no compassion for the child, for it is the child that offers the most fertile ground. How should the Black mother begin in this effort to unveil the psychological networks devised to destroy her children? She must first begin with the knowledge that she has been a victim of this design. She must first begin with a real knowledge of self, no matter how painful this knowledge may be.

Robert Staples: The Myth of the Black Matriarchy

In dealing with the question of the role of the black woman in the black struggle one must ultimately encounter the assertion that the black community is organized along matriarchal lines, that the domineering black female has been placed in a superordinate position in the family by the historical vicissitudes of slavery, and that her ascendency to power has resulted in the psychological castration of the black male and produced a host of other negative results that include low educational achievement, personality disorders, juvenile delinquency, etc. One of the solutions to the "Negro" question we hear is that black males divest themselves of this female control of black society and reorganize it along patriarchal lines which will eventually solve the problem created by black female dominance.

And one can easily understand how the typical black female would react when told that the problem of black liberation lies on her shoulders, that by renouncing her control over the black male, their other common problems such as inadequate education, chronic unemployment and other pathologies will dissipate into a dim memory.

The myth of a black matriarchy is a cruel hoax.

It is adding insult to injury to black liberation. For the black female, her objective reality is a society where she is economically exploited because she is both female and black; she must face the inevitable situation of a shortage of black males because they have been taken out of circulation by America's neo-colonialist wars, railroaded into prisons, or killed off early by the effects of ghetto living conditions. To label her a matriarch is a classical example of what Malcolm X called making the victim the criminal.[1]

To explode this myth of a black female matriarchy, one must understand the historical role of the black woman and the development of that role as it was influenced by the political and economic organization of American society. Like most myths, the one of a black matriarchy contains some elements of truth. Black women have not been passive objects who were satisfied with watching their menfolk make history. If they had been contented to accept the passive role ascribed to the female gender, then the travail of the past four centuries might have found the black race just as extinct as the dinosaur. It is a poor tribute to their historical deeds to

Reprinted from *The Black Scholar*, 1 (January-February, 1970), pp. 8-16. Copyright © 1970 by The Black Scholar.

[1]George Breitman, *Malcolm X Speaks*. New York: Merit Publishers, 1965.

characterize them as "sapphires," an opprobrious term that belies their real contribution to the black struggle.

Referring to black women as matriarchs is not only in contradistinction to the empirical reality of their status but also is replete with historical and semantic inaccuracies. It was in the study by J. J. Bachofen[2] that the term matriarchy was first employed. He was attempting to present a case for the high position of women in ancient society. His conclusion was that since free sexual relations had prevailed during that time and the fathers of the children were unknown, this gave women their leading status in the period he called "mother-right."

A matriarchy is a society in which some, if not all, of the legal powers relating to the ordering and governing of the family-power over property, over inheritance, over marriage, over the house—are lodged in women rather than men.[3] If one accepts this formal definition, the consensus of most historians is that "men reign dominant in all societies; no matriarchy (*i.e.*, a society ruled by women) is known to exist."[4]

From a historical perspective, the black woman has always occupied a highly esteemed place in black culture. The African woman who first reached the shores of the American continent was already part and parcel of the fabric of history. She was descended from women who had birthed some of the great militarists of antiquity and from whose number had come some of the most famous queens to sit upon the thrones of ancient Egypt and Ethiopia. Her exploits and beauty were remembered by Semitic writers and fused into Greek mythology.[5]

Despite her important historical role, there is little doubt about the respective authority patterns in the black family of the pre-slave period of African civilization. There, the family organization was patriarchal in character and was a stable and secure institution. E. Franklin Frazier described the African patriarchal family this way:

His wife and children gathered around him, and served him with as much respect as the best drilled domestics serve their masters; and if it was a fete day or Sunday, his sons-in-law and daughters did not fail to be present, and bring him some small gifts. They formed a circle about him, and conversed with him while he was eating. When he had finished, his pipe was brought to him, and then he bade them eat. They paid him their reverences, and passed into another room, where they all ate together with their mother.[6]

The ordeal of slavery wrought many changes in the family life of Afro-Americans, including the male and female roles. Family life of the African

[2] J. J. Bachofen, *Das Mutterrecht*, Stuttgart, 1861.

[3] Margaret Mead, *Male and Female*, New York: William Morrow and Company, 1949, p. 301.

[4] William Goode, *The Family*, Englewood Cliffs, New Jersey: Prentice-Hall, Inc., 1964, p. 14.

[5] John Hope Franklin, *From Slavery to Freedom*, New York: Random House, 1947.

[6] E. Franklin Frazier, *The Negro Family in the United States*, Chicago: University of Chicago Press, 1939, p. 7.

model was an impossibility when the slave's existence had to be devoted primarily to the cultivation and manufacture of tobacco and cotton. The buying and selling of slaves involved the splitting up of families, while the maintenance of discipline on the plantation prevented the husband and father from protecting his wife and children against his white masters and other more favored slaves. The financial value set on slave children and the rewards given to successful motherhood in cash, kind, and promotion from field slave to house slave gave an especially high status to the mother, a status which the father could only enjoy if placed in a position akin to that of a stud animal, this leading to a breaking of family ties and the degradation of family life still further.

Under the conditions of slavery, the American black father was forcefully deprived of the responsibilities and privileges of fatherhood. The black family's desire to remain together was subordinated to the economic interests of the slave-owning class. Only the mother-child bond continually resisted the disruptive effect of economic interests that dictated the sale of fathers away from their families. Not only did the practice of selling away fathers leave the black mother as the prime authority in the household but whenever the black male was present, he was not allowed to play the normal masculine role in American culture. Davie reports that:

In the plantation domestic establishment, the woman's role was more important than that of her husband. The cabin was hers and rations of corn and salt pork were issued to her. She cooked the meals, tended the vegetable patch, and often raised chickens to supplement the rations. If there was a surplus to sell, the money was hers. She made the clothes and reared the children. If the family received any special favors it was generally through her efforts.[7]

Just as in the society at large, power relationships in the family are aligned along economic lines. The power base of the patriarchal family is, in large part, based on the economic dependence of the female member. In the black slave family, the black woman was independent of the black male for support and assumed a type of leadership in her family life not found in the patriarchal family. At the same time, white society continued to deny black males the opportunity to obtain the economic wherewithal to assume leadership in the family constellation.

The reasons for this suppression of the black male are found in both the economic imperatives of slavery and the sexual value system of white America. In the early period of colonial America, the white family was strongly patriarchal and many of the income and property rights enjoyed by women and children were those 'given' to them by the husband or father. White women had primarily a chattel status, particularly in the Southern part of the country. They were expected to remain chaste until marriage while white

[7]Maurice Davie, *Negroes in American Society*, New York: McGraw-Hill, 1949, p. 207.

Southern males were permitted, or often encouraged, to sow their wild oats before, during and after marriage.[8]

A double standard of sexual behavior allowing premarital sex for men while denying it to women, always poses the problem of what females will provide the source of sexual gratification for bachelor males. There is adequate historical evidence that black slave women were forced into various sexual associations with white males because of their captive status. That physical compulsion was necessary to secure compliance on the part of black women is documented by Frazier, in relating this young man's story:

Approximately a century and a quarter ago, a group of slaves were picking cotton on a plantation near where Troy, Alabama, is now located. Among them was a Negro woman, who despite her position, carried herself like a queen and was tall and stately. The overseer (who was the plantation owner's son) sent her to the house on some errand. It was necessary to pass through a wooded pasture to reach the house and the overseer intercepted her in the woods and forced her to put her head between the rails in an old stake and rider fence, and there in that position my great-great-grandfather was conceived.[9]

Thus, the double-standard of premarital sexual behavior allowed the Southern white woman to remain "pure" and the bodies of the captive female slaves became the objects of their ruler's sexual passion. Consequently, black males had to be suppressed to prevent them from daring to defend the black woman's honor. For those black males who would not accept their suppression passively, the consequences were severe. As one person reports the story of his father's defense of his mother:

His right ear had been cut off close to his head, and he had received a hundred lashes on his back. He had beaten the overseer for a brutal assault on my mother, and this was his punishment. Furious at such treatment, my father became a different man, and was so morose, disobedient, and intractable, that Mr. N. decided to sell him. He accordingly parted with him, not long after, to his son, who lived in Alabama; and neither mother nor I ever heard from him again.[10]

During the period of slavery, the physical resistance of black males to the rape of their women was met with all the brutal punishment white society could muster. That they were not totally successful in their efforts to crush the black man is evidenced in the heroic deeds of Denmark Vesey, Nat Turner, Frederick Douglass, David Walker and others. The acts of these

[8] Arthur W. Calhoun, *A Social History of the American Family*, New York: Barnes and Noble, 1919.

[9] E. F. Frazier, *op. cit.*, p. 53.

[10] *Ibid*, p. 48.

black males are sometimes played down in favor of the efforts of Harriet Tubman, Sojourner Truth and other black females in securing the slave's freedom. Such favoritism can be expected of a racist society bent on perpetuating the myth of a black female matriarchy, with males pictured as ineffective husbands and fathers who are mere caricatures of real men. The literary castration of the black male is illustrated by the best selling novel, *The Confessions of Nat Turner*,[11] which generated much heat and little light, in terms of understanding one of the most important black revolutionists of his time.

The cultural stereotype of the domineering black woman belies the existence of the masses of black women who constituted a defenseless group against the onslaught of white racism in its most virulent sexual and economic manifestations. That black women are still involuntarily subjected to the white male's lust is reflected in the revelations of a white employer to John Howard Griffin, as reported in his book, *Black Like Me:*

He told me how all of the white men in the region crave colored girls. He said he hired a lot of them both for housework and in his business. "And I guarantee you, I've had it in every one of them before they ever get on the payroll."

"Surely some refuse," I suggested cautiously.

"Not if they want to eat—or feed their kids," he snorted. "If they don't put out, they don't get the job."[12]

Black women have frequently been slandered by the cultural folklore that the only free people in the South were the white man and the black woman. While there have been a few black women who have gained material rewards and status through the dispensation of their sexual favors to white men, the massive indictment of all black women for the acts of a few only creates unnecessary intra-group antagonisms and impedes the struggle for black self-determination.

Many proponents of the black matriarchy philosophy assert that the black female gained ascendency in black society through her economic support of the family. Although the unemployment rate of black males is disproportionately higher than that of white males, only a very small minority of black families with both parents present are dependent on the mother for their maintenance. It is a rather curious use of logic to assume that black females, who in 1960 earned an annual wage of $2,372 a year as compared to the annual wage of $3,410 for white women and $3,789 for black men,[13] have an economic advantage over any group in this society.

However, what semblance of black female dominance that is found in our society can be traced to the persistent rate of high unemployment among

[11] William Styron, *The Confessions of Nat Turner*, New York: Random House, 1967.

[12] John Howard Griffin, *Black Like Me*, New York: Signet, 1963.

[13] *United States Census of Population Report*, 1960.

black males which prevents them from becoming the major economic support of their family. The economic causes of female dominance are manifest. For instance, the percentage of black women in the labor market declines as the percentage of black males employed in manufacturing and mechanical industries is increasing. The effect of higher black male employment is the male's added responsibility for his family's support; the authority of the wife declines and that of the husband increases.

Many black men have not been permitted to become the kings of their castles. If black women wanted to work, there was always employment for them—even during depressions. Sometimes it was even a higher kind of work than that available to black men. Historically, black males have suffered from irregularity of employment more than any other segment of the American proletariat. Thus, they have been placed in a weak economic position which prevents them from becoming steady providers for their families. Any inordinate power that black women possess, they owe to white America's racist employment barriers. The net effect of this phenomenon is, in reality, not black female dominance but greater economic deprivation for families deprived of the father's income.

The myth of a black matriarchy was strengthened by the Moynihan Report released in 1965.[14] Moynihan's central thesis was that the black family was crumbling and that a major part of the blame lay with the black matriarchy extant in the black community. Some of the evidence cited would lack credibility to all but a group bent on making the victim responsible for the crimes of the criminal. Such sources of proof as the higher educational level of black females vis-à-vis black males conveniently overlook the alternative possibility—that many black males are forced to terminate their formal education early in order to help support their family. Instead, they cite the wholly unsupported statement by a "Negro" expert that, "Historically, in the matriarchal society, mothers made sure that if one of their children had a chance for higher education the daughter was the one to pursue it."[15] In a society where men are expected to have a greater amount of education and earn a higher income, it is difficult to imagine black women celebrating the fact that over 60 percent of the college degrees awarded American blacks are received by women. The end result of this disparity, according to one study, is that almost 50 percent of black female college graduates are married to men employed at a lower socio-economic level than their wives.[16]

Moreover, according to Moynihan and his cohorts, the black matriarchy is responsible for the low educational achievement of black males. In marshalling this arsenal of evidence, Moynihan was apparently unable to find any likelihood that the racist educational system, with its concomitant racist teachers, bore any responsibility for the failure of black males to reach acceptable educational levels by white standards. In the criminalization of the victim, countervailing evidence is dismissed out of hand. The fact that

[14] *The Negro Family: The Case for National Action*, United States Department of Labor, 1965.

[15] Whitney Young, *To Be Equal*, New York: McGraw-Hill, 1964, p. 25.

[16] Jean Noble, *The Negro Woman College Graduate*, New York: Columbia University Press, 1956, p. 64.

black schools are more likely to be housed in inadequate buildings, with inferior facilities, staffed by inexperienced and racist teachers and over-crowded,[17] only confuses the issue, especially when there is a matriarchal structure that is more handily blamed.

According to the "experts" on the black family, the black male is harshly exploited by the black matriarchy. Many black mothers, they report, express an open preference for girls.[18] This charge is confirmed by a white psycholo-gist, described by a major magazine as devoid of any racism, who states that black males have an inordinate hatred for their mothers.[19] Although there are research studies that reveal no sex-role preference on the part of black mothers,[20] it appears that the practitioners of white social science have not been content with pitting husband against wife but also wish to turn sons against mothers, brothers against sisters. The evidence for these assumptions is not only flimsy, but in some cases also non-existent. If the research is similar to other psychological studies, they have probably used a sample of ten blacks, who, on the verge of a psychotic breakup, wandered into their mental clinic.

These charges of black men hating their mothers must be very puzzling to the black mothers aware of them. They would be puzzled because they realize that if a preference is shown for any sex-role in the black family, it would more likely be expressed in favor of the male child. The problems of raising a black male child in a racist society have been great. Many black mothers out of fear—real or fancied—repressed the aggressive tendencies of their sons in order to save them from the white man's chopping block. For to act as a man in a society which feared his masculinity, the black male was subject to the force of brutal white retaliation. The black mother had to constantly live with the realization that her son might be killed for exercis-ing the prerogatives of manhood. For those black mothers who exorcised their son's aggressive drives out of concern for their safety, hatred seems to be an inappropriate, and most improbable, response.

In addition to the host of pathologies putatively generated by the black matriarchy, the familiar theory of a relationship between fatherless homes and juvenile delinquency is brought up again. While there is nothing inher-ently wrong with a woman heading a family, the problem arises when she tries to compete in a society which promotes, expects and rewards male leadership. Consequently, she is unable to bring to her family the share of the social and economic rewards received by father-headed households. It is this very factor that probably accounts for any discernible correlation be-tween mother-headed households and juvenile delinquency. The children in

[17] *Equality of Educational Opportunity*, United States Department of Health, Education and Welfare, Office of Education, 1966.

[18] Thomas F. Pettigrew, *A Profile of the Negro American*, Princeton, New Jersey: D. Van Nostrand, 1964, p. 16.

[19] The particular psychologist in question, Herbert Hendin, was quoted in *Newsweek*, November 17, 1966, pp. 119–120.

[20] Robert Bell, *The One-Parent Mother in the Negro Lower Class*, Unpublished paper presented to the Eastern Sociological Society, 1965.

a fatherless home are frequently relegated to the lowest living standards in our society. The problems facing husbandless women with children are compounded by the inequities in American society based on sex role ascriptions.

It is impossible to state that the black woman is just like the women of other races. Her history is different from that of the prototypical white woman and her present-day behavioral patterns have evolved out of her historical experiences. In general, she is more aggressive and independent than white women. There are studies that show that black females are more non-conforming than white females as early as age ten. The reason for her greater self-reliance is that it has been a necessary trait in order for her and her children to survive in a racist and hostile society. Moreover, the society has permitted her more self-assertion than the white female.

Among male chauvinists, aggressiveness per se may be considered an undesirable trait in women and should be restricted to the male species. But this is all part of the age-old myth about the inherent nature of woman as a passive creature. More often than not, it has served as a subterfuge for the exploitation of women for the psychological and material gain of the male species. Black women lose nothing by their greater tenacity. That tenacity has, historically, been a source of strength in the black community. While white women have entered the history books for making flags and engaging in social work, black women have participated in the total black liberation struggle.

While recognizing these differences, the question before us now is how much power do black women really have and how is it exercised? Power is commonly defined as the ability to dominate men, to compel their action even against their wishes.[21]

The black woman has often been characterized as a more powerful figure in the family because she participates more in making decisions about what kind of car to buy, where to go on a vacation, etc.[22] In certain cases, she is the only one to make major decisions. A closer inspection of her decision-making powers often reveals that she does not make decisions counter to her husband's wishes, but renders them because he fails to do so. The reason he defers to her in certain decisions is simply because she is better equipped to make them. Usually, she has more formal education than her mate and in matters relating to the white society, she knows her way around better. She is more familiar with the machinations of white bureaucracies since contacts with the white world have been more available to black women than to black men.

Making decisions that black men cannot, or will not, make is a poor measure of the power a black woman has in the family. The chances are good that no decisions are made which he actively opposes. The power of black women is much like American democracy—it is more apparent than

---

[21] Henry P. Fairchild, *Dictionary of Sociology and Related Sciences*, Totowa, N. J.: Littlefield, Adams and Co., 1965, p. 227.

[22] Robert O. Blood, Jr., and Donald Wolfe, *Husbands and Wives*, New York: The Free Press, 1960.

real. Power alignments are frequently based on the alternatives an individual has in a situation where there is a conflict of interests. It is here where the black male achieves the upper level of the power dimension.

Whenever a black man and black woman find themselves in objective and irremediable conflict, the best solution is to find another mate. The objective reality of black women is that black men are scarcer than hen's teeth. For a variety of reasons, there is an extremely low sex ratio in the black community, especially during the marriageable years—18 to 45 years.[23] This means that black women must compete for a relatively scarce commodity when they look forward to marriage. They are buyers in a seller's market. Black women, like all women, have their affectional and sexual needs. Many a black male's shortcomings must be tolerated for the sake of affection and companionship. In a sense, many black women have to take love on male terms.

The low sex ratio hardly allows black women to exercise any meaningful control over black men. In fact, as one black woman states:

As long as she is confined to an area in which she must compete fiercely for a mate, she remains the object of sexual exploitation and the victim of all the social evils which such exploitation involves.

In the Negro population, the excess of girls is greatest in the fifteen-to-forty-four age group which covers the college years and the age when most marriages occur . . . the explosive social implications of an excess of more than half a million Negro girls and women over fourteen years of age are obvious. . . . How much of the tensions and conflicts traditionally associated with the matriarchal framework of Negro society are in reality due to this imbalance and the pressures it generates.[24]

Another index of the matriarchy is simply the percentage of female-headed households in the black community. The Moynihan theory of the black matriarchy derives from his findings that 25 percent of all black families have a female head. This "proof" of a matriarchal family structure brings up many interesting questions, not excluding the important one: over whom do these women have control? Logically, the only power they have is to face a super-exploitation by the system of white racism that bi-parental black families do not encounter to the same degree.

The matriarchal myth is not always applied to only black families. A number of social scientists claim that suburban white families are matriarchal. They point out that the commuting father's disappearance during the day leaves the mother in charge of the home and children. As a result, the

---

[23]In New York City, for instance, there are only 75 black men for every 100 black women in about this same age range.

[24]Paul Murray, *The Negro Woman in the Quest for Equality*, paper presented at Leadership Conference, National Council of Negro Women (Washington D.C., November 1963), pp. 11-12, 12-18.

father's power is reduced in these areas, and he is relegated to enacting the "feminine" role of handyman.[25] This observation has prompted one person to suggest that exhorting black slum dwellers to emulate the presumably more stable white middle-class, restore father to his rightful place, and build a more durable family life will subsequently expose them to the threat of the suburban matriarchy.[26]

Any profound analysis of the black matriarchy proposition should reveal its fallacious underpinnings. Recognition of this fact raises the crucial question as to why white society continues to impose this myth on the consciousness of black people. This writer submits that it has been functional for the white ruling class, through its ideological apparatus, to create internal antagonisms in the black community between black men and black women to divide them and to ward off effective attacks on the external system of white racism. It is a mere manifestation of the divide-and-conquer strategy, used by most ruling classes through the annals of man, to continue the exploitation of an oppressed group.

In the colonial period of Algeria, the same situation existed wherein the colonists attempted to use the female population to continue their colonial rule. Fanon reports that the colonial administration devised a political doctrine for destroying the structure of Algerian society. By encouraging Algerian women to break the bonds of male domination in their society— setting male against female—the colonialists hoped to dilute the Algerian capacity for resistance. According to Fanon, it was:

the woman who was given the historic mission of shaking up the Algerian man. Converting the woman, winning her over to the foreign values, wrenching her free from her status, was at the same time achieving a real power over the man and attaining a practical, effective means of destroying Algerian culture.[27]

In contemporary America, a female liberation movement is beginning to gain impetus.[28] This movement is presently dominated by white women seeking to break out of the centuries-old bondage imposed upon them by the male chauvinists of the ruling class. Whether black women should participate in such a movement is questionable. Hatred of a social curse which is part and parcel of an exploitative society that discriminates not only against blacks but also women should not be confused with hatred of men. The adversary is not one sex or the other—it is the racist, capitalist system which needs, breeds and preys upon oppressions of all types.

Any movement that augments the sex-role antagonisms extant in the

[25] Ernest W. Burgess and Harvey J. Locke, *The Family*, New York: American Book Co., 1960, p. 112.

[26] Eric Josephson, "The Matriarchy: Myth and Reality," *The Family Coordinator*, 1969, pp. 18, 268–276.

[27] Frantz Fanon, *A Dying Colonialism*, tr. by Haakon Chevalier, New York: Grove Press, 1967, p. 39.

[28] See Evelyn Reed, *Problems of Women's Liberation*, New York: Merit Publishers, 1969, for one white radical's approach to the matriarchal origin of society question.

black community will only sow the seed of disunity and hinder the liberation struggle. Whether black women will participate in a female liberation movement is, of course, up to them. One, however, must be cognizant of the need to avoid a diffusion of energy devoted to the liberation struggle lest it dilute the over-all effectiveness of the movement. Black women cannot be free *qua* women until all blacks attain their liberation.

The role of the black woman in the black liberation struggle is an important one and cannot be forgotten. From her womb have come the revolutionary warriors of our time.[29] The revolutionary vanguard has a male leadership but the black woman has stepped beside her man engaged in struggle and given him her total faith and commitment. She has thrust herself into the life or death struggle to destroy the last vestige of racism and exploitation in the American social structure. In the process of continuing her life-long fight against racist oppression, the myth of her matriarchal nature will soon join the death agony of America's racist empire. Until that time arrives, the black woman should be revered and celebrated—not only for her historical deeds in the building of African civilization, in the struggle to maintain the black peoples of America as a viable entity—but for her contemporary role in enabling black people to forge ahead in their efforts to achieve a black nationhood.

[29]It is interesting to note that, despite unfounded rumors about the emasculation of the black male, the thrust of the black liberation struggle has been provided almost exclusively by a black male leadership. In selecting leaders of black organizations, black females inevitably defer to some competent black male, an act which shows how much they really prefer the dominating position they supposedly have in black society.

Gail A. Stokes: Black Woman to Black Man

Calling all Black men, calling all Black men, come in, Black man, come on in. . . .

I've heard your cry ringing from the Black Nationalist movements to the Muslim teachings of Elijah Muhammad. O.K., you've been put down and let down by the white man and his woman, and you are now pleading your case to the Black female nation. Well, show me what it is you have to offer.

In bygone times, you have cursed me and labeled me a wretched bitch because of my blasphemies against your name, your condition, your attitude. Yet these blasphemies were justified, because when I looked at you I saw a free slave thinking himself a free man, forgetting me and lusting after the white man, the white woman, the white status symbol.

My belly rose and swelled year after year from the implantations of your seed, while you cursed my pregnancies, forgetting that they were all mainly

Reprinted from *Liberator*, Vol. 8, No. 12 (December 1968), p. 17. By permission of the publisher. Copyright © 1968 by *Liberator*.

the product of your sexual pleasures. But you didn't mind letting the consequences rain heavily upon *my* nappy head.

Payday came on Fridays and you would stop off at the bar and throw the
babies' milk and food money across the counter like the big white spender.
Then to finish off what little cash was left, you'd go to the liquor store for
that cheap whiskey bottle from which you'd drink the rest of the night, or
sometimes you'd buy some smoke instead to illuminate your false feelings of
grandeur.

Me, I had to stomach it all. Along with the Black child inside of me that
neither I nor you wanted. I'd cry and plead and beg while taking you on your
all-too-familiar weekly tour of our dilapidated rooms with the dilapidated
furniture and our poor Black and starving children all over the junk that
they had peed on.

Where was the food and rent money going to come from? I couldn't get a
loan because I couldn't pay it back. The merchant in the corner grocery store
wouldn't let me charge any more because I couldn't pay the previous week's
bill. How could I help but wonder when you would ever use your head and
grow up, stand up, be a man? My insides were torn. I cursed you and began
my wailing, and all you could say was: "Shut up, goddamn it, shut up!"
"Lord, why don't you let me die?" I'd say to myself, but I was dead already. I
had been laid out in my coffin unknowingly the day I had married you, the
human being I thought I loved and who I thought loved me.

Now I've gone deaf, deliberately deaf to your calls, and all your illusions
of power. I will have no part of your power—Black, white, pink, or green.
Just give me my power, power to break away from . . . *you!*

You greet me with "My Black goddess," but you don't know how goddesses are treated. Can you really expect me to believe that you can treat me
that way? No sir, I will not accept your humble, feeble offerings. No, not
now. It's too late; I'm broken beyond repair. For if I extend my hand
towards yours, will you give me that feeling of secure femininity? Hell no,
for you, like the oppressor, have helped to make me a perpetual beast of
burden.

Of course, you will say, "How can I love you and want to be with you
when I come home and you're looking like a slob? Why, white women never
open the door for their husbands looking the way you Black bitches do."

I should guess not, you ignorant man. Why should they be in such a state
when they've got Black maids like me to do everything for them? There is no
screaming at the kids for her, no standing over a hot stove; everything is
done for her. And whether her man loves her or not, he provides . . . *provides*
. . . do you hear that, nigger? PROVIDES!

Yes, I know your pay isn't much and your opportunities are limited, but
when you squander away what little you do make and the same little that I
count on so desperately, how else can I react?

No money, no love, no pride—how can I be anything else but the evil bitch
that you call me. Can I smile when you come home bringing no six o'clock
happiness? Can I be beautiful when I am worthless? I look and I see no
survival for me, and this death of mine projects upon my young children.

The young babies know more about cussing and fussing than laughter, love and good times. The ugly mold has been set for us; and you, Black man, watch us turn to jelly. Into the mold will drain the life of our children, their children, and their children's children.

The oppressor has been determined to keep you running and so you in turn have been determined to keep me barefoot and pregnant. He keeps you under and you keep me under. For each blow that the Man rains on your head, you come home and rain triple blows upon my already weary and battered skull.

I cannot heed your calls now, because when I came to you with love and respected you in spite of your servitude, you passed me by unnoticed. Now you want to offer me dignity in all forms, but the Black love and dignity I want can not emerge in long gowns and covered heads. First you kept me looking like death standing in the corner looking for a place to die. Now you want to wrap me all up to show that you've at last really killed me and that you've no longer got a half-dead, whining bitch but a walking mummy.

7

Husbands and Wives

Lee Rainwater: Husband-Wife Relations

... Despite the high degree of premarital sexual activity and the rather high proportion of premarital pregnancies, most lower-class Negro men and women eventually do marry and stay together for a shorter or longer period of time. Marriage is an intimidating prospect and is approached ambivalently by both parties. For the girl it means giving up a familiar and comfortable home that, unlike some other lower-class subcultures, places few real restrictions on her behavior. (While marriage can appear to be an escape from interpersonal difficulties at home, these difficulties seldom seem to revolve around effective restrictions placed on her behavior by her parents.) The girl also has good reason to be suspicious of the likelihood that men will be able to perform stably in the role of husband and provider; she is reluctant to be tied down by a man who will not prove to be worth it.

From the man's point of view the fickleness of women makes marriage problematic. It is one thing to have a girl friend step out on you, but it is quite another to have a wife do so. Whereas premarital sexual relations and fatherhood carry almost no connotation of responsibility for the welfare of the partner, marriage is supposed to mean that a man behaves more respon-

From "The Crucible of Identity: The Negro Lower-Class Family," by Lee Rainwater, *Daedalus*, 95 (Winter 1965), pp. 251-255. Reprinted by permission from *Daedalus*, Journal of the American Academy of Arts and Sciences, Boston, Massachusetts. Lee Rainwater is Professor of Social Relations at Harvard University.

sibly, becoming a provider for his wife and children even though he may not be expected to give up all the gratifications of participation in the street system.

For all these reasons both boys and girls tend to have rather negative views of marriage as well as a low expectation that marriage will prove a stable and gratifying existence. When marriage does take place it tends to represent a tentative commitment on the part of both parties with a strong tendency to seek greater commitment on the part of the partner than on one's own part. Marriage is regarded as a fragile arrangement held together primarily by affectional ties rather than instrumental concerns.

In general, as in white low-class groups, the decision to marry seems to be taken rather impulsively. Since everyone knows that sooner or later he will get married, in spite of the fact that he may not be sanguine about the prospect, Negro lower-class men and women are alert for clues that the time has arrived. The time may arrive because of a pregnancy in a steady relationship that seems gratifying to both partners, or as a way of getting out of what seems to be an awkward situation, or as a self-indulgence during periods when a boy and a girl are feeling very sorry for themselves. Thus, one girl tells us that when she marries, her husband will cook all of her meals for her and she will not have any housework; another girl says that when she marries, it will be to a man who has plenty of money and will have to take her out often and really show her a good time.

Boys see in marriage the possibility of regular sexual intercourse without having to fight for it, or a girl safe from venereal disease, or a relationship to a nurturant figure who will fulfill the functions of a mother. For boys, marriage can also be a way of asserting their independence from the peer group if its demands become burdensome. In this case the young man seeks to have the best of both worlds.

Characteristic of both the Negro and white lower class is a high degree of conjugal role segregation. That is, husbands and wives tend to think of themselves as having very separate kinds of functioning in the instrumental organization of family life, and also as pursuing recreational and outside interests separately. The husband is expected to be a provider; he resists assuming functions around the home so long as he feels he is doing his proper job of bringing home a pay check. He feels he has the right to indulge himself in little ways if he is successful at this task. The wife is expected to care for the home and children and make her husband feel welcome and comfortable. Much that is distinctive to Negro family life stems from the fact that husbands often are not stable providers. Even when a particular man is, his wife's conception of men in general is such that she is pessimistic about the likelihood that he will continue to do well in this area. A great many Negro wives work to supplement the family income. When this is so the separate incomes earned by husband and wife tend to be treated not as "family" income but as the individual property of the two persons involved. If their wives work, husbands are likely to feel that they are entitled to retain a larger share of the income they provide; the wives, in turn, feel that the husbands have no right to benefit from the purchases they make out of their own money. There is, then, "my money" and "your money." In this situation the husband may come to feel that the wife should support the children out of her income and that he can retain all of his income for himself.

While white lower-class wives often are very much intimidated by their husbands, Negro lower-class wives come to feel that they have a right to give as good as they get. If the husband indulges himself, they have the right to indulge themselves. If the husband steps out on his wife, she has the right to step out on him. The commitment of husbands and wives to each other seems often a highly instrumental one after the "honeymoon" period. Many wives feel they owe the husband nothing once he fails to perform his provider role. If the husband is unemployed the wife increasingly refuses to perform her usual duties for him. For example one woman, after mentioning that her husband had cooked four eggs for himself, commented, "I cook for him when he's working but right now he's unemployed; he can cook for himself." It is important, however, to understand that the man's status in the home depends not so much on whether he is working as on whether he brings money into the home. Thus, in several of the families we have studied in which the husband receives disability payments his status is as well-recognized as in families in which the husband is working.

Because of the high degree of conjugal role segregation, both white and Negro lower-class families tend to be matrifocal in comparison to middle-class families. They are matrifocal in the sense that the wife makes most of the decisions that keep the family going and has the greatest sense of responsibility to the family. In white as well as in Negro lower-class families women tend to look to their female relatives for support and counsel, and to treat their husbands as essentially uninterested in the day-to-day problems of family living. In the Negro lower-class family these tendencies are all considerably exaggerated so that the matrifocality is much clearer than in white lower-class families.

The fact that both sexes in the Negro slum culture have equal right to the various satisfactions of life (earning an income, sex, drinking, and peer-group activity which conflicts with family responsibilities) means that there is less pretense to patriarchal authority in the Negro than in the white lower class. Since men find the overt debasement of their status very threatening, the Negro family is much more vulnerable to disruption when men are temporarily unable to perform their provider roles. Also, when men are unemployed the temptations for them to engage in street adventures which repercuss on the marital relationship are much greater. This fact is well-recognized by Negro lower-class wives; they often seem as concerned about what their unemployed husbands will do instead of working as they are about the fact that the husband is no longer bringing money into the home.

It is tempting to cope with the likelihood of disloyalty by denying the usual norms of fidelity, by maintaining instead that extra-marital affairs are acceptable as long as they do not interfere with family functioning. Quite a few informants tell us this, but we have yet to observe a situation in which a couple maintains a stable relationship under these circumstances without a great deal of conflict. . . .

With couples who have managed to stay married for a good many years, these peccadillos are tolerable although they generate a great deal of conflict in the marital relationship. At earlier ages the partners are likely to be both prouder and less inured to the hopelessness of maintaining stable relationships; outside involvements are therefore much more likely to be disruptive of the marriage.

The precipitating causes of marital disruption seem to fall mainly into economic or sexual categories. As noted, the husband has little credit with his wife to tide him over periods of unemployment. Wives seem very willing to withdraw commitment from husbands who are not bringing money into the house. They take the point of view that he has no right to take up space around the house, to use its facilities, or to demand loyalty from her. Even where the wife is not inclined to press these claims, the husband tends to be touchy because he knows that such definitions are usual in his group, and he may, therefore, prove difficult for even a well-meaning wife to deal with. As noted above, if husbands do not work they tend to play around. Since they continue to maintain some contact with their peer groups, whenever they have time on their hands they move back into the world of the street system and are likely to get involved in activities which pose a threat to their family relationships.

Drink is a great enemy of the lower-class housewife, both white and Negro. Lower-class wives fear their husband's drinking because it costs money, because the husband may become violent and take out his frustrations on his wife, and because drinking may lead to sexual involvements with other women. . . .

Finally, it should be noted that migration plays a part in marital disruption. Sometimes marriages do not break up in the dramatic way . . . but rather simply become increasingly unsatisfactory to one or both partners. In such a situation the temptation to move to another city, from South to North, or North to West, is great. Several wives told us that their first marriages were broken when they moved with their children to the North and their husbands stayed behind. . . .

The gains and losses in marriage and in the post-marital state often seem quite comparable. Once they have had the experience of marriage, many women in the Negro slum culture see little to recommend it in the future, important as the first marriage may have been in establishing their maturity and respectability.

Robert Staples: Educating the Black Male at Various Class Levels for Marital Roles

The purpose of this paper is to explore the necessity and feasibility of preparing the Black male, at various class levels, to take on the marital roles of husband and father. The specifics of a premarital educational program will not be dealt with in this paper. It is assumed that a premarital preparation program will focus on teaching the requisites that make for a happy and successful marriage. Instead, we will concentrate on some new dimensions of such an educational undertaking. Class distinctions should be emphasized, as they affect the nature of any premarital educational program devised to deal with this problem. Use of the concept of social class, when distinguished from cultural factors, dictates two levels of analysis by the family sociologist—separating the social phenomena associated with the group's position in the class hierarchy from the factors relevant to conditions germane to racial or cultural affiliation.

Not only is premarital preparation essential for Afro-American youth but for youth in general. There is a definite lack of continuity in American society between adolescence and adulthood, as many American males go from the family of orientation to the family of procreation without any supportive bridges from the society. However, while this problem may be extant for all youth, factors endemic to the nature of the Afro-American's life in American society lend a particular degree of urgency to preparing him to meet the requirements of his future marital roles.

In assessing the need for premarital preparation of Black males, one only has to refer to the various research studies on the Afro-American family in order to identify the problems besieging this subcultural group. It should be noted, however, that the Black male is neglected from a research point of view simply because he is more diffiuclt to reach than women, youth, and children.

Due to the realization of the importance of the race problem in this country, the family life of Afro-Americans has been studied more intensively than that of any other racial or nationality group in our society. But it is still a fact that the Black family remains more a talked about than a studied phenomenon, and more a researched than an assisted group. Moreover, many of these research studies are replete with oversimplifications of popular sterotypes which stabilize in the minds of family life educators a host of useless and invalidated generalizations.

The problems of the Black family, in a racial or cultural sense, have to be analyzed more from a historical perspective than a contemporary one. Most authorities on the subject are in agreement that the African ancestors of America's bondsmen had a stable and secure family unit. The majority of slaves came from West African societies which had patriarchal and patrilin-

Reprinted from The Family Coordinator, 30 (April 1970), pp. 164-167, by permission of the National Council on Family Relations.

eal forms of social organization. Descent was traced through male sex-links, and authority over the family was invested in the hands of male members of the society (Herskovits, 1928, pp. 137–138, 349–351, 280).

It was in the transplantation from Africa to the shores of the New World that the Black family underwent a radical reorganization of its structure, as a consequence of the vicissitudes of slavery. During the period of their enslavement, Black fieldhands were prevented from developing stable families by the policies of their white slavemasters. Families were torn asunder at the will of their owners; the mother-child unit was the bond around which the family developed as men were traded or sold without their families; and there was little opportunity for the development of masculine responsibility (Frazier, 1939, pp. 3–69).

Under slavery, the father's function was biological rather than sociological or economical. The mother reared and cared for the children, and they were considered hers. Not having to support his wife and children, some fathers failed to develop a feeling of responsibility for them (Davie, 1949). However, many slave fathers, and most freedmen, when allowed the opportunity, performed ably in the role of parent and nurtured their children into adulthood (Frazier, 1939, p. 20).

These historical factors are often cited as the causal antecedents of the matricentric family organization found in the Black communities throughout the United States. However, it seems that the one hundred years since slavery offer sufficient cause for understanding the basis of a female-centered family among Black people without the necessity of referring to the slavery period. In both a historical and a contemporary sense, Black males have suffered from irregularity of employment more than any other segment of the American proletariat. They are the last to be hired and the first to be fired from the menial jobs they commonly hold. Being in a weak economic position, they have seldom succeeded in becoming steady providers for their families so that they could form a stable family unit (Drake and Cayton, 1945, p. 585).

One of the principal effects of emancipation and redistribution of the Black population has been the differentiation of sex and family relations according to socio-economic status, especially in the towns and cities. The deviations in the character of the Afro-American family have been greatest in the lower class, due chiefly to its social isolation and economic position.

In general, the research evidence indicates a positive correlation between marital satisfaction and satisfaction with income. The same appears to be true of Afro-American marriages. The study by Blood and Wolfe revealed that among Afro-Americans the higher the husband's income the more satisfied his wife was with him (Blood and Wolfe, 1960, p. 34). Another survey of Black women reported that the higher the educational level, the greater the marital satisfaction (Bell, 1965). Gillete found that Black middle-class husbands participate more in the child care area than do white middle-class husbands (Gillete, 1960).

Present-day research investigations indicate that marital tensions are exacerbated among lower-class husbands and wives. In the first place, the conjugal relationship is seen from a negative point of view. Bell's study disclosed that not only was motherhood more highly valued than wifehood but some lower-class Black women actually reject the adult-female roles of both spouse and mother (Bell, 1965). In another investigation by Broderick, less than 75 percent of his Black male sample said they ever wanted to get married (Broderick, 1965).

Liebow, in his study of lower-class Black males, found a pervasive disenchantment with marriage among this group. Marriage was seen as a series of public and private fights between spouses; as creating problems of how to feed, clothe and house a wife and child; and as inducing anxiety about being unable to ward off attacks on the health and safety of their children (Liebow, 1967, pp. 109–110). Similarly, Blood and Wolfe discovered that 63 percent of their lower-class Black female sample would not marry if they had to do it over. They were also dissatisfied with their husbands as lovers and providers, and, in general, communication was poor between Afro-American spouses (Blood and Wolfe, 1960).

The writer's own research has confirmed these sex-role antagonisms in Afro-American marriages (Staples, 1967). Black women tend to see the male as irresponsible and exploitative. They definitely feel the Black male should take more of an active and responsible role in the areas of family activity. Conversely, many Black males tend to confuse sexual and social roles, and see explicitly female figures as masculine and authoritative. Therefore, their attitudes toward women are mistrust, hostility, and a resentful dependency (Kardiner and Ovesey, 1951).

While these same marital problems prevail in the white community, they appear in a more recurrent and aggravated form among Blacks because of the peculiar conditions under which Afro-Americans are forced to live. For this reason, it is more imperative to find ways of stabilizing and making more harmonious the Afro-American family structure.

Family life educators must address themselves to the development of nativist responses in the Black community. This recent movement, alternatively known as Black consciousness or nationalism, is presently relating itself to the legitimation of its subcultural patterns of behavior. It is concentrated in the urban centers of our society and is disproportionately popular among Black youth, the group around which any premarital education program would center.

The evolution of a sense of community among Afro-American youth is a prime factor to be considered by family life educators. Although the educational program may be carried out by primary or secondary groups, formal or informal associations, the medium of transmission must be Black-oriented, and, if possible, the educators should be male members of the Black community.

Afro-American males might best be prepared for their future marital roles by the inculation of pride in their African heritage, by a reminder of their forefathers' patrilineal and patriarchal form of family organization. Hopefully, this will generate those changes in the Black family which will enable the Black husband and father to play the role required of him.

Although the writer alluded to the weak economic position of the Black male as a key factor in sustaining Black family disorganization, this article does not relate to solutions dealing with this problem due to the political and economic realities of contemporary American society. Black nationalism is, in part, a realistic response to this nation's failure to bring about those necessary economic and social changes that would strengthen the role of the Black male vis-à-vis the family. Thus, there is little need to recapitulate on the necessity for this type of change, since previous exhortations have encountered a national unresponsiveness.

Based on this knowledge of past failures to deal with the basic etiological factors, the writer has concluded that the most pragmatic approach to preparing Black males for their marital roles would be a reincarnation or revitalization of their cultural heritage as it pertains to the family. This appears more practical because it relies more on the internal motivation of the individuals involved than on changes in the larger society. Concomitant with the increment in nativist sentiments among Black youth, it appears to be a more easily achieved objective.

The use of the term "patriarchy" may be somewhat misleading to some readers of the article. This does not imply a regression of the equalitarian family model now emerging in certain segments of the Black community, most notably among the middle-class strata, but rather means greater male participation in family activities, including economic support and socialization processes. If necessary, however, male dominance as a consequence of the psychological identification of Black males with African family systems is not excluded as a viable substitute for the female-dominated households that now prevail in certain segments of the Black community. There are few objections to this idea in the Black community—especially from Black females.

There are no stringent standards for the Black educators in a pre-marital education program. The writer's criterion for these educators is that they be able to provide successful father/husband models for Black youth and transmit the role expectations consonant with meeting their marital role requirements. Despite societal stereotypes of the monolithic disorganized Black family, the author feels that there is an adequate supply of Black husbands/fathers to meet the needs of a premarital education program for Black youth.

References

Blood, Robert O.,Jr., and Donald M. Wolfe. *Husbands and Wives: The Dynamics of Married Living.* New York: Free Press, 1960.

Broderick, Carlfred. "Socio-sexual Development among Urban Negroes and Whites." *Journal of Marriage and the Family,* 27 (May 1965), 200:203.

Davie, Maurice, *Negroes in American Society.* New York: McGraw-Hill, 1949.

Drake, St. Clair, and Horace Cayton, *Black Metropolis.* Chicago: University of Chicago Press, 1945.

Frazier, E. Franklin, *The Negro Family in the United States.* Chicago: University of Chicago Press, 1939.

Gillete, Thomas Lee, *Maternal Employment and Family Structure as Influenced by Social Class and Role.* Unpublished doctoral dissertation, University of Texas, 1960.

Herskovits, Melville, *The American Negro.* New York: Harper & Row, 1928.

Kardiner, Abram, and Lionel Ovesey, *The Mark of Oppression.* New York: Norton, 1951.

Liebow, Elliot, *Tally's Corner.* Boston: Little, Brown, 1967.

Staples, Robert, *The Lower-Income Negro Family in Saint Paul.* St. Paul: St. Paul Urban League, 1967.

Robert O. Blood, Jr., and Donald M. Wolfe: Negro-White Differences in Blue-Collar Marriages in a Northern Metropolis

That American Negro families differ generally from white families is well known (see U.S. Department of Labor, 1965). Higher rates of illegitimacy, desertion, and a matriarchal family pattern are familiar characteristics of Negro family life in general (e.g., Kephart and Monahan, 1952).

Relatively rare, however, are statistical analyses of Negro and white marriages which introduce status controls. How much of the difference results from the generally lower status of Negroes in American society?

A complete test of this question would require controlling on education, income, and occupation simultaneously.[1] This paper controls on occupation alone. An earlier version showed persistent differences between Negro and white marriages among blue-collar workers generally. In most of the following tables, an even finer occupational control is used so that comparisons can be made within the upper or lower half of the working class.

Nature of the Data

The 1955 Detroit Area Study, under the direction of the senior author, interviewed a representative sample of *731* wives in intact families living in the Detroit Metropolitan Area (Blood and Wolfe, 1960: Appendix A).

Reprinted from *Social Forces*, 48 (September 1969), pp. 59-63, with permission of the University of North Carolina Press. Robert O. Blood, Jr., is Professor of Sociology at Pindle Hill College. Donald M. Wolfe is a member of the faculty of Western Reserve University.

[1]Jessie Bernard (1966) analyzed the effect of occupation, income, and education on marital stability, using data from the 1960 Census. She found that despite these multiple controls, Negro marriages remain appreciably less stable than white marriages, especially at low-status levels.

Table 1. Husband's Mean Power by Occupation and Race

	Blue Collar		White Collar	
	Low	High	Low	High
White	5.07*	4.98*	5.34	5.52
	(162)	(162)	(79)	(151)
Negro	4.31*	4.60*	–	5.00
	(78)	(20)		(5)

Numbers in parentheses represent the number of families on which means are computed.
*The differences between white and Negro means for the blue-collar groups is statistically significant at the .01 level.

Sixteen percent of the sample, or *115* cases, involve Negro couples. *Ninety-six* percent of the husbands hold blue-collar jobs. By contrast, only *57* percent of the white husbands hold blue-collar jobs.

Within the working class, Negroes are skewed toward the poorest jobs. *Eighty-one* percent of the Negro blue-collar men but only *50* percent of their white counterparts hold low blue-collar jobs (operatives, unskilled and service). Our more refined occupational control separates low blue-collar workers from high blue-collar skilled workers and foremen.

Findings

How, then, do blue-collar Negroes compare with whites holding similar jobs?

Power Structure

Negro wives' matriarchal role should be clearly expressed in marital decision-making.

Table 1 shows that within each occupational category Negro husbands have less power than their white counterparts.[2] The difference is greatest at the low blue-collar level where Negroes are concentrated, but also appears at both the high blue-collar and high white-collar levels.

Detailed analysis of six of our eight decisions (omitting choice of the

Table 2. Balance of Power in Negro and White Blue-Collar Families

	Negro	White
Husband-dominant	17%	21%
Equal	33*	49*
Wife-dominant	39*	21*
Not ascertained	11	9
Total	100%	100%
Number of families	110	354

*Differences between percentages of Negroes and whites in these power categories are statistically significant at the .01 level.

[2] For the measure of power, see Blood and Wolfe (1960: 19-20).

husband's job and family doctor) shows that the difference in power structure is pervasive. Negro wives make all six decisions more often than white wives (Detroit Area Study, 1957).[3] One might expect wife-dominance to occur at the expense of husband-dominance. However, at low-income levels (under $4,000), Negro husbands also make more unilateral decisions about several topics (car, house, vacation, wife's work). Consequently, Negro families do not have significantly fewer dominant husbands but substantially fewer joint decision-makers.

Table 2 shows how wife-dominant Negro families appear at the expense of equalitarianism. The differences are so great that the modal pattern shifts from equalitarianism for white families to wife-dominance for Negro families.

Can the Negro wife's dominance be attributed to greater personal competence? In the population at large, the wife's power rises with participation in the labor force (Blood and Wolfe, 1960:40–41). This contributes to the Negro-white difference. However, the margin of employed Negro wives over white wives in these intact families is surprisingly small (25 percent versus 21 percent, a difference which is not statistically significant).

The Division of Labor

Our data show that Negro husbands do slightly *less* housework than white husbands—not enough less to be significantly different but enough to explode any notion that Negro husbands are domestic servants to their matriarchal wives.

Although for all practical purposes, there is no difference between races in

Table 3. Adherence to Traditional Sex Roles in the Division of Labor in Negro and White Blue-Collar Families

Adherence to Traditional Sex Roles	Negro	White
Masculine		
High	66%	68%
Moderate	15	16
Low	5	11
Not ascertained	15	5
Total	101%	100%
Feminine		
High	52%	43%
Moderate	26	30
Low	16	24
Not ascertained	5	3
Total	99%	100%
Number of families	110	354

*Differences between races in mean adherence to masculine roles are significant at the .05 level and in feminine roles at the .06 level of probability.

[3] Most of these "consumer" decisions correspond to the area of "purchases and living standards" where Middleton and Putney (1960) found a general tendnecy toward wife-dominance in Negro marriages by using the Strodtbeck technique. Presumably the Negro worker's occupational difficulties undermine his authority more extensively in economic decisions than in other areas.

the *proportion* of housework done by husband and wife, Table 3 shows that Negro couples stick more closely to the traditional sex-role assignments.[4] The traditional division of labor has technical advantages under ordinary conditions. When the wife stays home all day, she gains efficiency by specializing in the food–clothing–housecleaning complex, whereas male strength and mechanical aptitude lend themselves to exterior and repairing tasks. However, when wives go to work, the traditional division of labor tends to change. Working wives are less able to do their housework and need help from their husbands. Hence, in working-wife families, husbands tend to move into the wife's domain, lowering the wife's adherence to the feminine role in the domestic division of labor (Blood, 1963).

We have already seen that a slightly higher percentage of Negro wives are employed outside the home. On this basis we would expect Negro wives to be less able to fulfill the feminine housekeeping role. Yet Table 3 shows the opposite—Negro wives do more traditional tasks despite pressures to the contrary. While these differences are not large, they reflect a tendency for blue-collar Negro husbands to be less responsive to the wife's needs than white husbands. The differences become even more striking when viewed against the discovery that blue-collar Negroes work shorter hours than whites and therefore are more available to help out (*38* percent of the whites vs. only *25* percent of the Negroes work over 40 hours a week). Thus, an appreciable number of Negro wives must cope with the extra demands of home plus job without the expected compensatory assistance from their husbands.

Negro wives do not feel altogether hopeless about their husbands' vocational prospects, at least at the beginning of their married lives. Almost as many young Negro wives as white wives report that their husbands have mobility aspirations; but in later years Negro couples become disillusioned rapidly.

Table 4. Wife's Role in Blue-Collar Men's Occupational Mobility by Race

Wife's Mobility Role	Low Blue-Collar		High Blue-Collar	
	Negro	White	Negro	White
Active				
Housework	26%	19%	19%	17%
Thrift	13*	2*	5	2
Employment	9*	2*	14†	2†
Collaboration	3	2	5	2
Supportive	20*	37*	29	35
None	23	33	29	36
Not ascertained	4	5	—	5
Total	98%	100%	101%	99%
Number of families	89	178	21	176

*Differences significant at the .01 level.

†Difference significant at the .01 level.

[4]For the measure of the division of labor in household tasks, see Blood and Wolfe (1960: 49-52).

Table 5. Informative Companionship in Blue-Collar Marriages by Race

Frequency Husband Tells Wife about Events at Work	Low Blue-Collar		High Blue-Collar	
	Negro	White	Negro	White
Every day (300)	28%	41%	14%	36%
Almost every day (200)	15	20	29	19
Once or twice a week (50)	24	14	19	15
Once a month or more (10)	18	13	24	7
Less often (2)	16	7	10	19
Not ascertained	—	4	5	3
Total	101%	99%	101%	99%
Mean annual frequency	127*	216*	118†	161*
Number of families	89	178	21	176

Numbers in parentheses show weights used in computing mean annual frequencies.

*The difference between means is significant at the .01 level.

†This difference is significant at the .05 level.

A wife's role in furthering her husband's ambitions must be relatively indirect if he is a manual worker. Yet answers to the question, "What do you do to help your husband along in his work?" provide insights into the way the wife sees herself and her husband

Although not all the differences in Table 4 are statistically significant, Negro wives feel consistently more responsible than white wives. Fewer Negro women feel completely unable to help in any way. Fewer support the husband's own mobility efforts. Rather, they stress their own tangible contributions to family solvency and success. Keeping house for the husband may seem a rather indirect way of helping him get ahead but more Negro wives take credit for it. With money scarcer in Negro families, thrift assumes more functional importance. Money may be both saved and earned by the wife. Hence the same poverty which produces an emphasis on thrift also gives the wife's employment extra value. Note that the racial differential in mentioning the wife's employment is larger than the marginal difference in the proportion of wives actually employed outside the home.

Companionship

Making decisions and doing housework are compulsory aspects of married living. Other aspects of marriage are more optional. They include the uses to which leisure may be put if couples have the time and the inclination. Broadly speaking, these uses may be labeled companionship.

According to Table 5, Negro wives typically experience "informative companionship" with their husbands only once or twice a week whereas the median white wife does almost every day. This failure to engage in "chit-chat" is symbolic of the broader tendency for the Negro man to interact less with his wife.

Table 6. Therapeutic Utilization of Blue-Collar Husbands by Race

Frequency Wife Tells Husband Her Troubles after a Bad Day	Low Blue-Collar		High Blue-Collar	
	Negro	White	Negro	White
Always (4X)*	12%	25%	14%	22%
Usually (3X)	22	22	24	20,
About half the time (2X)	22	22	33	26
Seldom (1X)	34	15	19	20
Never (0)	9	13	10	10
Not ascertained	—	2	—	3
Total	99%	99%	100%	101%
Mean	1.96†	2.33†	2.14	2.24
Number of families	89	178	21	176

*Weights used in computing mean frequencies.
†Difference between means is significant at the .05 level.

Is this failure in communication one-sided? Is the husband passive but the wife talkative? Not the Negro wife. Table 6 shows that the modal low blue-collar Negro wife *seldom* tells her husband her troubles after she has had a bad day whereas her white counterpart *always* does.

From the Negro husband's point of view, this may be a good thing. Listening to a tale of woe may not be the most enjoyable way to spend one's leisure. But for the wife, not telling her troubles means not getting needed help. So here again the Negro wife is left to her own resources.

The correlation between Tables 5 and 6 suggests that companionship (or loneliness) tends to be reciprocal. In these white families, communication often goes both ways. In more of the Negro marriages, both partners fail to communicate. The Negro husband is not so much henpecked as segregated.

Marital Satisfaction

In every aspect of marriage which we have examined, Negro wives have been shortchanged. Hence, it is not surprising to find them relatively dissatisfied with their marriages. Indeed Table 7 shows three to four times as many white as Negro wives in the most enthusiastic category.

Table 7 shows that the median white wife is highly satisfied with her marriage whereas the typical Negro wife is only moderately satisfied. Not only are Negro wives objectively deprived but they resent it.

Conclusions

This comparison of Negro and white blue-collar marriages shows significant differences in many variables in the direction of greater deprivation for Negro wives. In decision-making they get less cooperation from their hus-

[5] For the measure of marital satisfaction, see Blood (1967: 251, 256).

Table 7. Wife's Marital Satisfaction in Blue-Collar Marriages by Race

Wife's Marital Satisfaction	Low Blue-Collar		High Blue-Collar	
	Negro	White	Negro	White
Very high	7%	20%*	5%†	21%‡
High	27	28	29	31
Moderate	36	30	38	30
Low	21†	10†	14	11
Not ascertained	9	12	14	7
Total	100%	100%	100%	100%
Number of families	89	178	21	176

*Difference significant at .01 level.
†Difference significant at .05 level.
‡Difference significant at .10 level.

bands so they must make more family decisions unaided. In the division of labor at home, their husbands less often come to their aid in difficult circumstances. In the leisure-time aspects of marriage, less interaction takes place between Negro husbands and wives. Negro men less often share their day's experiences with their wives and wives less often share their troubles in return. These objective deficiencies in marital interaction patterns are reflected in greater dissatisfaction of Negro wives with their mates.

References

Bernard, Jessie. "Marital Stability and Patterns of Status Variables." *Journal of Marriage and the Family*, 28 (November 1966), 421–439.

Blood, Robert O., Jr., "The Husband-Wife Relationship." In F. Ivan Nye and Lois W. Hoffman (eds.), *The Employed Mother in America*. Chicago: Rand McNally, 1963.

———. *Love Match and Arranged Marriage*. New York: Free Press, 1967.

Blood, Robert O., Jr., and Donald M. Wolfe. *Husbands and Wives: The Dynamics of Married Living*. New York: Free Press, 1960.

Detroit Area Study. "Consumer Decisions in Negro and White Detroit Area Families." Bulletin #1261. Ann Arbor: University of Michigan, 1957.

Kephart, William M., and Thomas P. Monahan. "Desertion and Divorce in Philadelphia." *American Sociological Review*, 17 (October 1952), 719–727.

Middleton, Russell, and Snell Putney. "Dominance in the Family: Race and Class Differences." *American Journal of Sociology*, 65 (May 1960), 605–609.

U.S. Department of Labor. *The Negro Family: The Case for National Action*. Washington, D.C.: Government Printing Office, 1965.

E. Franklin Frazier: The Black Bourgeoisie

Among the women of the black bourgeoisie there is an intense fear of the competition of white women for Negro men. They often attempt to rationalize their fear by saying that the Negro man always occupies an inferior position in relation to the white woman or that he marries much below his "social" status. They come nearer to the source of their fear when they confess that there are not many eligible Negro men and that these few should marry Negro women. That such rationalizations conceal deep-seated feelings of insecurity is revealed by the fact that generally they have no objection to the marriage of white men to Negro women, especially if the white man is reputed to be wealthy. In fact, they take pride in the fact and attribute these marriages to the "peculiar" charms of Negro women. In fact, the middle-class Negro woman's fear of the competition of white women is based often upon the fact that she senses her own inadequacies and short-comings. Her position in Negro "society" and in the larger Negro community is often due to some adventitious factor, such as a light complexion or a meager education, which has pushed her to the top of the social pyramid. The middle-class white woman not only has a white skin and straight hair, but she is generally more sophisticated and interesting because she has read more widely and has a larger view of the world. The middle-class Negro woman may make fun of the "plainness" of her white competitor and the latter's lack of "wealth" and interest in "society"; nevertheless she still feels insecure when white women appear as even potential competitors.

Both men and women among the black bourgeoisie have a feeling of insecurity because of their constant fear of the loss of status. Since they have no status in the larger American society, the intense struggle for status among middle-class Negroes is, as we have seen, an attempt to compensate for the contempt and low esteem of the whites. Great value is, therefore, placed upon all kinds of status symbols. Academic degrees, both real and honorary, are sought in order to secure status. Usually the symbols are of a material nature implying wealth and conspicuous consumption. Sometimes Negro doctors do not attend what are supposedly scientific meetings because they do not have a Cadillac or some other expensive automobile. School teachers wear mink coats and maintain homes beyond their income for fear that they may lose status. The extravagance in "social" life generally is due to an effort not to lose status. But in attempting to overcome their fear of loss of status they are often beset by new feelings of insecurity. In spite of their pretended wealth, they are aware that their incomes are insignificant and that they must struggle to maintain their mortgaged homes and the show of "wealth" in lavish "social" affairs. Moreover, they are beset by a feeling of insecurity because of their struggles to maintain a show of wealth through illegal means. From time to time "wealthy" Negro doctors are arrested for selling narcotics and performing abortions. The life of many a "wealthy" Negro doctor is shortened by the struggle to provide diamonds, minks, and an expensive home for his wife.

There is much frustration among the black bourgeoisie despite their privileged position within the segregated Negro world. Their "wealth" and "social" position cannot erase the fact that they are generally segregated and rejected by the white world. Their incomes and occupations may enable them to escape the cruder manifestations of racial prejudice, but they cannot insulate themselves against the more subtle forms of racial discrimination. These discriminations cause frustrations in Negro men because they are not allowed to play the "masculine role" as defined by American culture. They can not assert themselves or exercise power as white men do. When they protest against racial discrimination there is always the threat that they will be punished by the white world. In spite of the movement toward the wider integration of the Negro into the general stream of American life, middle-class Negroes are still threatened with the loss of positions and earning power if they insist upon their rights. After the Supreme Court of the United States ruled that segregation in public education was illegal, Negro teachers in some parts of the South were dismissed because they would not sign statements supporting racial segregation in education.

As one of the results of not being able to play the "masculine role," middle-class Negro males have tended to cultivate their "personalities" which enable them to exercise considerable influence among whites and achieve distinction in the Negro world. Among Negroes they have been noted for their glamour. In this respect they resemble women who use their "personalities" to compensate for their inferior status in relation to men.

In the South the middle-class Negro male is not only prevented from playing a masculine role, but generally he must let Negro women assume leadership in any show of militancy. This reacts upon his status in the home where the tradition of female dominance, which is widely established among Negroes, has tended to assign a subordinate role to the male. In fact, in middle-class families, especially if the husband has risen in social status through his own efforts and married a member of an "old" family or a "society" woman, the husband is likely to play a pitiful role. The greatest compliment that can be paid such a husband is that he "worships his wife," which means that he is her slave and supports all her extravagances and vanities. But, of course, many husbands in such positions escape from their frustrations by having extra-marital sex relations. Yet the conservative and conventional middle-class husband presents a pathetic picture. He often sits at home alone, impotent physically and socially, and complains that his wife has gone crazy about poker and "society" and constantly demands money for gambling and expenditures which he can not afford. Sometimes he enjoys the sympathy of a son or daughter who has not become a "socialite." Such children often say that they had a happy family life until "mamma took to poker."

Preoccupation with poker on the part of the middle-class woman is often an attempt to escape from a frustrated life. Her frustration may be bound up with her unsatisfactory sexual life. She may be married to a "glamorous" male who neglects her for other women. For among the black bourgeoisie, the glamour of the male is often associated with his sexual activities. The frustration of many Negro women has a sexual origin. Even those who have sought an escape from frustration in sexual promiscuity may, because of satiety or deep psychological reasons, become obsessed with poker in order to escape from their frustrations. One "society" woman, in justification of her obsession with poker, remarked that it had taken the place of her former preoccupation with sex. Another said that to win at poker was similar to a sexual orgasm.

The frustration of the majority of the women among the black bourgeoisie is probably due to the idle or ineffectual lives which they lead. Those who do not work devote their time to the frivolities of Negro "society." When they devote their time to "charity" or worthwhile causes, it is generally a form of play or striving for "social" recognition. They are constantly forming clubs which ostensibly have a serious purpose, but in reality are formed in order to consolidate their position in "society" or to provide additional occasions for playing poker. The idle, overfed women among the black bourgeoisie are generally, to use their language, "dripping with diamonds." They are forever dieting and reducing only to put on more weight (which is usually the result of the food that they consume at their club meetings). Even the women among the black bourgeoisie who work exhibit the same frustrations. Generally, they have no real interest in their work and only engage in it in order to be able to provide the conspicuous consumption demanded by "society." As we have indicated, the women as well as the men among the black bourgeoisie read very little and have no interest in music, art or the theater. They are constantly restless and do not know how to relax. They are generally dull people and only become animated when "social" matters are discussed, especially poker games. They are afraid to be alone and constantly seek to be surrounded by their friends, who enable them to escape from their boredom.

The frustrated lives of the black bourgeoisie are reflected in the attitudes of parents towards their children. Middle-class Negro families as a whole have few children, while among the families that constitute Negro "society," there are many childless couples. One finds today that "where the children are few, they are usually spoiled" in middle-class Negro families. There is often not only a deep devotion to their one or two children, but a subservience to them. It is not uncommon for the only son to be called and treated as the "boss" in the family. Parents cater to the transient wishes of their children and often rationalize their behavior towards them on the grounds that children should not be "inhibited." They spend large sums of money on their children for toys and especially for clothes. They provide their children with automobiles when they go to college. All of this is done in order that the children may maintain the status of the parents and be eligible to enter the "social" set in Negro colleges. When they send their children to northern "white" colleges they often spend more time in preparing them for what they imagine will be their "social" life than in preparing them for the academic requirements of these institutions.

In their fierce devotion to their children, which generally results in spoiling them, middle-class Negro parents are seemingly striving at times to establish a human relationship that will compensate for their own frustrations in the realm of human relationships. Devotion to their children often becomes the one human tie that is sincere and free from the competition and artificiality of the make-believe world in which they live. Sometimes they may project upon their children their own frustrated professional ambitions. But usually, even when they send their children to northern "white" universities as a part of their "social" striving within the Negro community, they seem to hope that their children will have an acceptance in the white world which has been denied them.

Part Three

The Family

Black women tend to regard children as a value in themselves, whether born in wedlock or not. This attitude may have its roots in the Black historical experience, when the social status and value of a slave woman largely depended upon her breeding capacity. Among plantation slaves, the assertion that a woman could not have children constituted a slur.[1] Motherhood signifies maturity and the fulfillment of one's function as a woman.

The selections in the section on child bearing deal with the normal concerns of the social scientist studying fertility and related factors in the female population. What is not mentioned, although of equal importance to the Black community, is the political implications of family planning efforts among Black citizens of this country—namely the possibility of genocide. While the relevance of genocide to a discussion of family planning may be challenged, it is nonetheless a subject of salient, and strongly debated, concern to Black people.

Genocide, the systematic extermination of a species or destruction of its culture, is nothing new to American society. When whites first entered the New World, at least 750,000 Indians inhabited North America. By 1850 the Indian population was reduced to 250,000.[2] This is, of course, a small

---

[1]Charles S. Johnson, *Shadow of the Plantation* (Chicago: University of Chicago Press, 1934), p. 58.

[2]Robert Staples, "Liberation or Extermination: The New American Dilemma," *The Correlator*, January-February 1968, pp. 4–6.

number of people compared to the millions of Black slaves who never survived the trip from Africa to the United States.

Black genocide can be achieved indirectly over a long period of time. One manner in which it may be accomplished is through the eminently respectable method of family planning. Although the problem is complex, there have been attempts in the past to legislate the compulsory sterilization of Black women. Some Black women on welfare have been forced to accept sterilization in exchange for a continuation of welfare benefits. These facts lend credence to the concept of genocide through birth control. Historically, birth control has already been employed to significantly reduce the Indian and Eskimo populations.

Moreover, some people who do not support social movements for Black equality are quite willing to give aid to family planning programs for breaking the cycle of poverty. The current government administration sees birth control as part of the solution to Black poverty; a massive campaign for "birth control" is being promoted not only in underdeveloped nonwhite areas of the world but also in Black communities in the United States. As one observer has noted, "Blacks are crying out for jobs and education and the government is pushing the pill. They want jobs and they get the pill."[3]

While the use of birth control is, ostensibly, a matter of free choice for Black women, there is a compulsory and seductive character to the family planning movement. It becomes coercive when Black women on welfare are warned not to have any more children or their financial assistance may be eliminated, or when Congress freezes the welfare money so that additional children of welfare mothers cannot receive aid. The family planning centers stimulate interest in birth control among the Black population by their conspicuous location in Black communities and their offer to give the pill free of charge to any Black woman who wants it. It is a lot easier, for instance, for Black women to get free contraceptives than to receive free food stamps. In addition, these family planning clinics are noticeably absent from many lower class white communities, where one would assume the need to be just as great.

The government's concern over the size of Black families curiously coincides with the growing numbers of Black people in this country's largest cities, where they threaten to achieve political ascendancy and alter power relationships. During the twentieth century many Blacks migrated from rural southern regions to urban areas in both the North and the South. Today the Black population is more highly urbanized than the white population. Moreover, the proportion of Blacks (31 percent) dwelling in the central cities of the 24 largest metropolitan areas is more than double the proportion of whites (15 percent). If the 1960 rates of population increase are sustained, Blacks would require a little over 30 years to double their number, while whites would need over 50 years.[4]

[3]"Black Doctors Speak Out," *San Francisco Chronicle*, August 18, 1968, p. 7.

[4]Philip M. Hanser, "Demographic Factors in the Integration of the Negro," in Talcott Parsons and Kenneth B. Clark (eds.), *The Negro American* (Boston: Beacon Press, 1965), pp. 71–101.

Many Blacks also believe that Black women have the inalienable right and responsibility to determine when it is in their best personal interest and in the interest of the Black liberation struggle to have children or not to have them.[5] It has been suggested that family planning clinics be controlled by Blacks and that Black women should be educated about the issues involved in birth control.

The article by Rainwater, taken from his book *Family Design*, deals with medical assistance for family limitation. It is interesting to note that he found Black wives more likely to have had some discussion of contraceptive measures with medical personnel—mostly at the initiation of the medical personnel. Rainwater speculates that physicians are more likely to see a case as a problem when the patient is Black—that they feel family limitation for Blacks more urgent than for whites.

Hill and Jaffe present a detailed picture of Black fertility behavior. They summarize various research findings on the family size preferences of lower income Blacks and assess the fertility and family planning practices of Black parents in light of the actual medical services which have been available to them. They subsequently examine the implications for both short-term and long-term programming of major health and social services to meet the needs of disadvantaged Black families.

Although motherhood is, of course, important to Black women, not all of them enjoy carrying out their maternal role. (Even during the slavery period, some Black women rejected their children because child bearing was often traumatic. Many slavemasters forced pregnant women to work as hard as the other slaves up to the arrival of the child. Afterward they frequently carried out dual roles on the plantation—laborer and mother.[6])

The frequent employment of the mother creates special problems in the socialization of the Black child, especially if we accept as valid the findings that Black husbands do not help their wives in the home.[7] According to several studies, lower class Black children are trained to be of little bother to their parents and are expected to mature early. Lower class Black children are liberated earlier for productive activity; children freed for work and economic independence are also freed from parental control. Thus, a great deal of socialization takes place within the peer group rather than the family environment.[8]

Like so many other aspects of the Black family, child rearing practices are seen as undesirable according to white standards. Researchers report that the working Black mother is inclined to be tired and irritable, which leads to impatience and insistence on immediate obedience by her children. What

[5] Frances M. Beal, "Double Jeopardy: To Be Black and Female," *New Generation*, Fall 1969, pp. 6–7.

[6] Cf. E. Franklin Frazier, *The Negro Family in the United States* (Chicago: University of Chicago Press, 1939), Ch. 3.

[7] Robert O. Blood, Jr., and Donald Wolfe, *Husbands and Wives* (New York: Free Press, 1960), pp. 110–111.

[8] Allison Davis and John Dollard, *Children of Bondage* (Washington, D.C.: American Council on Education, 1940); Abram Kardiner and Lionel Ovesey, *The Mark of Oppression* (New York: Norton, 1951), p. 72.

discipline the child gets is likely to be arbitrary and inconsistent; yet at the same time he is not offered appropriate rewards for obedience and conformity.[9]

Some of the child rearing practices of Blacks are common to all lower class groups. The tensions and stresses of lower class life affect the parent-child relationship as well as the husband-wife relationship. In the forties, a classical study of child rearing among whites and Blacks found that differences in child rearing practices between middle class and lower class Blacks were similar to those between middle class and lower class whites.[10]

Black child rearing does differ from that of whites in some respects, however. A basic difference in socialization practices is that Black parents have had to teach their children the role of "Negro." In the past, Black parents felt compelled to inculcate subordination to whites in their children. Black children were admonished to avoid fights or brawls with whites because this behavior was dangerous. Males, in particular, had all aggressive tendencies repressed by Black mothers for fear that acting aggressively toward whites could end in death.

While some undesirable socialization practices still exist, the love of Black mothers for their children is clear. In general, Black mothers raise their children with a greater ease than white mothers. Black children are seldom filled with the middle class neurotic traits of white children and avoid the status anxieties associated with some rigid middle class child-rearing practices.[11] Other observers have noted that neglect and abuse of children on welfare are more frequent among whites than Blacks[12] and that Black mothers are more accepting of retarded children than white mothers.[13]

In the section "Parental Roles and Socialization Practices," Schulz's article deals with a neglected figure in the Black family, the father. Schultz's study is exploratory and contains a limited number of cases. His conclusions, though only tentative, are that the role of father in the Black family is highly dependent on his ability to earn a living and his willingness to share that living with his family. Fatherhood, for him, is a precarious status, considering all the negative forces in the ghetto which affect this role.

In the next study, Blau found that Black mothers expose themselves less than white mothers to child rearing literature and other sources of information, regardless of class position and, in most cases, of educational level, but they are more often favorable toward experts. One reason for this finding is the low number of Blacks in the middle class. Thus, the new members of this class have fewer opportunities than their white counterparts for exposure to

---

[9]*Ibid.*

[10]Allison Davis and Robert J. Havighurst, "Social Class and Color Differences in Child Rearing," *American Sociological Review*, 11 (December 1946), pp. 698–710.

[11]Cf. Arnold W. Green, "The Middle-Class Male Child and Neurosis," *American Sociological Review*, 11 (February 1946), pp. 31–41.

[12]Elizabeth Herzog, "Some Assumptions about the Poor," *Social Service Review*, 37 (December 1963), pp. 400–407.

[13]Personal communication with Dr. Irving Tallman, Professor of Sociology at the University of Minnesota.

and assimilation of middle class modes of child rearing within their own racial group.

In the third study, Kamii and Radin investigated class differences in the socialization practices of Black mothers in the context of their child rearing goals. By direct observation of mother-child interactions in the home and a card sorting method of studying child rearing goals, these researchers concluded that middle and lower class Black mothers differ fundamentally not in their goals but in their socialization practices. Kamii and Radin then examine the relationship of these practices to the development of anaclitic identification, internal controls, and subsequent conformity to norms and discuss the implications of their conclusions for education.

Bell's study of 202 Black mothers in Philadelphia revealed that although the lower class Black male considered his marital and parental roles of little importance, the lower class Black woman believed the role of mother to be highly significant. Furthermore, she saw marriage as potentially dangerous because of the possibility that economic resources which could be used for taking care of children might be squandered by her husband.

The family is the crucial socializing agent in American society. It is within the family context that the child receives material and emotional support and the motivation to acquire the educational and occupational skills necessary for achieving socially acceptable goals. White racism, which has vitiated the family structure of many Blacks, has left its mark most conspicuously on Black youth.[14]

One result has been the large number of Black youths left without fathers. At any one time about 36 percent of Black children are living in homes with one or both parents missing, and less than one third of all Black youth reach 18 having lived all their lives with both parents.[15] The prevalence of fatherless homes among Blacks has led to several studies on fatherless Black children.[16] A common finding in these studies is that black youth from fatherless families are highly likely to exhibit negative self-esteem. Pettigrew, for instance, concluded that his sample of fatherless, working class, Black males felt more victimized, less in control of their environment, and more distrustful of others than working class males from intact homes.[17]

The Black individual's personality formation is contingent upon the majority society's view of himself. It is no wonder that Blacks are anomic, alienated, and lack hope for the future.

A challenge to the above propositions has been cogently put forth by one sociologist, who undertook a rigorous and systematic review of the literature on the personality formation of Blacks. After pointing out the theoretical and methodological weaknesses of much of this research, his answer was,

[14]David Ausubel and Pearl Ausubel, "Ego Development among Segregated Negro Children," in E. Harry Passow (ed.), *Education in Depressed Areas* (New York: Teachers College Press, 1963), pp. 100–135.

[15]Daniel P. Moynihan, *The Negro Family: The Case for National Action* (U.S. Department of Labor, March 1965), p. 16.

[16]Robert Staples, *The Fatherless Family and Child Personality Structure: A Theoretical and Methodological Assessment*, unpublished manuscript, 1969.

[17]Thomas F. Pettigrew, *A Profile of the Negro American* (Princeton, N.J.: Van Nostrand, 1964), pp. 19–20.

I suggest that, contrary to the traditional view, the racial conflict which has characterized relations between Blacks and whites in the United States has positive functions, as well, for the Negro sub-community. The repression leads to a measure of group solidarity instead of the commonly hypothesized group disorganization.

. . . Negroes are less likely to be personally disorganized than their white counterparts since they find themselves part of a solidary group. The solidary group helps one to confront the views and actions of the oppressive majority. . . . The Black man can rely upon a group which possesses a rather well articulated ideology which redefines the white man's actions and explains [his] lowly position.[18]

Whether the racism he encounters demoralizes him or not, he must still cope with problems unique to Black youth. For instance, although the unemployment rate for nonwhites is very high for all age groups, the greatest unemployment occurs in the younger age bracket. Unemployment among 14–19-year-old Blacks has exceeded 20 percent in every year since 1958.[19] We have already seen how success in Black marriages is heavily dependent on the male's ability to provide for his family. It is not surprising to find that almost 70 percent of all Black teenage marriages end in divorce.[20]

In the section "Personality Development and the Problems of Youth," Rainwater reveals the way in which white America structures reality so that other Blacks do the direct damage to the psyche of Black youth. It is within the context of family interaction that the Black child develops an identity—his conception of himself and his community's recognition of himself. According to Rainwater, the process of identity labeling in the Black family leaves the Black child with the self-image of a "bad" person. In the process of growing up, white racism, which denies his goodness, seems to confirm his family's earlier definition of him as an essentially bad person.

Himes's article examines some of the work-related problems of Black youth from lower class backgrounds. According to Himes, the work-related cultural deprivations of the lower class Black youth have both judgmental and realistic dimensions, influencing both his acceptance and his performance as a worker. His exclusion from the labor force deprives him of relevant work models, separates him from the work ethos, and alienates him from job ways, thus reinforcing realistic as well as judgmental deprivation.

In the next article, Coles examines the identity crisis of Black youth in the region of the country where the effects of caste are greatest—the South. From their formative years, he says, Black children must learn who they are, what they probably will be, where they cannot go, and what they cannot be. Such reality testing determines the child's sense of his own worth and his sense of the power of those who define his worth, and, consequently, of their worth.

---

[18]John D. McCarthy, *Race and Self-Esteem: A Potential Controversy*, a paper presented at the Pacific Sociological Meeting, Seattle, Washington, 1969, pp. 21–22.

[19]*Manpower Report of the President*, March 1965, p. 206.

[20]Cf. Carl Rowan, "The Tragedy of Teenage Marriages," *Ebony*, August 1961, pp. 61–68.

However, the perpetual attacks of whites on their physical and psychological being have not deterred Black youth from the struggle to secure liberation for their people.

Staples' case study gives us an in-depth view of the life of one Black youth in the ghetto. Written in 1966, this case study focuses on the alienation of one Black youth from his family and his society. It reveals how the mark of oppression can psychologically crush a Black adolescent who must find a sense of worthiness in a society which has stacked the cards against him. The program of economic and educational change that Staples mentions has not come about. But many of the nation's young people are actively working to bring about those changes in the American social structure which will make a healthier society for us all.

8

Child Bearing

Lee Rainwater: Medical
Assistance for Family Limitation

Family limitation and contraception have been at most only partly under formal medical control. For most of the history of this aspect of Western technology, medicine has had relatively little to do with family planning practices; the principal methods responsible for the great decline in births during the 19th century (coitus interruptus and douche) were more or less completely within the area of lay control, and the rise in use of the condom probably had more to do with the public health efforts of the armed services in two world wars than with the prescriptions of individual physicians. However, in the past two or three decades there has been a growth in the social definition of contraception as a medical rather than a purely lay affair, a development finally recognized officially by the American Medical Association in 1937. The development and popularization of methods which require medical assistance, such as the diaphragm, and advice in choosing among the methods available, probably contribute to the growing awareness of contraception as something one should discuss with a physician.

However, it would be incorrect to believe that most couples now rely on their physicians for advice in choosing and using family limitation methods.

Reprinted from Lee Rainwater, *Family Design* (Chicago: Aldine Publishing Company, 1965), pp. 244-251. By permission of the author and publisher. Copyright © 1965 by Social Research, Inc.

Table 1. Medical Discussion of Family Limitation

		None	With Physician as Out-Patient	Planned Parenthood Clinic	Post-Partum in Hospital
Middle class Protestants	(34)	6%	88%	12%	—
Middle class Catholics	(23)	30	59	8	4%
Upper-lower class whites	(26)	39	61	—	4
Upper-lower class Negroes	(24)	29	54	17	21
Lower-lower class whites	(24)	46	46	4	12
Lower-lower class Negroes	(29)	38	21	14	28

In Table 1 we present the proportions of several social groups who have had one or another kind of medical experience concerning family limitation. Among middle class Protestants, almost all wives have had some contact with physicians in which contraception was discussed. (No figures are presented for husbands' contacts since fewer than 5 percent of men say they have ever talked this over with their doctors; in its medical aspects contraception is very clearly a feminine matter in the eyes of our respondents, and husbands participate at second hand.) Middle class Catholics, of course, have had less contact with physicians both because they delay contraception longer and because they are likely to discuss the rhythm method with a physician only after experimenting with it on their own until there is a failure. Within the lower class, upper-lower class persons are more likely to have had medical contacts than are lower-lower class persons, but overall, Negro wives are slightly more likely to have had some medical discussion, in good part because discussion is initiated by medical personnel in hospitals. There is a religious difference in medical contacts only in the middle class; in the lower class Protestants and Catholics are equally likely to have had medical contact.

Table 2 reflects the type of medical contact the wife has had for those cases in which there has been some medical discussion. In the middle class

Table 2. Type and Situation of Medical Discussion

		Out-Patient of		Planned Parenthood	Post-Partum in Hospital
		General Physician	Obstetrician-Gynecologist		
White Middle class	(48)	29%	67%	12%	2%
Upper-lower class	(16)	81	19	—	6
Lower-lower class	(13)	69	15	8	15
Negro Upper-lower class	(17)	41	41	24	29
Lower-lower class	(18)	22	11	22	45

Table 3. Medical Discussion and Effective Contraceptive Practice in the Lower Class

		Has Had Discussion	Has Not Had Discussion
Negro effectives	(16)	87%	13%
White effectives	(17)	59	41
All ineffectives who want more children	(21)	57	43
All ineffectives who do not want more children	(42)	60	40

(regardless of religion) the practice seems well established that a wife seeks advice from a specialist. Among Protestants the practice of consulting with an OB-Gyn specialist at a premarital examination is quite common; among Catholics this kind of discussion tends to be delayed until later in the marriage when family limitation or spacing become real issues. The attraction of the specialist also accounts for the small number of middle class wives who patronize Planned Parenthood; their comments about the organization clearly indicate that they go there because they want to get the most expert advice available. Lower class whites tend to rely on their "family doctor" for contraceptive advice; about three quarters of them have discussed family limitation with this source and very few with any other source. Negroes rely much less on the general physician; upper-lower class Negro women are more likely to get the advice of specialists, either at Planned Parenthood or elsewhere. Lower-lower class Negro wives have their medical contacts most often in the hospital; a small minority consult Planned Parenthood or the family doctor, and very few seek out a specialist in any other setting.

Only 10 percent of lower class whites have discussed contraception with professionals in a hospital, while about 38 percent of the Negroes have done so. This is partly accountable by the fact that the Negro wives in our sample are likely to have so many children that they are singled out by their hospital physicians as "problem cases," but there is also the distinct possibility that their physicians are more likely to see a problem case where the patient's coloring is dark; that is, there is a sense of greater urgency about family limitation for Negroes than for whites. We have no evidence bearing on this point, of course, but this interpretation is consistent with the finding that few of the Negro wives say that they initiated the discussions that took place in the hospital; often they seem slightly intrigued but uneasy about them, and feel they are being "put on the spot."

Are those who have medical discussions more likely to be effective practitioners of contraceptions than those who do not? Tables 3 and 4 present data on this point. Clearly there is no difference in the effectiveness of those who have and have not had medical discussions. The one exception to the pattern involves Negro effectives, who apparently do more often seek out medical advice on how to effectively limit their families.

When we examine the kind of professional contact these wives have had (Table 4), some differences between effectives and ineffectives are apparent for Negroes, though not for whites. The Negro effectives are most likely to have contact with private specialists or with Planned Parenthood; Negro ineffectives are most likely to have had medical discussions in the hospital. It

Table 4. Type of Medical or Professional Setting and Effective Contraceptive Practices in
the Lower Class

| | | Out-Patient of | | | |
		General Physician	Obstetrician-Gynecologist	Planned Parenthood	Post-Partum in Hospital
Whites					
Effectives	(10)	80%	10%	—	20%
Ineffectives who want no more children	(10)	70	20	10	10
Negroes					
Effectives	(14)	29	43	36	21
Ineffectives who want no more children	(15)	40	—	13	67
All					
Ineffectives who want more children	(12)	67	42	—	—

would seem, then, that the post-partum discussions lower class women have
in hospitals are not particularly useful in directing them toward effective
contraception. This is partly because the discussion tends to come fairly late
in the game, after the wives involved are pretty well convinced that nothing
short of sterilization will help them, partly because they are uncertain as to
whether to take the advice as constructive or as insulting, and partly because
the communication is, as they remember it, often quite incomplete. Thus,
two Negro women who are ineffective after having had six and seven
children, respectively, recounted their hospital experiences (one in Chicago
and the other in Oklahoma City) as follows:

He just mentioned birth control, but he didn't say what kind. The doctor at the
[Cook] County [Hospital]. I asked him [about birth control] when I had my first. A lot
of women are skeptical about asking; they wish the doctor would hit on it. If he does,
then they feel freer to talk about it. [When should he bring it up?] With a woman
who has had miscarriages, or had babies too fast, or it would be bad for her health,
or she has just had children and children, too many.

Yes, the doctor at the hospital told me that as long as it didn't bother me [to have
many children] to go ahead but if it bother me he could make me stop. He said he
could tell me what to do but he didn't say what. If he thinks she need to stop he needs
to tell her; he knows what is best.

It is quite possible that the physicians who initiated the discussions with
these two women felt that the women did not seem interested. It is clear
from other comments by lower-lower class women that they tend to feel
rather distant from the physicians with whom they have contact and that the
physicians have to work hard to communicate effectively with this kind of
patient. Some of the underlying resistance which these women have, even
when they are interested in learning to limit the number of children they
have, will be apparent in the sections which follow on general attitudes

toward different kinds of family planning advice and programs. All of this is not to say, of course, that advice to women in hospitals is useless—its utility depends on the physician making a real effort, not a hurried one, to consult with the woman and help her understand that there really are available methods that *she* can use effectively. Also, since the method most commonly recommended in these situations, the diaphragm, is probably the most difficult one for lower class women to adopt and use effectively, medical discussion has tended to be fruitless. Now that the much simpler oral contraceptive is available, medical contact in hospitals probably offers more promise of helping at least some women move from ineffective to effective practice.

After asking respondents about their own contacts with physicians, we asked them the following general question about how free a physician should be in initiating advice on contraception:

Some doctors don't discuss contraception with women unless the women herself brings it up, even though they feel she needs to learn about it. What do you think of that?

Taking together the women's own experiences and their statements in response to the question above, we gain some insight into different ways of relating to physicians. Within the lower class, upper-lower class women seem to make efforts to relate fairly closely with their physicians, and this probably makes it easier for them to ask for and accept contraceptive advice. Thus, upper-lower class women are more likely to mention the pleasant personal qualities of their family doctors:

A Protestant woman: The doctor told me about the diaphragm and suppositories. He's a general doctor. After my second baby he told me when I went in for the six weeks checkup. I always feel at ease with him; he's the type that puts you at ease. I always say when I'm going to see him I'm not going to see a doctor: I'm going to see an uncle.

A Catholic woman: After the second child he said to use rubbers. He was very friendly and nice to talk to. He's just a medical doctor, not a specialist or anything. No one ever told me anything before that. I think they should. A young girl that's married, he should talk that over with her. Some religious person wouldn't believe in anything but the cycle so he wouldn't tell them. So depending on the doctor, he could talk—he knows his patient and how the patient feels and can decide whether to tell.

On the other hand, lower-lower class women seldom speak of their physicians in this way—they reflect more distance in their comments, more suspicion, and more vulnerability to shame or insult; some women are hopeful that the physician will overcome this barrier and help them. Others are more standoffish:

A Negro woman: I've never talked to him about it. I wouldn't mind discussing it but that's no sign I'd use anything. If he thinks she needs it he should bring it up cause he's her doctor and most women would be embarrassed to bring up something like that. . . .

I never talked about it except about the diaphragm with our family doctor and then the doctor at the [Planned Parenthood] Center where I got the diaphragm. As far as I'm concerned I was sort of glad he brought it up because I had thought about it but if a person just brings it up sort of casual like you don't think as much. A doctor can say and you pay attention because you know they know what they're talking about.

. . . At this point we want only to note that many lower-lower class women find their contacts with physicians (as with hospitals) both barren of emotional gratification and not very helpful. Often they do not explicitly blame the doctor (they did not expect anything else), but their comments on later questions about how medical people should help them suggest something of what they were wishing for.

Adelaide Cromwell Hill and Frederick S. Jaffe: Negro Fertility and Family Size Preferences— Implications for Programming of Health and Social Services

The subtlest and most pervasive of all influences are those which create and maintain the repertory of stereotypes. We are told about the world before we see it. We imagine most things before we experience them. And those preconceptions, unless education has made us acutely aware, govern deeply the whole process of perception. . . .There is another reason, besides economy of effort, why we so often hold to our stereotypes when we might pursue a more disinterested vision. The systems of stereotypes may be the core of our personal tradition, the defenses of our position in society. . . . Any disturbance of the stereotypes seems like an attack upon the foundation of the universe. It is an attack upon the foundations of our universe, and, where big things are at stake, we do not readily admit that there is any distinction between our universe and the universe. A world which turns out to be one in which those we honor are unworthy, and those we despise are noble, is nerve-racking. There is anarchy if our order of precedence is not the only possible one. For if the meek should inherit the earth, if the first should be the last, if those who are without sin alone may cast a stone, if to Caesar you render only the things that are Caesar's, then

Reprinted from *The Negro American*, Talcott Parsons and Kenneth Clark (eds.), (Boston: Beacon Press, 1967), pp. 160-204, with permission of the American Academy of Arts and Sciences. Adelaide Cromwell Hill is Assistant Professor of Sociology at Boston University. Frederick S. Jaffe is Vice-President for Program Planning, Planned Parenthood Federation of America.

the foundations of self-respect would be shaken for those who have arranged their lives as if these maxims were not true. . . .

Walter Lippmann, *Public Opinion*

Several years ago, Cornell sociologist J. Mayone Stycos evaluated fertility control efforts in developing nations and found that a principal obstacle to acceleration of programs is rooted, not simply in objective conditions, but in the *subjective explanations* which the elite and ruling classes of most countries offer for the high fertility of lower class groups. He identified a complex of related attitudes summed up in the expression "procreation is the poor man's recreation." These attitudes have three major components: (1) Lower class parents do not *care* how many children they have; or (2) They *want* many children; and (3) They have an *unusually active sex drive* uninhibited by a sense of morality or social responsibility, which derives from their basic "nature," variously defined as primitive, child-like, animal-like, amoral and/or immoral. Stycos found that although the evidence in the developing countries at that time (and since reinforced substantially) contradicted each of these postulates, the social policies advocated by the elites followed from their own unfounded preconceptions. Thus they placed less emphasis on measures aimed at modifying economic and social conditions (including the availability of family planning services). Rather, they advocated confronting high fertility among the lower classes primarily by "more direct" measures such as "teaching 'self-control,' reducing sexual frequency by state-provided avenues of sublimation, and the reduction of illegitimacy by legal, religious and social pressures." He concluded that "the initial and perhaps major hurdle" which must be surmounted for the expansion of fertility control in the developing countries is the attitude of their elite ruling classes.[1]

Stycos' model of upper class stereotypes blocking the development of sound policies and programs is focused on experience with fertility control efforts, but has considerable relevance for a broader range of problems in both the developing countries and the United States. It offers an especially useful insight in the current discussion of the problems of impoverished Negro families stimulated by the Department of Labor study, *The Negro Family: The Case for National Action*, because (1) these problems are most frequently defined precisely in terms of the different fertility behavior of the Negro poor, and (2) upper class biases about lower class fertility (which Stycos found to be universal in all societies) are in this case reinforced and augmented by racial biases as well.

The basic facts outlining the trend of white-nonwhite fertility changes since World War II are hardly in dispute. The postwar baby boom was the result of increased levels of fertility among all Americans, but was more

[1] J. M. Stycos, "Obstacles to Programs of Population Control—Facts and Fancies," *Marriage and Family Living*, 25:1, February 1963.

pronounced among Negro families. Nonwhite fertility increased very rapidly in the late 40's and continued at quite high levels until 1957, when it began to decline along a path parallel to the decline in white fertility. In the last several years, in fact, there has been a somewhat larger decline in nonwhite fertility rates than in white rates. Nevertheless, in 1963 nonwhite fertility was still 40% higher than white—144.8 births per thousand women aged 15-44 compared to 103.7.[2]

Through painful experience, demographers have learned to avoid offering simplistic explanations for complex changes over time in fertility behavior. Investigators are currently attempting to elucidate both the causes of the baby boom itself and the widening of fertility differentials by color, which is especially puzzling because it occurred at a time when the nonwhite population was becoming increasingly urbanized, achieving higher educational levels, and improving on some socio-economic indices. These are changes, of course, which in many societies have, in the long run, been associated with declining fertility levels.

To some observers, however, the postwar widening of the fertility gap is "proof" of nothing more or less than an all-pervasive pathology among impoverished Negroes—a pathology which has become internalized, is self-perpetuating, and has produced in "zoological tenements" of the urban ghetto a state of "biological anarchy."[3] Such a conclusion generates "remedies" quite similar to those which Stycos found were advocated by elites in developing nations: more efficacious exhortation of the poor to be more responsible, coupled with a variety of pressures, not excluding punitive and coercive measures (such as compulsory sterilization of mothers of out-of-wedlock children) which have thus far been regarded by most Americans as impermissible.

In the United States, as in the developing countries, the available evidence contradicts the essential premises of this kind of instant demography. A *detailed* examination of recent nonwhite fertility behavior reveals a far different picture—one of considerable underlying (but for the most part thwarted) aspiration for family limitation and upward mobility. It is our view that this is of the highest significance for structuring sound—and humane—programs in a variety of problem areas for those Negro families which are disadvantaged and economically deprived. In this paper, we will attempt a closer look at nonwhite fertility, summarize research findings on the family size preferences of impoverished Negroes, and assess the fertility and family planning practices of Negro parents in the context of the actual medical services which have been available to them. From this analysis, hopefully, will emerge some implications for both short- and long-term programming of major health and social services to meet the needs of impoverished Negro families.

[2] A. S. Lunde, "White—Nonwhite Fertility Differentials in the United States," *Health, Education and Welfare Indicators*, September 1965.

[3] T. H. White, *The Making of the President, 1964*, New York: 1965, pp. 221-242.

A Closer Look at Fertility Behavior

Negro families in the United States are not divided simply into a group of relatively successful middle class families, on the one hand, and a large, undifferentiated group of impoverished and disorganized families on the other. There is a growing group of well-to-do Negroes at the top and a wide variety of types of middle class families within the Negro community. There are also significant socio-economic sub-groups among low income Negro families, as among all families, such as a stable blue collar working class. Even in a slum, a great diversity of family structure is found.[4]

If likes are to be compared with likes, therefore, it is essential that differential fertility be analyzed among comparable groups. Thorough studies of postwar trends in white-nonwhite fertility reveal that when various measures of socio-economic status are held constant, white-nonwhite differences in fertility are either reduced very significantly, eliminated entirely or, in some cases, even reversed. In Chicago in 1950, "almost all of the difference between white and nonwhite total fertility could be accounted for by differences in socio-economic status."[5] For the nation as a whole in the same year, when fertility rates were compared by educational status, the same result was found.[6] Ten years later, the 1960 census showed that nonwhites with four years of high school education have about the same number of children as whites, while those with four years of college have fewer. When fertility is compared by occupational status and income, there is still a gap between white and nonwhite rates. However, the gap is narrowed considerably in the occupation and income categories above the most impoverished level; for example, while nonwhite mothers ages 45–49 with incomes below $2,000 have one third more children than comparable whites, in the income brackets above $3,000 the difference is cut in half.[7]

These analyses strongly suggest that continuing high fertility is more a consequence of the Negro's disproportionately low socio-economic status than of any other factor. This conclusion is reinforced when one unique variable—southern farm background, with its particular blend of rural and regional influences—is independently traced. Current higher fertility levels among nonwhites are the result partly of the *unusually* high fertility of the minority of nonwhite couples who presently live in the rural South and partly of the *moderately* high fertility of the many nonwhite couples who were born on southern farms and have since emigrated. "When we come to nonwhite couples with *no* previous southern farm residence, we find average past and expected numbers of births that do not differ significantly from

[4]Cf. H. Lewis, "Child Rearing among Low-Income Families," reprinted in L. A. Ferman *et al*, eds., *Poverty in America*, Ann Arbor: 1965; and "The Family: Resources for Change," Agenda Paper prepared for Planning Session for the White House Conference "To Fulfill These Rights," November 1965.

[5]E. M. Kitagawa and P. M. Hauser, "Trends in Differential Fertility and Mortality in a Metropolis—Chicago," in E. W. Burgess and D. Bogue, eds., *Contributions to Urban Sociology*, Chicago: 1964, pp. 74–5.

[6]A. and E. Lee, "The Future Fertility of the American Negro," *Social Forces*, 37:3, March 1959, p. 229.

[7]Lunde, *op. cit.*, p. 28.

those of white couples. *In other words, by the time nonwhite couples are one generation or more removed from the rural South, their fertility is very much like that of the white population.*"[8] This finding[9] of the 1960 Growth of American Families study is especially significant in light of the fact that Negroes who are one generation or more removed from the rural South are still subject to continuing discrimination in employment, income, housing, education, and health services which does not affect their white counterparts;[10] as St. Clair Drake has so aptly put it, they continue to be victims of "a system of social relations [which] operates in such a way as to deprive them of a chance to share in the more desirable material and nonmaterial products of ... society [and which deprives them of] the same degree of access which others have to the attributes needed for rising in the general class system."[11]

In addition to the general improvements in economic and social conditions which sparked the overall postwar baby boom, the nonwhite rate of growth seems to have been substantially affected by the medical advances of the last several decades in a manner not too different from the way in which sharp reductions in mortality rates have been the prime cause of the population explosion in developing countries. The medical advances which increased significantly the child bearing and infant survival potential of nonwhites include the greater proportion of nonwhite deliveries occurring in hospitals, an increase from approximately 18% of births in 1935 to 89% in 1964; the rapid fall in the incidence of diseases which often caused sterility; and the general decrease in maternal, neonatal, and fetal mortality since 1935.[12] The immediate effect of an increase in child bearing potential among a population "which is not widely employing sophisticated methods of birth control" is a very rapid increase in birth rates.[13]

Finally, much of the fertility differential is explained by a higher proportion of larger families among nonwhites. Fifth or higher order births totaled nearly one third of all nonwhite births—almost twice the proportion for white women.[14] (However, since 1960, nonwhite rates for fifth and higher

[8] A. A. Campbell, "Fertility and Family Planning among Nonwhite Married Couples in the United States," *Eugenics Quarterly*, 12:3, September 1965, pp. 126, 131, emphasis added.

[9] The 1960 census confirms the findings of sample surveys which show that the excess of nonwhite over white fertility is concentrated in the South. While all ever-married nonwhite women aged 18–39, regardless of socio-economic status, living outside the South had only 11% more children than white women, the differential in the South was 42%, ranging from 34% in southern urban areas to 64% on southern farms. 1960 Census PC (1)-1D, Table 249.

[10] It would be interesting to study comparable segments of the major immigrant groups—e.g., Irish, Italians, Northern Europeans, Eastern Europeans, Jews, etc., who came from rural backgrounds—to determine how long it took these groups to approximate the child bearing patterns of urban America, and which groups achieved this adaptation within one generation after arriving in the United States.

[11] St. Clair Drake, "The Social and Economic Status of the Negro in the United States," *Daedalus*, 94:4, Fall 1965, p. 772.

[12] Cf. especially R. Farley, "Recent Changes in Negro Fertility," paper presented at Population Association of America, April 1965. The relative difference between white and nonwhite rates of maternal, neonatal, and fetal mortality has in fact increased since 1950, but nonwhite rates were in absolute terms so high in the mid-30's that the decline was significant enough to enhance nonwhite child bearing potential; e.g., nonwhite maternal mortality declined from 875.5 per 100,000 live births in 1935–39 to 98.1 in 1963.

[13] Farley, *op. cit.*

[14] Lunde, *op. cit.*, p. 31.

order births have declined more rapidly than white rates for similar birth orders.) The significance of this finding is indicated by Mollie Orshansky's observation that "the larger the family, the greater the poverty hazard for children. . . . Of the 15 million children being reared in poverty, 6½ million or 43% were growing up in a home with at least 5 youngsters under age 18. Indeed the poverty rate among families rose sharply from 12% when there was one child in the home to 49% when there were 6 or more children. . . . *The poverty rate for all families with 5 or 6 children is three and a half times as high as for families with 1 or 2 children.*"[15]

Since 1957, both white and nonwhite fertility has declined, but there has been a slightly larger drop in nonwhite rates; between 1959 and 1963 there was a decrease of 11.2 births per thousand nonwhite women ages 15–44 compared to 10.2 per thousand white women.[16]

The Question of Illegitimacy

Detailed examination of white-nonwhite fertility trends also requires something better than mechanical repetition of the *registered* rates of out-of-wedlock births by color, which are often seized upon to support the image of widespread pathology, rampant sexuality, and galloping family disintegration among Negroes. Apart from the fact that even these registered rates are almost never analyzed by socio-economic status (which would help to compare likes with likes), it is clear that knowledgeable population scholars have serious doubts of their validity. The expert committee convened by the National Center for Health Statistics and the Census Bureau to scrutinize all aspects of the collection and interpretation of fertility data points out that the published rates are certainly incomplete because some out-of-wedlock births are not registered as such; the committee concludes ruefully that "*the most that can be said* about the illegitimacy figures is that they indicate the minimum extent of illegitimacy."[17] Clearly the opportunity for under-registration and misstatement of legitimacy status is more available to whites than to nonwhites, if only because of the disproportionately greater reliance of nonwhites on public and charity hospitals where concealment is extremely difficult.

There has been one systematic study thus far which attempts to illuminate the extent of white-nonwhite differences in *out-of-wedlock conceptions* (an index that might be more indicative than *registered illegitimate births* of the actual state of differential unmarried sexual activity unprotected by contraception). In this careful study linking marriage certificates and birth records in Detroit, coupled with a mail survey, the ratio found in 1960 was one out-of-wedlock *conception* among whites to three among nonwhites, as com-

---

[15] M. Orshansky, "Who's Who among the Poor: A Demographic View of Poverty," *Social Security Bulletin*, July 1965, pp. 14–15, emphasis added.

[16] *Vital Statistics of the United States, 1963*, Volume I, "Natality," Table 1–2, pp. 1–4.

[17] National Center for Health Statistics, *Fertility Measurement: A Report of the United States National Committee on Vital and Health Statistics*, September 1965, p. 8, emphasis added.

pared to a ratio of one to eight for registered illegitimate *births*. The study also showed that while most pregnant whites married *before* the birth of the child, a substantial proportion of nonwhite "illegitimate" children are legitimized *after* birth by subsequent marriage of the consanguineal parents. The investigator concluded that "the dramatic difference between white and nonwhite illegitimate births, then, is as much or more a function of fewer marital resolutions before the birth of the child [among nonwhites] as it is a function of higher illegitimate conceptions." In other words, precipitous marriages among whites and illegitimate births among nonwhites are largely different adjustments to the same underlying trend of rising out-of-wedlock conceptions.[18]

It should be pointed out that even this striking reduction in the color differential does not fully correct the impression given by the illegitimacy statistics, since this study does not take into account the considerably higher proportion of whites who resort to illegal abortion when they become pregnant out of wedlock,[19] nor does it estimate illegitimate births to women *remaining* single which are registered as legitimate. It seems reasonable that if adequate data on differential utilization of abortion and concealment were combined with the findings of this study on forced marriages, the differential between white and nonwhite rates of out-of-wedlock *conceptions* would be reduced even further or might well become negligible, even without controlling for socio-economic status.

This is not to dismiss the fact that a significant proportion of Negro children are born in a status branded illegitimate, nor to deny the serious social consequences which result. It suggests, however, that formation of sound policies aimed at equalizing the outcomes of out-of-wedlock conceptions can be based only on an honest confrontation of the total reality and not merely a fragment. Despite the vast expressed concern over the increasing incidence of illegitimacy, there is little demand for comprehensive studies which would illuminate the central operative factors: the extent of unmarried sexual activity among different socio-economic groups, the true incidence of out-of-wedlock pregnancy, and the different adjustments (e.g., abortion, concealment, forced marriage, illegitimate birth, adoption) to out-of-wedlock pregnancy. There is in fact considerable resistance to confronting the limited knowledge we do have, as can be seen in the opposition to extending publicly financed family planning services even to unmarried *mothers*, which would help somewhat to equalize access to contraceptive guidance between the unmarried poor and non-poor.

Indeed, perhaps nothing better illustrates elitist and class-biased attitudes,

---

[18] W. F. Pratt, "Premarital Pregnancy in a Metropolitan Community," paper presented at Population Association of America, April 1965. Since nonwhites have repeated out-of-wedlock births more often than whites, the published rates of illegitimate *births* give a misleading impression of the numbers of *women* involved. When repeaters are taken into account, the color differential is reduced even further: Pratt found that in Detroit the proportion of nonwhite *women* ever experiencing illegitimate conception is only about twice as high as among whites.

[19] P. H. Gebhard *et al., Pregnancy, Birth, and Abortion,* New York: 1958.

such as Stycos found in the developing countries, than our society's differential treatment of the issues of sexual morality and illegitimacy. Almost without exception, and whatever the author's point of view, books, magazine and newspaper articles, and TV shows about sexual morality and/or immorality are concerned with what are regarded as lowered sexual standards in a middle or upper class setting (*Sex on Campus, Sex in Suburbia, Sex and the Single Girl, Sex in the Office,* etc.). It is the *changed nature* of the sexual activity itself which is criticized, approved, or explained, and the psychodynamic impact of this change in "relationships" of boy to girl, man to woman, husband to wife. It is striking that the question of illegitimacy is almost never raised in this setting since it is presumed (sometimes wrongly) that middle class couples have access to effective contraception and, if they slip, to competent abortion. (A report by a distinguished group of psychiatrists on *Sex and the College Student* discusses, matter of factly, not merely the availability of contraception—"many college students view contraceptive information as a right that is due them"—but also the resort to abortion either at the hands of illegal practitioners or on dubious legal grounds or in a foreign country where the operation is legal. Apparently these alternatives, and precipitous marriage, dispose of most campus pregnancies since, the report states, "the few unmarried pregnant college women who decide to carry their babies to term usually then give them up for adoption."[20])

In the context of lower class (and usually nonwhite) behavior, on the other hand, illegitimacy is *always* discussed; it is *never* seen as a different adjustment to the same sexual revolution which has changed the attitudes and practices of all Americans in the last 40 years, but rather is presumed to be the outcome of a historic, unchanged, and unchanging lower class promiscuity that can only be dealt with moralistically and punitively. Deluged by this veritable flood of double-standard literature (Freud and interpersonal relationships for the upper class, Calvin and judgmentalism for the lower), James Baldwin has been led to comment: "White people seem to ask us, if they ask us anything, 'Come into my nightmare with me; be like me; have abortions instead of illegitimate children.' "[21] To our knowledge, no one has yet responded to the policy implications of his observation.

Family Size Preferences

It is clear from the data that socio-economic and educational status, and particularly the influence of fertility patterns of the rural South, continue to play a decisive role in shaping nonwhite fertility trends. Several investigators[22] suggest that the gap in white-nonwhite fertility will be narrowed as

[20] Group for the Advancement of Psychiatry, *Sex and the College Student*, New York: 1965, pp. 43–55.
[21] *Life*, May 24, 1963.
[22] Lunde, *op. cit.*; Lee and Lee, *op. cit.*; Farley, *op. cit.*

general socio-economic conditions improve, as more Negroes move from the rural South, and as higher educational levels are achieved by nonwhites. These conclusions are reinforced by the findings of the 1960 Growth of American Families study, which provides, for the first time, a nationwide view of the family size preferences of nonwhite parents. The study demonstrates that nonwhite wives want *fewer* children than white wives. The average number wanted by nonwhite respondents was 2.9, compared to 3.3 by the white wives. (Only the small number of nonwhite wives currently living on southern farms expressed a desire for more children than their white counterparts; for the South as a whole, both groups wanted an average of 3.0). Furthermore, 46% of nonwhites said they wanted no more than 2 children, compared to 29% of whites.[23]

These findings are based on a national sample survey of married women of child bearing age now living with their husbands, but they are confirmed by numerous local studies which investigated family size preferences without regard to formal or present marital status: In Chicago, twice as many nonwhites as whites said they wanted only two children,[24] and 90% of a group of AFDC mothers of out-of-wedlock children said they did not want to have the child.[25] In Florida, 70% of a predominantly Negro group of public health maternity patients said they wanted to have no more children.[26] In New Orleans, 56% of a sample of very low income Negroes said they wanted no more than three children, 94% said they thought family planning services should be made available to the medically indigent, and 75% of those between 15 and 34 expressed a desire for more information themselves.[27] Confirmation is also provided by the Greenleigh study of poverty in Detroit, which surveyed 2,081 low income, largely Negro households to identify the services the impoverished families required to ameliorate poverty. The survey showed that family planning services ranked sixth in a listing of 28 needed services, outranked only by such obvious needs as financial assistance, job training, help with children's school problems, and day-care facilities.[28]

Response to Family Planning Services

The above studies, though demonstrating that impoverished Negro parents almost uniformly express a strong desire for effective family limitation,

[23]P. K. Whelpton, A. A. Campbell, and J. Patterson, *Fertility and Family Planning in the United States*, Princeton (in press).

[24]A. O. Blair, "A Comparison of Negro and White Fertility Attitudes," Master's thesis submitted at University of Chicago, 1963.

[25]Greenleigh Associates, *Facts, Fallacies, and Future*, 1960.

[26]R. L. Browning and L. L. Parks, "Child bearing Aspirations of Public Health Maternity Patients," *American Journal of Public Health*, 54:1831, November 1964.

[27]J. D. Beasley, C. L. Harter, and A. Fischer, "Attitudes and Knowledge Relevant to Family Planning among New Orleans Negro Females," paper presented at American Public Health Association, October 1965.

[28]Greenleigh Associates, *Home Interview Study of Low-Income Households in Detroit, Michigan*, 1965.

may perhaps be viewed with skepticism because they represent mere verbal expression. They are, however, confirmed by the response of impoverished Negro parents in those communities where family planning services are made available to them with dignity, energy, and skill. Privately organized Planned Parenthood centers in some 120 communities are still the main birth control clinics available to low income families in the U.S.; among the 282,000 patients served by these centers in 1964, the largest single group—47%—was Negro. The birth control program initiated by the District of Columbia Health Department is described as "one of the most popular programs that we have."[29] In two hospital clinics operated by the University of Buffalo Medical School for low income patients, 88% of the patients are nonwhite—a significantly higher proportion than in the hospitals' other medical services.[30] Similar findings are reported from North Carolina,[31] Grady Hospital in Atlanta, Georgia, and in the 14 birth control clinics located in New York City's municipal hospitals, which has experienced a remarkable increase of more than 150% in new patients seen during the last year alone.[32] In a hospital-centered maternity care project in Augusta, Georgia, a nurse tells of the response of patients to the offer of contraception: "Almost everyone who is told about it wants it."[33] In Chicago, nonwhite birth rates dropped 22% in the last five years—an "extraordinary" decline—as a result of an intensive program of birth control service and education, the difference between white and nonwhite fertility has declined by one fourth.[34]

Perhaps the most significant finding to date is contained in a recently published study from the Chicago Planned Parenthood clinic of more than 14,000 low income patients on oral contraception; 83% of the patients were nonwhite, nearly half had not completed high school, one out of six was a welfare recipient. Between 70 and 83% of the patients (72 to 84% of nonwhite patients) continued to take the pills regularly 30 months after they came to the clinic.[35] This is an astonishingly high retention rate for *any* procedure requiring continuous self-administration of medication, and is testimony to the readiness of the poor generally, and particularly the Negro poor, to respond to well-conceived, energetically delivered voluntary programs employing modern contraceptive methods.

[29]M. Grant, testimony, *Hearings on District of Columbia Appropriations for 1966—H. R. 6453*, Subcommittee of Committee on Appropriations, U.S. Senate, 1965, p. 590.

[30]J. Lippes, and C. L. Randall, "Participation of Area Hospitals in Family Planning," in S. Polgar and W. Cowles, eds., *Public Health Programs in Family Planning*, a supplement to *American Journal of Public Health*, January 1966.

[31]E. Corkey, "A Family Planning Program for the Low-Income Family," *Marriage and the Family*, 26:4, November 1964.

[32]A. S. Yerby, personal communication.

[33]K. Close, "Giving Babies a Healthy Start in Life," *Children*, 12:5, September-October 1965, p. 181.

[34]D. Bogue, *West Side Fertility Report*, Community and Family Study Center, University of Chicago (in press).

[35]R. Frank and C. Tietze, "Acceptance of an Oral Contraceptive Program in a Large Metropolitan Area," *American Journal of Obstetrics and Gynecology*, 93:122, September 1, 1965. The difference between 70% and 83% is explained by assignment of the small number of patients lost to follow-up, with the lower figure representing the minimum number of continuing users and the larger the maximum.

The operative consideration here lies in the combination of proper conception and energetic delivery of the service.[36] The most successful demonstration projects have, to one degree or another, been considerably different from the kind of medical care which impoverished Negroes normally receive. Instead of compelling patients to sit for hours on end in dingy waiting rooms, appointments are often scheduled (as in private practice), and efforts are made to offer a bright and cheerful atmosphere. Many clinics are located in the heart of impoverished neighborhoods, not halfway across town, and sessions may be scheduled at night or other unusual times to fit patients' needs. Staff members are urged to refrain from imposing their attitudes and values upon patients, and nonprofessional workers have been employed to interpret to potential patients how family planning can help them to realize *their* desires about family size. Baby-sitting services are sometimes provided. Fees are adjusted to what the patient can afford. And, perhaps most significant, clinics are not segregated by color.

Medical Care for the Negro Poor

Through these and other fairly simple innovations, efforts have been made in the best clinics to approach the atmosphere of mutual respect and understanding which governs private medical practice, and impoverished Negro parents have responded. But they have not often been given the opportunity. While most Americans of higher income are easily able to secure competent and sympathetic guidance in fertility control from their private physicians if they desire it, the Negro poor have to depend very heavily on charity or tax-supported medical facilities, which for the most part still do not make family planning services available.

This denial is but one aspect of what Commissioner Alonzo S. Yerby has vividly described as "a two class system of health care" that gives the poor medical services which are piecemeal, inadequate, underfinanced, uncoordinated, and offered without compassion or concern for the dignity of the individual.[37] But the Negro poor do not share equally even in this inferior system of medical care, though there is ample evidence that their health needs are greatest. Citing current rates of perinatal mortality as an example, Yerby demonstrates that "in terms of health, there is a special disadvantage to being a Negro in the United States which transcends being poor."[38]

---

[36]Cf. N. T. Gray, *Recruiting Low-Income Families for Family Life Education Programs*, Child Study Association, 1965; and J. S. Martin, "The Implementation of Family Planning: Experiences in an Urban Community," paper presented at District V. American College of Obstetricians and Gynecologists, Cleveland, October 30, 1965.

[37]A. S. Yerby, "The Disadvantaged and Health Care," paper presented at White House Conference on Health, November 3, 1965; and "The Problems of Medical Care for Indigent Populations," *American Journal of Public Health*, 55:1212, August 1965. Cf. also M. A. Glasser, "Extension of Public Welfare Medical Care: Issues of Social Policy," *Social Work*, October 1965; L. H. Berry, "Disadvantaged Populations," paper presented at White House Conference on Health, November 3, 1965; and A. Yankauer, "Maternal and Child Health Problems," *The Annals*, September 1964.

[38]"The Disadvantaged and Health Care," *op. cit.*

The net effect of this double discrimination is to discourage impoverished Negroes from seeking preventive and diagnostic medical care, and to confine their care to those emergency and chronic conditions which make medical services absolutely necessary.[39] Among those who do get some medical care, one out of three visits to a physician among Negroes occurs in a hospital outpatient clinic, compared to one out of ten among whites.[40] Even this understates the extent of the deprivation in regard to family planning services, since Negroes rely more heavily on public or charity medical facilities during the child bearing period, when the subject of family planning normally comes up. Data from the National Center for Health Statistics shows that in 1963–4, 48.6% of nonwhite hospitalizations for delivery were in government institutions, compared to 23.7% of white hospitalizations.[41] In New York City between 1955 and 1959, 82% of married nonwhites delivered their babies in municipal hospitals or on ward services of voluntary hospitals, compared with 14.5% of whites.[42] In Washington, D.C., in 1961, 75% of nonwhite births were staff cases.[43] In 1961, 57% of Negro live births in California occurred in county hospitals, compared to 13% of white.[44] The 1961 report of the Obstetrical Statistical Cooperative, based on 66,000 discharges at approximately 20 hospitals in New York, New Haven, Hartford, Philadelphia, San Francisco, Baltimore, and other cities, showed that nearly 94% of nonwhite deliveries were on ward service, compared to 35% of whites.[45]

These figures make clear that the vast majority of nonwhite mothers do not have ready access to a private physician during the child bearing period. They help explain the findings of the 1960 GAF study that despite their expressed interest in family limitation, only 59% of nonwhite couples had used *some* method of fertility control, compared to 81% of whites, and that nonwhites relied much more on methods which are relatively low in effectiveness (douche, jelly and vaginal suppositories) and do not require "medical advice, which is generally less available to nonwhite than to white wives."[46] The 1960 study, of course, was conducted before the introduction of oral pills and intrauterine devices, which, in the clinical reports noted above, have proved to be particularly acceptable to low income couples

---

[39] W. Cowles and S. Polgar, "Health and Communication in a Negro Census Tract," *Social Forces*, 10:3, Winter 1963.

[40] National Center for Health Statistics, *Volume of Physician Visits by Place of Visit and Type of Service—U.S. July 1963–June 1964*. June 1965, p. 8.

[41] P. S. Lawrence, personal communication (special tabulation of data from National Center for Health Statistics).

[42] J. Pakter *et al.*, "Out of Wedlock Births in New York City, No. 1—Sociologic Aspects," *American Journal of Public Health*, Vol. 51, No. 5 (May 1961).

[43] F. Oppenheimer, "Population Changes and Perinatal Mortality," *American Journal of Public Health*, Vol. 52, No. 2 (January 1961).

[44] State of California, Department of Public Health Birth Records.

[45] Obstetrical Statistical Cooperative, *1961 Combined Report*.

[46] Campbell, *op. cit.*, p. 129.

generally[47]—but which require competent medical guidance and prescription.

Thus the denial of birth control services to the Negro poor is an integral part of the denial of adequate medical services in general and during the child bearing period in particular—a discrimination which has contributed to the continuation of doubled and quadrupled rates of infant and maternal mortality for nonwhites as compared to whites. Furthermore, the higher rate of nonwhite fertility, caused in part by unequal access to adequate fertility control services, in turn tends to keep these mortality rates high, since maternal and infant mortality and morbidity increase significantly with increasing parity and with shorter intervals between births, and the incidence of prematurity is considerably higher when the interval between pregnancies is less than 12 months.[48]

Implications for Programs for the Disadvantaged Negro Family

These, then, are some of the main features of the current Negro fertility picture. Fertility levels among Negroes are substantially higher than whites, reflecting the disproportionately low socio-economic status of the Negro community and particularly the influence of southern farm background. Negro parents in all socio-economic groups (except the few now living on southern farms) express a consistent desire for smaller families than do whites. In those few communities where skillful and sympathetic birth control services have been made available to impoverished Negroes, the response has been considerable. Adequate instruction in fertility control, however, is still beyond the reach of the poor because tax-supported and charity medical agencies do not yet generally offer these services. The Planned Parenthood Federation of America estimates that there are some 5 million American women in families with incomes below $3,000 a year— about one fourth Negro—who are in their child bearing years, fertile, and not pregnant or seeking a pregnancy at any given time, and who thus may be considered the minimum patient load for subsidized contraceptive services in the United States. Approximately 500,000 of these women are estimated to receive contraceptive services either from Planned Parenthood Centers or public agencies, leaving 4.5 million women not now being served.[49]

What are the implications of these related findings for programming of health and social services?

First, it seems clear that voluntary family planning services must be made

---

[47]Workers in Planned Parenthood Centers credit the doubling of patient loads in the last five years to the much greater acceptability of the new methods among low-income couples. For a discussion of the importance of type of contraceptive method in understanding family planning behavior of the poor, see S. Polgar, "The Impact of New Contraceptive Methods in Impoverished Neighborhoods of New York," paper presented at Population Association of America, April 1965.

[48]These relationships were demonstrated in classic studies by such investigators as Jacob Yerushalmy in the early '40's. The extensive recent literature has been summarized in F. S. Jaffe and S. Polgar, "Medical Indications for Fertility Control," Planned Parenthood Federation of America, 1954 (mimeographed).

[49]F. S. Jaffe, "Financing Family Planning Services," American Journal of Public Health (in press).

available to impoverished Americans generally, and to the Negro poor, in order to give them a genuine opportunity to carry out *their* desires in regard to family size. The implementation of comprehensive family planning services should result, fairly rapidly, in fewer unwanted conceptions, and over a longer term, in reduced rates of maternal and infant mortality and morbidity. Many observers believe that there would also be significant social consequences, such as a decrease in desertion and divorce, as more couples learn that it is possible to control at least part of their life circumstances.[50]

Family planning is not a panacea for all the problems of poverty and dependency, nor is it a substitute for massive social programs to enable impoverished Negroes to obtain jobs, increase income levels, enlarge educational opportunities, and otherwise improve their living conditions. But the reduction of poverty and dependency will not be slowed significantly, no matter how comprehensive these programs, unless the poor, white and nonwhite, are also able to have only the number of children they want. In the spectrum of urgently needed programs, family planning is one which is achievable relatively quickly and easily: With modern methods, we have sufficient knowledge and technology; it is a relatively simple and inexpensive aspect of medical care; the number of patients to be served is quite limited; and most important, the poor have shown considerable readiness to respond to this service.[51] It is not necessary to remold basic attitudes or develop new aspirations among impoverished Negroes, but to provide the means of realizing aspirations they already have.

This does not mean that *any* kind of program will work automatically. If the program is proffered with racist overtones, if it is coupled with constant threats to sterilize unmarried mothers on welfare, if it is presented as a punitive means of reducing relief costs, and if the mere request for birth control is taken as *prima facie* evidence that there's a "man in the house," thus jeopardizing the woman's eligibility for public assistance, the response is likely to be negligible. Moreover, this kind of program gives credence to those groups in the Negro community who reject family planning as an effort by the white majority to reduce Negro power. In spite of these vocal attacks by some individuals and nationalist organizations, it is significant that militant Negro political figures have given outstanding leadership during the last several years in campaigns to modify restrictive laws or liberalize public policies on birth control in such states as New York, Illinois, Michigan, Maryland, and Wisconsin.

A second implication of this analysis is that the extension of birth control services will require a very considerable expansion in the maternity care services—and in the full spectrum of health services—which are available to

[50]Without attempting to state a causal relationship for which adequate studies have not been done, Orshanky (*op. cit.,* p. 16) comments on the interaction between high fertility and family breakdown: "What cannot be said is how often the poverty itself may have antedated and even contributed to the family dissolution. Age for age, mothers without a husband present have borne more children than women still living with a husband. Knowing that it is often the worker with low earnings potential who has the larger family, one can only wonder about the possible relation between too many children, too little family income and the breakup of a marriage." See also Lewis, "The Family: Resources for Change," *op. cit.,* p. 7.

[51]Cf. F. S. Jaffe, "Family Planning, Public Policy and Intervention Strategy," *Journal of Social Issues* (in press).

the Negro poor. This expansion must involve both the development of additional facilities and considerable improvements in the quality and comprehensiveness of the services provided, and in the arrangements for their organization and delivery. In other words, it will require significant movement toward ending the "two class system," certainly as far as maternity care is concerned.

The Modernization Process

Expansion of family planning services and improvements in maternity care would directly affect fertility itself. We believe, however, that there are less obvious underlying implications for a much wider range of services. Here it may be useful to draw on the understanding, which is emerging among students of population problems in the developing countries, of the "basic unity of the modernization process."[52] This concept, which means that economic and social development on the one side and declining fertility on the other are integrally related parts of the same process of modernization, may be of use in understanding the full significance of the expressed desires of the Negro poor for effective family limitation. For the concept is based upon the premise that social, cultural, and psychological readiness for fertility control does not and cannot take place unless it is a part of social, cultural, and psychological readiness for general economic and social development. In simple terms, the readiness of parents for family planning reveals a desire to insure a better life for the children—a theme which is repeated continually in interviews among parents in all countries and ethnic groups who express an interest in fertility control. Thus the readiness of the Negro poor for family limitation confirms Hylan Lewis's finding that "a major aspiration of low-income parents for their children is to see that their children do better in life—especially in jobs, education, and family behavior—than they have been able to do themselves."[53]

That impoverished Negroes have profound hopes for their children's futures ought to be obvious in the light of the civil rights revolution. Yet in most health, social, and educational services, it is often maintained that the poor and the Negro poor are "unmotivated" to take advantage of services which they need and would benefit by. It is our view that the expressed and demonstrated readiness of the Negro poor for fertility control is but one aspect of a readiness for a wide variety of measures aimed at improving mobility, and suggests that the response will be considerable to genuine services which are properly organized and delivered.[54] The task is to use our

---

[52] I. Taeuber, "Future Population Trends," paper presented at United Nations World Population Conference, September 1965.

[53] "The Family: Resources for Change," op. cit., p. 18.

[54] The potentially strategic role of medical agencies is suggested by Greenleigh (Home Interview Study, op. cit., p. 10) and by Dean Julius Richmond who observes: "Health personnel with an interest and competence in dealing with the social probelms of their patients, and operating in a setting providing personalized, dignified care, may find they have a unique entree to helping families to deal with their social and psychological problems." ("Infants and Children," paper presented at White House Conference on Health, November 3, 1965.)

intelligence, imagination, and affluence to restructure existing service systems—health, welfare, education, etc.—in order to fulfill these hopes and not thwart them.

Far from revealing disintegration and unrelieved pathology, current trends in Negro fertility attitudes and behavior suggest a substantial reservoir of aspiration and indeed of strength on which positive service programs for impoverished Negro families can be based. In this country, as in the developing nations, such programs can be developed only with a genuine understanding of real human beings in the real world, and not with elitist stereotypes which, in the U.S. too, appear to be "the initial and perhaps major hurdle" to be surmounted.

The authors wish to acknowledge with gratitude the suggestions and criticisms of Arthur A. Campbell, National Center for Health Statistics; Lisbeth Bamberger, Office of Economic Opportunity; Bruce Jessup, M.D., Department of Health, Education and Welfare; Lincoln Day, Yale University; and the following staff members of Planned Parenthood Federation: Steven Polgar, Ph.D., Mrs. Naomi Thomas Gray, Mrs. Jeannie Rosoff, and Richard Lincoln.

9

Parental Roles and
Socialization Processes

David A. Schulz: Variations in the
Father Role in Complete Families
of the Negro Lower Class

In spite of the fact that there are numerous studies of the Negro in America, very few have been concerned primarily with the family.[1] Those that have taken the family as a central concern[2] have not been based upon intensive studies such as, for example, Oscar Lewis' studies of poor families in Mexico.[3] Indeed, it is common to think of lower-class Negro families in

Reprinted with permission from *Social Science Quarterly*, 49 (December 1968), pp. 651-659.

[1] Studies such as Allison Davis and John Dollard, *Children of Bondage* (Washington, D.C.: American Council of Education, 1940); Abram Kardiner and Lionel Ovesey, *The Mark of Oppression* (New York: Norton, 1951); and Hertha Reise, *Heal the Hurt Child* (Chicago: University of Chicago Press, 1962) concentrate on the children. Those such as Kenneth Clark, *Dark Ghetto* (New York: Harper and Row, 1965); Hylan Lewis, *Blackways of Kent* (Chapel Hill: University of North Carolina Press, 1955); and St. Clair Drake and Horace Cayton, *Black Metropolis* (New York: Harcourt, Brace and World, 1945) consider the family as a small portion of a much broader concern for community studies, although Lewis does develop a family typology based on genealogical data.

[2] For example E. Franklin Frazier's *The Negro Family in the United States* (Chicago: University of Chicago Press, 1939) is based largely upon census data and other gross indices of family life combined with the author's own intuitive interpretation of their meaning. It is not based on an examination of how particular families function. The one intensive participant observation study of the Negro lower class by Elliot Liebow (*Tally's Corner* [Boston: Little, Brown, 1967]) only touches upon the family as its main concern is with "corner men."

[3] *The Children of Sanchez* (New York: Random House, 1961) and *Five Families* (New York: Science Editions, Inc., 1962).

terms of a simple "fatherless-complete" typology.[4] Consequently Hylan
Lewis had to say recently, "in focusing on family homes . . . the present
father tends to be forgotten. Forgotten also is the fact that we know very
little about him."[5]

Negro family structure has been studied more intensively in the Caribbean. Here the work has been motivated to a large extent by a concern to
determine if patterns of nonresidential mating do or do not indicate a
breakdown or "disorganization" of the family—a concern originating in the
markedly high rates of illegitimacy.[6]

Several types of mating patterns are described. Hyman Rodman, for
example, found that the natives of Coconut Village distinguished between
three types of "marital" relations: "friending," "living," and "married."[7]
Friending was a nonresidential pattern similar to one called "visiting" by
Roberts and Braithwaite.[8]

The concern of the present study, however, is to describe and analyze
some of the variations in the husband-father role in the category that is
ordinarily thought of as "married."[9]

The Sample

The field work focused upon 10 lower-class Negro families living in a
large public housing project in a midwestern city. Five of the families were
complete, five were fatherless.[10] The age of the parents ranged from 33 to
55. All except two families had teenage children living in the households.
The size of the families varied from six to 18 persons and the households
from five to 18 persons. The latter included some kin at times but no other

[4]This tendency is heightened by the accessibility of Census data. A good idea of the extent to which this
dichotomy is considered central to the study of the lower-class Negro family is provided in Thomas
Pettigrew, *Profile of the Negro American* (Princeton, N.J.: D. Van Nostrand, Inc., 1964) on page 15 and
following. The issue of the relevance of this simple typology was brought forward in the controversy over
the Department of Labor's *The Negro Family: The Case for National Action*, now attributed to Daniel
Patrick Moynihan.

[5]Lee Rainwater and William Yancy, *The Moynihan Report and the Politics of Controversy* (Boston: MIT
Press, 1967), p. 322.

[6]For a summary of this work see Raymond T. Smith, "Cultural and Social Structure in the Caribbean:
Some Recent Work on Family and Kinship Studies" in *Comparative Studies in Society and History* (The
Hague, The Netherlands: Mouton & Co., Oct., 1963).

[7]"Marital Relationships in a Trinidad Village," *Journal of Marriage and Family Living*, 23 (May, 1961),
pp. 166–170.

[8]"A Cross-Mating Table for a West Indian Population," *Population Studies*, 14:3 (1961).

[9]John F. Cuber and Peggy B. Harroff develop a fivefold typology of marriage for the upper middle class
that parallels in several respects this attempt, particularly in their discussion of the "conflict habituated" type
of marriage which seems similar to this study's "indiscreet free-man." See "The More Total View: Relationships Among Men and Women of the Upper Middle Class," in Hyman Rodman, ed., *Marriage, Family and
Society: A Reader* (New York: Random House, 1961).

[10]In the project 54 percent of the families were headed by females. See Jerome Stromberg, *A Preliminary
Report on Housing and Community Experience: Occasional Paper # 1* (St. Louis: The Social Science
Institute of Washington University, 1966). Lefcowitz estimates that only about 23 percent of the entire
lower-class Negro family population was headed by females in 1960. See "Poverty and Negro-White Family
Structure," paper presented to the White House Conference, "To Fulfill These Rights," 1965.

boarders. Although about 88 persons lived in these households during most of the study, only three of the households remained relatively stable in size. Data were collected on all household members and most family members.

Methodology

The majority of the data on these households were collected by means of participant observation[11] and open-ended interviewing. While the researcher did not live with the families, he did spend about 250 ten-hour days on site interacting with the family members in various ways—sometimes obviously studying them and asking direct questions, at other times just enjoying their company at home, in a bar, or on the street. Extensive biographies were taken of all parents and many teenaged members of the households, and the assessment of the role played by the father in each household was based upon information obtained from most, if not all, family members plus observations of family interaction. All periods of the waking day were covered in most families, and in one the researcher was invited to spend the night.

Whenever possible a tape recorder was used to record conversations and interviews. Notes were made on all encounters. To supplement the information obtained from family members and to provide additional perspectives on the families, data were obtained from the files of the Housing Authority, the schools, and the police.

A Typology of Marginality

As an exploratory study attempting to document the variety to be found in lower-class Negro family life, the first objective was to describe each family. This objective alone could easily result in ten case studies. Indeed, each family has enough distinctive characteristics to be considered by some researchers as a separate culture.[12] To dichotomize the 10 families simply into "complete" and "fatherless," however, is to grossly oversimplify. A useful compromise can be achieved if one looks at the husband-father role in terms of several significant variables: (1) the "strength" of the conjugal bond, (2) the support given by the father to his family and (3) the relationship of the father to the children. At this stage of the research, none of these variables was rigorously defined or measured, but an immense amount of qualitative data[13] has enabled the researcher to make and support judgments about the relative placement of these families along the dimension of

[11] In point of fact neither detached observation nor totally immersed participation was ever achieved; the working balance always tended toward one or the other pole.

[12] Jules Henry, "An Anthropological Approach to Cultural Idiosyncratic and Universal Factors in Behavior," *American Anthropologist.*

[13] The researcher's personal notes on observations and interviews exceed 2,500 type-written pages and the data on the larger study exceed 20,000 pages.

adult male marginality. The 10 families suggest six types. This article describes the three types of "complete" families.[14]

The Indiscreet Free-man

The most marginal type of father observed is the indiscreet free-man.[15] What is apparent in his relationship to his family is a split in allegiance between his legitimate family and one or more "illegitimate" families. This outside interest is continually paraded before his wife and family either in a constant, chiding reference to the "other woman" or by the deliberate eigineering of an encounter with her. His interests outside the family are reflected in his spending on behalf of the other woman and, if he has had children by her, a regular amount of money may be set aside each month in their behalf—regardless of whether or not the court has intervened—or, more commonly, he will buy shoes, clothing, and gifts for them from time to time. Such a father's interests have repercussions upon his legitimate children, creating an intensified kind of sibling rivalry with his "outside" children who, in some instances, are known personally by his legitimate children. Life within such families is thus one of constant conflict and bickering. That the family stays intact at all is probably related to (1) the advancing age of the wife which, combined with her many children, makes her less and less attractive to other men and more and more destined to head a household should her husband leave, (2) her continuing hope that he will reform his ways, and (3) his positive, if sporadic contributions in support and affection to his family.

Two families fit this type: the Pattersons and the Boikens. Illustration from the Patterson case will suffice. They had been married 22 years; he was 45, she was 42. They had 18 children including eight "outsiders."[16] All but two were his by other women. Their present household included eight children in age from 9 to 19. Mr. Patterson's earnings as a machine operator for a local automobile manufacturer accounted for $5,593 of the family's $6,072 annual income; his wife's earnings accounted for the balance. He was in complete charge of the money and allowances, expecting his wife to live within her allowance, adequate or not.

About four years ago he left his family to live with another woman by whom he sired two children. Prior to that, in 1965, his wife had had him put in the workhouse for six months for nonsupport while he was living with

---

[14] The researcher is greatly indebted to Lee Rainwater's "notes" entitled "Three Patterns of Separateness and Connectedness in Lower-Class Families: A Typology" although the typology presented in this study is a modification of his. The sixfold typology derived from these families is as follows: monogamous, discreet free-man, indiscreet free-man, quasi-father, supportive biological father, and supportive companion. A seventh and most marginal type, the pimp, was described by the family members but not observed. The last four types are discussed in David A. Schulz and Lee Rainwater, "The Role of the Boyfriend in Lower-Class Negro Life," paper presented to the Midwest Sociological Society, Des Moines, Iowa, 1967.

[15] This type resembles the type of father described as Jesus Sanchez by Lewis in *Children of Sanchez.*

[16] As the term is used in the project it means "outside a particular relationship" which ordinarily terminated in marriage—not simply "outside of wedlock."

another woman. His spending, even when he was at home, extended to his several "outside" children, a fact that was fully and painfully known by his wife and legitimate children. When he was at home he generally was shunned by his family and usually ate alone.

He once commented on his marriage:

I would say that if I had to do it all over again, I don't think I would select this route that I have gone. It hasn't been too pleasant at all times. I mean there's a ruling to everything. You can't run what's in the house and what's on the outside of the house both at the same time . . . so I don't know whether I came in the house too much or whether I stayed on the outside too long. It's a problem somewhere. . . . I don't think it would get serious enough where it would cause another separation. . . . [You] make the best out of what you have. . . . I can walk, shun them, a lot easier than the other person could shun me.

His wife's account of their marriage reflected his indiscretion more vividly:

Well before we came to the city my husband and I were separated three times on the sake of fighting. He used to fight me all the time. He was in the city about nine months before I came. When I came up he was living with another woman at my uncle's house. . . . I have never walked out in front of him, but this lady he used to live with, he have had her right out in front of my door. . . . I asked him not to do it again because he seemed like he was boasting about it. And the next time he did it . . . I got a gun and started down the steps and he ran down there by the car. But by the time I got down under the building he had done pulled off.

His relationships with his children were also strained, particularly those with his older boys, who generally took the side of their mother against him. Their oldest boy once lived with the family, but he moved out about midway in this study in order to avoid a fight with his father, who at the last encounter had "hit him up side of the head with a shoe." After that Patterson's wife claimed that when he walked in the door, "the actual sight of him made me nervous . . . because I had a fear of his ways."

The older girls, on the other hand, tried to cover up the family feuding as much as possible, stressing the fact that their father "will still give" to them. His 18-year-old daughter, B., noted "every family has its ups and downs . . . some parents be arguing and fighting all the time . . . but they don't hardly quarrel. . . . One of them will walk away from it. I guess because they have us and don't want to be setting a bad example in front of us." The implied denial could not, even for B., cover up Patterson's obvious and flagrant infidelity, which lay at the base of the family conflict. Mr. Patterson's indiscretion as a free-man made his home all but intolerable for him, and a source of embarrassment and hurt for his wife and children as well.

The Discreet Free-man

In contrast to the indiscreet free-man, the discreet free-man's "cutting out" is clearly a secondary concern, which he does not use to antagonize his wife and children. As a result his indiscretions are understood and both partners are likely to admit "we get along well enough." His relationship to his children is not particularly impaired as a result of his interests outside the home and they often look upon him as an ideal father. Typically, just as he is able to cover up or minimize his activities with other women, so also he is able to carry on deviant activities such as gambling or pimping without these appreciably interfering with his home life. The relationship can be considered as a separate type, therefore, because it does not result simply from the fact that the "old man" has not been caught yet. His indiscretions are known to his wife and family, but he manages in such a way as not to antagonize them, and thus maintains a relatively comfortable relationship with his legitimate family, which persists over time.

Two families fit this type: The Washingtons and the Bardwells. The Washingtons can provide the illustration. The researcher knew them for over three and one-half years and only toward the end of the study discovered why he knew comparatively little about them. Mr. Washington, 51, and seven of his boys had long police records connected mainly with gambling and narcotics. The father had once been "sent up" for possession of lottery equipment. Nevertheless, the home was neat, well kept, and his children well mannered. An impression of warmth and intimacy was characteristic of their interactions. He and his wife, who was 47, had been married 26 years and for 19 of these years Mr. Washington had been the major wage earner. During the time of the study he supplemented his wife's earnings as a domestic through efforts at odd jobs and through gambling. Neither source of income was reported in the family's annual income of $4,370. The Washingtons had 12 children including two "outsiders" born before they married.

Mr. Washington said that he had managed to stay married 26 years because "we don't raise a lot of cain. If a little something happens we don't jump down each other's throat." He expressed his conception of marital fidelity in a way that implied he "cuts out" but does not play the field and does not brag about his antics in front of his wife:

I am this type of fellow. I talk to anyone before my wife or behind my wife. But just to go out and say I've got a bunch of women and that type of thing, that's all baloney. . . . I see some women that look good to me, sure, and if you push it you can get caught in the right corner and you might step out. You're human and you're a good one if you don't. If you just go out and strive directly for that then you're going to find somebody that wants to do these things. The average woman that does it ain't doing it because she likes to but because she wants to do something just like you . . . something different . . . it's not a big deal.

His wife presented a complementary picture of tolerating his discreet outside activities:

I think I've been a nice lady. I ain't bragging on myself, but it takes a steady head I guess. I never was a wild person and like to get in the streets. I stayed home and took care of my children . . . I didn't leave my children to nobody.

One impressive indicator of the control parents were able to exercise over themselves and their children was their willingness not to exchange gifts as Christmas time. Mr. Washington said, "It's pretty rough when you know everybody else is receiving them and giving them and you're not . . . but if you understand life . . . you just have to grit your teeth and say, 'Well we doing the best we can, and thank the Lord.' "

Finally, instead of denouncing his delinquent children, as many parents did, Mr. Washington said of his oldest boy, who had the longest record, "He's just another one of my kids regardless of the troubles he's been in. Maybe he made a mistake and maybe he didn't. Maybe he just got the wrong break. That happens too. Sometimes to the best of people."

The family, despite what went on outside, was a central concern for all its members, and Mr. Washington's discretion in handling what went on outside was a major factor in its continuing relative stability.

The Monogamous Father

The last type of father is called the monogamous type because he is proud of the fact that he is able to say, "Where you see me, you will see my wife." This type, although rare in fact, is reflected in the data in numerous references to its desirability. In such a family the father does not "cut out" and if he has had any "outside" children they are the result of youthful indiscretions and not of his violation of monogamous marriage. His home and family are his major concerns and receive his constant attention. Typically, such fathers have good relationships with their children and high status in the family regardless of their ability to earn a living.

Only one family fitted this type in the data: the Fraziers. They had been married 20 years, were the least urbanized of the families studied (lived in the city only seven years) and were the only family in which the father was younger than the mother. He was 37, she 40. He, nevertheless, was an advocate of the patriarchal type of family and his wishes in this regard were respected.[17] Because of illiteracy and a fear of the streets the family spent

[17] In his article "The Impact of Urban Civilization upon Negro Family Life," *American Sociological Review*, 2 (1939), E. Franklin Frazier described a type of family organization originating in rural southern communities of Negro, white, and Indian ancestry that was relatively isolated from the main currents of Negro life and that maintained a strictly patriarchal tradition. The Fraziers seem to have been influenced by this tradition.

most of its time inside the small row apartment it had rented in the heart of the city—the last of five residences in which they lived during the last two years of the study. Mr. Frazier received disability checks and his wife received ADC, giving the family an annual income of $4,896 for a family of 11.

For both of the Fraziers "cutting out" was unheard of. They believed that for the parents to do so would result in their complete inability to control their children. Mr. Frazier said:

I have been to lots of houses and I've seen some pretty rough deals with kids. I'll tell you what that come from. That comes from mother and daddy. If you do any and everything over your child you can't expect no better can you? . . . I don't let my children see me do no wrong thing. . . . I'm not playing [cutting out]. I ain't got nane that can tell you that today. They ain't never seen daddy come in here drunk, cussing, clowning, or nothing. They'll tell you that right now. Daddy is going to come in here as he leaves.

Being thus strong believers in teaching children by example rather than precept, both Fraziers labored to keep themselves respectable "in front of the children" for they knew that the accusation "Mamma, you and Daddy do it" had no acceptable reply—"It ain't nothing for us to say." Thus despite his educational handicaps and his poor earning power, Mr. Frazier was very well thought of in his family and his children were well behaved. The Frazier family was a warm, intimate shelter from the harsh realities of the street and if they had the legitimate earning capacity to become upwardly mobile, such a family would have followed the style of living more characteristic of the working-class nuclear family. Ironically, however, given their economic status, their conception of appropriate family living was a handicap in teaching the children how to cope with the world in which they found themselves. Thus they obtained a degree of intimacy at the expense of acquiring effective survival techniques.

Marginality and the Mode of Legitimating Authority

An interesting aspect of the internal dynamics of these families was the fact that each type of father made his claim to hold authority in the household on somewhat different grounds.

(1) The monogamous father tended to legitimate his authority on the basis of two more or less equal aspects of his relationship to the external world: his ability as an adequate provider (or the fact that his inability to provide was "understood"), and his ability to say, "There ain't nane that can speak slack of me"—that is, he was an adequate model for respectable behavior. He was not an adaptive strategist because he had been able to

"make it" by legitimate means and because his principles prohibited him from being one.

(2) The "discreetly free" fathers, on the other hand, tended to legitimate their authority within the household on the basis of being warm, loving "pals" to their children and expressive companions to more instrumentally oriented wives. They tended also to be able to muster respect for their ability to cope with the environment by means of manipulative strategies such as gambling, "working game" on friends, and discreet affairs with other women, which provided them with victories their sons would have liked to emulate. They were, or at one time had been, adequate providers and their current disability was understood by their families. They expressed concern for "skeletons" in the family closet, indicating they would have liked to draw upon past respectable behavior to provide an example for their children, but could not.

(3) The "indiscreet" fathers had least control over their children because they had little to justify their authority. If they were able to provide for their family, this ability was marred by their split in allegiance. If they were unable, their disability was not accepted and they had to prefabricate an instrumental role in order to protect themselves in this vulnerable area—thus Mr. Boiken, though unemployed, thought of himself as earning $150 a week, the amount earned by the construction crew with which he once worked. They generally had little justification for authority on the basis of their expressive ability, and none as a model for traditional respectable behavior.

Conclusion

In an exploratory study based primarily upon such a small number of families the conclusions drawn can only be suggestive. However, the father in lower-class Negro families does not appear to be simply subordinate to his wife, as the term "matriarchal" would indicate and the term "matrifocal" might imply. His status, these data suggest, depends not only upon his capacity to earn a living and his further willingness to share that living with his family, but also upon the degree of his adherence to the norms of monogamous marriage, his ability to cope with the harsh realities of the ghetto, and his capacity to be a pal to his children. The family that seems best able to survive as a family unit in a situation where there is little hope of upward mobility or of sufficient income from legitimate sources is the family that is best able to cope with its environment as it presents itself. In such a family the father is typically the discreet free-man.

The cohesiveness of such families in spite of their extreme openness to the life of the street was a source of constant amazement to the researcher, and the extent of the father's influence, particularly as a model for effective coping behavior, was greater than expected.

Zena Smith Blau: Exposure to
Child Rearing Experts: A
Structural Interpretation of Class-
Color Differences[1]

The writings of experts bearing on diverse realms of behavior, transmitted by the mass media, constitute a major mechanism for the diffusion of new information and ideas in contemporary societies. As yet, however, we have achieved little systematic understanding of the social processes by which exposure to this source of innovation comes about, or about the related problem of the processes that lead to the adoption of the ideas advocated.

In a recent article reviewing the present status of research concerning the diffusion of innovation Katz, Levin, and Hamilton comment that "very few studies have been done on the basic problem of comparing the ways in which different kinds of structural arrangements within a group condition the diffusion of a given item."[2] They go on to suggest some of the ways in which social structures may condition the diffusion process. Their idea that social structure implies, among other things, the existence of boundaries which differentiate "the frequency and character of social relations"[3] and thus constitute barriers to diffusion comes very close to the central problem with which the present paper deals—the analysis of selected structural attributes of class-color groups and how they facilitate or hinder the exposure of their members to the writings of a body of experts in the realm of child-rearing. More specifically, the substantive problem is to provide a structural interpretation of a pattern of differences between Negro and white middle- and working-class mothers in their exposure to the writings of child-rearing experts, in their attendance at child-care classes, and in their attitudes toward experts.

Child-rearing studies have repeatedly shown that the class position and educational level of mothers condition their exposure to diverse sources of formal and informal information and advice.[4] Although these findings were based, for the most part, on samples of white women, there was every reason

Reprinted from *American Journal of Sociology*, 69 (May 1964), pp. 596-608, with permission of the author and The University of Chicago Press. Copyright 1964, The University of Chicago. Zena Smith Blau is Professor of Sociology at The University of Illinois.

[1]This study was supported in part by National Institute of Mental Health, Public Health Service Research Grant 07316–01, and in part by a grant from the University of Illinois Graduate College Research Board. I also wish to acknowledge the assistance of Arlene Krieger and former Dean Emily C. Cardew, of the University of Illinois College of Nursing, and the advice of James A. Davis, Jacob J. Feldman, and Harold Levy, of the National Opinion Research Center, during early phases of the research.

[2]Elihu Katz, Martin L. Levin, and Herbert Hamilton, "Traditions of Research on the Diffusion of Innovation," *American Sociological Review*, XXVIII (April, 1963), 248.

[3]*Ibid.*, p. 247.

[4]See, e.g., Martha Sturm White, "Social Class, Child Rearing Practices, and Child Behavior," *American Sociological Review*, XXII (December, 1957), 704–12; Melvin L. Kohn, "Social Class and Parent-Child Relationships: An Interpretation," *American Journal of Sociology*, LXVIII (January, 1963), 471–80; and esp. Urie Bronfenbrenner, "Socialization and Social Class through Time and Space," in Eleanor F. Maccoby,

to believe that they would apply as well to Negro women of similar class position and educational level.

Indeed, color differences in the realm of child-rearing had largely ceased to be a matter of specific research interest after Davis and Havighurst reported, in a pioneering study published in 1946, that they found few differences in the child-rearing practices of Negro and white mothers who occupied similar class positions.[5] Although their study did not deal with the problem of exposure to experts' writings it seems to have been assumed by the researchers who followed them that the pattern of findings would extend to this kind of behavior as well. However, in the last decade several studies of class differences in the child-rearing patterns of white mothers have reported findings which contradict those of Davis and Havighurst.[6] Whatever the reason for these discrepancies, they suggest the need for taking a new look at the problem of class-color differences in child-rearing, and especially for bringing to bear on this question some of the new modes of sociological analysis that have been developed since the appearance of the early Chicago study.

The study of which the present paper is a part does not replicate the content of the Davis and Havighurst study, but it has a similar sample design.[7] A quota sample of 224 mothers, selected on the basis of race, class position,[8] and parity, was interviewed during the period of confinement on the maternity floors of three large, centrally located hospitals in Chicago during 1961–62. One section of the interview schedule contained a series of questions about the extent and nature of respondents' exposure to various mass media and to child-rearing content in these sources. Some of these data are presented in the analysis that follows.

Exposure to Child-Rearing Literature

An index of the extent of exposure to child-rearing literature was obtained by combining the scores assigned to answers to three questions: the fre-

---

Theodore M. Newcomb, and Eugene L. Hartley (eds.), *Readings in Social Psychology* (New York: Henry Holt & Co., 1958), pp. 400–425, which presents a review of many child-rearing studies and a provocative discussion of how reading the experts may promote changes in child-rearing.

[5] Allison Davis and Robert J. Havighurst, "Social Class and Color Differences in Child Rearing," *American Sociological Review*, XI (1946), 698–710.

[6] E.g., Robert K. Sears, Eleanor E. Maccoby, and Harry Levin, *Patterns of Child Rearing* (Evanston, Ill.: Row, Peterson & Co. 1957), and White, *op. cit.*; for an interpretation of these inconsistencies see Bronfenbrenner, *op. cit.*

[7] The original design called for fifty cases each of middle-class and working-class white and Negro mothers, one third having had only one child and the rest having had more than one. However, we could not locate as many Negro middle-class mothers as planned (although we remained in the field longer in an attempt to do so), and decided instead to obtain more interviews with women in the other three class-color categories in order to prevent undue shrinkage of the sample. Conclusions based on so small a sample, particularly of Negro middle-class mothers, are admittedly tentative and are presented merely as hypotheses which still need to be tested on a more adequate sample.

[8] The index of class position is based on husband's occupation. Respondents whose husbands are engaged in non-manual occupations are classified as middle class, and those whose husbands are in manual occupations are defined as working class.

Table 1. Child-Rearing Media Exposure Scores in Four Class-Color Groups (Percent)

Exposure	Middle Class		Working Class	
	White	Negro	White	Negro
Low	13	32	38	56
Medium	19	47	30	18
High	48	21	32	6
Total percent	100	100	100	100
No. of cases	(83)	(19)	(56)	(66)

quency with which respondents read child-rearing articles (1) in their daily newspapers and (2) in magazines, and (3) whether they have read Dr. Benjamin Spock's book, *Baby and Child Care.*[9] "High" exposure (a score of 3 or 4) signifies regular readership of child-rearing articles in at least one of the mass media, and of Spock's book. "Medium" exposure (a score of 1 or 2) indicates regular readership of such articles in at least one of the mass media, or only of Dr. Spock's book; and "low" exposure (a score of 0) indicates that a respondent has not read Spock and does not ordinarily read child-rearing articles.[10]

Table 1 shows that the extent of exposure to child-rearing literature is influenced by both the class position and color of mothers. White mothers expose themselves more to this kind of literature than Negro mothers, both in the middle and in the working class, and exposure is more prevalent in the middle class than in the working class, independent of skin color. In other words, the woman with no regular exposure to child-rearing literature is highly exceptional in the white middle class, considerably less so in the Negro middle class and white working class, but in a majority in the Negro working class.[11] The difference between Negro and white mothers in *extent* of exposure to child-rearing content stems in part from the difference be-

[9] The individual questions were cross-tabulated and scored in the following way: a score of 1 each was given if a respondent regularly read child-rearing articles in a daily newspaper or in any magazine mentioned, and a score of 2 was given to those who had read Dr. Spock's book, on the assumption that the latter covers at least as wide a range of content and has at least as much impact as the other two sources taken together. Respondents were also asked about their exposure to the well-known pamphlet, *Infant Care,* published by the U.S. Children's Bureau, but so few had read it (33 respondents) that it was not included in the exposure index. Two open-ended questions concerning other sources read by respondents yielded even fewer returns.

[10] No value judgment that mothers ought to read child-rearing literature is implied here, nor are any a priori assumptions made about the impact of this literature on the child-rearing practices of mothers variously located in the social structure. The latter problem will be dealt with in a forthcoming paper.

[11] The Negro-white differences in exposure to child-rearing content are not due to differences in extent of exposure per se to newspapers and magazines. Analysis of scores on a mass-media exposure index, based on the frequency of newspaper and magazine reading, indicates that the exposure of respondents varies primarily with class position and only slightly with color. Thus the proportions of respondents who read both a newspaper and a magazine regularly, or one regularly and the other occasionally, are 82 percent among whites and 79 percent among Negroes in the middle class and 59 percent and 54 percent, respectively, in the working class. Also of interest is our finding that none of the Negro respondents exposes herself *exclusively* to Negro publications. Only five respondents read the *Chicago Defender,* the local daily Negro newspaper (which, incidentally, does not carry a column on child care) and all these also read at least one of the four daily Chicago newspapers.

tween them in the *kind* of media to which they expose themselves, specifi-cally their use of Dr. Spock's book. Separate analysis of the proportions who have read this book shows that among white middle-class mothers the overwhelming majority (77 percent) have read the book, but in the Negro middle class the proportion is strikingly smaller (32 percent): indeed it is lower than in the white working class (48 percent). The smallest proportion of Spock readers is found among Negro working-class mothers (12 per-cent).[12]

It is well known, of course, that book readership is more widespread in the middle class than in the working class, particularly among the better edu-cated. Higher education, in turn, is more widespread among whites than among Negroes in the middle class. For example, among middle-class re-spondents in our study only 8 percent of the whites but 37 percent of the Negroes have not completed high school and 69 percent and 21 percent, respectively, have had some college education. In the working class, on the other hand, the level of education of white and Negro mothers is virtually identical. Fifty-five percent in each color group have not completed high school; and 9 percent and 8 percent, respectively, have had some college education. But the differences in exposure to Dr. Spock's book between Negroes and whites persist, for the most part, even when educational back-ground of respondents is controlled. Table 2 shows that at each educational level in both classes the proportion of mothers who have read Spock is higher among whites than among Negroes, although in the middle class the size of the differences between the two color groups diminishes considerably as educational level rises. In the working class, the difference in readership between Negroes and whites is greatest among high-school graduates. It can

Table 2. Percentage Who Read Spock, by Class, Color, and Educational Level

	Education*			Difference	
Class and Color	Grades 8–11 (1)	High-School Graduate (2)	Attended College (3)	Col.(2) Minus Col. (1)	Col. (3) Minus Col. (2)
Middle class					
White	57 (7)	68 (19)	82 (57)	11	14
Negro	0 (7)	37 (8)	†	37	—
Difference	57	31			
Working class					
White	39 (31)	60 (20)	60 (5)	21	0
Negro	8 (36)	12 (35)	40 (5)	4	28
Difference	31	48	20		

*N's are given in parentheses.

†Three of the four Negro middle-class respondents who attended college have read Dr. Spock's book.

[12] Respondents were first asked whether they had ever heard of Dr. Spock's book. The proportions who had never heard of the book were only 5 percent in the white middle class, but 37 percent in both the Negro middle class and the white working class, and 65 percent in the Negro working class. It is interesting that, although identical proportions of white working-class and Negro middle-class women knew about the book, fewer in the latter group had read it.

also be seen that, while each of the three variables—class, color, and educational level—independently affects exposure to Spock's book, the magnitude
of differences between Negro and white mothers in most cases is greater
than between mothers of comparable educational background in the two
classes, or between respondents at different educational levels within the
same class. It is noteworthy that in the middle class the differences in the
proportions of Negro and white mothers who have read Spock diminish
considerably as educational level increases. But in the working class the
largest difference between Negro and white mothers occurs among the high-
school graduates, because the proportion of white mothers who have read
Spock is as high in this group as among those with some college education,
whereas among Negro mothers this proportion is considerably higher
among the college-educated than among high school graduates. In other
words, readership of this source of child-rearing information varies more
with education among Negro than among white mothers. But it is apparent
that educational differences do not account for the large variance between
the two color groups with respect to readership of Spock's book.[13]

Attendance at Mothers' Classes

The pattern of differences between Negro and white mothers in exposure
to child-rearing literature also extends to their attendance at mothers'
classes, which many hospitals run for the benefit of maternity patients.
Patients are ordinarily invited to attend classes during either their pregnancy or confinement, and in some cases at both times. The decision to
attend or not is left up to the patient with the result, as a number of studies
have shown, that middle-class women attend these classes more frequently
than working-class women.[14]

Respondents in the present study were asked: "Have you ever attended
any classes or groups dealing with the care of infants either before or since
you have had your baby?" Mothers who had not attended classes were
asked: "Were you ever approached or invited to join such a group or class?"
These questions were asked to ascertain whether differences in attendance
might reflect class or color bias on the part of hospital personnel rather than
self-selection on the part of respondents themselves.

Table 3 shows that higher proportions of white than of Negro mothers
attended classes, regardless of class position, and that attendance varied
little with class position. The differences between the two color groups
evidently do not reflect discriminatory treatment of Negro maternity patients, since the proportion of those not invited to join classes is no higher
among Negro than among white respondents.

[13]Similar differences occur between Negro and white respondents of like class position and educational
background on the composite index of exposure (see Table 6).

[14]See, e.g., D. Mann, L. Woodward, and N. Joseph, *Educating Expectant Parents* (New York: Visiting
Nurse Service, 1961), and A. Yankauer, W. Boek, E. Shaffer, and D. Clark, "What Mothers Say about
Childbearing and Parent Classes," *Nursing Outlook,*VIII (October, 1960), 563–65.

Table 3. Attendance at Mothers' Classes, by Class and Color (Percent)

		Middle Class		Working Class	
Invited	Attended	White	Negro	White	Negro
Yes	Yes	52	21	42	21
	No	13	63	18	38
No	No	35	16	38	36
No answer	No	0	0	2	5
Total per cent		100	100	100	100
No. of cases		83	19	56	66

Attitudes toward Experts

The question arises whether the pattern of differences between Negro and white mothers in their exposure to formal sources of information may simply reflect different evaluations on their part of the importance of expert advice in the realm of child care and child-rearing. One might expect that the greater exposure of white mothers, particularly those in the middle class, to various sources of information reflects a belief on their part that they can thereby enhance the effectiveness of their behavior in the maternal role, while Negro women may expose themselves less to such sources because they are less inclined to share this opinion. The data, however, contradict this assumption.

Respondents were asked: "Some mothers feel it's important to find out what the experts (like doctors, psychologists, etc.) have to say about raising children while others don't think that is necessary. What do you think?" Responses were classified as generally favorable (e.g., "experts have more knowledge or experience"), unfavorable (e.g., "I don't believe in raising children by the book" or "mothers know best"), or ambivalent (e.g., "it does not hurt to get their ideas, but I'll use my own judgment"). Table 4 shows, contrary to expectation, that favorable attitudes toward child-rearing experts are expressed more frequently by Negro mothers in both the middle and the working class. Negative sentiments, on the other hand, occur slightly more often among whites. Ambivalent attitudes are more frequent among middle-class women, both white and Negro, than among those in the working class.

Table 4. Attitude toward Experts, by Class and Color (Percent)

Attitude toward Child-Rearing Experts	Middle Class		Working Class	
	White	Negro	White	Negro
Favorable	45	63	52	62
Ambivalent	23	16	12	5
Unfavorable	31	21	32	27
NA	1	0	4	6
Total percent	100	100	100	100
No. of cases	83	19	56	66

That Negro women express favorable attitudes toward child-rearing experts more often than white women, regardless of class position, but typically expose themselves less to such informational sources seems contradictory and might even be dismissed as simply another instance of the known tendency of respondents in low-prestige groups to express agreement more readily, regardless of item content, in the interview situation.[15] But some recent evidence of a similar order suggests another explanation, which turns out to be more fruitful for understanding the dynamic interplay of attitudes and behavior toward experts among mothers in different social contexts.

In a recent National Opinion Research Center study of public attitudes toward medical care, Feldman found that people who have more contact with physicians are also more critical of them than those with less contact.[16] More recently, in a study of attitudes toward fluoridation in a Massachusetts community, Gamson and Schuman reported that respondents who accord physicians high-prestige rankings in comparison with other professionals also express hostile sentiments toward them more frequently than those who give them lower rankings.[17] One explanation for this ambivalence suggested by the authors is that "the very standards that lead to high prestige may cause physicians to be judged against criteria that are exceedingly difficult to meet. The stronger a respondent feels about the importance of such standards the more he is likely to accord prestige to physicians as against other occupations but to judge physicians severely by these same standards."[18]

By the same token, white mothers may be more prone than Negro mothers to express ambivalence toward child-rearing experts precisely because they depend more on them for guidance, as indicated by the fact that they expose themselves more to the writings of experts. Indeed, a comparison of mothers' attitudes toward experts according to mothers' exposure scores in each of the four class-color groups lends support to this interpretation (see Table 5). It shows that in each class-color group, the proportion who express ambivalence toward experts is greater among respondents who have high- or medium-exposure scores than among those with low-exposure scores. The original differences noted in Table 4 between Negro and white mothers virtually disappear in the middle class, and become smaller in the working class, among respondents who expose themselves to experts' writings.

Among those with low exposure to this literature, on the contrary, the differences in ambivalence and particularly in negativism between white and Negro women become *more* pronounced. Unfavorable sentiments are voiced more often by mothers who do not read the experts in three of the four groups—all except the middle-class Negroes. But among mothers with low exposure negative attitudes are expressed considerably more often by

---

[15]See, e.g., Gerhard E. Lenski and John C. Leggett, "Caste, Class, and Deference in the Research Interview," *American Journal of Sociology*, LXV (March, 1960), 463–67.

[16]Jacob J. Feldman, "What Americans Think about Their Medical Care," American Statistical Association, Proceedings of the Social Statistics Section Meeting (December, 1958).

[17]William A. Gamson and Howard Schuman, "Some Undercurrents in the Prestige of Physicians," *American Journal of Sociology*, LXVIII (January 1963), 463–70.

[18]*Ibid.*, p. 469.

Table 5. Percent Ambivalent and Percent Unfavorable toward Experts, by Exposure Score, Class, and Color

Exposure	Middle Class				Working Class			
	White		Negro		White		Negro	
Percent of total with medium and high scores	87		68		63		44	
			Percent Ambivalent					
Low	18	(11)	0	(6)	10	(21)	0	(37)
Medium and high	24	(72)	23	(13)	14	(35)	10	(29)
			Percent Unfavorable					
Low	55	(11)	17	(6)	43	(21)	33	(37)
Medium and high	28	(72)	23	(13)	26	(35)	21	(29)

whites, particularly in the middle class, than by Negroes. This suggests that the woman who does not "read the experts" but is located in a social millieu where this practice is prevalent feels called upon to justify her deviance by denigrating experts. Thus, in the white middle class where the pattern of reading child-rearing literature is most prevalent, women with low-exposure scores are most often negative toward experts.[19] In the white working class where this pattern is less widespread women with low exposure scores exhibit negative attitudes correspondingly less often. Exposure to experts' writings is least prevalent among Negro mothers in the working class. Consequently, Negro women who do not read this literature do not feel constrained to rationalize their indifference to expert opinion by denying its value. This difference in social context may well explain why Negro women with lower exposure scores express hostility toward experts considerably less often than their white counterparts.

Class Mobility and Color Differences

The pattern of high exposure to the writings of child-rearing experts is more prevalent among white middle-class mothers than among Negro middle-class mothers with a similar amount of formal education (see Table 6).[20] In fact, even white working-class women who have not completed high school have high-exposure scores nearly as often as women with more education in the Negro middle class. Differences in the constitution of the middle classes and the working classes in the two color groups, and their implications for acculturation to middle-class modes of behavior, may help to explain the differences noted above.

[19] The proportion of mothers in the Negro middle class who express negative sentiments is lower than in the white middle class, as expected. But contrary to expectation, it is also lower than in the other strata.

[20] The sample contains four cases of Negro middle-class mothers who have had some college education. Only one of them has a high-exposure score compared to 58 percent among *white* middle-class respondents who have attended college.

Reliance on experts' writings is part of a larger complex of orientations and modes of behavior that differentiate the child-rearing patterns of middle-class mothers from those in the working class in white society.[21] We would therefore expect to find this pattern more prevalent among women of middle-class origin than among those of working-class origin who have moved into the middle class.[22] Table 7 shows that high exposure is in fact considerably more frequent among the stationary members of the white middle class (59 percent) than among the upwardly mobile (32 percent). Her newly won middle-class status does not automatically lead a woman to emulate the less visible forms of behavior that prevail among her established class peers. The acculturation process in this realm of behavior, as in others, requires opportunities for association with established members of the middle class in the course of which social pressure can be exerted upon the new members to adopt middle-class ways. Since the stationary members constitute the majority in the white middle class, such social opportunities would seem to be readily available to the upwardly mobile woman. And the fact that the tenure of the stationary members in the middle class has been of longer duration and that they are apt to be better educated further enhances their ability to influence the incoming members of their group. Thus, the pattern of reliance on experts could be expected to spread by degrees among the upwardly mobile as they acquire longer tenure in their new position, resulting in closer conformity to the behavior of their stationary peers.

A comparison of the exposure scores of upwardly mobile white women with those of similar origin who have remained in the working class constitutes a crude test of this hypothesis. Although there is little difference in high exposure, the proportion with some exposure (high or medium) is considerably greater among the upwardly mobile (89 percent) than among stationary members of the working class (55 percent), which indicates that the former have assimilated the middle-class pattern to some degree—although not to the full extent, since *high* exposure is less widespread among them than among the stationary members of the middle class. Thus, the data lend support to our hypothesis concerning the acculturation effects that accompany upward mobility into the white middle class.

[21] That this practice is in fact more prevalent in the white middle than working class has been shown by a number of studies besides this one. See, e.g., White, *op. cit.*, and Kohn, *op. cit.* The latter study also contains a suggestive interpretation of these observed patterns of differences as reflections of differences in the value systems that prevail among the two strata.

[22] Class origin is defined by father's occupation when the respondent was sixteen years old. Respondents are classified as stationary members of the middle class if their fathers and husbands are in non-manual occupations, and as upwardly mobile members if their father did manual work but their husband does non-manual work. In the working class, downwardly mobile respondents are those whose fathers did non-manual work but whose husbands are manual workers, and stationary respondents are those whose fathers and husbands are manual workers. There is some variation in the age composition of these groups. Thus, the proportion over twenty-five years old in the white middle class is 58 percent among stationary respondents and 45 percent among the upward mobiles; in the white working class this proportion is 30 percent among stationary respondents and 27 percent among downward mobiles; and among Negroes it is 24 percent among the upward mobiles and 44 percent among stationary working-class respondents. However, the pattern of differences in exposure shown in Table 7 persists even when age is controlled (except that there are too few cases of older upwardly mobile Negroes to make meaningful comparisons).

Table 6. Percentage Distribution of Exposure Scores, by Class, Education, and Color

Education and Color	Exposure			Total N
	High	Medium	Low	
	Middle Class			
Grades 8–11				
White	29	29	42	7
Negro	0	43	57	7
High-school graduate or higher				
White	50	40	10	76
Negro	33	50	17	12
	Working Class			
Grades 8–11				
White	29	19	52	31
Negro	6	30	64	36
High-school graduate or higher				
White	36	44	20	25
Negro	6	47	47	30

Table 7. Percentage Distribution of Exposure Scores, by Class, Color, and Mobility

	Percent	Exposure			Total	Total N*
		High	Medium	Low		
		White				
Middle class:						
Stationary	65	59	28	13	100	53
Upward mobile	35	32	57	11	100	28
Working class:						
Stationary	79	29	26	45	100	42
Downward mobile	21	36	55	9	100	11
		Negro				
Middle class:						
Stationary	10		†		†	2
Upward mobile	90	24	41	35	100	17
Working class:						
Stationary	98	7	38	55	100	60
Downward mobile	2		†		†	1

* The class origin of ten respondents could not be ascertained, and these cases are excluded from the analysis.

† Among the Negro respondents are only two cases of stationary middle-class members and one case of a downwardly mobile member. All three of these respondents have medium exposure.

The constitution of the Negro middle class differs sharply from that of the white middle class, and therein may lie the explanation, at least to some degree, of the differences in the extent to which their members expose themselves to child-rearing literature. Owing to the long history of pervasive economic and social discrimination against Negroes in our society the size of the established Negro middle class has traditionally been much smaller than its white counterpart, both in absolute and in relative terms. Since World War II, however, employment opportunities for Negroes in non-manual occupations have increased with a corresponding increase in the numbers who have recently moved from the working class into the middle class.[23] Indeed, in our sample fully 90 percent of the middle-class Negro women come from working-class backgrounds, in contrast to 35 percent in the white middle class. Owing to their insignificant number,[24] the stationary members of the Negro middle class are not in a position to exert any appreciable effect on the behavior of the upwardly mobile members of their class. And since the barriers of segregation allow for little, if any, informal association between members of the two color groups the upwardly mobile Negro woman is also cut off from the influence exerted by stationary members of the white middle class.

As a result, the acculturation of Negro upwardly mobile women to the modes of behavior that prevail in the middle class is likely to proceed at a slower pace than in the case of upwardly mobile whites, and this is exemplified by the differences between them in the extent of their exposure to the writings of child-rearing experts (see Table 7). In contrast to only one-tenth of the upwardly mobile whites, over one-third of the upwardly mobile Negroes have low exposure to this kind of literature.[25]

Analysis of the composition of the white working class also helps explain why even in this stratum exposure to experts' writings is more widespread than in the Negro middle class, despite the fact that the latter contains a larger proportion of better educated women. Although the large majority (79 percent) of white working-class respondents are stationary members of their stratum, the rest (21 percent) were reared in the middle class and subsequently moved down into the working class. A comparison of the exposure scores of the downwardly mobile and stationary members of the white working class (see Table 7) shows that a higher proportion (91 percent) of the former have high or medium scores than of the latter (55 percent). And it is the presence of this downwardly mobile contingent that

[23] This is not meant to imply, of course, that the size of the Negro middle class approaches that of the white middle class, even relative to the total Negro population, but only that the proportion of the Negro middle class with working-class origins is larger than the corresponding proportion in the white middle class. The analysis assumes that this is true for the Chicago population at large as well as for our sample, which is admittedly small and not representative.

[24] The tiny number of stationary middle-class Negroes (2) and of downwardly mobile working class Negroes (1) in our sample makes impossible some comparisons corresponding to those in the white group and results in some unavoidable gaps in the analysis.

[25] When age is controlled this difference becomes even more pronounced among younger women (under twenty-six): only 27 percent of the upwardly mobile whites compared to 77 percent of the upwardly mobile Negroes have low-exposure scores.

largely accounts for the greater prevalence of high exposure in the white working class than in the Negro middle class. For in the latter group the proportion with low-exposure scores (35 percent) is less than among the stationary members of the white working class (45 percent). But downwardly mobile white working-class mothers expose themselves considerably more to experts' writings than upwardly mobile Negro middle-class women, an indication that former social ties with her middle-class family and friends are maintained to some extent by the downwardly mobile woman who thereby remains subject to middle-class influences to a greater degree than the upwardly mobile Negro middle-class woman. But the data also suggest that the impact of middle-class influence on downwardly mobile women has waned, since only 36 percent of them have high exposure to child-rearing literature in contrast to 59 percent of their former class peers, those who have retained their middle-class status.

However, although the downwardly mobile white mother shows evidence of being negatively influenced by her association with her new class peers, she may also act, to some degree, as a carrier of middle-class patterns of behavior to the stationary members of the working class with whom she develops social ties. For the stationary members of the white working class expose themselves more to child-rearing literature than stationary members of the Negro working class, despite the fact that the educational level of the members of the two strata is similar. But in the Negro working class in our sample there are virtually no downwardly mobile respondents (2 percent) and consequently here the chances of exposure to middle-class social influences are most limited.

Summary and Conclusions

Exposure to informational sources in the realm of child-rearing was shown to be more widespread among white than among Negro mothers, regardless of class position. This pattern of Negro-white differences persists even when respondents' educational level is taken into account. But Negro women tend to express favorable sentiments toward child-rearing experts more often than white women, despite the fact that they expose themselves less to their writings. Simultaneous analysis of these two variables revealed that in all four class-color groups women with high or medium exposure were more prone to express ambivalence toward experts than those with little or no exposure. But an interesting pattern of differences was observed in the incidence of negative attitudes between the two color groups: among women with low exposure, whites were more often negative toward experts than Negroes, but no such differences were noted among women with higher exposure. This suggests that the prevalence of a pattern of behavior in a group conditions the relationship between behavior and attitudes among its individual members. Where reading child-rearing literature is a widespread practice, as it is among white mothers, the very prevalence of this pattern within the group operates as a pressure toward conformity upon the individual. In *this* social context, *not* to read the experts constitutes a deviant act, and women who do not conform to the pattern of exposure feel constrained to justify their deviance by denigrating experts. But in a group where this practice is rare, as is the case among Negro mothers, the woman who does not read the experts is under no social or psychological pressure to provide rationalizations for her abstinence.

Analysis of the differences in the proportions of stationary and upwardly mobile members in the two middle classes helps to explain why the pattern of reading child-rearing literature is less widespread among Negro women, even the better educated Negroes, than among whites. The existence of a stationary majority in the white stratum creates numerous opportunities for upwardly mobile women to become exposed to middle-class modes of behavior such as "reading the experts." And association with these better educated, more prestigeful members in their stratum constitutes the source of social pressure through which new members become acculturated to these middle-class ways. In contrast, the Negro middle class contains an overwhelming majority of upwardly mobile members. Thus the new member has fewer opportunities than her white counterpart for exposure to, and assimilation of, middle-class modes of behavior within her own color group, and the barriers of segregation forestall her exposure to these influences through association with the stationary members of the white middle class. Indeed, even white working-class mothers may have a better chance of exposure to middle-class influences through their association with the downwardly mobile members of their stratum. But the Negro working-class mother is removed from even this source of influence, since there are virtually no downwardly mobile women in her stratum.

That economic discrimination and social segregation are major impediments to the acculturation of the Negro masses to urban middle-class culture is well known. Our analysis helps to specify *how* these practices operate to delay this process even among middle-class, better educated Negroes. Cognizant as we all are of the existence of a dual stratification system, we tend to think of the Negro and white class systems as similar though separate. Our findings suggest that there may be a number of structural differences between them that differentiate not only the rate with which middle-class norms diffuse among their members but also the amount of strain that accompanies the acculturation process. These differences in social structure mediate the effects that upward mobility and higher education exert on the attitudes and behavior of their individual members, not only in the realm of child-rearing, but probably in other realms of behavior as well. In other words, although the existence of a dual stratification system constitutes a grave social liability to a society that espouses democratic values, it constitutes an opportunity, while it persists, for the social scientist to make systematic comparisons between two class systems within a common cultural framework and thereby to gain a better understanding of how specific structural variables, present to a different degree in the two class systems, condition the diffusion of various kinds of norms, practices, and innovations among the members similarly situated within them. By the same token, it would undoubtedly prove fruitful to study the impact of desegregation on these processes by comparing their effects on Negroes who have gained opportunities for informal association with their white counterparts and on those similarly located in their class system for whom such opportunities still do not exist.

Constance K. Kamii and Norma J. Radin: Class Differences in the Socialization Practices of Negro Mothers

Much has been learned about socioeconomic class differences in child-rearing practices since the publication of "Social Class and Color Differences in Child-Rearing" by Davis and Havighurst.[1] However, research in this area has been handicapped by two serious limitations. First, almost all the data have been obtained in interviews. As Yarrow[2] pointed out, information obtained in interviews is subject to many systematic distortions. She urged researchers to use direct observation of interactions rather than continuing to rely on personal accounts of past events.

The second limitation was pointed out by Kohn,[3] who stated that many investigations have focused on insignificant variables, e.g., severity of toilet training and weaning, and that socialization practices must be understood in the context of parental values, or goals. He believes, for example, that the investigation of frequency of physical punishment becomes meaningful only in the context of what goals the parents are attempting to teach.

The two limitations described above are particularly evident in research on the child-rearing of lower-lower class Negro mothers. While problems of deportment at school have been known for some time to be class-related,[4] neither the child-rearing goals of disadvantaged[5] Negro mothers nor the

Reprinted from *Journal of Marriage and the Family*, 29 (May 1967), pp. 302-310, by permission of the National Council of Family Relations and the authors. Constance Kamii is Research Associate, Ypsilanti Public Schools, Ypsilanti, Michigan. Norma Radin is Assistant Professor of Social Work at the University of Michigan.

This paper is based on part of the senior author's doctoral dissertation entitled *Socioeconomic Class Differences in the Preschool Socialization Practices of Negro Mothers* (University of Michigan, 1965), which is obtainable from University Microfilms, Inc., 313 North First Street, Ann Arbor, Michigan.

[1] Allison Davis and Robert J. Havighurst, "Social Class and Color Differences in Child-Rearing," *American Sociological Review*, 11 (December, 1946), pp. 698-710.

[2] Marianne R. Yarrow, "Problems of Methods in Parent-Child Research," *Child Development*, 34 (March, 1963), pp. 215-226.

[3] Melvin L. Kohn, "Social Class and Parent-Child Relationship: An Interpretation," *The American Journal of Scoiology*, 68 (January, 1963), pp. 471-480.

[4] Robert J. Havighurst, P. H. Bowman, G. P. Liddle, C. Y. Matthews, and J. V. Pierce, *Growing Up in River City*, New York: John Wiley, 1962; Robert J. Havighurst and Hilda Taba, *Adolescent Character and Personality*, New York: John Wiley, 1949; and August B. Hollingshead, *Elmtown's Youth*, New York: John Wiley, 1949.

[5] The terms "lower-lower class" and "disadvantaged" are used interchangeably in this paper.

parent-child interactions through which norms are transmitted have been clarified. Hess[6] and Caldwell[7] are studying the nature of mother-child interactions among disadvantaged Negroes in direct observations. Hess's investigation, however, has centered around the cognitive environment of these children, and Caldwell's work has focused primarily on children younger than three years of age.[8]

The present investigation was an attempt to gain an understanding of the antecedents of lower-lower-class Negro children's deportment problems while keeping in mind the limitations of traditional methodology. Since deportment problems are closely related to the lack of inner controls, the variables shown by other investigations to be crucial for the internalization of norms were studied. The general hypothesis was that lower-lower- and middle-class mothers are basically similar in their child-rearing goals but that only lower-lower-class mothers interact with children in ways that perpetuate the need for external controls. Direct observation was made of mothers interacting with their preschool children in their own homes, and the observed behavior was then interpreted in the context of the mothers' child-rearing goals. The goals and behaviors of two groups of Negro mothers were compared so as to hold race constant in these socioeconomic class comparisons. The hypotheses tested were:

1. Lower-lower-class mothers' child-rearing goals generally do not differ from those of middle-class mothers.

2. Lower-lower-class mothers are less responsive than middle-class mothers to the *explicit* socio-emotional needs children express.

3. Lower-lower-class mothers initiate fewer interactions with children than do middle-class mothers in ways that meet children's *implicit* need for companionship and affection.

4. Middle-class mothers use *bilateral* techniques more often than do lower-lower-class mothers to influence children to behave in desired ways (i.e., consulting, gently requesting, explaining, using psychological manipulations, sensitizing children to mothers' feelings, and preventively reminding); lower-lower-class mothers use *unilateral* techniques more often than middle-class mothers (i.e., commanding, bribing, physically enforcing, and coercing).

5. Middle-class mothers reward children more often than lower-lower-class mothers for behaving in desirable ways; lower-lower-class mothers use negative

---

[6]Robert D. Hess and Virginia Shipman, "The Cognitive Environment of Urban Preschool Children," Interim Report, U.S. Department of Health, Education and Welfare: Children's Bureau, 1966.

[7]Bettye M. Caldwell, Leonard Hersher, Earle L. Lipton, Julius B. Richmond, George A. Stern, Evelyn Eddy, Robert Drachman, and Albert Rothman, "Mother-Infant Interaction in Monomatric and Polymatric Families," *The American Journal of Orthopsychiatry*, 33 (July, 1963), pp. 653–664; and Bettye M. Caldwell and Leonard Hersher, "Mother-Infant Interaction during the First Year of Life," *Merrill-Palmer Quarterly*, 10 (1963), pp. 119–128.

[8]The published work of both Caldwell and Hess concern observations outside the home in laboratory-type situations. Both researchers are currently engaged in observations in the homes. Caldwell has so far used home observations "primarily for the development of techniques rather than for arriving at generalizations about the nature of the interaction" (personal communication).

reinforcement more often than middle-class mothers when children behave in undesirable ways.

The above hypotheses were derived from a variety of previous studies with samples of Caucasian populations in which the middle class was compared with the lower class, i.e., the working class. Thus, the conclusions found in the literature concerning "lower-class" whites were used as a starting point for the present investigation of "lower-lower-class" Negroes. The first hypothesis concerning child-rearing goals was based on Kohn, who concluded that "middle- and working-class parents share a broadly common set of values—but not an identical set by any means."[9] The second and third hypotheses related to children's socio-emotional needs were derived from Bronfenbrenner[10] and Sears, Maccoby, and Levine,[11] who showed that middle-class mothers are more affectionate than lower-class mothers and that children who have received emotional support manifest a strong "conscience." The fourth hypothesis pertaining to influence techniques was based on Bronfenbrenner,[12] who showed that lower-class parents use more "power," and Spiegel,[13] who argued that unilateral power is less likely than bilateral approaches to lead to the internalization of decisions. The final hypothesis concerning what mothers do *after* the child engages in desirable or undesirable behavior was derived from Swanson[14] and Sears, Maccoby, and Levine.[15] Both of these authors stressed the importance of positive reinforcement to the internalization of parental values and advanced the concept of anaclitic identification as a link between child-rearing practices and the development of inner controls. This link will be discussed after the presentation of the results.

Method

Samples

A total of 40 Negro mothers of four-year-old children living in Ypsilanti and Ann Arbor, Michigan, were included in the study. Half of them were

[9] Kohn, *op. cit.*, p. 471.

[10] Urie Bronfenbrenner, "Toward a Theoretical Model for the Analysis of Parent-Child Relationships in a Social Context," in *Parental Attitudes and Child Behavior*, ed. by John C. Glidewell, Springfield, Ill.: Charles C. Thomas, 1961, pp. 90–109.

[11] Robert R. Sears, Eleanor E. Maccoby, and Harry Levin, *Patterns of Child Rearing*, Evanston, Ill.: Row-Peterson, 1957.

[12] Bronfenbrenner, *op. cit.*

[13] John P. Spiegel, "The Resolution of the Role Conflict within the Family," in *The Patient and the Mental Hospital*, ed. by Milton Greenblatt, D. J. Levinson, and R. H. Williams, New York: The Free Press, a division of the Macmillan Co., 1957, pp. 545–564.

[14] Guy E. Swanson, "Determinants of the Individual's Defenses against Inner Conflict: Review and Reformulation," in *Parental Attitudes and Child Behavior*, ed. by John C. Glidewell, Springfield, Ill.: Charles C. Thomas, 1961, pp. 5–41.

[15] Sears, *et al.*, *op. cit.*

Table 1. Characteristics of the Lower-Lower and Middle-Class Samples

	Lower-Lower Class (N = 20)	Middle Class (N = 20)	Significance of Difference
Average age of mother	25.7	30.5	.05
Average number of years of schooling completed by mother	10.1	14.2	.01
Average number of years of schooling completed by father	8.8	17.5	.01
Presence of father in home	25%	100%	.01
Average number of children in family	4.6	2.8	n.s.
Average number of children older than the four-year-old	2.6	0.95	.05
Average number of children younger than the four-year-old	1.0	0.85	n.s.
Number of boys in sample	9	8	n.s.

lower-lower-class mothers defined as those receiving public assistance. The other half were middle-class mothers defined as those having husbands with middle-class occupations.[16] While the lower-lower-class group was a random sample selected by the Bureau of Social Aid, the middle-class sample could not be selected by the same procedure, as middle-class Negro mothers of four-year-old children were few in number and difficult to find. This sample was obtained by following various professional contacts. Although the difference in sample selection was a serious limitation, it was seen as unavoidable and did not preclude the drawing of tentative conclusions in this early phase of research. None of the disadvantaged mothers refused to be interviewed, while one of the middle-class mothers on the original list stated that she was not interested in participating.

As can be seen from Table 1, which shows some relevant characteristics of the two groups of mothers, the two samples differed significantly in many class-related respects.

Procedure

The primary method of this investigation was the observation of how mothers coped with their preschool children while the senior author conducted interviews in the home. In order to insure the presence of the child in the same room, the investigator asked to have the child present, explaining that the child and the mother would be asked shortly to perform a color-sorting task. The investigator then set up a tape recorder and, to create

---

[16] Four teachers, three social workers, two physicians, two psychologists, two engineers, a lawyer, an Air Force officer, a chemical technician, a postal carrier, an architect, a speech pathologist, and an accountant were included.

problems which the mother had to handle, asked the mother one question after another, thereby holding her attention. The child was excluded from the conversation and inevitably became restless. How the mother interacted with this restless child was the focus of this study.

The second part of the procedure dealt with child-rearing goals. The mother was presented with 18 cards, each stating a child-rearing goal. Both the 18 goals and the assessment technique were an adaptation of Kohn.[17] In the present study, the mother was asked to sort the 18 cards into three piles— one pile for the most important six goals, another pile for the second most important six, and a third pile for the least important six qualities.

The third and final part of the procedure consisted of asking the mother to ask her child to sort colors, a task which was only an excuse for keeping the child in the same room.

All the mother-child interactions which related to children's socio-emotional needs and to mothers' influence techniques were typed from the tapes and the investigator's notes as soon after the interview as possible. In order to equate the two samples in length of observation time, all the interactions which took place after the first 30 minutes of each interview were discarded, since the shortest interview lasted 30 minutes. The data pertaining to mothers' behavior were thus based on a total of 600 minutes for each group, as there were 20 mothers in each sample. All the mothers' interactive behaviors were then coded[18] in relation to the children's socio-emotional needs and with regard to influence techniques. An example of the former is a mother's reaction to the child's showing something to her. An example of the latter is the mother's request that the child be quiet.

Inter-coder reliability was obtained by having another coder randomly spot-check the coding from the typed material, and 88 percent agreement was obtained. This reliability could be increased to 99 percent when the coding on which there was disagreement was discussed.

Assessment and Statistical Analysis

Three types of data were obtained in this study: (a) data on child-rearing goals obtained from the sorting of 18 cards into three equal piles, (b) observation data based on a system of coding interactions, and (c) interview data. Only the first two types of data are presented in this article because of limitation of space.

Child-rearing goals. The child-rearing goals were scored by assigning three points to a card placed in the pile of "the *most* important," two points to a card placed among "the *next* most important," and one point to a card placed among "the *least* important" goals. The scores of each group of 20 mothers were then averaged for each card, yielding a minimum possible mean score of 1.0 and a maximum possible mean score of 3.0. The significance of the difference between the two means was tested with the t-test.

[17]Kohn, *op. cit.*

[18]Appendix A of the dissertation, pp. 124–137, gives scoring criteria.

Table 2. Socioeconomic Class Differences in Relative Emphasis on 18 Child-Rearing Values

Lower-Lower Class Rank	Child-Rearing Value	Lower-Lower Class Mean	Middle-Class Mean	Difference*	Significance†
1.0	That he is honest.	2.74	2.95	−0.21	n.s.
2.0	That he is happy.	2.60	2.65	−0.05	n.s
3.0	That he obeys his parents well.	2.54	2.50	+0.04	n.s.
4.0	That he obeys his teachers well.	2.49	2.00	+0.49	n.s.
5.0	That he is neat and clean.	2.34	1.95	+0.50	.05
6.0	That he has good manners.	2.44	2.20	+0.24	n.s.
7.0	That he has a good education.	2.39	2.35	+0.04	n.s.
8.0	That he has self-control.	2.05	2.20	−0.15	n.s.
9.5	That he is dependable.	2.00	2.55	−0.55	.001
9.5	That he is considerate of others.	2.00	2.85	−0.85	.001
11.5	That he is a good student.	1.99	1.80	+0.19	n.s.
11.5	That he is liked by adults.	1.99	1.10	+0.89	.001
13.0	That he is ambitious.	1.54	1.80	−0.26	n.s.
14.0	That he is curious about things.	1.45	1.80	−0.35	n.s.
15.0	That he is able to play by himself.	1.40	1.30	+0.10	n.s.
16.0	That he is affectionate.	1.30	1.45	−0.15	n.s.
17.0	That he is able to defend himself.	1.25	1.35	−0.10	n.s.
18.0	That he is popular with other children.	1.20	1.20	0.00	

*(Lower-lower class mean)–(middle-class mean).
†t test, 2 tail.

This method of assessing values has advantages and disadvantages. It enables mothers of both socioeconomic classes to express their goals in the same way regardless of verbal skill, but it limits the range of possible scores. The second question to be raised regarding the validity of the assessment method is whether or not a person's statement that something is of value to him can be accepted. The alternative of direct observation may not be satisfactory either, for, as Robin Williams said:

No student of human conduct can accept uncritically, as final evidence, people's testimony as to their own values. Yet actions may deceive as well as words, and there seems no reason for always giving one precedence over the other.[19]

Interactions (observation data). After mothers' interactive behaviors were coded, each mother was given a score on each interaction category, indicating how many times she used that technique during the 30-minute period of observation. The statistical test used to confirm or reject the null hypotheses related to mother-child interactions was the Kolmogorov-Smirnov two-sample test, which tests the agreement between two cumulative distributions.[20]

[19] Robin Williams, *American Society*, New York: Alfred Knopf, 1951, p. 378.
[20] Sidney Siegel, *Nonparametric Statistics*, New York: McGraw-Hill, 1956, p. 127.

The method of observation used in the present investigation had some serious limitations. The presence of the investigator undoubtedly affected observable behavior, and neither the same set of stimuli of the laboratory nor standardized tests were used. However, it was felt that both groups of mothers put forth their best behavior; and some genuine, representative behaviors were bound to emerge during an interview of 30 minutes, no matter how well people tried to present themselves. It was also felt that observation in the natural environment would be more meaningful than in the artificial setting of the laboratory.

Results

Child-Rearing Goals

Table 2 shows the child-rearing goals of the two groups of mothers in descending order for the lower-lower class, from the most important to the least important goals. The values of the two groups can be said to be quite similar, but some differences were observed. Statistically significant differences in relative emphasis were obtained on four of the 18 goals—considerateness (p<.001) and dependability (p<.001), which were stressed by the middle class, and being liked by adults (p<.001) and neatness and cleanliness (p<.05), which were stressed by the lower-lower class.

In general, however, the data can be said to lend support to the hypothesis stated earlier concerning child-rearing goals. For the most part, the two groups of mothers accorded priority to the same qualities of honesty, happiness, obedience to parents, and a good education.

Interactions (Socialization Practices)

Table 3 shows the reactions of the two groups of mothers to children's directly expressed socio-emotional needs. It can be concluded from this table

Table 3. Reactions of Lower-Lower- and Middle-Class Mothers to Children's Directly Expressed Needs

		Lower-Lower Class		Middle-Class		Significance of Difference Between
		Frequency	Percent	Frequency	Percent	Proportion
Child's need-expressing behavior		101	100	233	100	
Mother's reaction	Meeting need	46	46	171	73	.05
	Partially meeting need	20	20	34	15	—*
	Not meeting need	35	35	28	12	—*

*A comparison was not made, because the comparison of "meeting need" made subsequent comparisons no longer independent of the first comparison.

Table 4. Lower-Lower- and Middle-Class Mothers' Mother-Initiated Behavior which Met Children's Implicit Needs

	Mean Frequency		
	Lower-Lower Class (N = 20)	Middle Class (N = 20)	Significance of Difference*
Mother-initiated interaction	0.45	1.20	.05
Continuing interaction	0.90	1.15	n.s.
Verbal communication of affection	0.20	1.35	.01
Non-verbal communication of affection	0.40	1.45	n.s.
Sharing activity	0.25	0.65	n.s.

*Kolmogorov-Smirnov test.

that the data support the hypothesis stating, "Lower-lower-class mothers are less responsive than middle-class mothers to the *explicit* socio-emotional needs children express."

The socioeconomic class differences in mothers' need-meeting responses are actually more dramatic than are indicated by the above analysis of mothers' *reactions* to children's demands. The mean frequency of children's attempts at eliciting a reaction was 11.65 for the middle class and 5.05 for the disadvantaged class (p<.05, rank-sums test). It can thus be said that middle-class children not only *receive* gratifying responses significantly more frequently when they attempt to receive such responses but also *seek* gratifying responses significantly more often than do lower-lower-class children. The difference in frequency of gratifying responses per unit time yielded a ratio of almost 4:1.

Table 4 concerns *mother-initiated* interactions related to children's *implicit* need for companionship and affection, e.g., her initiating a conversation with the child. The middle-class mean was higher in every subcategory, and, as can be seen from Table 4, statistically significant differences were obtained in "mother-initiated interaction," "verbal communication of affection," and "non-verbal communication of affection." The hypothesis "Lower-lower class mothers initiate fewer interactions with children than do middle-class mothers in ways that meet children's *implicit* need for companionship and affection" can thus be said to be confirmed by the data.

The various techniques used by mothers to attempt to influence children's behavior can be seen in Table 5. Statistically significant differences were obtained both in "commanding" and in "consulting."[21] While not all the influence-technique categories showed significant differences, it can be said that middle-class mothers were found to use more bilateral techniques and that disadvantaged mothers tended to use more unilateral techniques.

[21]"Consulting" refers, for example, to saying, "Do you want to go get your book?" where the mother gives the child a choice and an opportunity to make a decision.

Table 5. Influence Techniques Used by Lower-Lower- and Middle-Class Mothers*

Influence Technique	Total Lower-Lower-Class Frequency (N=20)		Total Middle-Class Frequency (N=20)		Significance of Difference†
Verbal techniques					
1. Requesting					
a. Gently or politely		58		64	n.s.
(1) Without explanation	(49)		(42)		—
(2) With explanation	(9)		(22)		—
b. In a commanding manner		83		26	.05
(1) Without explanation	(77)		(23)		.05
(2) With explanation	(6)		(3)		—
c. With irritation		9		2	n.s.
(1) Without explanation	(7)		(2)		—
(2) With explanation	(2)		(0)		—
2. Consulting		4		27	.01
3. Psychological manipulations		36		53	n.s.
a. Coaxing	(21)		(19)		—
b. Humoring	(0)		(2)		—
c. Evaluating	(5)		(3)		—
d. Distracting or offering a substitute gratification or alternative	(7)		(14)		—
e. Offering aids for self-control	(1)		(5)		—
f. Ignoring	(0)		(5)		—
g. Others	(2)		(5)		—
4. Offering bribes		3		0	n.s.
5. Warning or threatening		14		4	n.s.
a. Loss of love	(0)		(0)		—
b. Loss of things or privilege	(0)		(0)		—
c. Physical punishment	(7)		(2)		—
d. "Exile"	(7)		(0)		—
e. Others	(0)		(2)		—
Physical enforcement		10		11	n.s.
1. Casual	(4)		(2)		—
2. Forceful	(6)		(9)		—
Total		217		187	

* Frequency during a total of 600 minutes of observation (30 minutes with each of 20 mothers).

† Kolmogorov-Smirnov test.

It can be observed from Table 5 that the techniques most frequently used by lower-lower-class mothers were, in descending order of frequency, commanding without explanation (35 percent), requesting gently without explanation (25 percent), coaxing (ten percent), and warning or threatening (six percent). Middle-class mothers were found most frequently to use gentle requests without explanation (22 percent), consulting (14 percent), gentle requests with explanation (12 percent), and commanding without explanation (12 percent). The limited repertoire of the disadvantaged mothers

Table 6. Positive and Negative Reinforcement Used by Lower-Lower- and Middle-Class Mothers

| | Mean Frequency | | |
	Lower-Lower Class (N = 20)	Middle Class (N = 20)	Significance of Difference*
Negative reinforcement†	0.55	0.10	n.s.
Positive reinforcement‡	0.05	0.80	.05

*Kolmogorov-Smirnov test.
†Includes punishing and other gentler expressions of disapproval.
‡Includes verbal and physical rewards.

becomes evident when it is seen that 60 percent of all their attempts to influence children consisted of only two categories, i.e., commanding and gently requesting without explanation.

Table 6 concerns mothers' behaviors *after* the occurrence of children's desirable or undesirable behavior. As can be seen from this table, the data lend support only to the first half of the hypothesis stating, "Middle-class mothers reward children more often than lower-lower-class mothers for behaving in desirable ways; lower-lower-class mothers use negative reinforcement[22] more often than middle-class mothers when children behave in undesirable ways."

It can be argued that the observed differences in socialization practices which have so far been described are due not to social class but to other class-related variables such as the number of children in the home and the presence of the father in the home. Two subsamples of mothers matched for number, sex, and birth order of children were therefore obtained, and their socialization practices were compared. The class differences remained essentially the same. No comparison was made of two subsamples matched for the presence of the father in the home because of the small number of families in the lower-lower-class sample with fathers in the home. The very absence of a father is in itself a lower-lower-class characteristic, and the significance of such a comparison would be open to question.

Discussion

Caution must be exercised in interpreting the findings of the present investigation. Although some types of maternal behavior were found typically in the homes of middle-class Negroes and others, typically in disadvantaged Negro homes, not all mothers demonstrated the characteristics of their strata. Social class is thus not a determinant of behavior but a statement of probability that a type of behavior is likely to occur.

A comparison of the most important goals for the middle- and lower-

[22]"Negative reinforcement" includes all types of punishment as well as gentler expressions of disapproval.

lower-class mothers suggests that, although the basic values of both classes are similar, middle-class mothers expect obedience to be combined with considerateness, whereas disadvantaged mothers want complete obedience to those in authority.[23] These findings are consistent with Kohn,[24] Bernstein,[25] and Hess's[26] conclusion that the lower class tends to control children by appealing to status or authority, e.g., "Don't talk to your mother like that," and "You must mind your mother," whereas the middle class tends to appeal to the regulator's feelings and to the child's guilt feelings, e.g., "It upsets me when you talk like that." This seemingly minor difference between obedience and considerateness is highly significant, because emphasis on good behavior through obedience depends on the presence of authority figures and not on the development of inner controls in the child.

With regard to mother-child interactions, the conclusions of the present study were: (a) middle-class mothers are more bilateral and disadvantaged mothers are more unilateral in their influence techniques; (b) middle-class mothers reward children considerably more frequently than disadvantaged mothers for behaving in desirable ways; and (c) middle-class mothers gratify children's socio-emotional needs considerably more often than disadvantaged mothers.

The influence techniques used by disadvantaged mothers may in part account for the lack of inner controls observed in school among lower-lower-class children. According to Spiegel,[27] bilateral approaches are likely to lead to the internalization of expectations, while unilateral approaches are not. In fact, according to Spiegel, unilateral approaches like coercion often result in defiance and rebellion. It can be speculated that the bilateral approach of "consulting" observed in middle-class homes leads to the internalization of maternal expectations, while the unilateral approach of commanding, which typifies disadvantaged mothers, perpetuates the need for external controls.

Inferences which may be made from the findings of the present study tend to support Swanson's view[28] that anaclitic identification is more effective in inhibiting impulses than identification with the aggressor. Anaclitic identification, or identification motivated primarily by the child's anxiety over the loss of his parents' love, requires the practices which were observed among middle-class mothers, i.e., reward for "good" behavior and gratification of socio-emotional needs. According to Swanson, these positive elements in the parent-child relationship tip the balance between the potential gratification and the potential pain of transgression. On the other hand, identification with the aggressor is motivated primarily by the child's desire to avoid

[23] As can be seen from Table 2, "that he obeys his teachers well" was stressed considerably more by lower-lower-class mothers.

[24] Kohn, *op. cit.*

[25] Basil Bernstein, "Social Class, Speech Systems, and Psychotherapy," *The British Journal of Sociology*, 15 (March, 1964), pp. 54–64.

[26] Hess and Shipman, *op. cit.*

[27] Spiegel, *op. cit.*

[28] Swanson, *op. cit.*

punishment, and impulse control is therefore dependent upon external forces.

The middle-class Negro child, who is rewarded frequently and appears to develop emotional dependence on his mother, is known to behave, in general, in accordance with society's norms. The lower-lower-class Negro child, whose socio-emotional needs are not met and who does not develop an emotional dependence on his mother, is known, in general, to fail to behave in accordance with society's norms. It may be speculated that these elements are linked [as shown in the chart below].

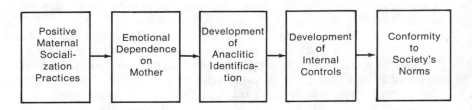

If the above theoretical links are correct, they suggest that compensatory education must include an attempt to alter the socialization practices of disadvantaged mothers, along with a program to foster verbal development (such as that recommended by Bereiter and Engelmann[29] and a curriculum to build a cognitive foundation (such as that being developed by Deutsch[30] and Kamii [31]). Efforts to change child-rearing patterns can be made both on the high school level, before the girls become mothers, and as part of a preschool program, when disadvantaged children are still young enough to benefit from changes in their mothers' behavior. In addition, schools with a large proportion of disadvantaged children may have to alter some of the teachers' child-management techniques. Efforts must be made to foster the internalization of external controls, rather than merely suppressing undesirable behavior.

The alleviation of reality pressures (e.g., poverty and poor employment as described, for example, by Jeffers[32]) is necessary to lessen the feeling of alienation from society among the disadvantaged. However, teachers and social workers must also make an effort to go beyond the amelioration of

[29]Carl Bereiter and Siegfried Engelmann, *Teaching Disadvantaged Children in the Preschool,* Englewood Cliffs, N.J.: Prentice-Hall, 1966.

[30]Martin Deutsch, "Facilitating Development in the Preschool Child: Social and Psychological Perspectives," *Merrill-Palmer Quarterly of Behavior and Development,* 10 (1964); and Martin Deutsch, *Reversing Deprivation Effect in the Preschool Child: Description of a Demonstration Research Program for a Therapeutic Curriculum,* Special Project Section, National Institute of Mental Health, 1962, mimeographed.

[31]Constance K. Kamii and Norma L. Radin, *A Framework for a Preschool Curriculum Based on Some Piagetian Concepts, Journal of Creative Behavior* (in press); and Hanne D. Sonquist and Constance K. Kamii, "The Application of Some Piagetian Concepts to Teaching in a Preschool for Disadvantaged Children," in press, to appear in *Young Children,* March, 1967.

[32]Camille Jeffers, *Living Poor: A Participant-Observation— The Study of Choices and Priorities,* Ann Arbor: Ann Arbor Publishers, 1967.

external reality, as the changing of external conditions will not necessarily result in the child's development of inner controls, which are essential for his success in school and, later, on a job.

The investigation described in this paper has the limitations of small samples of a middle-class group which was not randomly selected. As a preliminary study, however, it did demonstrate the feasibility of direct observation in the homes and the delineation of crucial variables in mother-child interactions. Further work is necessary with larger, random samples and longer periods of observation. The hypothesis advanced above concerning the internalization of external controls must also be subjected to similar investigations with Negro fathers and with Caucasian mothers and fathers of various socioeconomic strata.

A problem closely related to the internalization of external controls is the development of the achievement motive. The lower class has been known for some time to be less able than the middle class to internalize standards of excellence.[33] The two elements of achievement and deportment are interrelated from the standpoint of personality theory as well as for the social mobility of the disadvantaged child, but each needs to be studied separately before being combined into a complex analysis.

Summary and Conclusions

Class differences in the socialization practices of Negro mothers were investigated in the context of their child-rearing goals. Direct observation of mother-child interactions in the homes and a card-sorting method of studying child-rearing goals led to the conclusion that middle- and lower-lower-class Negro mothers do not differ fundamentally in their goals but that they do differ considerably in their socialization practices. Middle-class mothers were found to gratify children's socio-emotional needs, to use bilateral influence techniques, and to reward children for desirable behavior significantly more often than lower-lower-class mothers. The relationship of these practices to the child's internal controls and conformity to society's norms was discussed, with anaclitic identification as a theoretical link. These conclusions appeared to suggest ways in which efforts might be made by schools to foster the development of inner controls in disadvantaged children.

[33] Bernard C. Rosen, "The Achievement Syndrome: A Psychocultural Dimension of Social Stratification"; and Elizabeth Douvan, "Social Status and Success Strivings"; both in *Motives in Fantasy, Action and Society*, ed. by John W. Atkinson, Princeton: Van Nostrand, 1958, pp. 495–517.

Robert R. Bell: The Related Importance of Mother and Wife Roles among Black Lower-Class Women

While sociologists often generalize about *the* American family, there is beginning to emerge a body of research data indicating significant variations in American family patterns. Of increasing importance for the family sociologist is the analysis and delineation of family types by social class and racial background factors.[1] The evidence increasingly suggests that there are important differences between Black and white family patterns in the lower class and that the Black lower-class family must be seen as a part of a Black lower-class subculture. "Subculture" is used to refer to a subdivision within American society that forms a functioning unity of values and behavior patterns that have an integrated impact on participating individuals.[2] The concept of subculture implies that all groups in American society share many factors in common, but that the *areas of difference* peculiar to a given subculture are the focus of major interest at a given time.

The Black lower class may be viewed as an ongoing and pervasive subculture. That is, it provides a meaningful social setting for most of its members who are a part of the subculture from birth to death and who are influenced by subcultural patterns in a variety of ways. The time span makes the Black lower-class subculture different from most other pervasive subcultures that influence members for only specific time spans during the life cycle; for example, delinquent or adolescent subcultures, prison subcultures, etc.

In this paper the discussion is limited to some patterns related to the family in the Black lower class and *not* to the general Black lower-class subculture. We will first examine some recent research findings that provide a brief description of an important family form to be found in the Black lower-class subculture. Second, we will present some research findings with regard to one aspect of the Black lower-class family—the relatively high importance of the mother role and low importance of the wife role.

Pattern in the Black Lower-Class Family

It is clear that the Black lower-class subculture in general, and the family in particular, have maintained patterns for many years different from the "ideal" American definitions of society and the family. For example, the

---

A paper presented at the Groves Conference on Marriage and the Family, San Juan, Puerto Rico, April 1967. Reprinted with permission of the author. All rights reserved. Robert Bell is Professor of Sociology at Temple University.

[1]One study that compares Black and white families in the lower class is Lee Rainwater, *Family Design* (Chicago: Aldine Publishing Co., 1965).

[2]See Julius Gould and William L. Kolb, *A Dictionary of the Social Sciences* (New York: Free Press, 1964), pp. 167–168.

importance of the female-head family among Blacks has its roots in the slavery system and was further developed and maintained by the caste system of the Afro-American in the South following the Civil War. During that period the Black male was often limited in family involvement because of low economic opportunity and because the climate of racial prejudice made his participation as the family head extremely difficult. Historically, there were also important differences in the socialization of Black men and women with regard to family values. For example, Hauser has pointed out that the "Black female, in household interaction with middle-class white families of the South as well as the North, has acquired attitudes and norms of behavior which have led her to look down upon any Black male without similar exposure."[3] As a result the Black male was generally excluded from contact with middle-class family role models.

Some researchers several decades ago suggested that as Blacks increasingly migrated to urban areas, especially in the North, such subcultural family characteristics as the female-head family and illegitimacy would decrease.[4] However, the evidence clearly indicates that these characteristics have not been reduced by the Northern and urban migration of Blacks.[5] For example, today the female-head Black families constitute 23 percent of all families in urban areas but only 11 percent in rural farm areas.[6] It is apparent that an important characteristic of the family in the Black lower class continues to be the major role importance of the mother. This implies a number of other peculiar role and behavior characteristics related to the great importance of the mother in the Black lower-class family.

The commonly accepted values with regard to marital roles in the American middle class place great stress on love as a prerequisite for entering marriage and as basic to the continuance of marriage defined as successful. An important aspect of the middle-class value with regard to love as basic to the success of marriage is that marital love makes the husband-wife relationship the exclusive one for meeting the sexual needs of either partner. Any deviation from this exclusive relationship of marital sex is often defined as threatening, especially to the wife, of the overall marital love relationship. Other middle-class marriage values are that both spouses find some satisfactions through companionship with one another and that the husband will be the primary breadwinner.[7] In the middle-class rearing of children the mother has the primary role, but the father very often performs what is believed to be an important supplementary parental role. We will briefly

---

[3] Philip M. Hauser, "Demographic Factors in the Integration of the Negro," *Daedalus*, Fall 1965, p. 854.

[4] See John Dollard, *Caste and Class in a Southern Town* (New York: Anchor Books, 1957); St. Clair Drake and Horace R. Cayton, *Black Metropolis* (New York: Dryden Press, 1951); and Arnold Rose, *The Negro in America* (Boston: Beacon Press, 1958).

[5] See M. Elaine Burgess and David O. Price, *An American Dependency Challenge* (Chicago: American Public Welfare Association, 1963); and Lewis, *op. cit.*, pp. 108–137.

[6] *The Negro Family*, Office of Policy Planning and Research, U.S. Department of Labor, March 1965, p. 64

[7] For a discussion of these points see Robert R. Bell, *Marriage and Family Interaction* (Homewood, Ill.: Dorsey Press, 1963), Chs. 10, 11.

discuss some research findings that indicate that these general middle-class values are often not values (with related behavior) common to the Black lower-class family.

There have been a number of studies indicating that husband-wife roles and patterns of interaction in the lower class are quite different from those of the middle class. In the Black lower class the notion of love as a prerequisite to marriage and as a condition for its successful maintenance is not a strong value. There is also strong evidence that companionship in marriage is not a strong value or behavior pattern in the lower class. Lack of marital companionship is reflected in the general patterns of sex-segregated activities. For example, lower-class partners tend to maintain old friendship and kinship ties rather than reorganize ties after marriage to make the spouse a part of one social network.[8] Herzog has pointed out that lower-class men and women are likely to see themselves as opposed to each other and belonging to quite different worlds.[9]

Rainwater found in a study of conjugal role relations in the lower class similar patterns for both Blacks and whites, with "segregated" conjugal roles the case for both groups.[10] Rainwater also found that "the husband participates minimally and in specialized ways around the home, the wife carries the responsibility for the home and children largely by herself, and she seldom participates with her husband in outside activities."[11] Besner points out that the lower-class husband seems to want periodic reassurance of some authority, while at the same time demanding freedom to come and go at will.[12] As a result the lower-class husband often takes on a quasi-patriarchal role—demanding the traditional patriarchal role rights but filling few of the traditional role responsibilities.

Recent research indicates that the lower-class husband is not only tangential to family functioning but that very often his wife prefers it that way. Rainwater writes that "in spite of the worrying she may do about the possibility of her husband straying away from home and thus depriving the family of its source of support and measure of respectability, the lower-lower-class wife seems to find handling the family on her own to her liking, or at least consistent with what she has learned to expect from living in her particular social world."[13]

What may be the single most important characteristic of the Black lower-class marriage relationship centers around the breadwinner role. The difficulties of finding jobs and maintaining employment have long been recognized as a major problem for the Black lower-class male. The ratio of

[8]See Albert K. Cohen and Harold M. Hodges, Jr., "Characteristics of the Lower-Blue-Collar Class," *Social Problems*, Spring 1963, p. 320; and Arthur Besner, " Economic Deprivation and Family Patterns, " *Welfare in Review* (Welfare Administration), September 1965, p. 22.

[9]Elizabeth Herzog,"Some Assumptions about the Poor," *Social Service Review*, December 1963, p. 399.

[10]Rainwater, *op. cit.*, p. 32.

[11]*Ibid.*, p. 56.

[12]Besner, *op. cit.*, p. 22.

[13]Rainwater, *op. cit.*, pp. 59–60.

nonwhite unemployment is highest among men between the ages of twenty-five and thirty-four, the years of child rearing in the family.[14] But even when the Black male is employed, his income is just half of that of the white male—in 1963 the average income for Black men was $2,400 as compared with $4,800 for white men.[15]

Because the Black lower-class male has restricted opportunities to fill the family breadwinner role, the Black lower-class woman has a high involvement in combining occupational roles with that of her wife and/or mother roles. In March, 1964, 48 percent of the Black women married with husband present, as compared to 33 percent of the white women, were in the labor force. When there was no husband present, 50 percent of the Black women and 39 percent of the white women were in the labor force.[16]

The nonwhite/white ratio of labor-force activity for women is greatest in the age range twenty-five to thirty-four. As Moynihan points out, "the unemployment ratio of nonwhite to white women is *lower* than average in just those middle years when it is highest for nonwhite males,"[17] As pointed out, the earnings of Black males are about half those of white males; however, Black women have improved their income position relative to white women in all regions of the United States except the South, so that they are now practically equal.[18] "At the same time that Black women were closing the income gap, more were working. Between 1950 and 1960 the female proportion of the Black labor force rose from 35.1 percent to 40.2 percent. By 1964, women accounted for 41.3 percent of the nonwhite labor force.[19] That Black women very often combine family roles with work roles is illustrated by the fact that 57 percent of nonwhite women with children six to seventeen years of age are in the work force.[20]

It seems clear that one major characteristic of the Black lower-class family is that of the wife taking over or supplementing the male breadwinner role by working. When the mother does not work and there is no father present, the breadwinner role is often taken over by the government. In 1961 not quite half of all children receiving ADC (Aid to Dependent Children) were Black.[21] For the Black lower-class woman the realities of her world often suggest that marriage has limited possibilities for acquiring a husband to fill the breadwinner role. On the one hand, because of a combination of unstable, unskilled occupations and racial minority status, the Black lower-class male has little success or security in an occupational role. On the other hand,

[14]Daniel Patrick Moynihan, "Employment, Income, and the Ordeal of the Negro Family," *Daedalus,* Fall 1965, p. 757.

[15]"Negro Population: March 1964," *Current Population Reports,* Series p-20, No. 142, October 11, 1965, p. 1.

[16]*Ibid.,* p. 6.

[17]Moynihan, *op. cit.* p. 761.

[18]*Ibid.,* p. 756.

[19]*Ibid.,* p. 757.

[20]*Ibid.,* p. 762.

[21]Moynihan, *op. cit.,* p. 762.

the lower-class Black mother receiving ADC who decides to marry may be gambling her control over a stable low income against an income that may be even lower and less stable by shifting through marriage to economic dependence on a husband.[22]

The Black lower-class woman's strong commitment to the mother role is illustrated in several ways. First, there is little if any stigma attached to becoming a mother outside of marriage. That this is common is seen in the statistic that in 1963 24 percent of all nonwhite births in the United States were illegitimate.[23] Another illustration of the Black woman's strong commitment to having children is reflected in her low induced abortion rates. "Among the grade school and high school educated women, the Black wives have lower rates of induced abortion than do whites, despite the fact that the Black wives have higher conception rates."[24]

One obvious consequence of the Black woman's limited involvement in marriage, along with her high commitment to the mother role, is that the Black lower-class family is often made up of only the mother and her children. In 1962, 23 percent of all Black families were units with a female head, as compared to 9 percent of white families.[25] It has been estimated that only about one third of all Black youth reach age eighteen having lived all their lives in families with both parents present.[26] In a previous study we suggested that in the Black lower class the female-head family "may in reality be the most efficient and functional family type. This is suggested because the presence of the husband-father may in the long run more negatively than positively affect the mother and her children, and, because the female head is supported within the Black lower class by a long tradition and acceptability, it presents minimal social stigma."[27] To enter marriage for the middle-class "ideals" of economic security, love or companionship, and to have children has limited significance for many Black lower-class women. It is possible that many Black lower-class women would like to marry for middle-class "ideals," but their experience and observations clearly indicate that the middle-class "ideals" have little correlation with the realities of marriage they see in the world around them.

Research Findings

Our discussion thus far has pointed out some of the characteristics of the Black lower-class family. However, one purpose of this paper is to investigate a particular area of the family—the relative importance of marital

---

[22] See Sydney E. Bernard, "The Economics and Social Adjustment of Low-Income Female-Headed Families," Report of Research Project, Welfare Administration, Grant No. 004, 1964, p. 8.

[23] Moynihan, *op. cit.*, p. 762.

[24] Paul H. Gebhard, et al., *Pregnancy, Birth, and Abortion* (New York: Harper, 1958), p. 165.

[25] *The Negro Family*, p. 62.

[26] Moynihan, *op. cit.*, p. 761.

[27] Robert R. Bell, "The One-Parent Mother in the Negro Lower Class," *Eastern Sociological Meetings*, New York, April 1965, p. 14.

versus parental roles for the Black woman. As we have pointed out there are a number of factors suggesting that for many Black women the wife role has limited significance, while the role of mother has correspondingly greater significance. Furthermore, we hypothesized that women in the Black lower-lower class would show a higher rejection of marriage than women in the upper-lower class.

The population to be discussed consists of 202 Black mothers, each with at least two children, one of whom was in nursery school or kindergarten, and who lived in three elementary school districts in Philadelphia. The three school districts are essentially alike and may be described as almost totally Black and on the basis of demographic data, classified as lower class.[28] The interviewing was done by three Black female graduate students using a schedule consisting of 102 items.

The index of social class used in this paper is that of the woman's education. The traditional indices of social class based on the husband's education, occupation, income, etc., could not be used with this sample, where many women had no husband. The rationale for using the education of women as an index of social class has been discussed in previous papers.[29] In the discussion that follows, the women are divided into a "low" status group ($N = 75$), those having nine years of education or less, and a "middle" status group ($N = 122$), with 10 to 12 years of education. We have previously offered evidence for our suggestion that the "low" status group is representative of the Black lower-lower class while, the "middle" status group predominantly represents the upper-lower class.[30] It is the lower-lower class that we believe predominantly constitutes the Black lower-class subculture. We will also, at several points in the discussion that follows, present some data from another study now under way. This data will be with regard to 100 Black and 100 white women, all of whom have at least four years of higher education with a baccalaureate degree

Marriage

For better or for worse, the "low" status women first experience marriage at slightly younger ages than do "middle" status women. The mean age at first marriage for the "low" was 18.2 years and for the "middle" status women was 18.8 years. (By contrast, the Black college graduate women married at a mean age of 23.5 years.) Another way of showing the young age at first marriage is that among the "low" status women 34 percent were married at age 16 or younger as compared with only 14 percent of the "middle" status women.

When the women were asked what they liked best about being married, 60 percent of the "low" and 40 percent of the "middle" gave the response of

---

[28]Robert R. Bell, "Lower Class Negro Mothers' Aspirations for Their Children," *Social Forces*, May 1965, p. 495.

[29]*Ibid.*, pp. 495–496.

[30]*Ibid.*, pp. 494–500.

"nothing." Interaction between husband and wife, so important to middle-class marriages, was mentioned by only one fourth of the "low" and one third of the "middle" status women.

When the women were asked to rate their own marriages, there were no significant differences, with 43 percent of the "low" and 50 percent of the "middle" status women rating their marriages as either "very good" or "good." It is of interest that the sample of Black college graduate women did not rate their marriages any higher than did the less-educated Black women. Fifty-one percent of them rated their marriages "very good" or "good," as compared to 80 percent of the white college graduate women. The same pattern as above appears with regard to the women's assessment of their marriage as compared to other marriages they knew. Stating that they felt theirs was "better" were 32 percent of the "low," 45 percent of the "high," 38 percent of the Black college graduates, and 68 percent of the white college graduate women.

The respondents were also asked: "If you had it to do all over would you ever marry?" The answer of "yes" was given by only 36 percent of the "low" and by 64 percent of the "middle" status women. "Yes" was given by 88 percent of the Black college graduate women and 100 percent of the white college graduates. The respondents were also asked the more specific question: "If you had it to do all over would you marry the same person you did marry?" For the "low" status respondents 35 percent asnwered "yes," as did 59 percent of the "middle" status women. However, for the Black college graduate women, only 46 percent answered "yes." It appears that the low status Black women rejected *both* marriage in general and specific marriages. By contrast, the college graduate Black women accepted the general value of marriage *but* tended to reject their specific marriage experiences. Finally, the white college-educated women suggested a very high level of accepting *both* marriage in general and their specific marriage experiences.

To more specifically test the relative importance of marriage and parental roles, we asked the respondents the following: "If you could only be a wife or mother (but not both), which would you choose?" The wife role was selected by only 16 percent of the "low" and 24 percent of the "middle" status women. Among the college graduate women the wife role was selected by 50 percent of the Black women and by 74 percent of the white women.

The data suggest that marriage has limited importance to Black women at all educational levels, although as one moves up in education, marriage takes on importance for an increasing proportion of Black women. It is also possible that if education were held constant at all levels, Black women would show a greater rejection of marriage than would white women. This appears to be a reasonable suggestion, given the negative aspects of marriage for Black women in the past as well as the present.

Parenthood

On none of our items with regard to parent-child relationships did we find any significant differences in the responses given by "low" and "middle" status Black women. In general we found a high value for both groups associated with being a mother. For example, when the respondents were asked what they liked "most" about being a mother, 72 percent of the "low" and 78 percent of the "middle" said to "love and help their children."

The mothers were asked about the contribution of the father to caring for the child when he was one year of age. The father's role was minimal; for example, it was found that 39 percent of the "low" and 29 percent of the "middle" status fathers "never fed the baby," and 27 percent of the "low" and 17 percent of the "middle" status fathers never "played with" or "held the child." Yet when the mothers were asked how they felt about what the father did, only 19 percent of the "low" and 27 percent of the "middle" described the father's participation as "not enough." It appears that for both mother groups the father does relatively little in taking care of his children, but his minimal participation is generally accepted by the woman. It may be that a husband playing an active father role would represent deviant behavior in the Black lower class.

Summary

Our data would suggest that for the Black lower-class male *both* marriage and parental roles are frequently of minimal importance. By contrast, for the Black lower-class woman the marriage role is of little importance, but the parental role is very often of high significance to her. It is quite possible that for some Black lower-class women, marriage is not only viewed as negative in itself, but also as potentially dangerous to the parental role as she actually fills it. That is, to get married may mean for some Black women the possibility that their limited economic and personal resources needed for taking care of their children will be drained off by the husband. Our evidence indicates that for a number of Black lower-class women there is not just antipathy toward marriage, but rather a real feeling of hostility because it is often seen as making the difficult situation of daily living even more difficult.

10

Personality Development and
the Problems of Youth

Lee Rainwater: Identity Processes
in the Family

Up to this point we have been examining the sequential development of family stages in the Negro slum community, paying only incidental attention to the psychological responses family members make to these social forms and not concerning ourselves with the effect the family forms have on the psychosocial development of the children who grow up in them. Now we want to examine the effect that growing up in this kind of a system has in terms of socialization and personality development.

Household groups function for cultures in carrying out the initial phases of socialization and personality formation. It is in the family that the child learns the most primitive categories of existence and experience, and that he develops his most deeply held beliefs about the world and about himself. From the child's point of view, the household *is* the world; his experiences as he moves out of it into the larger world are always interpreted in terms of his particular experience within the home. The painful experiences which a child in the Negro slum culture has are, therefore, interpreted as in some sense a reflection of this family world. The impact of the system of victimization is transmitted through the family; the child cannot be expected to

From "The Crucible of Identity: The Lower-Class Negro Family," by Lee Rainwater, *Daedalus*, 95 (Winter 1965), pp. 258-264. Reprinted by permission from *Daedalus*, Journal of the American Academy of Arts and Sciences, Boston, Massachusetts.

have the sophistication an outside observer has for seeing exactly where the villains are. From the child's point of view, if he is hungry it is his parents' fault; if he experiences frustrations in the streets or in the school it is his parents' fault; if that world seems incomprehensible to him it is his parents' fault; if people are aggressive or destructive toward each other it is his parents' fault, not that of a system of race relations. In another culture this might not be the case; if a subculture could exist which provided comfort and security within its limited world and the individual experienced frustration only when he moved out into the larger society, the family might not be thought so much to blame. The effect of the caste system, however, is to bring home through a chain of cause and effect all of the victimization processes, and to bring them home in such a way that it is often very difficult even for adults in the system to see the connection between the pain they feel at the moment and the structured patterns of the caste system.

Let us take as a central question that of identity formation within the Negro slum family. We are concerned with the question of who the individual believes himself to be and to be becoming. For Erikson, identity means a sense of continuity and social sameness which bridges what the individual "*was* as a child and what he is *about to become* and also reconciles his *conception of himself* and his community's recognition of him." Thus identity is a "self-realization coupled with a mutual recognition."[1] In the early childhood years identity is family-bound since the child's identity is his identity *vis-à-vis* other members of the family. Later he incorporates into his sense of who he is and is becoming his experiences outside the family, but always influenced by the interpretations and evaluations of those experiences that the family gives. As the child tries on identities, *announces* them, the family sits as judge of his pretensions. Family members are both the most important judges and the most critical ones, since who he is allowed to become affects them in their own identity strivings more crucially than it affects anyone else. The child seeks a sense of valid identity, a sense of being a particular person with a satisfactory degree of congruence between who he feels he is, who he announces himself to be, and where he feels his society places him. He is uncomfortable when he experiences disjunction between his own needs and the kinds of needs legitimated by those around him, or when he feels a disjunction between his sense of himself and the image of himself that others play back to him.

"Tell It Like It Is"

When families become involved in important quarrels the psychosocial underpinnings of family life are laid bare. One such quarrel in a family we have been studying brings together in one place many of the themes that seem to dominate identity problems in Negro slum culture. The incident illustrates in a particularly forceful and dramatic way family processes

[1] Erik H. Erikson, "Identity and the Life Cycle," *Psychological Issues*, Vol 1, No. 1 (1959).

which our field work, and some other contemporary studies of slum family life, suggests unfold more subtly in a great many families at the lower-class level. The family involved, the Johnsons, is certainly not the most disorganized one we have studied; in some respects their way of life represents a realistic adaptation to the hard living of a family nineteen years on AFDC with a monthly income of $202 for nine people. The two oldest daughters, Mary Jane (eighteen years old) and Esther (sixteen) are pregnant; Mary Jane has one illegitimate child. The adolescent sons, Bob and Richard, are much involved in the social and sexual activities of their peer group. The three other children, ranging in age from twelve to fourteen, are apparently also moving into this kind of peer-group society.

When the argument started Bob and Esther were alone in the apartment with Mary Jane's baby. Esther took exception to Bob's playing with the baby because she had been left in charge; the argument quickly progressed to a fight in which Bob cuffed Esther around, and she tried to cut him with a knife. The police were called and subdued Bob with their nightsticks. At this point the rest of the family and the field worker arrived. As the argument continued, these themes relevant to the analysis which follows appeared:

1. The sisters said that Bob was not their brother (he is a half-brother to Esther, and Mary Jane's full brother). Indeed, they said their mother "didn't have no husband. These kids don't even know who their daddies are." The mother defended herself by saying that she had one legal husband, and one common-law husband, no more.

2. The sisters said that their fathers had never done anything for them, nor had their mother. She retorted that she had raised them "to the age of womanhood" and now would care for their babies.

3. Esther continued to threaten to cut Bob if she got a chance (a month later they fought again, and she did cut Bob, who required twenty-one stitches).

4. The sisters accused their mother of favoring their lazy brothers and asked her to put them out of the house. She retorted that the girls were as lazy, that they made no contribution to maintaining the household, could not get their boy friends to marry them or support their children, that all the support came from her AFDC check. Mary Jane retorted that "the baby has a check of her own."

5. The girls threatened to leave the house if their mother refused to put their brothers out. They said they could force their boy friends to support them by taking them to court, and Esther threatened to cut her boy friend's throat if he did not cooperate.

6. Mrs. Johnson said the girls could leave if they wished but that she would keep their babies; "I'll not have it, not knowing who's taking care of them."

7. When her thirteen-year-old sister laughed at all of this, Esther told her not to laugh because she, too, would be pregnant within a year.

8. When Bob laughed, Esther attacked him and his brother by saying that both were not man enough to make babies, as she and her sister had been able to do.

9. As the field worker left, Mrs. Johnson sought his sympathy. "You see, Joe, how hard it is for me to bring up a family. . . . They sit around and talk to me like I'm some kind of a dog and not their mother."

10. Finally, it is important to note for the analysis which follows that the following labels—"black-assed," "black bastard," "bitch," and other profane terms—were liberally used by Esther and Mary Jane, and rather less liberally by their mother, to refer to each other, to the girls' boy friends, to Bob, and to the thirteen-year-old daughter.

Several of the themes outlined previously appear forcefully in the course of this argument. In the last year and a half the mother has become a grandmother and expects shortly to add two more grandchildren to her household. She takes it for granted that it is her responsibility to care for the grandchildren and that she has the right to decide what will be done with the children since her own daughters are not fully responsible. She makes this very clear to them when they threaten to move out, a threat which they do not really wish to make good nor could they if they wished to.

However, only as an act of will is Mrs. Johnson able to make this a family. She must constantly cope with the tendency of her adolescent children to disrupt the family group and to deny that they are in fact a family—"He ain't no brother of mine"; "The baby has a check of her own." Though we do not know exactly what processes communicate these facts to the children it is clear that in growing up they have learned to regard themselves as not fully part of a solidary collectivity. During the quarrel this message was reinforced for the twelve-, thirteen-, and fourteen-year-old daughters by the four-way argument among their older sisters, older brother, and their mother.

The argument represents vicious unmasking of the individual members' pretenses to being competent individuals. The efforts of the two girls to present themselves as masters of their own fate are unmasked by the mother. The girls in turn unmask the pretensions of the mother and of their two brothers. When the thirteen-year-old daughter expresses some amusement they turn on her, telling her that it won't be long before she too becomes pregnant. Each member of the family in turn is told that he can expect to be no more than a victim of his world, but that this is somehow inevitably his own fault.

In this argument masculinity is consistently demeaned. Bob has no right to play with his niece, the boys are not really masculine because at fifteen and sixteen years they have yet to father children, their own fathers were no goods who failed to do anything for their family. These notions probably come originally from the mother, who enjoys recounting the story of having her common-law husband imprisoned for nonsupport, but this comes back to haunt her as her daughters accuse her of being no better than they in ability to force support and nurturance from a man. In contrast, the girls came off somewhat better than the boys, although they must accept the label of stupid girls because they have similarly failed and inconveniently become pregnant in the first place. At least they can and have had children and therefore have some meaningful connection with the ongoing substance of life. There is something important and dramatic in which they participate, while the boys, despite their sexual activity, "can't get no babies."

In most societies, as children grow and are formed by their elders into suitable members of the society they gain increasingly a sense of competence and ability to master the behavioral environment their particular world presents. But in Negro slum culture growing up involves an ever-increasing appreciation of one's shortcomings, of the impossibility of finding a self-sufficient and gratifying way of living. It is in the family first and most devastatingly that one learns these lessons. As the child's sense of frustration builds he too can strike out and unmask the pretensions of others. The result is a peculiar strength and a pervasive weakness. The strength involves the ability to tolerate and defend against degrading verbal and physical aggressions from others and not to give up completely. The weakness involves the inability to embark hopefully on any course of action that might make things better, particularly action which involves cooperating and trusting attitudes toward others. Family members become potential enemies to each other, as the frequency of observing the police being called in to settle family quarrels brings home all too dramatically.

The conceptions parents have of their children are such that they are constantly alert as the child matures to evidence that he is as bad as everyone else. That is, in lower-class culture human nature is conceived of as essentially bad, destructive, immoral. This is the nature of things. Therefore any one child must be inherently bad unless his parents are very lucky indeed. If the mother can keep the child insulated from the outside world, she feels she may be able to prevent his inherent badness from coming out. She feels that once he is let out into the larger world the badness will come to the fore since that is his nature. This means that in the identity development of the child he is constantly exposed to identity labeling by his parents as a bad person. Since as he grows up he does not experience his world as particularly gratifying, it is very easy for him to conclude that this lack of gratification is due to the fact that something is wrong with him. This, in turn, can readily be assimilated to the definitions of being a bad person offered him by those with whom he lives. In this way the Negro slum child learns his culture's conception of being-in-the-world, a conception that emphasizes inherent evil in a chaotic, hostile, destructive world.

Joseph S. Himes: Some Work-Related Cultural Deprivations In Lower-Class Negro Youth

For lower-class Negro youths just entering the labor market, three conditions are institutionally depriving: age, race, and social class. Since age tends to affect white and Negro youths alike, it may be omitted in the following discussion. Race and social class are, of course, not the same. For Negroes, however, race tends to determine class, and, in fact, the two are almost inseparable.

In the present discussion, cultural deprivation is understood to refer to residual personality characteristics that issue from socialization under specific institutionalized preconditions. In the case of lower-class Negroes, the significant institutionalized preconditions include, among others, color segregation, material discrimination, inferior or collateral social status, disparaging social evaluations, chronic social frustrations, and a substantively distinct subculture. From socialization under such preconditions, the individual emerges as a functioning member of his social world. Certain dimensions of the functional adjustment to his effective social world, however, constitute cultural deprivations in terms of the standards and demands of the larger world from which he is more or less excluded.

The work-related residual cultural deprivations of lower-class Negro youths taken at the point of entering the labor market have both judgmental and realistic dimensions. Judgmentally, deprivation refers to the absence or distortion of those knowledges, social graces, and levels of sophistication that "typical" young people are expected to exhibit. For example, culturally deprived young Negroes are said to be awkward and ill-at-ease, loud and boisterous, uncouth or gauche in manner, improperly dressed, limited in general knowledge, unsophisticated, and the like. These and similar phrases indicate that Negro youths differ in many respects from a generally accepted model or standard.

Stated judgmentally, deprivations signify cultural deviation rather than absolute cultural lacks. Lower-class Negro youths reveal the knowledge, social traits, and personality characteristics of the racial group and social class from which they emerge. Such characteristics seem to have more relevance for social acceptance than for specific job performance. For example, gauche manners or lack of sophistication may have little or no relevance for operating a machine or performing a technical task. However, such behavior may decisively influence the individual's chances of securing a job or his relations with associates in the work situation.

In terms of the reality dimension, some cultural deprivations represent genuine lacks as defined by minimal demands of the economy and specific

Reprinted from *Journal of Marriage and the Family* (November 1964), pp. 447-451, by permission of the National Council on Family Relations and the author. Dr. Joseph Himes is Professor of Sociology at the University of North Carolina, Greensboro.

Paper originally presented at the Groves Conference on Marriage and the Family, Knoxville, Tennessee, April 1964.

occupations. For example, inability to read and to understand and follow directions is decisively handicapping for many modern jobs. Functional illiteracy of this kind is not limited, of course, to lower-class Negroes, although their race and social class make them peculiarly vulnerable to this cultural deprivation.

A number of studies have examined the nature, extent, and consequences of realistic cultural deprivations such as functional illiteracy, lack of basic education, inadequacy of mathematical and scientific skills, adolescent character defects, and so on.[1] Some other work-related cultural deprivations constitute incidental residual consequences of exclusion of Negroes from the basic work life of the economy. They appear as group-linked, trained incapacities and function to handicap youthful Negroes when they enter the labor market.

Two local situations may serve to symbolize the institutionalized exclusion of Negro workers from important sectors of the national work force. In Piedmont, North Carolina, furniture and textile manufacture are basic, traditional industries. Historically, virtually no Negro workers are employed in production jobs in either industry. In Durham, within Piedmont, North Carolina, although some Negroes work as insurance executives and bankers in all-Negro concerns, none is employed as stock broker or advertising executive. The extent of Negro exclusion from the nation's work force is well known and has been documented elsewhere.[2] In the following paragraphs, three residual work-related cultural deprivations issuing from job exclusions of Negro workers are examined briefly.

Irrelevant Work Models

Lower-class Negro children are denied the experience of daily association with parents, relatives, neighbors, friends, and peers who manufacture textiles and furniture and who deal in securities or plan advertising campaigns. There is none of the casual talk and informal interaction that imperceptibly and inadvertently introduce the child to the role of the worker and the world of work in factory and office. Unlike their lower-class, poor white cohorts, such Negro children cannot, in routine socialization, acquire and identify with the roles of workers in factory and office. Rather they must rely on the formal institutions, the mass media and secondhand gleanings of Negro servants for glimpses into the world of work symbolized by the furniture factory and the brokerage office. In a revealing comment on transmission of the female role in American families, Talcott Parsons stresses the importance of the availability of the mother model in casual informal contacts with girl children in the home: ". . . It is possible from an early age to initiate girls directly into many important aspects of the adult feminine role.

[1] Among other sources, see Michael Harrington, *The Other America*, New York: Macmillan, 1962; and James Bryant Conant, *The American High School Today*, New York: McGraw-Hill, 1959.

[2] See E. Franklin Frazier, *The Negro in the United States*, New York: MacMillan, 1939, Chapter XXIII; and Robert C. Weaver, *Negro Labor*, New York: Harcourt, Brace, 1946.

Their mothers are continually about the house and the meaning of many of the things they are doing is relatively tangible and easily understandable to a child. It is also possible for the daughter to participate actively and usefully in many of these activities.. . . ."[3]

Excluded from casual though meaningful contacts with modern workers, the lower-class Negro child cannot identify by internal role taking and anticipatory socialization with the worker models that are symbolized by the furniture maker and stock broker. Such experiences are as much beyond his social reach as if they were prohibited by law. Whatever knowledge and skill and character he may bring to the modern labor market, he cannot present those fringe cultural characteristics that come from being "bred to the job."

However, it must not be thought from the foregoing that the lower-class Negro youth comes to the job market culturally empty handed. He brings with him the residues of learning and the precipitates of identification with those occupational models that exist in reality within his racial and class world. For most, casual and informal childhood experiences have been with unskilled and service workers in city and country. But terms like "technology," "automation," and "white collar" tend to show how irrelevant this Negro youth's work-related cultural baggage is for the modern labor market.

Exclusion from Work Ethos

Workers who are restricted to the fringes of the occupational structure tend to be excluded from the tenets and rationalizations of the work ethos. They cannot perceive the linkage between effort and advancement. For example, the Negro janitors and maids in furniture factories and brokerage offices cannot expect to become production, office, or managerial workers as a result of hard work and self-improvement. The lower-class Negro child sees none of his parents, relatives, neighbors, friends, and peers moving up the occupational ladder. Hard work and extra effort may be a necessary condition of keeping a job. But neither hard work nor self-improvement leads to a promotion. What then is the value of hard work, extra effort, and self-improvement?

The work reserved for Negroes has no intrinsic goodness or importance. The worker does not have a sense of the relation of his job to any total scheme or large goal of the enterprise. Both he and his job are marginal to the aims of the business and to the philosophy of business. If he is loyal or dedicated, and many are, his reaction is likely to be personal rather than ideological. Such work is often uninspiring, fatiguing, and sometimes even deadening.

In family and neighborhood, Negro lower-class workers are prone to act out negative responses to the job. In casual talk and informal relations with

[3] Talcott Parsons, "Age and Sex in the Social Structure of the United States," *American Sociological Review*, 7 (October 1942), p. 605.

their children, they say in effect that work is neither good nor promiseful of better things. In spite of the teachings of the social institutions and the mass media, they believe that work is simply work, an unpleasant though necessary condition of staying alive. They go to the job in the morning with reluctance and escape from it at day's end with relief.

Such workers and their children are often alleged to be "apathetic" or "lazy." But these words are social evaluations, not real explanations. From one perspective, they mean that lower-class workers and their children have not entered into the Protestant middle-class work ethos. They have not seen that work is good, that more education leads to greater opportunities, and that increased effort results in job advancements. From another perspective, such judgments reveal a pragmatic realism. The experiences of many lower-class Negroes demonstrate that self-improvement and increased effort tend to multiply and intensify their frustrations and unhappiness.

The lower-class Negro child relies upon the formal institutions, the mass media, and various adventitious personal experiences to acquire the tenets and rationalizations of the work ethos. In this respect, he is disadvantaged *vis à vis* his white cohort, whose childhood observations demonstrate the validity of hard work and self-improvement as preludes to advancement in the world of work. When he enters the labor market, therefore, the lower-class Negro youth is initially handicapped by a cultural deprivation with consequences which may accumulate with the passage of time.

Alienated from Job Ways

Family and neighborhood experiences of lower-class Negro children tend to alienate them from the distinctive ways of factory and office. They do not overhear relatives, neighbors, and friends in the "shoptalk" about incidents, people, and things of the job. They cannot acquire familiarity with office and factory tools by playing with daddy's briefcase or tool kit. No casual talk and informal relations introduce them to the jargon, costumes, bearing, manners, and attitudes of office and shop. They have no childhood experiences that acquaint them with the general layout, daily routines, general atmosphere, and occupational *dramatis personae* of an industrial workshop or business office.[4]

Furthermore, lower-class Negro children cannot acquire from their occupationally marginal parents the ideologies and values of labor unions. Thus, they do not apprehend the sense of structured competition and cooperation that marks awareness of labor-management relations. They are not bred to that robust labor union conviction that the worker, if not his work, is good

---

[4] I still remember vividly how alien and unprepared I felt the first days in the aircraft factory during the war. The overwhelming and incessant racket, the inescapable glaring lights, and the sense of frantic perpetual motion distracted and terrified me. Everything and everybody was strange. The jargon—socket wrench, bonding cable, duralium, lock nut, etc. — was a foreign tongue. It took me days to find my way around and to feel at home in the factory. My experiences were duplicated by many other novices to the production line.

and dignified and important. These children are alien to the experience of group solidarity and secular collective destiny that distinguish the American labor movements. They cannot acquire from daily experience the definitions and justifications of legitimate individual and collective goals and values that are transmitted by the labor movement.

Finally, family patterns and daily habits of lower-class Negroes and their children are seldom conditioned by the long arm of production and office jobs. Work shifts, pay periods, over-time requirements, vacation schedules, and the like, seldom shape the routines of family life and daily activities. The climate of family relations is not affected by the vagaries of the politics of the job, for Negro workers are outside the occupational power system. These children and their families are passed by in the drama of the strike, the diversions of the industrial recreational program, or the securities and protections of pension systems.

Exclusion from these and other social extensions of the factory and office job tends to induce a further cultural deprivation among lower-class Negro youths. It appears as a trained unreadiness for smooth transition from family, school, and neighborhood to the social world and technical roles of work. For these youths, the workshop or the business office is a world apart, an alien and intimidating social milieu.

Conclusion

Race and class establish institutionalized preconditions under which lower-class Negro youths are socialized to certain work-related cultural deprivations. Some are judgmental in character and influence the individual's acceptance as a worker. Realistic deprivations, however, tend to handicap the individual in actual job performance. Exclusion of lower-class Negroes from important sectors of the work force constitutes one institutionalized precondition and eventuates in a series of work-related cultural deprivations. The three examined here briefly include socialization to irrelevant job models, exclusion from the prevailing work ethos, and alienation from the culture of the modern factory and office.

Robert Coles: Children and Racial Demonstrations

For the past three years I have been studying young people of the South— white and Negro as they initiate various kinds of social change, from entering desegregated schools to picketing lunch counters, libraries or town office buildings. . . . My old interest in children under stress was stimulated

Reprinted from *The American Scholar*, 34 (Winter 1964-1965), pp. 78-92, with permission of the author. Robert Coles is a research psychiatrist at the Harvard University Health Service.

by this moment in our national life which found children seeking or taking on a variety of stressful roles in one social and political crisis after another; and so I returned South . . . living in Atlanta, where I could observe school desegregation as it developed, meeting weekly with the nine pioneering Negro youths and with a like number of their white classmates. From Atlanta I traveled to New Orleans for monthly interviews with the four Negro girls, a few others who followed their steps the next year, and a handful of their white schoolmates and teachers. I moved elsewhere over the South in those years, devoting a good deal of time to talking with young people involved in the sit-in movement and segregationists who were opposing desegregation through organizations and demonstrations of their own . . . .

It was not easy for me as a white psychiatrist to get to know such facts, let alone learn more generally the emotional ties and strains at play in Negro families. It is easier to observe them sociologically, then categorize: they are matriarchal families whose members are underprivileged, ill-educated people, relatively deprived of cultural traditions and roots. Even descriptions of the anger and frustration common to most of these families may fail to account for the origin of these feelings in the special, grinding humiliations constantly faced. We may easily understand a Negro's instant anger before a threatening state trooper, but fail to see that from their first years Negro children must learn who they are, where they may not go, what they most probably will be and cannot be. Such lessons of reality become psychological facts—surely as important as social and economic ones—which determine the child's sense of his own worth, his sense of the power of those who define his worth, and consequently, of their worth.

If the Negro child's life is one of having to learn how to confront a future of unrelenting harassment, his intimidated parents must prepare him for it. They must teach their child a variety of maneuvers and postures to cope with his baffling lot. By seven or eight most Negro children know the score, and I have seen them draw only faintly disguised pictures of the harsh future awaiting them. Yet such a future can be either harsh and purposeless or harsh but at least with some promise that the pain endured will contribute to the eventual end of its causes. . . .

Until now nonviolence has come naturally to Negroes, because the only choice has been turning their suffering in upon themselves, converting it to sullen despair. Negroes are not becoming angry. They have always been angry. We are fortunate that for the moment their anger has found constructive expression. Other kinds have been shown waiting in the wings, fierce reminders that the real alternative to the remarkable lack of impulsivity and fragility in these children is the violence, delinquency and addiction of some of their more injured peers or elders.

Suffering also can ignore the color line. In a sense white and Negro children have more in common with each other than with their parents. They share an historical moment that can be painful to them regardless of race. I have watched white school children in the South suffer with shame as they slowly begin to realize what Negro classmates must endure. Even some

frantic segregationists experience guilt, an unconscious kind which sometimes accumulates large enough in a particular child to change his racial
attitudes. Most Southerners simply turn away, in apathy or defensive rationalizations; or they watch. They watch in surprise as these Negro youths
contain themselves under the repeated provocation of hecklers. "Where did
they ever learn to behave like that?" I was asked by a white girl of seventeen
who watched her town's police club a Negro girl two years her junior. She
went on to express her covert sympathy with the girl by saying, "I don't
think any girl of her age really wants to cause trouble."

Yet there are records of violence and antisocial behavior from children,
both younger and older than that Negro girl, which go back into the Middle
Ages and persist through our time. School children once were armed and the
word "truant," which I hear applied to so many Negro children trying to
become American citizens, comes from a Latin word describing a wandering student. Such youths were readily accepted by many societies until their
freedom slowly began to threaten the more stable order of life demanded by
the rising bourgeoisie. The nineteenth century, that sober era when upper-
class children were most precious and least indulged, was amply touched by
juvenile crime and violence. The earliest records of the Children's Aid
Society of New York (founded in 1854) mention many instances of both.
Across the seas student groups—such organizations as Young Italy and
Young France of the 1830's and 40's—were forming the rebellious vanguard to spreading nationalism. Today's protesting Negro youths, despite
their supposed lack of "civilization" and their susceptibility—even if at a
segregated distance—to twentieth-century liberalism, with all its supposed
encouragement to lowered standards for obedience, are much less violent
and wild, much more controlled or "repressed" than their nineteenth-cen-
tury counterparts in Western Europe; and despite the hardships of their
race's special exploitation, they seem no less sturdy.

Indeed, there are no easy correlations between parental ideology, class or
race and "successful" child development. Many children the world over
have revealed a kind of toughness and plasticity under far from favorable
conditions that make the determined efforts of some parents to spare their
children the slightest pain seem quite ironic. Despite our wealth and its
advantages for our children, despite our constant interest in their "welfare,"
we so far have produced no general flowering of humanity. Of course
middle-class breast-beating is always tempting, and can be easily justified by
a glance at our all too numerous hoody, self-indulgent youths. In contrast, the
affluent section of our society has also produced—in the Peace Corps, in the
Northern college youths who have joined the civil rights movement—a
remarkable kind of idealistic youth, many of whom have achieved their own
virtue by rejecting their parents' too obvious materialism. Similarly, I have
come to know reliable and productive Negro children from the most desolate
homes. Their parents are tired, beaten, and sometimes very unattractive in
speech and action. But such parents produce their fair share of delinquent
children, too. . . .

Regardless of *our* ideas about Negro youths and what they think and believe or how they should behave in their childhood, most of the students I know are surprisingly little concerned with ideology, and their parents even less so. With more success these parents and children will have the various choices that make thinking and planning appropriate. "Right now," one of them grimly told me, "I don't do much figuring, and I don't worry about what's going to happen to me. I just try to get into those lunch counters, and my parents, they don't much care one way or the other. I mean they do, but they don't know, to tell the truth, what we're doing." Moreover, it is an ironic fact that many Negro children have had much wider latitude in street play than their white counterparts. There has been until recently much less reason for a Negro parent to restrict his child to study and discipline. This very "freedom" of the poor child whose parents do not have faith in the future has allowed some of these children to make their very spontaneous street demonstrations.

To many of these children their parents have not merely lost hope, but are deeply compromised by virtue of their long, if historically necessary, submission to the white world. If I needed instruction on the ways Negro leaders—college presidents, businessmen, ministers, political leaders—have had to truckle to their white counterparts, then go wearily homeward with their pittance, these youths have given it eagerly and bitterly. In a sense these students are their race's first truly independent spokesmen, asserting a critical role, one perhaps unique in America, toward the Negro adult community similar to that played by students in other countries where education is rare, and freedom is being newly sought or has only recently been won.

I have said that these demonstrations—picketing stores and braving the subsequent white "justice" of hoses, dogs, truncheons, electric prodding poles, courtrooms, trials, jails, criminal records—do not necessarily cause psychological collapse or psychiatric symptoms in these teen-aged youths. I have stressed that we must understand their behavior in its meaning for them. Yet, when we try to evaluate the meaning of their behavior for us, we often flounder in our own problems. We are a generation that looks very carefully at motives. The most common interest I hear from many concerned people is one that asks what *kind* of person takes on this hard life of protest, of demonstration and frequent arrest. Such curiosity is partly related to our fear that these youths will be hurt by the trials they assume. But our upper middle-class culture is more generally curious about why people do things— and which people do what things. It is anxious to use such knowledge, too, for its children's sake. Tentative psychological hypotheses become for many a code of dogmatically held rights and wrongs, to be assiduously implemented in the child's training and education, in the general atmosphere that surrounds him.

Well, who are these "children" and what are their motives? They are all kinds—seekers, wanderers and rebels; children who are men, young men sometimes acting in very childish ways (they are not always demonstrating, but they are always human). How do they compare with youths the world over? Like them they have restless energy and spells of anxious hesitation. Like them they seek expression and may in moments fear it, too. Some of them are controlled and studious, and others are delighted, if a bit surprised, to find themselves *both* lawbreakers and heroes. Every year high schools and colleges all over the world witness school riots, "panty raids," or youths engaged in clamorous political activities based upon widely different ideological convictions. Delinquency is worldwide, and class wide, too. The Mayor of Nairobi recently remarked upon its occurrence there. It plagues the Borstal boys in England as well as our own young, those from slums to those in elegant suburbs. How do we compare the youthful spirit that causes a destructive riot in Princeton with that which caused the young white students in Oxford, Mississippi, to shout their vulgar defiance of Federal law? In a Northern city I recently watched a group of youths about fourteen or fifteen years old scream various obscenities at a Negro couple moving into their neighborhood. What marked off their impulses, motivations and problems from those of the youthful Negro and white demonstrators in the South or North?

Some of the differences are clear. Many of those youths taking part in racial demonstrations are better integrated psychologically as well as racially. They act out of deep moral convictions, and in a spirit of sensitivity and thoughtfulness. In contrast, other youths, in Oxford or Chicago, are squalid, mindless toughs, acting out of careless impulsivity. But for many of both groups the differences are less psychological than social and cultural. Young men and women whom we today might call "children" fought on *both* sides in the Civil War; Napoleon had his brave drummer boys; and English children read of a boy who was a hero in the Battle of Jutland. . . . I doubt very much, however, whether we shall find a final judgment upon these youths that rests upon psychiatric analysis of motives, and if a small but influential segment of our society asks for it too exclusively, that is a problem in itself. . . .

Whatever their motives, these hopeful children of the sit-ins are not willing to accept the prevailing values of a segregated society. They are committed to action, dedicated to affirming new values. Their actions are what make them guileless and powerfully innocent, and their actions occurring in our particular time; because it is this very time that is their essential catalyst, enabling them to strike out and claim, successfully, once forbidden territory. They have not been the first Negro youths to dream of freedom, to want cafeteria coffee, to covet revenge. They are not the first to delight in their parents' anxiety and fear and try for their own social action. If they are white, they are not the first youths to flout powerful customs and try to build their very own. Until recently, however, many children died young, families were more authoritarian in structure, social controls were perhaps firmer in societies not only more simple and compact, but further apart in time and space. Until recently, moreover, the Negro was not free enough, or secure enough even to conceive of the true security of real freedom. Now he is; it is a mere beginning, but a crucial and historic one. In all its social, political and cultural senses, the historical moment allows the translation of the possible or potential into the actual. The chance for such translation is strikingly similar to the conditions that seem to make some individuals more able and productive than others. After all, the chief complaint of most of our mentally ill is not that life is hard, or even painful, but that it is both of these without a sense of fulfillment—their dreams seem out of touch with the reality of their lives. As psychiatrists we must help our patients understand their dreams and help them dream other dreams, those sensible and realistic ones that we now call "goals." But goals must find their destiny, and this destiny will always be outside our offices, in the midst of the world and its particular moment and nature.

These children who protest and demonstrate want for themselves what in this country is no scarcity for many others—freedom and work, a share in our wealth, a proper place in our social and cultural life. Since the beginning of history racism has afflicted many corners of our earth. Vast armies have moved from continent to continent, tribes and castes have moved within continents, conquering and in turn being conquered. The United States is the first country founded on the exile of those from other nations, and it is now the first country to begin to come to terms with genuine freedom and equality across racial lines for so large a number of people. It is not an easy job, and at times we look across history in heavy guilt. Yet these children in their present irrepressible confrontation of all of us are very much part of us. There is something historically special about what they are doing, and politically special about how they are doing it; and I would think something very "healthy," too, for them and for their country as a democracy. They are forcing us to face our proper destiny.

Robert Staples: Childhood in a Black Ghetto: A Case Study

John Blue, Jr., 18 years old, was born in Richmond, Virginia. He is of Black ancestry, possesses a tenth-grade education, and was reared in the Baptist Church by his parents. John is the fourth of five children born to John and Dorothy Blue. His mother is a maid and his father a postal worker. Some six years ago, John's parents were divorced, and he now lives with his mother, older sister, and younger brother in St. Paul, Minnesota. Junior, as he is called, has another older sister who is married and lives in Minneapolis and an older brother who is presently serving with the armed forces in Vietnam. Mr. Blue, Sr., continues to reside in Virginia by himself and does not contribute to the support of his children.

Of those living at home, Junior's younger brother, age 17, is in his last year of high school. His older sister, age 20, dropped out of school four years

Originally prepared for the Studies in Racism Series under the sponsorship of Professor Talmadge Anderson, Director, Department of Black Studies, Washington State University, May 1966. This is the first publication of this article. All rights reserved. Permission to reprint must be obtained from the publisher.

ago and currently works as a Nurse's Aide at a local hospital. Junior, who also failed to complete high school, currently works at odd jobs—when he can find work—washing cars, hauling trash, and so on. His difficulty in finding employment is compounded by the fact that he has a rather long record of encounters with the law.

His last offense resulted in a year's jail term at the local reformatory. He and some other boys beat up a white man and robbed him. After his release from jail, he has not worked steadily and manages to earn only enough money for clothes and recreation.

Physical Description, Health, and Development

Junior is tall, lanky, and awkward. He is about six feet two inches tall and does not carry his height well. His clothes appear to be too large for him, and he walks with a heavy step. He weighs about 140 pounds and, with the exception of hay fever, has no chronic illnesses. Mrs. Blue explained that Junior had been a rather small lad until the age of 15, when his greatest growth occured.

Junior seems to have completed his physical development, since he has not grown taller in the last two years. His voice is rather low, and he speaks in a gruff tone. Although he has some facial hair, he does not shave and is anxious for the day when he can grow a beard like his idol, Malcolm X.

Junior is also sexually mature. Most of the primary and secondary sex characteristics have appeared within the average amount of time. He would seem to be neither an early nor late maturing adolescent. Although he views a beard as a sign of masculinity, he seems to be content for the moment to have his unusual height show his maleness within his peer group. This gives him a special status in his primary group relationships and facilitates his leadership role.

A Typical Day

On most days, when Junior is not working, he gets up around 10 o'clock. By that time, everyone else in the house has left for school or work. He fixes some breakfast and then sits around the house listening to a local rhythm and blues radio station. Frequently, some of his friends, who are also high school dropouts, drop by and talk about what they did together the previous night.

While talking together, they usually smoke cigarettes and drink beer if they have the money to buy any. Sometimes they pretend to fight with each other and generally laugh it up. When playing around, they do not bother Junior, since one does not jest with a person of his leadership status.

Early in the afternoon, they leave the house for a poolroom, where they play pool and listen to the jukebox if they have the money. If they don't, they just stand in front of the poolroom and continue their horseplay. When school gets out, the girls come by the poolroom, and the boys begin their "rap."

Around 5 or 6 o'clock, when Junior's mother returns from work, he goes home for dinner and then returns to the streets to hang around. In the evening he stands around on the corner talking to his friends. When he deviates from this pattern, he rides around in one of his friends' cars or indulges in sexual activity with his girlfriend.

His typical day consists of idling around his home and the streets. When asked about why he did not try harder to find employment, he stated:

I don't see no use in going downtown anymore to look for a job. After all, it costs 50 cents to take the bus down there, and I can do something a lot better with that money. Everytime I go down there, I just get the runaround. Those old prejudiced white people ain't going to help you find a job. When I go there, they ask me if I got a high school diploma. Then they want you to take a lot of tests and you still don't get a job.

Because he cannot find employment, Junior has become resigned to a life of idleness. He has given little thought to what he will do in the future because he sees little opportunity for improving his life chances.

Intellectual Performance

Until the age of eleven, Junior attended an all-Black school in Virginia. At that time he was considered an average pupil with normal intellectual development. When he came to St. Paul, he was in the first year of junior high school, and his fellow students and his teachers were mainly white. He did very well in his first year, but afterward his grades began to drop lower and lower up to the time he dropped out of high school.

His main interests in school were in shop courses. Although he enjoyed working on cars and doing carpentry, bricklaying, and other manual jobs, his grades in these courses were not good because he had a high rate of absenteeism, frequently disrupted the class by horseplay with his classmates, and was disrespectful to his teachers.

It should not be assumed because of Junior's interest in vocational courses that he lacks any academic potential. During his three years in junior high school, he received straight A's in his English courses. His mother explained that he wrote beautiful themes in his English classes. Somewhat embarrassed at this revelation, Junior remarked that he got such good grades in English by sweet-talking the teacher.

His attitude toward school is mostly negative. He said,

I used to like school when I was in Virginia with all my friends and I knew all my school teachers and they really helped you learn. When I came to St. Paul I had to go to school with all these "paddies" and all the teachers were white. The "paddies" would look down on all the "brothers" because they thought they were better than us. And the teacher usually favored them. When I got to be around fifteen years old, I didn't let them mess over me like I used to—so I got suspended from school a lot. I wasn't learning very much anyway—so I just quit. I also knew that there were no good jobs for Negroes anyway.

Talking to Junior gives the impression that he does possess the skills necessary for academic success. He is an avid reader of the Black newspapers and can regurgitate anything he has read in them. In addition, he can remember thousands of baseball and football statistics and knows the lyrics of a large number of rhythm and blues songs.

Nonintellectual Interests and Habits

Many of Junior's interests have already been described. Most of his time is taken up by same-sex peer relationships. He plays pool during the day and listens to rhythm and blues day and night. Although he is interested in sports, he states that he does not participate in any sports activities because he is not in real good shape. He has no hobbies in the normal sense of the word. A strong theme of his peer discussions is sexual activity with the high school girls.

Social Development

Junior grew up in a home riddled by conflict between his mother and father, conflicts sometimes marked by physical violence. He had a very tenuous relationship with his father, who was seldom at home. He described his early home life this way:

I would not say I had a real happy childhood. My father was very strict with us, he wouldn't allow us to stay up at night and watch television or do anything. In fact, we wouldn't even have had a television set if it wasn't for my mother. My father always provided us with a place to live and food to eat—but that's about all. We only saw him late at night when he came in from work, he never took us anywhere, and he wouldn't buy a car so we could go out for rides like other kids.

In contrast, Junior has had a very close relationship with his mother. He described his mother as always doing what she could for her children. When she divorced his father, they moved to St. Paul, where she had some relatives. Once there she got a job as a domestic worker and supported her children entirely on her earnings. When he spent a year in the local reformatory, his mother came to see him every visiting day until he was released. However, his warm relationship with his mother is strained by her anguish at his idleness. She feels that he should get a job so that he can stand on his own two feet.

Junior's relationship with his siblings is one of aloofness and antagonism. He does not interact at all with his older sister because he knows she does not approve of his present behavior. There is a great deal of conflict between him and his younger brother. This conflict arises out of their totally different personalities. Ken is a very sensitive person. He likes to read and watch television, and he is constantly fighting with Junior about his playing the radio so loud and about Junior's friends hanging around the house. Junior calls Ken a square but admits that he might make it because "he's got something upstairs."

Junior seldom mentions his older brother and oldest sister. They are both away from home now; even when they did live there, they were so much older that he had little interaction with them. When talking about his older brother, Junior shows a mixture of admiration and resentment. He is proud of his brother because he finished college and is now an army captain serving in Vietnam. However, when his brother comes home, he is apparently very critical of Junior for having dropped out of school and not working. Junior's reaction is that he just doesn't understand that not all people are alike. Just because he worked hard and finished college doesn't mean everybody can do it.

Because Junior is tall and aggressive, he has a quasi-leadership status in his peer group. His friends always look him up; he never seeks them out. He also has a high status because of his alleged number of sexual conquests. His rap is considered the best in the community, and his steady old lady is a real fox. When together with his male friends, they constantly discuss their sexual activity, real and imagined. Girls are referred to as bitches and whores in an undiscriminating way. It is assumed that all girls are susceptible to a good rap; any girl who does not indulge in sexual activity is considered a social deviate.

One can discern an inordinate amount of interest in sexual activity that is not consonant with a "normal" sex drive. Much of their sexual behavior is oriented toward the status acquired in their subculture by having sexual intercourse with a girl. On the girl's part, she expects to be seduced by most of the boys that she meets but attempts to save her sexual favors for her old man of the moment. Junior sees sex as a form of pleasure and gives little consideration to the girl as an individual. He sees love and marriage as something he is not yet ready for.

Psychological Functioning and Personality Development

Junior is a classic example of the effects of oppression. Born into a caste system that demeans his worth as an individual, he has adjusted by retreating into a culture which provides some ego gratification and which remains outside the pale of the dominant group's value system. Conflict is apparent in his adjustment to this caste system. On the one hand he extols the virtues of being Black and on the other has his hair straightened to conform to at least one value of the dominant white culture.

Many of Junior's problems stem from the lack of a male role model. Because of his tenuous relationship with his father, he has a poor image of the adult male world, and, for him, masculinity is defined in terms of the number of his sexual conquests.

Because he lives in a society which labels him inferior and denies him sufficient means to attain socially valued goals, his internal identity is one of an inferior individual even though he acts aggressive. Since he is consigned to a ghetto from which he feels there is no escape, he asserts that his identity is that of other Black people who are joining together to ward off the destructive effects of the American system of racism. In evaluating himself, he uses the norms of his peer group while unconsciously accepting the identity given him by white society, that of an invisible man. Sometime later, he may vent his resentment at white society's denial of his humanity and his masculinity by participating in a rebellion or by committing another crime. Or perhaps he will displace his aggression by attacking another Black person.

Summary and Evaluation

John Blue, Jr., is a product of the American system of racism which relegates Blacks to an inferior social status. The fact that he has grown up in a fatherless world also derives from the caste system, which has rendered almost half of all Black children, at some time in their lives, fatherless. The historical experiences of slavery and subsequent racial segregation have vitiated the Black family structure.

In his social development, Junior was emancipated early from parental control. Because his mother worked, much of his socialization into the values of his culture was done by his same-sex peer group. His early childhood experiences were in the South, where he could develop his identity within the well-defined structure of the Southern cultural system. While he was going to school there, his Black teachers may have provided him with role models that encouraged his learning in school. The primary group character of the Southern Black community may have provided him with adequate reinforcement for adjusting in the normative manner of many Southern Black youths.

Once he left the warm environment of his Southern community, he faced the more subtle caste system of St. Paul, Minnesota. From the stable Southern culture he had known, he was thrust into the amorphous racial atmosphere of a Northern city. The consequence was an ambivalence toward the white world which was diffused into a generalized hostility toward all whites. Consequently, he cannot be motivated by white teachers or counseled by white probation officers. He has resigned himself to the status of a have-not Black man in a country of affluence. He has an identity, but it is not a positive one. A transformation in his self-concept can only come about through a program of economic and educational change which will provide the experiences for a healthier identity for Junior and all the other Black Americans like him.

Part Four

Problems

The Black family has always been perceived as an institution beset with problems. In the view of some authorities these problems—unemployment, poverty, and so on—in turn repercuss in the arena of family behavior, causing what they believe to be a vicious circle with no end in sight. A more fruitful approach to the problems aspect of Black family life would be to isolate those factors in the social structure that threaten the Black family and to ascertain how their amelioration or elimination would improve the functioning of Black families.

In this section, labeled "Problems," the first group of articles deals with interracial dating and marital behavior. The inclusion of this topic in this section will probably be questioned, since there is considerable disagreement over whether interracial unions do constitute a problem. In an ideal society, individuals date and marry people without regard to considerations of race; in a society permeated with a racist ethos, such unions are virtually impossible. In this society, race is an important criterion in the selection of sex and marriage partners. Moreover, it can act as either a propelling or a repulsive force—causing individuals to either select or reject others on the basis of racial membership.

However, when Blacks were first introduced to the Americas, race was less important as a basis for excluding potential marriage partners. The first Blacks brought to this country were largely males, who had the status of indentured servants. They fraternized with white indentured servants in an atmosphere of equality, devoid of racism. There were numerous marriages between Black and white indentured servants. Even after the advent of slavery, interracial unions continued to take place. The white male–Black female associations—coercive and voluntary—are quite well-known. Less well-known are the associations between Black male slaves and free white women. The extent of their association is best indicated by the fact that certain Southern states felt compelled to pass laws making any white female a slave who had a child by a slave.

Marriage between individuals implies an equality of the people involved. In a society predicated on racial inequality, such a mixture of the races was not only considered undesirable but was legally prohibited until recent times. Since these laws separated Blacks and whites on the intimate, social level, once the barrier was lifted, they frequently related to each other on the basis of cultural stereotypes—especially Black men and white women. Thus, some Black men saw white women as virgin goddesses, with whom sex relations took on the character of eating forbidden fruit. For white women, Black men were super-studs, possessed with inexhaustible sexual energy and potent sexual equipment. Seeing a relationship between people in terms of cultural symbols deprives the relationship of its humanity. Once the cultural myths are destroyed, the individuals must seek out new ways of relating to each other or dissolve the relationship.

In the selection from Hernton's book *Sex and Racism in America*, he discusses the influence of sex on race problems, stating that the anxieties of the white male about the Black male's having sexual access to white women is an important influence on America's racial barriers. In addition, Hernton makes the somewhat dubious assertion that whites are unable to relate to Blacks except in a sexual context—conscious or unconscious.

The article by Staples describes some of the factors influencing Black-white sex relations. The article says that, in general, Black males and white females, having been barred from sexual union in the past, have an inordinate sexual attraction for each other. Some of the reasons for the mutual appeal, the realities of interracial sexual unions, and some of the problems connected with them are discussed.

In the next article, David Heer examines some of the data on interracial marriages in the United States. Although his research was confined to four states, I believe that his findings are applicable to other parts of the country. In general, he found that interracial marriages are increasing, that most of them involve Black men and white women, and that the marriages involve spouses from the same social class. Previous studies of intermarriage have found that the rate of marriage outside the group varies inversely with the proportion of potential partners belonging to that group—for example, in a city with a small percentage of Catholics, more Catholics marry non-Catholics than in a city with a much higher percentage of Catholics. In the analysis of his data, Heer confirms this hypothesis with whites but not with Blacks. Since potential marriage partners tend to be selected within a small geographical area, the residential segregation of Blacks and whites makes the hypothesis inoperative in this case.

Heer's conclusion, that "any increase in Negro-white marriage is likely to bring Negroes nearer to equality with whites," may be seriously challenged. Interracial marriages have continued to increase since Heer's article was written. A survey in *Newsweek* magazine revealed that over 20 percent of white college students have dated a member of another race.[1] Around this same time, the National Advisory Commission on Civil Disorders reported that this country was moving toward two societies, Black and white, separate and unequal.[2] Thus, interracial dating and marriage are not valid barometers of racial equality. For a long time the ban against them was a symbol of the racial caste system in this country, but inequality of the races is more closely related to the position of Blacks in the economic organization of American society.

In the past, the Black family was torn asunder by the economic imperatives of slavery. The aftermath of slavery again found Black families the victim of a chaotic and irresponsible economy. Black males have persistently been denied equal access to certain occupations, and their employment has been irregular in the menial jobs they have been allowed to hold. Since it is acknowledged that the negative features of family life are more frequently found in the lower income strata, it is easy to understand how Black families are affected by the ramifications of unemployment, underemployment, and low income.

The article by Moynihan presents an array of statistics related to the economic plight of the Black family. He discusses the effect of employment and income problems on the Black family, giving special attention to the problem of the underemployment of the Black male and the "overemployment" of the Black female. I must, again, question Moynihan's interpretation of his data and the conclusions that ensue. He starts off by asserting that middle class Blacks are doing very well and actually have a preferred position in the job market. This is a curious use of logic, since the objective figures available show that the income gap is larger between Black and white college graduates than it is between Black and white graduates of the eighth grade.

Moynihan also cites the failure of Blacks to achieve acceptable educational goals and the role of Black family structure in their lack of educational success. This sort of analysis has led to the emphasis on better education and job training to close the gap between Blacks and whites. However, according to another government official:

The lower educational level of some minority groups is a factor in their lower occupational status, but statistical analyses using two different approaches show that it accounts for only about one third of the difference in occupational ranking between Black men and majority men. The inevitable conclusion is that the other two thirds must be attributed to discrimination, deliberate or inadvertent.[3]

---

[1] "The New Mood on Campus," *Newsweek*, December 29, 1969, p. 44.

[2] *Report of the National Advisory Commission on Civil Disorders* (New York: Bantam Books, 1968).

[3] Charles Markham, Deputy Assistant Secretary for Metropolitan Development in the Department of Housing and Urban Development, quoted in *The Afro-American*, March 7, 1970, p. 1.

A similar analysis comes from Sheppard and Striner in the next selection. Like Moynihan, they cite the large family sizes of Blacks as a significant factor in perpetuating the crisis of Black family disorganization. Their argument that reducing the number of children in Black families will increase their opportunities is a spurious one. Large families are a function of poverty, not the reverse. The opportunities for Blacks to achieve socially acceptable goals have simply not existed, regardless of whether they had one child or 20. Moreover, the exhortations to Blacks to reduce their family size creates a certain amount of ambivalence in those of us who are aware of the possibly genocidal aspects of family planning efforts in the Black community.

The selection from *The Report of the National Advisory Commission on Civil Disorders* gives us another statistical portrait of the Black family and its economic problems. Of course, a statistical comparative study can only describe the problem and does not provide much insight into the causes of the variables involved.

Many of the selections in this reader could be included in the section on family disorganization, since traditional social science research has largely focused on the "pathological" characteristics of the Black family. Generally, the areas of family disorganization are divorce, desertion, separation, the fatherless family, illegitimate childbirths and prostitution.

Very little is known about the divorce rate of Blacks except that it is much higher than in the white population. One interesting aspect of divorce among Blacks is the fact that the higher the level of education among Blacks, the higher the divorce rate. The reverse is true for whites. A possible explanation is that poorly educated Blacks do not use the divorce courts as much, due to the costs involved, and resort more to desertion or separation.[4] For instance, this writer found that 8.7 percent of Black women, in Minnesota, were separated but not divorced from their husbands, in contrast to only 1.6 percent of white women.[5]

The issue of illegitimate children is confounded by other factors, namely the Western world's moral code demanding that children be produced only inside the socially approved contract of marriage. And as one group of expert statisticians concluded, "the most that can be said about the illegitimacy figures is that they indicate the minimum extent of illegitimacy."[6] In the case of the unwed Black mother, the fact that she becomes pregnant before marriage may be perceived as an adaptation to the vicissitudes of Black life in the urban ghettoes of America.

Much of the gap between the illegitimate birth rate of Blacks and whites can be attributed to less use of contraception, less use of abortion, differences in reporting illegitimate births, and a larger number of whites marrying

---

[4]Cf. William Goode, *After Divorce* (New York: The Free Press, 1956).

[5]Robert Staples, *The Lower-Income Negro Family in Saint Paul* (St. Paul: St. Paul Urban League, 1967), p. 23.

[6]National Center for Health Statistics, *Fertility Measurement: A Report of the United States Committee on Vital and Health Statistics*, September, 1965, p. 8.

before the birth of the child.[7] The remaining differences can be explained by the importance of motherhood to Black women. Even in the pre-slavery period of African society, the love of the African mother for her children was unsurpassed in any part of the world.[8] What this means is that the Black woman articulates her love of her children regardless of the legitimacy of their conception. This value of children apparently supersedes status considerations; even middle class Black women prefer to keep an illegitimate child rather than give it up for adoption or resort to an abortion.

In the first article in this section, C. Eric Lincoln examines some of the problems faced by fatherless Black families. This writer agrees that female-headed households encounter many difficulties but believes it is not necessarily related to father absence per se but rather to the national oppression of women. The role of the male adult in the family is so marginal that his absence affects mainly the economic functioning of the family. Black females left alone without the male's income encounter serious difficulties in maintaining a decent standard of living, and these difficulties lead to more difficulties in other areas of family functioning.

Hallowell Pope's article deals with unwed mothers and their sex partners. His article diverges from most research on this subject, since he asserts that these prepregnancy relationships with the alleged father cannot be described as deviant, exploitative, or lacking exposure to the normal social controls. Major differences he found between his Black and white subjects were that Blacks have more permissive premarital sexual attitudes and are less committed to legitimate childbirth and that the Black female is less desirous of getting married than the white female. These factors help explain findings that the Black unwed mother, in comparison to the white unwed mother, was more often in a long-term relationship with the father of her child but less often planning marriage.

The article by Staples discusses some of the history of Black prostitution, its characteristics, and the problematic aspects of commercialized sexual relations. While it is fashionable in some quarters to glorify the Black prostitute as a super-exploited member of the Black community, this occupation is beset with hazards and a variety of exploitations.

The last article, by Harry Edwards, compares two different types of lower class Black families—the Christian and the Black Muslim. His findings on the stability of Black Muslim families are interesting in light of prevalent theories concerning the organization of the lower class Black family. Although the Black Muslim families had lower class characteristics, they were middle class in many other respects—particularly with regard to such issues as sex practices, the value of education, and personal hygiene.

[7] Elizabeth Herzog, "Is There a Breakdown of the Negro Family?" *Social Work*, January 1966, pp. 1–8.

[8] E. Franklin Frazier, *The Negro Family in the United States* (Chicago: University of Chicago Press, 1939), p. 33.

11

Black and White: Sex and Marriage

Calvin Hernton: The Sexualization
of Racism

More than two decades ago, a Swedish social scientist was invited to America for the purpose of conducting perhaps the most thorough study of the race problem ever undertaken. The social scientist was Gunnar Myrdal. As it turned out, he produced a monumental work entitled *An American Dilemma*.

One of the most interesting aspects of the race problem was formulated by Myrdal into a schema which he called "The Rank Order of Discrimination." When Myrdal asked white Southerners to list, in the order of importance, the things they thought Negroes wanted most, here is what he got:

1. Intermarriage and sex intercourse with whites
2. Social equality and etiquette
3. Desegration of public facilities, buses, churches, etc.
4. Political enfranchisement
5. Fair treatment in the law courts

From *Sex and Racism in America*, by Calvin Hernton (Garden City, N.Y.: Doubleday and Company, 1965), pp. 3-8. Reprinted with permission. Calvin Hernton is Writer-in-Residence at Central State University.

6. Economic opportunities[1]

The curious thing about this "Rank Order" was that when Myrdal approached the Negroes, they put down the same items as did the whites, but with one major change—they listed them in the direct *reverse* order!

Today the same reverse positions are still maintained with equal vigor by both whites and Negroes. While I am not going to charge either group with being totally dishonest, I am going to assert that neither whites nor Negroes were or are being completely honest with themselves. For, of the various facets of the race problem in America, there is no doubt that the sexual aspect is as much a "thorn in the side" to Negroes as it is to whites. Both groups, for their own special reasons, are hideously concerned about it.

The white man, especially the Southerner, is overtly obsessed by the idea of the Negro desiring sexual relations with whites. The Negro man is secretly tormented every second of his wakeful life by the presence of white women in his midst, whom he cannot or had better not touch. Despite the severe penalties for associating with white women—lynching, castration, electrocution—Negroes risk their lives for white flesh, and an occasional few actually commit rape. On the other hand, the white man, especially in the South, cannot seem to adhere to his own laws and customs prohibiting interracial intercourse—he insults, seduces, and rapes Negro women as if this were what they exist for. A preponderance of racial violence takes the form of sexual atrocities against not only black women but black men as well.

In the North, Midwest, and West, where there are few legal barriers against race mixing, many Negroes and whites suffer social ostracism and castigation for engaging in interracial relations.

What does all of this mean? It means that the race problem is inextricably connected with sex. More and more in America, everything we make, sell, handle, wear, and do takes on a sexual meaning. Matters dealing with race relations are no exception. The Madison Avenue "hidden persuaders" and the "organization men" of the commercial world are functioning now in such an all-pervasive way that virtually no area of social reality, no facet of our psyches, can escape the all but total sexualization of American life. In nearly every television commercial, in every fashion magazine, on the "center pages" of our newspapers, on billboard, bus, and subway ads, in the tabloids of scandal, on the covers and pages of every "cheap" magazine—there is but one incessant symbol: the naked or half-naked white woman. The scantily clad white woman is irresistibly enticing as the ubiquitous sex symbol of our times. Sex pervades everything.

The sexualization of the race problem is a reality, and we are going to have to deal with it even though most of us are, if not unwilling, definitely unprepared.

---

[1]Gunnar Myrdal, *An American Dilemma*, 7th ed. (New York: Harper & Row, 1944), Vol. I, pp. 60–61.

A tall, dark Negro boards the subway at 42nd Street in New York City. He takes a seat in the corner away from everybody. He pulls from his hip pocket a magazine; he looks around carefully, then opens the cover and instantly becomes engrossed. He turns the pages slowly, almost as if transfixed in and by some forbidden drug. There are naked women in various "naughty" poses on every page of the magazine. Their skin is white. A white man enters and stands beside the Negro. Quickly the Negro snaps the magazine shut, tucks it into his pocket, lays his head back and closes his eyes, probably to dream or to have a nightmare.

"I can't hardly sit by a Negro woman," said a white man who served as an informant for this book. "I can't be comfortable in their presence. I mean I get excited. They don't even have to be good-looking. I can't help but get erect no matter what kind of looking Negro she is."

I have before me the October (1963) issue of the *Science Digest*. There is a picture of a Negro on the cover. The caption reads:

The Negro
HOW HE'S
DIFFERENT
WHY
WHITES
FEAR HIM[2]

Inside, on one of the pages, it says that the thing whites fear most about Negroes is that Negroes have an uncontrollable urge to mate with the sisters and daughters of white men. White men, especially Southerners, are afraid of the so-called superior, savage sexuality of the Negro male, and they are dead set against any measures that will lift the Negro's status, because they are certain that such measures will bring the Negro one step nearer to the white woman's bedroom. Meanwhile it is a common saying in the South among white males that "a man is not a man until he has slept with a nigger."

Listen to the advice a Negro woman in Mississippi gave reporter John Griffin, who she thought was a stranger to the way of white folks in the South.

... well, you know you don't want to even look at a white woman. In fact, you look down at the ground or the other way ... you may not know you're looking in a white woman's direction but they'll try to make something out of it.... If you pass by a picture show, and they've got women on the posters outside, don't look at them either .... Somebody's sure to say, "Hey, boy—what are you looking at that white gal like *that* for?"

---

[2]My italics.

[3]John Griffin, *Black Like Me* (New York: Signet Books, 1963), p. 60.

The white man's self-esteem is in a constant state of sexual anxiety in all matters dealing with race relations. So is the Negro's, because his life, too, is enmeshed in the absurd system of racial hatred in America. Since racism is centered in and revolves around sex, the Negro cannot help but see himself as at once sexually affirmed and negated. While the Negro is portrayed as a great "walking phallus" with satyr-like potency, he is denied the execution of that potency, he is denied the most precious sexual image which surrounds him—the white woman. The myth of the sanctity of "white womanhood" is nothing more than a myth, but because this myth is acted upon *as if* it were real both by blacks and whites alike, then it *becomes* real as far as the behavior and sensitivities of those who must encounter it are concerned.

The sexualization of racism in the United States is a unique phenomenon in the history of mankind; it is an anomaly of the first order. In fact, there is a sexual involvement, at once real and vicarious, connecting white and black people in America that spans the history of this country from the era of slavery to the present, an involvement so immaculate and yet so perverse, so ethereal and yet so concrete, that all race relations tend to be, however subtle, *sex* relations.

It is important to see how the racism of sex in America has affected the sexual behavior of blacks and whites toward one another, and how black and white people perceive each other and themselves sexually as a result of living in a world of segregation and racial bigotry. As Negro and Caucasian, male and female, what do we mean to each other as sexual beings?

I am reminded of the way the policemen, during the historic march on Washington in 1963, constricted their eyes, tightened their faces, and fondled their sticks every time an interracial couple passed them in that mammoth parade. I am further reminded that when the marchers were yelling for F-R-E-E-E-E-DOM, for jobs, civil rights, equality of education, and the rest, a young Negro leaped in the air and shouted out—"S-E-X!" Perhaps he was a "crackpot." Even so, can one be certain that he was not an omen for our times? I am not certain, for I submit that, secretly, for many Negroes and whites, sexual liberty is as precious and sought-after as any other freedom. As the other barriers to freedom fall down, sexual liberty will become increasingly important in our society.

Robert Staples: Negro-White Sex: Fact and Fiction

Several years ago a controversial book was published, entitled *Sex and Racism in America*. The central theme of the author, Calvin Hernton, was that the race problem in the United States is inextricably connected with sex. Among the statements in the book were charges that the white man is

Reprinted from *Sexology Magazine*, 35 (August 1968), pp. 46–51. Copyright 1968 by Sexology Corporation.

obsessed with the idea that Negroes desire sexual relations with whites and that Negro males are secretly tormented with unfulfilled sexual desires for white women whom they cannot have.

Hernton overstated his case. But it is clear that sexual relations between the races is a subject of much concern to many Americans.

The Swedish economist Gunnar Myrdal, while making his famous study of American race relations, asked white Southerners to list, by order of importance, the things they thought Negroes wanted most.

Heading the list of what whites thought Negroes wanted were intermarriage and sexual intercourse with whites. When Negroes were asked the same question, intermarriage and sexual intercourse with whites were ranked *last* among their desires in life.

Many Negroes feel that white fear of sex between the races is a barrier to their achieving equality in other areas. Recently, ex-football star Jim Brown was quoted as saying that the one big reason Negro athletes encountered racial prejudice was white women.

"It's a major factor why black and white players don't socialize," he said, "because sooner or later they are going to be in some situations involving women. The black athlete who is desirable to white women is going to run into all kinds of trouble."

The taboo on interracial sex relations is mostly centered around Negro men having relations with white women. It is not as strong for white men. One reason for this is that white men and Negro women have engaged in sex relations since the first Negro female slaves entered this country.

Some Negro slave women were forced to engage in sexual relations with their white masters; others did so out of desire. Children resulting from these interracial sexual unions are always considered Negroes; the unions were so common that they produced a much lighter-skinned American Negro than his African ancestor.

Traditionally, white fear of interracial relations has focused on the desire to avoid "mongrelization" of the races. Such a fear lacks any scientific basis. Experts on the subject of racial types seriously question that a pure race ever existed on this universe.

One such authority, Dr. Ashley Montagu (who drafted the statement on race for UNESCO and is now a Consultant for *Sexology*), notes that "the whole population of the world is hybrid and becoming increasingly so." At any rate, the high rate of racial mixing in the past almost certainly casts doubt on any pure race theory for the United States.

Since the interracial sex taboo is mostly centered around Negro men—white women, it is not strange that these two groups may have a certain curiosity about the sex ability of each other. Inflaming this curiosity are the sexual stereotypes mutually held by Negroes and whites about each other as sexual partners.

The common stereotype of the Negro male is that he possesses an overly large penis and has an abnormal sex drive. Because of his oversized penis, this notion goes, he supposedly can satisfy women in a way that men of other races cannot.

While it is true that many Negro males are preoccupied with the sexual conquest of women (so of course are many white males), the reasons are more psychological than biological. Sexual conquest of women is generally seen as a sign of masculinity in American culture and being masculine, in a sexual sense, is very important to Negro males because the ordinary symbols of masculinity have often been denied them in the past.

Many authorities on Negro family life, Dr. E. Franklin Frazier, for example, have asserted that the Negro male's sexual prowess has been a means of overcoming his inferior social status in American society.

In their classical study of the Negro personality. Kardiner and Ovesey concluded that "the common stereotypes about the sexual potency of Negro males are generally myths." Repressions and inhibitions use up so much mental energy, they said, that it is only natural that there would be disturbances in the Negro male's sex life.

In addition, the stereotype about the oversized penis of the Negro male has been weakened by some recent scientific evidence. It has been noted that, although the penis of the Negro male is larger than that of his white counterpart when flaccid, there is no significant difference between the penis size of the two groups when in an erect form. Besides, penis size is of very little importance in making a man an adequate sex partner and has no relationship to his sex drive.

Just as these sexual stereotypes may stimulate the curiosity of white women, the Negro male may be equally attracted by the concept of sacred white womanhood. Especially in the South, the penalties for having sex with a white female were extremely severe and her forbidden fruit status could only add to the natural attraction that most men feel toward the opposite sex.

Regardless of the social taboos, sex relations do take place between the races—most noticeably in the North. There are indications that Negro female–white male marriages are just as likely to occur as Negro male–white female marriages. The same may be true of illicit sexual relations.

Because of the social taboos on any intimate association between members of different races, there may be various motives for the people who establish such a relationship.

First of all, we must assume that Negroes and whites may be equally attracted to each other as sexual partners. Too often it is believed that the Negro partner is most desirous of the white partner because of the higher social status of whites in this society.

Yet the taboo on Negroes as sexual mates may give them a certain mysterious quality which also stimulates the sexual appetite of whites.

Whatever the reason, interracial dating appears most often in certain situations and among certain types of people. One authority on dating patterns in America, Dr. Lee G. Burchinal, reports that interracial dating may occur disproportionately among very different categories of young people.

In cities and especially among university students and professional people, he says, racial equality and integration are widely supported. Among these groups interracial dating occurs with increasing frequency and inter-racial marriage becomes increasingly likely.

There are white people, mostly in the North, who do not make a deliber-ate effort to exclude Negroes from the possibility of sexual intimacy. Such people usually come from radical or liberal family backgrounds, and they themselves are often dedicated to liberal causes.

Where interracial sex relations occur, problems can arise that are unique to this type of relationship. Especially in interracial sexual activity among unmarried couples, the possibility of an illegitimate child poses special problems. If the mother is white and unmarried, she may be reluctant to have what is usually considered a Negro child which she must raise by herself. This means she must have an illegal abortion or give birth to the baby and then put it up for adoption.

A unique situation has emerged in states like Minnesota, where the major-ity of Negro babies put up for adoption have white mothers. In such cases, it is very difficult to find prospective adoptive parents for children that are products of an illicit interracial sexual union.

Many people, of both races, feel that any white female who has sex relations with a Negro male may be of a low moral character or is mentally deficient. As a result, they are reluctant to adopt the children of such unions because they fear that the child may have inherited some of his mother's "bad" traits.

Despite the problems inherent in interracial marriages, such unions ap-pear to be increasing. The U.S. Supreme Court ruling of 1967 that all laws prohibiting marriage between members of different races are unconstitu-tional, along with the status gains for Negroes in the sixties, influence this increase.

It has also been noted that most partners in this type of marriage are in the same educational brackets as their spouses. Despite this increase, Negro-white marriages are still less than one percent of all marriages in the United States.

Little research is available on the success of interracial marriages. Author-ities who have studied the subject generally have concluded that these marriages have a fairly good chance of survival. The external pressures faced by interracial couples are often great but do not appear to be over-whelming.

From the evidence at hand, one can say that as the social, economic and political barriers that have traditionally separated whites and Negroes con-tinue to disappear, both the concrete and psychological barriers between their sexual activities will also diminish.

David M. Heer: Negro-White
Marriage in the United States

In the last year or two tremendous popular interest in the United States has been aroused in the subject of Negro-white intermarriage. Fifteen years ago Negro protest leaders soft-pedalled talk of such marriage and claimed they were interested only in jobs and votes. Conservative whites were comforted by Gunnar Myrdal's report that, although the ban on intermarriage was for them the most important aspect of the caste system, for Negroes it was the least important of the various forms of discrimination they were forced to suffer.[1]

Very recently, however, the attitude of many Negro leaders toward intermarriage has changed. Increasingly such leaders, particularly the younger ones, are asking, "Why not?" The marriage in 1963 to a fellow white student of the first Negro admitted to the University of Georgia shocked many conservative whites. Intransigent whites have also become alarmed by the possibility that in the very near future the United States Supreme Court will decree that state legislation banning interracial marriage is illegal.[2] This possibility arises because the Supreme Court has recently ruled in favor of an interracial couple from Florida convicted for illegal cohabitation under the state's law against miscegenation. A further ruling by the Supreme Court interdicting state bans on racial intermarriage would allow such marriage in the 19 states, mostly but not entirely Southern, where it is now prohibited.[3]

There are several reasons why Negro-white marriage is sociologically important. However, one of these reasons may be singled out for special attention.

Intermarriage and Negro-White Status
Difference

Most Negro thinking tended earlier to isolate political and economic deprivation from the social deprivation symbolized par excellence by white attitudes toward racial intermarriage. However, restrictions on racial intermarriage may be closely linked to the economic inequality that Negroes in

Reprinted from *Journal of Marriage and the Family*, 28 (August 1966), pp. 262-273, by permission of the National Council on Family Relations and the author. Dr. Heer is Professor of Biostatistics and Demography, School of Public Health, Harvard University.

[1] Gunnar Myrdal, *An American Dilemma*, New York: Harper, 1944, pp. 57–67.

[2] Arthur Krock, "The Debate on Miscegenation," *The New York Times*, September 9, 1963, and Arthur Krock, "In the Nation," *The New York Times*, December 8, 1964.

[3] These 19 states are Alabama, Arkansas, Delaware, Florida, Georgia, Indiana, Idaho, Kentucky, Louisiana, Mississippi, Missouri, North Carolina, Oklahoma, South Carolina, Tennessee, Texas, Virginia, West Virginia, and Wyoming. Since 1944 the following states have eliminated their miscegenation statutes: Arizona, California, Colorado, Maryland, Montana, Nebraska, Nevada, North Dakota, Oregon, South Dakota, and Utah.

our society endure. Kingsley Davis has identified the main social functions of the family as the reproduction, maintenance, placement, and socialization of the young.[4] Let us focus our attention on the placement function of the family in the contemporary United States, i.e., on the consequences which birth into a given family has for the youngster's future social position. First it is obvious that the transfer of wealth in the United States is largely accomplished by bequeathal from one family member to another. The possession of wealth not only entitles one to receive regular monetary interest; it is also a source of power, credit, and prestige. Secondly, although objectively recognized merit may be the predominant criterion for the matching of job applicants to job vacancies, influence and family connections are also quite important. In the building trades, for example, jobs cannot be obtained without admittance to the union's apprenticeship program. In many instances it is almost impossible to obtain entrée into the apprenticeship program unless one is a son or other close relative of a union member. Thirdly, entrée into elite positions in modern industrial societies is most easily obtained by those who are born into a family having relatively high status.[5] Birth in a high status family provides the financial means for obtaining advanced education, and it also gives one a sense of familiarity with the activities and functioning of high status society. This familiarity not only reduces the fear of interpersonal contacts in such a society but also increases the motivation to become a full participant.

In summary, being born into one family rather than another is a very important determinant of one's eventual social status. How may this fact affect the relative status of Negroes and whites in the United States? Consider first the pattern of familial inheritance. On a per capita basis white persons hold a far higher share of the nation's wealth than do Negroes. The formal and informal prohibitions on intermarriage serve to perpetuate this pattern of inequality because they make it unlikely for a Negro to inherit wealth from any white person. Secondly, Negroes are by and large excluded from those jobs to which entrance is strongly determined by "connections." This occurs simply because those jobs are usually held only by whites. Thirdly, the lack of close relatives among whites affects the socialization of Negro youth. Specifically, it prevents many of them from having an easy familiarity with the terrain of the social world of white persons and hence makes them afraid to apply for jobs demanding such familiarity even when their technical qualifications are completely satisfactory.

Thus a relaxation of the norms militating against Negro-white marriage should serve to reduce the status gap between Negroes and whites. This is not to say that a substantial increase in Negro-white marriage would necessarily soon bring Negroes into equality with whites. As we shall show later, the present frequency of marriages involving Negro grooms and white brides is considerably greater than the frequency of marriages involving

---

[4]Kingsley Davis, *Human Society*, New York: Macmillan, 1949, pp. 394–396.

[5]Joseph A. Kahl, *The American Class Structure*, New York: Rinehart, 1953, pp. 276–298.

white grooms and Negro brides. Perhaps upward social mobility would be more probable for a male child if he had a white father and a Negro mother rather than the reverse. The father is more likely than the mother to teach the son the terrain of the occupational world of white persons; therefore if job entrance is determined by particularistic factors, a white father will be of greater advantage than a white mother. Also, children of mixed marriages may encounter discrimination not only from white persons but also from other Negroes, because they are a product of a marriage not generally approved.[6]

Furthermore, it is not clear that an increased amount of Negro-white marriage is a necessary prerequisite for the elimination of Negro-white status differences. Americans of Jewish faith, with very low rates of intermarriage, have achieved a socioeconomic status at least as high as the rest of the population despite the fact that most of them are the recent descendants of poor immigrants.[7]

Thus the strength of the link between low frequency of Negro-white marriage and the Negro's inferior socioeconomic status is uncertain. Nevertheless, because the inferior status of the Negro is now of such concern, it is important for sociologists to maintain a close temperature reading concerning data on Negro-white marriage in the United States.

Analysis of State Data

Unfortunately, current data on this subject are very incomplete. At the present time, there are 31 states in which marriage between whites and Negroes is legal. However, in only three states is there any officially published record of such intermarriages: Hawaii, Michigan, and Nebraska. For selected years prior to 1960 the state of California made public a cross-tabulation of marriages by race of bride and race of groom, but this practice was discontinued in 1960 because of new legislation prohibiting a record of race on marriage licenses.[8]

For the period from 1950 to the time this paper was prepared, the only data on interracial marriages tabulated by state offices of vital statistics were as follows: California for 1955, 1957, 1958, and 1959; Hawaii, 1956–64; Michigan, 1953–63; Nebraska, 1961–64. In this paper we shall analyze these data and compare them with some data for earlier years. We shall not

[6]According to the results of a recent Gallup Poll (*Boston Globe*, March 11, 1965) 48 percent of adult Americans approve of laws making interracial marriage a crime. The percentage of various subgroups who approve such laws were as follows: Negroes outside the South, 14 percent; Southern Negroes, 30 percent; whites outside the South, 42 percent; Southern whites, 72 percent.

[7]Data on the current socioeconomic status of American Jews and on Jewish intermarriage patterns can be found in Donald J. Bogue, *The Population of the United States*, New York: The Free Press, 1959, pp. 694–709. Data on the status of immigrant Jews in the late 19th and early 20th centuries are summarized in Oscar and Mary F. Handlin, "A Century of Jewish Immigration to the United States," *American Jewish Yearbook*, Vol. 50 (1948–49), pp. 1–84.

[8]Personal communication from Dr. Hugh Carter, Chief, Marriage and Divorce Statistics, Division of Vital Statistics, National Center for Health Statistics, U.S. Public Health Service.

be concerned with other types of interracial marriage, such as between whites and Orientals.[9]

Some readers may question the quality of the official data on Negro-white marriage. On the one hand, it might be argued that social sanctions against such marriages are so severe that the reported number of such marriages would be less than the actual number. The difference between actual and reported numbers would then consist of marriages in which the race of one partner was consciously misreported on the marriage license. On the other hand, it might be argued that, because the true number of Negro-white marriages is very small, the reported number exceeds the actual number because of accidental misreporting of race for one partner on the marriage license. Since no study has yet been made of the validity of the reported numbers of interracial marriages in any of these states, some caution is warranted in the interpretation of the reported data.[10]

Much of the previous work on interracial marriage has focused on Negro-white marriages as a proportion of all marriages involving Negroes or as a proportion of all Negro brides and grooms to the exclusion of Negro-white marriages as a proportion of all marriages involving whites or of all white brides and grooms. Since a time series of intermarriage rates for which the base is Negro brides and grooms might show an entirely different trend from one in which the intermarriage rates had as their base the number of white brides and grooms, we shall present here intermarriage rates for both whites and Negroes.

In Table 1 we show six sets of reported data: (1) the proportion of white brides and grooms marrying Negroes, (2) the proportion of white grooms with Negro brides, (3) the proportion of white brides with Negro grooms, (4) the proportion of Negro brides and grooms marrying whites, (5) the proportion of Negro grooms with white brides, and (6) the proportion of Negro brides with white grooms.[11] Data are presented for the states and

---

[9]An excellent description of the current California data on interracial marriages of all types is found in Larry D. Barnett, "Interracial Marriage in California," *Marriage and Family Living*, 25:4 (November 1963), pp. 424–427, and of the recent data for Hawaii in Robert C. Schmitt, "Demographic Correlates of Interracial Marriage in Hawaii," *Demography*, Vol. II (1965), pp. 463–473. Data on interracial marriage of all types for Los Angeles County, California, are found in John H. Burma, "Interethnic Marriage in Los Angeles, 1948–1959," *Social Forces*, 42 (December 1963), pp. 156–165.

[10]Our data refer only to registered marriages between whites and Negroes. They do not take into account the unknown number of relatively stable sexual unions between whites and Negroes which are not legally registered as marriages. Data on the total number of sexual unions between whites and Negroes might show different patterns from the data on legal unions presented here.

[11]The previous literature on intermarriage is confused by the fact that there are two different ways of computing intermarriage rates. Many studies compute an intermarriage rate in which the numerator is the number of intermarriages and the denominator is the number of marriages in which either bride or groom is from the ingroup. In other studies the numerator is the number of brides and/or grooms intermarrying and the denominator is the number of brides and/or grooms in the ingroup. Intermarriage rates computed by the two different procedures can be quite dissimilar. In this study the second procedure is used. For a further discussion of the two ways of measuring intermarriage see Hyman Rodman, "Technical Note on Two Rates of Mixed Marriage," *American Sociological Review*, 30 (October 1965), pp. 776–778.

It should also be noted that if for either whites or Negroes the number of brides who intermarry is equal to the number of grooms who intermarry, the proportion of brides and grooms marrying into the other race will be the average of the separate figures for out-marriages of brides and grooms. On the other hand, if for either whites or Negroes the number of brides who intermarry is substantially less or greater than the

Table 1. Negro-White Intermarriage Percentages for Available States and Years (Base for Each Percentage is in Parentheses)

A. White Brides and Grooms

Percentage of:

State and Year	White Brides and Grooms Marrying Negro Brides and Grooms	White Grooms Marrying Negro Brides	White Brides Marrying Negro Grooms
California			
1955	0.14 (150,770)	0.06 (75,235)	0.21 (75,535)
1957	0.17 (167,926)	0.06 (83,809)	0.28 (84,117)
1958	0.17 (174,211)	0.08 (86,998)	0.26 (87,213)
1959	0.21 (183,563)	0.09 (91,643)	0.33 (91,920)
1955–59	0.17 (676,470)	0.07 (337,685)	0.27 (338,785)
Hawaii			
1956	0.13 (3,127)	0.00 (1,820)	0.31 (1,307)
1957	0.20 (2,994)	0.00 (1,721)	0.47 (1,273)
1958	0.10 (2,898)	0.06 (1,662)	0.16 (1,236)
1959	0.22 (3,201)	0.11 (1,821)	0.36 (1,380)
1960	0.24 (3,387)	0.16 (1,908)	0.34 (1,479)
1961	0.29 (3,429)	0.11 (1,898)	0.52 (1,531)
1962	0.24 (3,811)	0.05 (2,070)	0.46 (1,741)
1963	0.27 (4,004)	0.14 (2,162)	0.43 (1,842)
1964	0.38 (4,230)	0.13 (2,305)	0.68 (1,925)
1956–64	0.24 (31,081)	0.09 (17,367)	0.43 (13,714)
Michigan			
1953	0.07 (97,517)	0.04 (48,748)	0.10 (48,769)
1954	0.06 (94,516)	0.04 (47,246)	0.09 (47,270)
1955	0.08 (101,684)	0.05 (50,858)	0.11 (50,858)
1956	0.09 (103,972)	0.04 (51,971)	0.13 (52,001)
1957	0.07 (100,242)	0.01 (50,091)	0.14 (50,151)
1958	0.09 (100,583)	0.05 (50,269)	0.13 (50,314)
1959	0.10 (106,901)	0.04 (53,420)	0.16 (53,481)
1960	0.10 (111,122)	0.06 (55,544)	0.14 (55,578)
1961	0.11 (115,046)	0.05 (57,487)	0.18 (57,559)
1962	0.12 (118,157)	0.05 (59,044)	0.19 (59,113)
1963	0.15 (124,152)	0.07 (62,027)	0.23 (62,125)
1953–63	0.10 (1,173,892)	0.05 (586,673)	0.15 (587,219)
Nebraska			
1961	0.00 (21,080)	0.00 (10,542)	0.00 (10,538)
1962	0.00 (21,408)	0.00 (10,708)	0.00 (10,700)
1963	0.01 (22,498)	0.01 (11,257)	0.02 (11,241)
1964	0.02 (22,902)	0.01 (11,452)	0.03 (11,450)
1961–64	0.01 (87,888)	0.00 (43,959)	0.01 (43,929)
New York (excluding New York City)			
1921	0.04 (84,027)	0.01 (41,999)	0.06 (42,028)
1922	0.03 (83,782)	0.02 (41,885)	0.05 (41,897)
1923	0.04 (87,164)	0.03 (43,572)	0.06 (43,592)
1924	0.06 (84,769)	0.03 (42,367)	0.10 (42,402)
1921–24	0.04 (339,742)	0.02 (169,883)	0.07 (169,919)

Table 1. Negro-White Intermarriage Percentages for Available States and Years (Base for Each Percentage is in Parentheses)

B. Negro Brides and Grooms

Percentage of:

Negro Brides and Grooms Marrying White Brides and Grooms	Negro Grooms Marrying White Brides	Negro Brides Marrying White Grooms
2.21 (9,514)	3.36 (4,815)	1.02 (4,699)
2.14 (13,198)	3.47 (6,691)	0.78 (6,507)
2.20 (13,458)	3.35 (6,812)	1.02 (6,646)
2.58 (14,877)	3.96 (7,549)	1.16 (7,328)
2.30 (51,047)	3.56 (25,867)	1.00 (25,180)
6.45 (62)	9.09 (44)	0.00 (18)
9.52 (63)	13.33 (45)	0.00 (18)
4.35 (69)	4.08 (49)	5.00 (20)
9.33 (75)	9.80 (51)	8.33 (24)
13.79 (58)	14.71 (34)	12.50 (24)
13.33 (75)	16.00 (50)	8.00 (25)
13.04 (69)	17.78 (45)	4.17 (24)
12.79 (86)	14.81 (54)	9.38 (32)
16.16 (99)	20.31 (64)	8.57 (35)
11.28 (656)	13.53 (436)	6.82 (220)
0.75 (8,929)	1.09 (4,479)	0.40 (4,450)
0.78 (7,818)	1.10 (3,922)	0.46 (3,896)
0.80 (9,578)	1.12 (4,806)	0.48 (4,772)
0.89 (9,979)	1.32 (5,013)	0.46 (4,966)
0.76 (9,837)	1.37 (4,949)	0.14 (4,888)
0.94 (9,573)	1.37 (4,808)	0.50 (4,765)
1.01 (10,566)	1.62 (5,318)	0.40 (5,248)
1.01 (10,877)	1.39 (5,458)	0.63 (5,419)
1.13 (11,368)	1.76 (5,724)	0.48 (5,644)
1.20 (11,625)	1.90 (5,853)	0.49 (5,772)
1.56 (11,972)	2.34 (6,033)	0.77 (5,939)
1.01 (112,122)	1.53 (56,363)	0.48 (55,759)
0.00 (693)	0.00 (346)	0.00 (347)
0.00 (800)	0.00 (401)	0.00 (399)
0.39 (766)	0.52 (384)	0.26 (382)
0.67 (745)	1.07 (374)	0.27 (371)
0.27 (3,004)	0.40 (1,505)	0.13 (1,499)
3.21 (936)	5.63 (480)	0.66 (456)
2.52 (1,151)	3.60 (582)	1.40 (569)
2.17 (1,796)	2.87 (905)	1.46 (891)
2.63 (1,974)	4.09 (1,003)	1.13 (971)
2.56 (5,857)	3.87 (2,970)	1.21 (2,887)

years mentioned previously, and, for comparison, also for New York State (excluding New York City) for the years 1921–24.[12] All data are tabulated by area in which the marriage license was issued rather than by area of residence of bride or groom prior to marriage. This fact introduces an unknown amount of bias into our data. It is possible, for example, that many couples who live in states where Negro-white marriage is illegal obtain the license for such a marriage in some state where it is legal. No doubt, however, not all of these couples return to live in their former state of residence.

Of the four states with recent data, Hawaii has the highest reported incidence of Negro-white intermarriage. The rank of the remaining states in descending order of Negro-white intermarriage is California, Michigan, and Nebraska. This rank order holds true regardless of which of the six columns of data is examined. For whites of both sexes, the highest reported interracial marriage rate in each of the four states was as follows: Hawaii, 0.38 percent; California, 0.21 percent; Michigan, 0.15 percent; and Nebraska, 0.02 percent. For Negroes of both sexes the highest interracial marriage rate in each of the four states was: Hawaii, 16.16 percent: California, 2.58 percent; Michigan, 1.56 percent; and Nebraska, 0.67 percent. Thus, there is considerable variation among these states in the reported proportions of interracial marriage. In addition to the familiar case of Hawaii, the contrast between Michigan and California is also noteworthy. These are both large industrial states with similar proportions of Negro population. In 1959, the latest year in which data are available for both states, the proportion of Negro-white marriages in California was more than double that in Michigan according to each of the six indices shown in Table 1.

Table 1 also reveals a differential incidence of Negro-white marriage by sex, manifested in previous data on interracial marriage. Specifically, for each of the four states recording Negro-white marriages, marriages between Negro men and white women are much more common that those between white men and Negro women. For example, for California in 1959 the intermarriage rate of white grooms was 0.09 percent and that of white brides 0.33 percent. Similarly, the interracial marriage rate of Negro grooms was 3.96 percent and of Negro brides 1.16 percent.

Reasons for the differential incidence of interracial marriage by sex have been advanced by Kingsley Davis and Robert Merton.[13] Davis proposed two explanations. First, if, as he believed, marriages between Negro men and

---

number of grooms, then the percentage for both sexes will not equal the unweighted average for each sex but will be influenced more heavily by the intermarriage percentage for the sex having the greater proportion intermarrying. In the present case, the percentage of Negro brides and grooms marrying white brides and grooms is more heavily influenced by the percentage of Negro grooms marrying white brides than by the percentage of Negro brides marrying white grooms.

[12]J. V. DePorte, *Marriage Statistics*, Albany: New York State Department of Health, 1928.

[13]Kingsley Davis, "Intermarriage in Caste Societies," *American Anthropologist*, 43 (July–September 1941), pp. 388–395; and Robert K. Merton, "Intermarriage and the Social Structure: Fact and Theory," *Psychiatry*, 4 (August 1941), pp. 361–374.

white women largely involved Negro males of high social status and white women of low social status, then the groom could trade his class advantage for the racial caste advantage of the bride. This was also Merton's explanation. Secondly, Davis believed that marriages between a white man and a Negro woman would be relatively rare simply because the norms allowed white men to take sexual advantage of Negro women without marrying them. Subsequent research has failed to establish that marriages between Negro men and white women most frequently involve a groom of high scoial class and a bride of low social class.[14] Most such marriages in fact appear to involve spouses from the same class position. Thus further research is necessary to attain a satisfactory explanation for the sex differential in Negro-white marriage.

In view of the interest in the question of whether the trend in interracial marriages is upward or downward, it is unfortunate that, for the four states for which we have recent statistics, we have no data for earlier years. For the areas—mostly cities—for which we have earlier statistics, the recent data are not readily available. Therefore, no valid comparison of the rate of interracial marriage in the contemporary period with that one or two generations back is possible. The best we can do is to compare the recent data in the four states of California, Hawaii, Michigan, and Nebraska with available earlier data from other places. It is apparent from Table 1 that the rate of Negro-white marriage for Negroes in New York State (excluding New York City) in the early 1920's was higher than the recent rates for either Michigan or California. On the other hand, the intermarriage rate for whites is higher in Calfiornia and Michigan in the recent period than in New York State 40 years ago. As will be explained later in greater detail, this result is attributable to higher proportions of Negroes in the present populations of California and Michigan than in New York State some 40 years ago.

The Negro-white intermarriage rate for Negroes in Hawaii during 1964 was higher than any previously recorded rate for members of that race in any part of the United States during any time period. The closest competitor to Hawaii in this respect is the city of Boston in the period of 1900–1904. For Boston during this period the proportion of Negro grooms marrying white brides was 13.7 percent as compared with 20.3 percent in Hawaii in 1964, and the proportion of Negro brides marrying white grooms was 1.1 percent as compared with 8.6 percent in Hawaii in 1964.

We are on somewhat surer ground when we try to investigate the trend of interracial marriage in the United States within the last few years. The available data shown in Table 1 for the four states of California, Hawaii, Michigan, and Nebraska are certainly not conclusive, but they give a strong indication of the probable trend during recent years.

First, we may compare the intermarriage rates during the first and final year in the series for each state according to each of the six indices. For each state the higher interracial marriage rates invariably occur during the final

[14] Joseph Golden, "Characteristics of the Negro-White Intermarried in Philadelphia," *American Sociological Review,* 18 (April 1953), pp. 177–183.

Table 2. Measures Indicating the Correlation of Negro-White Intermarriage with Time, for
Michigan, 1953–1963

	Whites			Negroes		
	Both Sexes	Males	Females	Both Sexes	Males	Females
Product-moment correlation coefficient	+.909*	+.517	+.937*	+.893*	+.916*	+.505
Slope of regression line (percent per year)	+.007*	+.003	+.009*	+.066*	+.111*	+.025

* Significantly different from 0 at .01 level.

rather than the initial year of the series. Thus for these four states there is an
indication of an upward trend in interracial marriage. Because we have not
only an 11-year time series but also a large base population for Michigan, a
more refined measurement of increase in interracial marriage can be made
for that state. The association between interracial marriage and time was
investigated for Michigan by means of product-moment correlation analysis. Table 2 presents the coefficients of correlation and the slopes of regression for the six indices of interracial marriage in Michigan. All six indices
show an increase of the interracial marriage rate with time, but they vary in
the consistency of this increase. For four of the indices, i.e., those for whites
of both sexes, white women, Negroes of both sexes, and Negro men, the
trend in interracial marriage has been one of very steady rise, as shown by
correlation coefficients with time greater than 0.89 (P.01 that *rho* equals 0).
On the other hand, the trends for white men and for Negro women show a
less consistent increase over the 11-year interval. The coefficient of correlation for white men is only 0.52 and that for Negro women is 0.51. In
Michigan the most pronounced increase in Negro-white marriage has been
in those marriages involving Negro men and white women.

The recent data pointing to an upward trend in Negro-white marriage are
of enhanced interest because statistics for previous periods in the United
States indicated a decreasing trend in such marriages.[15] For example, data
are available concerning interracial marriage rates for both whites and
Negroes in the city of Boston for the period from 1900–1938. These indicate an almost continuous decline in the intermarriage rate for both whites
and Negroes. The most drastic decline occurred between 1900–04 and
1914–18, when the interracial marriage rate per 100 Negro marriages
dropped from approximately 14 to approximately 5. Wirth and Goldhamer
have attributed this decline in the city of Boston to the fact that in the
nineteenth century the city was the center of the abolitionist movement and
was "unusually and almost sentimentally receptive to Negroes." As the pro-
Negro sentiments fostered during and after the Civil War declined in their
intensity, the willingness of whites to marry Negroes declined correspond-

[15] The best summary of previous data on Negro-white marriage in the United States is contained in
Louis Wirth and Herbert Goldhamer, "The Hybrid and the Problem of Miscegenation," in *Characteristics of
the American Negro*, ed. by Otto Klineberg, New York: Harper, 1944.

ingly. Data for New York State (exclusive of New York City) also indicated a small decline from 1922–24 to 1934–36 in Negro-white marriages as a proportion of all marriages involving Negroes. No data were provided concerning the trend of interracial marriage for whites during this period.[16]

The sharp decline in Negro-white intermarriage in Boston after the turn of the century was almost entirely due to a decline in marriages involving Negro grooms and white brides. The proportion of Negro grooms marrying white brides in Boston declined from 13.7 percent in the period 1900–04 to 3.2 percent in the period 1914–38. On the other hand, the proportion of Negro brides marrying white grooms declined only from 1.1 percent to 0.7 percent.[17] Together with the recent Michigan experience, these data suggest that the volatile element in Negro-white intermarriage may be the marriage between the Negro male and the white female and that the interracial marriage rate between white males and Negro females may remain relatively constant.

Negro-White Intermarriage and Racial Distribution

It has been well-established that, for given religious groups, the rate of marriage outside the group varies inversely with the proportion of all potential marriage partners belonging to that group. For example, Locke, Sabagh, and Thomes have shown that for each of the Canadian provinces in 1954 there was a perfect inverse rank order correlation between the percentage of Catholic brides and grooms having interfaith marriages and the percentage of the total population of each province that was Catholic.[18] In addition, Glick has shown for the United States that religious distribution helps to explain the fact that there is a higher proportion of interfaith marriage among couples where at least one spouse is Catholic than among couples where at least one spouse is Protestant.[19]

Religious distribution differences affect the proportion of interfaith marriages in a mechanical fashion: increased availability of marriage partners of differing religion and decreased availability of partners of the same religion cause interfaith marriage to increase, and vice versa. As yet, however, no research has been done to determine if racial distribution affects the proportion of interracial marriage in the same way. Fortunately, it was possible to obtain data on Negro-white marriages for each county in California for the year 1959. Since these counties contain varying proportions of Negro and white population, it was possible to determine the associations between Negro-white intermarriage proportions and racial distribution.

[16] *Ibid.*, pp. 276–280.

[17] *Ibid.*, p. 282.

[18] Harvey J. Locke, Georges Sabagh, and Mary Margaret Thomes, "Interfaith Marriages," *Social Problems*, 4 (April 1957), pp. 329–333.

[19] Paul C. Glick, "Intermarriage and Fertility Patterns among Persons in Major Religious Groups," *Eugenics Quarterly*, 7 (March 1960), pp. 31–38.

Altogether there are 58 counties in California. Since the counties lying outside of metropolitan areas often have very small populations and in particular very small Negro populations, they have been combined in various ways. Areal correlations were performed using as units the 17 counties lying within a Standard Metropolitan Statistical Area in 1960 and combinations of the remaining counties, using as additional units the nine State Economic Areas [20] lying wholly outside a Standard Metropolitan Area.[21]

Coefficients of correlation were computed between actual Negro-white intermarriage proportions and the proportions which would be expected if marriages took place at random without regard to race. For white grooms the expected proportion was simply that of all brides who were Negro; for white brides it was the proportion of all grooms who were Negro. For white brides and grooms the expected proportion of Negro-white marriage was defined as the weighted sum of the expected proportion of white grooms marrying Negro brides and of white brides marrying Negro grooms, the first term weighted by the proportion of grooms among all white brides and grooms and the second term weighted by the proportion of brides among all white brides and grooms. For Negro grooms the expected proportion was that of all brides who were white; for Negro brides that of all grooms who were white; for Negro brides and grooms the expected proportion was defined as a weighted sum of the expected proportions of Negro grooms marrying white brides and of Negro brides marrying white grooms.[22] Table 3 shows the relevant data for each of the 26 areal units.

The six correlation coefficients show that the relationships between actual white intermarriage proportions and the proportions expected if marriage took place without regard to race are strongly positive and significantly different from 0 at the .01 level. In contrast, the relationships between actual and expected Negro intermarriage proportions are all very low. For white grooms the correlation between actual and expected proportion was +0.77, for white brides +0.79, and for white brides and grooms +0.85. On the other hand, the correlation for Negro grooms was –0.08, for Negro brides +0.16, and for Negro brides and grooms +0.01. Thus, among these areal units racial distribution is a good predictor of variation in white intermarriage proportions but fails to predict variation in Negro intermarriage proportions.

Why is racial composition a good predictor for whites but not for Negroes in these California areas? The apparent reason is that these areas show very

[20] For a definition of the counties included in each of these nine State Economic Areas, see U.S. Bureau of the Census, *United States Census of Population, 1960,* Final Report PC (3)–1A. "State Economic Areas," Washington, D.C.: U.S. Government Printing Office, 1963, p. 464.

[21] Even with the combination of nonmetropolitan counties into State Economic Areas, the problem of small numbers of Negro brides and grooms was not solved. Three State Economic Areas each had fewer than 50 Negro brides and grooms in 1959. In State Economic Areas 1, 2, and 9 there were respectively 6, 20, and 16 Negro brides and grooms.

[22] The concept of an expected interracial marriage rate for a given area implies that area is a closed marriage market. To the extent that persons select partners from outside the area or to the extent that both bride and groom obtain the marriage license from an areal jurisdiction in which neither resides, the model of a closed marriage market departs from reality.

little variation in the proportion of all potential partners who are white. In no area is the proportion of grooms or brides who are white less than 82 percent. Hence for Negroes the expected proportions of Negro-white marriage have only a small variance relative to their mean. On the other hand, for whites the expected proportions of Negro-white marriage display high variability with respect to their mean. If there were as much variability in the proportions of all brides and grooms who were white as in the proportions Negro, the proportions expected on the basis of random choice might be as good predictors of interracial marriage for Negroes as for whites.[23] Thus the low correlations obtained for the Negroes do not disturb the general conclusion that the actual proportion of an ingroup who marry into an outgroup is a direct function of the proportion of all potential partners belonging to that outgroup.

In previous work Paul C. Glick and the present writer have employed the concept of the ratio of actual proportion intermarried to the expected proportion intermarried if marriages took place at random without regard to ingroup-outgroup differences.[24] Variation in the ratio of actual to expected Negro-white intermarriage proportions implies that differences in the proportion of interracial marriages are due to some factor or factors additional to that of racial distribution.

For the California data shown in Table 3, the ratios of actual to expected Negro-white marriages for white grooms are in all cases almost identical to those for Negro brides, and those for white brides to those for Negro grooms. The ratio for whites of one sex will be identical to that for Negroes of the other sex whenever Negroes of one sex have the same tendency to marry persons of other races, such as Chinese, Japanese, Filipinos, and Indians. The white rate for one sex will be lower than the Negro rate for the other sex whenever whites of one sex have a greater tendency than Negroes of the other sex to marry persons of races other than white or Negro; the white rate for one sex will be higher than the Negro rate for the other sex whenever whites of one sex have a lesser tendency than Negroes of the other sex to marry persons neither white nor Negro. Because of the near identity of the California ratios for whites of one sex with those for Negroes of opposite sex, further analysis will be limited to the ratios for whites.

Causes of Variation in Ratios of Actual to Expected Intermarriage

Differences between California areas in the ratio of actual to expected Negro-white marriage may be caused in part by migratory marriage or by errors in recording. Among other possible explanations, one of the most

[23]For a general discussion of this issue, see H. M. Blalock, *Causal Inferences in Nonexperimental Research*, Chapel Hill: University of North Carolina Press, 1964, pp. 44–52.

[24]Paul C. Glick, *op. cit.*, and David M. Heer, "The Trend of Interfaith Marriages in Canada: 1922–1957," *American Sociological Review*, 27 (April 1962), pp. 245–250.

Table 3. Actual Negro-White Intermarriage Percentages and Expected Percentages According to Racial Distribution for 17 Metropolitan Counties and Nine Non-Metropolitan State Economic Areas of California, 1959

Area	White Grooms			White Brides		
	Num-ber	Percentage Marrying Negro Brides		Num-ber	Percentage Marrying Negro Grooms	
		Actual	Expected		Actual	Expected
Metropolitan counties:						
Alameda	4,280	0.26	14.13	4,267	0.35	14.32
Contra Costa	1,408	0.14	9.21	1,410	0.35	9.47
Fresno	2,386	0.00	4.95	2,404	0.42	5.30
Kern	1,756	0.00	6.21	1,761	0.00	6.16
Los Angeles	34,294	0.12	9.95	34,384	0.40	10.17
Marin	545	0.00	4.84	545	0.18	5.02
Orange	3,496	0.06	2.06	3,499	0.06	2.03
Riverside	1,946	0.05	4.84	1,953	0.31	5.13
Sacramento	2,326	0.09	2.77	2,330	0.30	3.02
San Bernardino	2,642	0.04	3.90	2,650	0.19	4.04
San Diego	7,098	0.02	4.23	7,119	0.17	4.39
San Francisco	5,522	0.22	9.80	5,551	0.90	10.43
San Joaquin	1,088	0.00	6.74	1,102	0.54	7.31
San Mateo	1,690	0.00	3.78	1,697	0.12	3.89
Santa Barbara	1,173	0.09	2.46	1,175	0.17	2.54
Santa Clara	3,299	0.03	1.71	3,308	0.12	1.83
Solano	568	0.35	14.58	579	1.04	15.16
Non-metropolitan State Economic Areas:						
1	1,209	0.00	0.25	1,205	0.00	0.25
2	1,075	0.09	0.91	1,078	0.09	0.91
3	2,413	0.04	3.54	2,436	0.25	3.77
4	1,044	0.10	1.50	1,046	0.10	1.50
5	1,511	0.00	2.50	1,517	0.00	2.50
6	1,876	0.00	3.73	1,879	0.00	3.73
7	1,268	0.00	2.65	1,272	0.24	2.88
8	4,536	0.13	7.15	4,560	0.42	7.41
9	1,194	0.00	0.66	1,193	0.00	0.66

Table 3. Actual Negro-White Intermarriage Percentages and Expected Percentages According to Racial Distribution for 17 Metropolitan Counties and Nine Non-Metropolitan State Economic Areas of California, 1959

Negro Grooms			Negro Brides		
Num-ber	Percentage Marrying White Brides		Num-ber	Percentage Marrying White Grooms	
	Actual	Expected		Actual	Expected
736	2.04	83.05	726	1.52	83.30
148	3.38	90.21	144	1.39	90.08
136	7.35	93.61	127	0.00	92.91
116	0.00	93.52	117	0.00	93.26
3,990	3.41	87.67	3,901	1.03	87.44
29	3.45	94.29	28	0.00	94.29
73	2.74	97.28	74	2.70	97.19
106	5.66	94.44	100	1.00	94.10
74	9.46	94.99	68	2.94	94.82
112	4.46	95.63	108	0.93	95.34
330	3.64	94.65	318	0.31	94.38
691	7.24	83.80	649	1.85	83.36
89	6.74	90.55	82	0.00	89.40
70	2.86	94.38	68	0.00	93.99
31	6.45	96.23	30	3.33	96.07
63	6.35	96.00	59	1.69	95.73
104	5.77	84.40	100	2.00	82.80
3	0.00	99.01	3	0.00	99.34
10	10.00	98.45	10	10.00	98.17
97	6.19	94.75	91	1.10	93.85
16	6.25	97.94	16	6.25	97.75
39	0.00	97.24	39	0.00	96.86
73	0.00	95.97	73	0.00	95.81
38	7.89	96.44	35	0.00	96.13
367	5.18	92.08	354	1.69	91.60
8	0.00	97.79	8	0.00	97.87

important may be the residential segregation of Negroes and whites within the area of reference. The ratio of actual to expected Negro-white marriage controls for variation in racial distribution between counties or State Economic Areas, but not for racial distribution within the county or area. Moreover, it is well-known that potential marriage partners tend to be chosen largely from among those living a very small distance away.[25] Hence the residential segregation of whites from Negroes within our areas may also be of considerable importance.[26] Specifically we may hypothesize that the greater the residential segregation of whites from Negroes within an area, the lower will be the ratios of actual to expected Negro-white marriage. Another factor which may be important in explaining areal differences in these ratios is the social status of the area's Negro community relative to that of the area's white community. We may suppose that the higher the relative status of the Negro community, the higher will be the ratio of actual to expected intermarriage.[27] A final factor which may cause variation in these ratios is the tolerance of the white community. These last three factors are presumably not independent. The degree of residential segregation may, for example, affect and be affected by the level of tolerance of the white community and the relative social status of the Negro community.

Measures of the tolerance of the white community in each of our California areas are not available. However, for the 17 metropolitan counties of California we can compute a measure of the degree to which Negroes are residentially segregated from whites, and for eight large California Standard Metropolitan Statistical Areas (consisting of a single one of our metropolitan counties or some combination of these) we can obtain a measure of the relative social class standing of the Negro community. The degree to which Negroes are residentially segregated from whites was measured by the coefficient of dissimilarity,[28] computed from 1960 census data on the number of white and Negro persons living in each census tract. This coefficient, the possible values of which vary from 0 to 100, indicates the proportion of Negroes who would have to move into a different census tract in order for the areal distribution of Negro population to be identical to the areal distribution of the white population. Table 4 shows the value of this

[25] For a review of studies on this topic, see A. M. Katz and R. Hill, "Residential Propinquity and Marital Selection: a Review of Theory, Method and Fact," *Marriage and Family Living*, 20 (1958), pp. 27-34.

[26] For an excellent and detailed study of patterns of Negro residential segregation in the United States, see Karl E. and Alma F. Taeuber, *Negroes in Cities*, Chicago: Aldine, 1965. For a theoretical argument relating intermarriage rates to degrees of residential segregation see James M. Beshers, *Urban Social Structure*, New York: The Free Press, 1962, especially chapters 5 to 7. For empirical data showing very strong direct relationships for several cities between the degree of residential segregation of foreign-born Americans in a subarea of the city and the proportion of native Americans of foreign or mixed parentage in that subarea whose parents are both foreign-born (presumed to be a rough measure of propensity to marry within the foreign-born group), see Stanley Lieberson, *Ethnic Patterns in American Cities*, New York: The Free Press, 1963, pp. 156-158.

[27] For a review of studies showing the strong degree to which marriages are endogamous within social status groups, see William M. Kephart, *The Family, Society, and the Individual*, Boston: Houghton Mifflin, 1961, pp. 279-281.

[28] For technical discussions of the coefficient of dissimilarity and other segregation indices, see Otis Dudley Duncan and Beverly Duncan, "A Methodological Analysis of Segregation Indexes," *American Sociological Review*, 20 (April 1955), pp. 210-217; and Karl E. and Alma F. Taeuber, *op. cit.*, pp. 195-245.

Table 4. Index of Residential Segregation between Negroes and Whites in 1960 and Ratio of Actual to Expected Negro-White Marriage for White Brides and Grooms in 1959, for the 17 Metropolitan Counties of California

County	Index of Residential Segregation	Ratio of Actual to Expected Intermarriage
Santa Barbara	.598	.052
Solano	.625	.047
Santa Clara	.661	.045
Riverside	.687	.036
San Francisco	.702	.055
Kern	.723	.000
Sacramento	.726	.066
San Bernardino	.737	.028
Fresno	.759	.041
San Joaquin	.765	.038
Orange	.793	.029
Alameda	.794	.021
San Diego	.795	.021
San Mateo	.835	.016
Contra Costa	.852	.027
Marin	.863	.018
Los Angeles	.889	.026

segregation index for each of the 17 metropolitan counties in California in 1960 and the area's 1959 ratio of actual to expected Negro-white marriage for white brides and grooms. The correlation between these two variables is −0.57 (P.05). Thus considerable support is given to the hypothesis that areal variation in residential segregation causes variation in Negro-white marriage proportions after controls have been instituted for the effects on intermarriage of differences in racial composition between areas.

The social status of the Negro community relative to that of the white community in each area where data were available was measured by computing the ratio between the proportion of employed white males in white-collar occupations and the proportion of employed Negro males in such occupations in 1960.[29] Thus a high ratio is an indicator of low relative status for Negroes and vice versa. The relevant data are shown in Table 5. The coefficient of correlation between this measure of relative status and the ratio of actual to expected intermarriage among white brides and grooms for the California SMA's was −0.83 (P.02). This finding gives strong support to our hypothesis that variation in the relative social status of Negroes and whites provokes variation in Negro-white intermarriage proportions when the latter are controlled for the effect of differences in racial composition between areas. However, because this high correlation is based on only

[29]The source of data for these ratios was U.S. Bureau of the Census, *United States Census of Population: 1960*, Volume I, Part 6 (California), tables 74 and 78, and Volume II, Part 1C (Nonwhite population by race), table 55. Professionals, managers and proprietors except farm and clerical and sales personnel were defined as being in white-collar occupations. Ideally it would have been desirable to compute additional measures of social status of Negroes relative to whites, such as relative educational attainment and relative income. However, comparable measures of educational attainment and of income were not available separately for the Negro and white populations of the California SMSA's from the published volumes of the 1960 Census.

Table 5. Ratio of the Proportion of All Employed White Males in White-Collar Occupations to the Proportion of All Employed Negro Males in White-Collar Occupations in 1960 and Ratio of Actual to Expected Negro-White Marriage for White Brides and Grooms in 1959, for 8 SMSA's in California

SMSA	Ratio of White Proportion White-Collar to Negro Proportion White-Collar	Ratio of Actual to Expected Intermarriage
Sacramento	2.15	.066
Los Angeles-Long Beach	2.45	.026
San Jose	2.62	.045
San Bernardino-Riverside	2.91	.032
San Francisco-Oakland	3.12	.036
San Diego	3.32	.021
Fresno	3.35	.041
Bakersfield	3.59	.000

eight cases, further research based on a larger number of cases would be desirable.

Ratio of Actual to Expected Negro-White Marriage for States

We may also calculate the ratio of actual to expected intermarriage from the recent data for the four states of California, Hawaii, Michigan, and Nebraska and the earlier data for New York State (excluding New York City). Table 6 shows the ratio of actual to expected rates of Negro-white marriage for white and Negro brides and grooms, for white and Negro grooms, and for white and Negro brides. On examining the ratios of actual to expected interracial marriage for differences between states, we find that for both whites and Negroes the highest ratios by far are for the state of Hawaii. Far lower are the ratios for the other three states with recent data. However, the ratios for California are considerably higher than for Michigan; those for Nebraska are smaller. The ratios for New York State (excluding New York City) in the early 1920's were about as high as those for California during the last decade.

The data in Table 6, which eliminate the effect of differences in racial composition, may be compared with the data in Table 1, with no such control. Logically, the order of areas in the ratios of actual to expected intermarriage should be very much more similar to the order of areas with respect to intermarriage proportions for the minority group than to the order of areas with respect to intermarriage proportions for the majority group. This principle is borne out in the present data. For example, according to Table 1, the intermarriage proportions for white brides and grooms in New York State in the early 1920's are approximately one-quarter those for California in the 1950's, whereas the intermarriage proportions for Negro brides and grooms are just slightly higher. Table 6 shows the ratios of actual

Table 6. Ratios of Actual Negro-White Marriage to Proportion Expected on the Basis of Racial Distribution for Available States and Years

State and Year	Whites			Negroes		
	Brides and Grooms	Grooms	Brides	Brides and Grooms	Grooms	Brides
California						
1955	.024	.010	.036	.024	.036	.011
1957	.024	.009	.039	.024	.038	.009
1958	.024	.012	.037	.024	.037	.011
1959	.029	.012	.044	.028	.044	.013
1955–59	.025	.010	.039	.025	.039	.011
Hawaii						
1956	.232	.000	.365	.229	.359	.000
1957	.333	.000	.511	.333	.513	.000
1958	.147	.143	.154	.151	.156	.142
1959	.310	.229	.350	.304	.352	.227
1960	.444	.348	.523	.436	.521	.343
1961	.426	.234	.553	.427	.554	.223
1962	.393	.114	.561	.385	.560	.110
1963	.370	.250	.457	.375	.462	.249
1964	.458	.217	.613	.454	.611	.215
1956–64	.348	.191	.467	.343	.467	.186
Michigan						
1953	.008	.005	.012	.008	.012	.004
1954	.008	.005	.012	.008	.012	.005
1955	.009	.006	.013	.009	.012	.005
1956	.010	.005	.015	.010	.014	.005
1957	.008	.001	.016	.008	.015	.002
1958	.010	.006	.015	.010	.015	.005
1959	.011	.004	.018	.011	.018	.004
1960	.011	.007	.016	.011	.015	.007
1961	.012	.006	.020	.012	.019	.005
1962	.013	.006	.021	.013	.021	.005
1963	.017	.008	.026	.017	.026	.008
1953–63	.011	.006	.017	.011	.017	.005
Nebraska						
1961	.000	.000	.000	.000	.000	.000
1962	.000	.000	.000	.000	.000	.000
1963	.003	.003	.006	.004	.005	.003
1964	.006	.003	.010	.007	.011	.003
1961–64	.003	.000	.003	.003	.004	.001
New York (Excluding New York City)						
1921	.036	.009	.053	.032	.057	.007
1922	.022	.015	.036	.026	.037	.014
1923	.020	.015	.030	.022	.029	.015
1924	.026	.013	.043	.027	.042	.012
1921–24	.024	.012	.041	.026	.039	.012

to expected Negro-white marriage in New York State to be almost identical to those in California.

As before, the causes of the rather marked differences between these four states in the ratios of actual to expected Negro-white marriage may be differences between them in Negro-white residential segregation, in the relative social status of Negroes and whites, and in the tolerance of the white community. It is difficult to test these speculations. Data on white tolerance of racial intermarriage are not available for any of these states. Furthermore, suitable data on the residential segregation of Negroes from whites for areas as large as states are also lacking. Data on the ratio of the proportion of employed white males in white-collar occupations to the proportion of employed Negro males in such occupations in 1960 were available for California, Michigan, and Nebraska, but not for Hawaii. For California this ratio was 2.55, for Michigan 2.81, and for Nebraska 2.91.[30] The ranking of the three states on this ratio is inverse to their ranking on the ratio of actual to expected proportions intermarrying. Thus the hypothesis that the relative social status of Negroes affects the rate of Negro-white intermarriage is again given support.

Table 6 also reveals that the ratio of actual to expected Negro-white marriage appears to be rising in each of the four states for which we have current data. The trend can again be measured with greatest assurance in Michigan. For that state, coefficients of correlation between ratios of actual to expected intermarriage and time were computed. For white brides and grooms and for Negro brides and grooms, the coefficient of correlation between the ratios and time was $+0.88$ (P.01), for white grooms $+0.43$, for white brides $+0.93$ (P.01), for Negro grooms $+0.91$ (P.01), and for Negro brides $+0.51$. The corresponding regression coefficients were .0007, .0002, .0012, .0012, and .0002. Thus the greatest increases in the Michigan ratios have occurred for white brides and Negro grooms.

The trend of increase in the ratios of actual to expected Negro-white marriage observed in these four states may be due in part to recent decreases in the residential segregation of Negroes and whites. Karl and Alma Taeuber show that for 64 of 109 cities in the United States the index of residential segregation between whites and non-whites was lower in 1960 than in 1950. Moreover, 35 of the 45 cities with an increasing index of segregation were in the South. Among the 64 cities in the North and West, only ten had an increase in the segregation index. For example, in the city of Detroit the segregation index (derived from city block data) decreased from 88.8 in 1950 to 84.5 in 1960.[31]

The increase in ratios of actual to expected intermarriage in these states may also be caused by decreasing divergence between the socioeconomic status of Negroes and whites. The ratio of white employed males in white-

---

[30] The ratios for Michigan and Nebraska involve a comparison of white with nonwhite proportions since data on the occupation of Negro males were not available. However, Negroes constitute 97.3 percent of the nonwhite population in Michigan and 80.2 percent of the nonwhite population of Nebraska, with most of the remainder being American Indians.

[31] Karl E. and Alma F. Taeuber, *op. cit.*, pp. 39–44.

collar occupations to Negro employed males in such occupations in 1950 was computed for Michigan, California, and Nebraska. In all of these states the ratio was higher in 1950 than in 1960. In California the 1950 ratio was 2.93 compared with 2.55 in 1960; for Michigan, 3.24 compared with 2.81; and for Nebraska, 3.23 compared with 2.91.[32]

Finally, the increase in ratios of actual to expected intermarriage in these states may possibly result from an increase in tolerance for such marriages. The writer was not able to find any survey data concerning attitudes toward Negro-white marriage for a year prior to 1963. However, nationwide longitudinal survey data on attitudes toward residential and school integration reveal a very substantial liberalization of opinion. For example, in 1942 only 30 percent of white persons in the United States favored white and Negro students in the same schools, but this proportion rose to 49 percent in 1956 and to 62 percent in 1963.[33] The sharp increase in the acceptance of school integration makes plausible the hypothesis that negative attitudes toward intermarriage have also softened.

Implications of a Rising Trend in Negro-White Marriage

In this paper it has been argued that Negro-white status differences will be reduced if further intermixture between Negroes and whites occurs. Racial intermarriage in the United States does appear to be increasing. Is it plausible to assume that the increase in Negro-white marriage will soon accomplish substantial racial intermixture? The answer to this is probably negative. It is hard to imagine a set of conditions under which Negro-white marriage rates would increase so rapidly as to achieve any large intermingling within the next 100 years. Thus the evident recent trend of increase in Negro-white marriage will not of itself soon bring Negroes to full equality with whites.

Nevertheless, any increase in Negro-white marriage is likely to bring Negroes nearer to equality with whites. Moreover, certain trends may be operating in interaction with Negro-white marriage to reduce the status gap between the races. For example, reductions in residential and school segregation may operate not only directly to decrease Negro-white status differences but also indirectly by increasing the frequency of Negro-white marriage. In addition, it is likely that any decreasing difference in status between Negroes and whites may increase the intermarriage rate and thus cause still further equalization.

[32]The data for 1950 were computed from U.S. Bureau of the Census, *Census of Population: 1950*, Volume II, Parts 5, 22, and 27, table 77.

[33]Herbert H. Hyman and Paul B. Sheatsley, "Attitudes towards Desegregation," *Scientific American*, 211 (July 1964), pp. 16–23.

12

Socioeconomic Characteristics

Daniel P. Moynihan: Employment, Income, and the Ordeal of the Negro Family

The civil rights revolution of our time is entering a new phase, and a new crisis. In the first phase, the demands of the Negro American were directed primarily to those rights associated with the idea of Liberty: the right to vote, the right to free speech, the right to free assembly. In the second phase, the movement must turn to the issue of Equality. From the very outset, the principal measure of progress toward equality will be that of employment. It is the primary source of individual or group identity. In America what you do is what you are: to do nothing is to be nothing; to do little is to be little. The equations are implacable and blunt, and ruthlessly public.

For the Negro American it is already, and will continue to be, the master problem. It is the measure of white bona fides. It is the measure of Negro competence, and also of the competence of American society. Most importantly, the linkage between problems of employment and the range of social pathology that afflicts the Negro community is unmistakable. Employment not only controls the present for the Negro American; but, in a most profound way, it is creating the future as well.

Reprinted by permission from *Daedalus*, Journal of the American Academy of Arts and Sciences, Boston, Massachusetts, Volume 94, Number 4 (Fall 1965), pp. 745-770.

Table 1. Unemployment Rates

	1930	1940	1950
White	6.6%	14.1%	4.5%
Nonwhite	6.1%	16.9%	7.9%
Ratio, nonwhite to white	.92	1.20	1.76

The current situation and recent trends pose a problem of interpretation which may not have been much noticed. It is that in terms of employment and income and occupational status it is quite possible the Negro community is moving in two directions, or rather that two Negro communities are moving in opposite ones. Obviously such a development would be concealed—cancelled out—in aggregate statistics that list all "nonwhites" together. Anyone with eyes to see can observe the emergence of a Negro middle class that is on the whole doing very well. This group has, if anything, rather a preferred position in the job market. A nation catching up with centuries of discrimination has rather sharply raised the demand for a group in short supply. One would be hard put to describe a person with better job opportunities than a newly minted Negro Ph.D. In a wide and expanding range of employment, there would seem to be no question that opportunities for some are rather more equal than for others, and that for the first time in our history the Negro American is the beneficiary of such arrangements. These facts are reflected in the steadily raising level of Negro aspirations and in efforts by the Negro to acquire the education and training that are the cartes d'identité of the Great American Middle Class.[1]

At the same time there would also seem to be no question that opportunities for a large mass of Negro workers in the lower ranges of training and education have not been improving, that in many ways the circumstances of these workers relative to the white work force have grown worse. It would appear that this in turn has led to, or been accompanied by, a serious weakening of the Negro social structure, specifically of the Negro family. It could be that this situation has gone on so long that the Negro potential is already impaired; in any event it would hardly seem possible to doubt that if it persists much longer the capacity of the Negro community to make the most of its opportunities will be grievously diminished. Measures that would have worked twenty years ago may not work today, and surely will not work twenty years hence. A crisis of commitments is at hand.

The moral grandeur of the Negro revolution makes it more than normally difficult to speak of these matters; yet it demands that we do so. The plain physical courage which the Negro leaders and their followers have shown in recent years ought at least to summon in the rest of us the moral courage to inquire just how bad things may have become while we were occupied

[1]In 1964 the number of corporation personnel representatives visiting the campus of Lincoln University in Pennsylvania was twice that of the graduating class. Inasmuch as half the class was going on to graduate school, the representatives of American business outnumbered their potential recruits by four to one. For an excellent survey, see Dorothy K. Newman, "The Negro's Journey to the City," *Monthly Labor Review*, May-June 1965. See also *The New York Times*, May 30, 1965.

elsewhere. It is probable that such inquiry will be resented by some and misused by others. So be it. The important fact is that it is not likely to cause any great harm if things turn out not to be so bad as they appeared. On the other hand, if present indications are correct, the only hope we have is to state them and face up to them.

Unemployment

The primary measure of the problem of Negro employment is the rate of unemployment.[2] It is here that the deterioration of the Negro position is most conspicuous. What has happened is that over the past thirty-five years the rate of Negro unemployment, from being rather less than that of whites, has steadily moved to the point where it is now regularly more than twice as great, while, of course, the over-all unemployment rate in the United States has remained higher than that of any other industrial democracy in the world. (As I write, unemployment in Japan is less than 1 percent.)

The decennial census shows the steady rise in the ratio.[3]

There is a sense in which this two-to-one ratio has not so much been a situation which has developed among Negroes, as it has been a relation that has long existed for Negroes in certain circumstances, and more and more Negroes have found themselves in those circumstances in recent years.

In 1930, 41 percent of Negro males were engaged in agriculture where, if incomes were low, so was unemployment. If the South is taken out of the 1930 census data, thereby measuring employment among predominantly urban Negroes, a 1.6 to 1 unemployment ratio appears: white 7.4 percent, nonwhite 11.5 percent. By 1940 the two-to-one ratio outside the South had emerged: 14.8 percent for whites, 29.7 percent for nonwhites. Since 1930 the proportion of Negroes living in cities has almost doubled. It is now nearly 75 percent—greater than that of whites. Correspondingly, the two-to-one unemployment ratio has since become general—one of the seemingly fixed ratios of our economy.

The unemployment rate is, of course, a vertical measure—recording the situation at any given moment. The true impact of unemployment in the

---

[2] A statistical note is necessary here. A great deal of data taken to refer to Negroes in fact refers to a larger group, all of whose members are classified as "nonwhite," as opposed to "white." These are the two main categories into which the population is divided in most ongoing statistical series collected by the federal government, as, for example, the employment series. Only in the decennial census is the nonwhite group broken down into subgroups. In 1960 Negroes were 92.1 percent of all nonwhites. The remaining 7.9 percent were made up largely of Indians, Japanese, and Chinese. An important fact is that with respect to almost all economic and social data, Chinese and Japanese (who together make up 3.4 percent of nonwhites) are at the opposite end of the spectrum from Negroes. Japanese and Chinese have twice as large a proportion of their population going to college as do whites; Negroes have a little less than half. Negroes have twice as high a rate of unemployment as do whites; Chinese and Japanese have half. In 1960, 21 percent of Negro women who had ever married were separated, divorced, or had their husband absent for other reasons, as against 7 percent of Japanese and 6 percent of Chinese. A consequence of these figures is that statistics for nonwhites generally understate the degree of unemployment among Negroes as well as the extent of family disorganization, and the gap that separates them from the white world. In this study the terms "Negro" and "nonwhite" are *not* used interchangeably, but rather refer to the smaller or larger group, as the case may be.

[3] The 1930 census was taken in the spring of the year before the full effects of the depression were felt. Data are not strictly comparable with those of later years, but ratios are valid.

Negro community can be measured accurately only in horizontal terms—the experience of unemployment over time. Here the facts emerge as something near disastrous. In 1958 only half of the nonwhite males who worked at any time during the year worked a full 50 to 52 weeks; in 1963, only 55 percent. Fewer than a third of the nonwhite women who worked during 1963 had a full year's employment. In some measure these statistics reflect the flexibility of the American work force. White rates, 67 percent for males and 38 percent for females during 1963, are also low. At the same time, the degree to which Negroes are forced into this pattern of intermittent employment is unmistakable. In 1964 nonwhites held 10 percent of the full-time and the voluntary part-time jobs in nonfarm industries, but they accounted for 27 percent of those working part-time involuntarily for economic reasons. This situation has shown no improvement since 1957. In sum, after an extended period of unprecedented economic growth, the Negro experience in the labor market remains hazardous and intermittent in the extreme.

Occupational Patterns

In contrast to the experience of unemployment, the occupational patterns of Negro workers have clearly improved over the past three and one-half decades. Slowly they are coming into line with the white work force; but they have a long way to go. The most dramatic and important movement has been out of agriculture. Over one third of the Negroes were in agriculture in 1930; less than one tenth in 1960. This movement has been accompanied by migration northward: approximately 70 percent of the Negro workers were in the South in 1930 and about 50 percent in 1960.

Employment of nonwhite farmers and farm managers has declined substantially over the past decade, falling much more rapidly than employment in that category generally. There were 389,000 nonwhites in this group in 1954, only 145,000 a decade later—a drop of 63 percent.

It should be noted, however, that the decline of Negro farmers was not matched by a similar decline in Negro hired farm laborers. During the decade in which nonwhite farmers and farm managers fell by 63 percent, nonwhite farm laborers and foremen fell only 14 percent, from 589,000 to 506,000. As a result, the proportion of nonwhites in this employment category actually rose slightly, from 23.6 percent in 1954 to 23.8 percent in 1964. This has been accompanied by increasing rates of unemployment—tenants and sharecroppers, no matter how low their income and living standards, are not so subject as hired farm workers are to unemployment or, possibly, to a decline in social stability.

At the other end of the spectrum, employment of nonwhite professional and technical workers has increased sharply over the past decade, growing more rapidly than employment in any other major occupational group. Between 1954 and 1964, employment of nonwhite professional workers increased from 217,000 to 499,000, a growth of 130 percent.

The rate of increase in employment of nonwhite clerical workers was

Table 2

	1930	1940	1950	1960
Percent of nonwhite civilian labor force which is in the South	71.9	72.8	63.0	53.3
Percent of experienced labor force which is in agriculture				
White	19.2	16.1	11.4*	6.2
Nonwhite	36.5	30.7	19.5*	9.1

* Based on those employed rather than total labor force.

exceeded only by that for professionals during the past decade. The number all but doubled, to a total of 572,000 in 1964, with a corresponding increase in the nonwhite proportion of all clerical workers to 5.4 percent. A similar movement occurred among nonwhite craftsmen and foremen, whose numbers increased by two thirds during the decade, from 316,000 to 525,000. Their proportion accordingly rose from 3.8 percent to 5.8 percent. A perhaps significant ratio is to be seen here. Among professional, clerical, and skilled workers, nonwhites steadily improved their position in the decade following the Korean War, rising to 5.8, 5.4, and 5.8 percent of the respective groups. From about one third of their proportionate share, they moved up to about one half. Each group has now rather more than a half million members. By and large they make up the Negro middle class, for whom things have unmistakably been getting better.

By far the largest group of nonwhite workers are those classified as operatives—the blue-collar workers of the nation's industry. Their number, 1,520,000 in 1964, was almost exactly that of professional, clerical, and skilled workers combined. Their numbers increased very little over the decade, less than 16 percent.

There were slightly more than one million nonwhite private household workers in 1954, an increase of 13 percent over the decade. During this period, however, the nonwhite proportion of such workers dropped from 51.4 percent to 43.6 percent.

Service workers (except private household workers) provide another large field of employment for nonwhites. Their number grew by one third during the decade of 1954–64, to a total of 1.4 million, but their proportion of the over-all total declined slightly to 20 percent. However, an increasing proportion of nonwhite men are employed in service occupations. The proportion rose from 14 percent in 1959 to 17 percent in 1963. Those with very much education were leaving service employment, but nonwhite men with little education were moving into it rapidly. From 1959 to 1963 the percent of nonwhite high school graduates employed in service occupations declined from 23 to 14. In the same period, the percentage rose for nonwhite men with an elementary education from 11 to 19.

Among laborers (except farm and mine) there was an actual decline in nonwhite employment over the same period, the total dropping 4 percent to 974,000. The nonwhite proportion of the over-all total also declined slightly.

Negroes fare badly in the category of sales workers, for all that their situation may be improving. In 1964 there were 136,000 nonwhite sales workers, representing 3.1 percent of the total. This represented an increase of better than 50 percent in a decade.

Without question, however, the most conspicuous failure of Negroes to win their way in the world has been in the related field of managers, officials, and proprietors. Once again the number of nonwhites in this category increased by nearly half over the decade, but the end result was only 192,000 positions, representing only 2.6 percent of the total, as contrasted with 2.3 percent in 1955. Taking away Asians would diminish the number still further, to only about 140,000 Negro positions.

It could well be that Negro Americans are arriving in the nation's cities at a time when opportunities for establishing small businesses are declining, a parallel to the decline in manufacturing jobs, and another example of the problem of the timing of the Negro migration. No other immigrant group came upon the scene at a moment of declining employment opportunities. But given the absence of any tradition of Negro entrepreneurship, the scarcity of entrepreneurial opportunity has worked virtually to exclude Negroes from this singularly important echelon of employment. Only 6.5 percent of nonwhite males with one or more years of college are working in this field, as against 22.7 of whites. In over-all terms present-day Negroes, as newly arrived migrants in the great urban areas of the nation, present an employment pattern strikingly similar to that of past migrant groups. For example, first-generation and second-generation Italian immigrants recorded in the 1900 census had almost precisely the occupational pattern of Northern Negroes sixty years later.

The basic question concerning the future employment of Negroes is whether the pattern of opportunity is shifting to make it easier or more difficult for them to move into line with the work force in general. We must also question whether or not the existing patterns of employment are affecting the Negro potential for taking advantage of the opportunities which arise in the future.

Income

The patterns of Negro employment are directly related to those of income. Negro income has risen substantially in recent years, as has employment. But the gap between Negro and white income is not closing; it is widening. And the problems that follow are made more savage by a soaring population.

The principal problem, and the proper focus of public concern, is that of the Negro male worker. His plight does not seem to improve. Income rises. Year-round, full-time workers gained almost $1,000 in the short period

Table 3. Occupations of Italians in 1900 Compared with Northern Negroes in 1960

	Total	Planters, Farmers, Overseers	Professional Services, Trade, and Transportation	Manufacturing and Mechanical	All Others
Italians, 1900	100%	2%	21%	32%	45%
Negroes, North, 1960	100%	*	23%	32%	45%

*Less than 1%.

from 1957 to 1963. But positions relative to white workers did not improve significantly, nor did the chances of being a year-round full-time worker.

The family income of nonwhites, relative to that of whites, rose steadily during the 1940's, peaked in the 1950's at about 57 percent, and has since fallen back. Of late the ratio has remained frozen in a two-to-one proportion reminiscent of the unemployment rates. During the period 1949 to 1959 the ratio of the median income of Negro men to that of white men declined in every region of the nation. The ratio went from .75 to .72 in the Northeast, from .50 to .47 in the South, and from .53 to .52 in the country as a whole.[4] From 1959 to 1963 the position of the Negro male appears to have improved somewhat in these terms, but the roughly two-to-one proportion was maintained.

In 1963 the median income of nonwhite males had risen to $2,507, as against $4,816 for whites. However, the Negro position remained precarious in the extreme. Six out of ten nonwhite farmers earned less than $1,000, fewer than one in ten earned over $3,000. Over half the nonwhite males earned less than $3,000. Only 1.2 percent of nonwhite males earned over $10,000—approximately 70,000 persons in all the United States, of whom as many as 25,000 were probably Chinese or Japanese. The impact of unemployment on nonwhite income is unmistakable. In 1963 those nonwhite men who worked year-round full-time earned a median income of $4,019—almost two thirds the white median of $6,245. However, only 49.7 percent of nonwhite men with income in 1963 actually worked a full year, as against 60.1 percent of whites.

The Ordeal of the Negro Family

The cumulative result of unemployment and low income, and probably also of excessive dependence upon the income of women, has produced an unmistakable crisis in the Negro family, and raises the serious question of whether or not this crisis is beginning to create conditions which tend to reinforce the cycle that produced it in the first instance. The crisis would

[4] Alan B. Batchelder, "Decline in the Relative Income of Negro Men," *Quarterly Journal of Economics*, LXXVIII (Nov. 1964), 525-548.

probably exist in any event, but it becomes acute in the context of the extraordinary rise in Negro population in recent years.

At the time of the founding of the nation, one American in five was a Negro. The proportion declined steadily until it was only one in ten by 1920, where it held until the 1950's when it began to rise. Since 1950 the nonwhite population has grown at a rate of 2.4 percent per year, compared with 1.7 percent for the total population. One American in nine is nonwhite today. If the rates of growth between 1950 and 1964 continue, one in eight will be nonwhite by 1972. In 1964 among children under the age of fourteen, 15 percent were nonwhite. Under one year of age, 16.4 percent were nonwhite: one in six. Although white and nonwhite fertility rates have declined somewhat since 1959, the nonwhite/white ratio of 1.42 has not narrowed. Between 1950 and 1960 the size of the white family changed very little, while that of nonwhites increased from 4.07 persons to 4.30 persons.

Perhaps most significantly, the gap between what might be called the generation rate between white and nonwhites is particularly wide. Negro women not only have more children, but have them earlier. Thus in 1960, there were 1,247 children ever born per thousand ever-married nonwhite women fifteen to nineteen years of age, as against only 725 for white women, a ratio of 1.7. The effect of this burgeoning population on family life is accentuated by its concentration among the poor. In 1960 nonwhite mothers age thirty-five to thirty-nine with family income over $10,000 had 2.9 children; those with less than $2,000 had 5.3. A peculiar and possibly important phenomenon, which might be termed the Frazier effect, after the distinguished author of *Black Bourgeoisie*, is that Negro upper-class families have fewer children than their white counterparts, while lower-class families have more. In 1960 nonwhite women (married once, husband present) age thirty-five to forty-four married early to undereducated laborers had 4.7 children, as against 3.8 for white women in the same situation. But nonwhite women in that age bracket, married at twenty-two or over to professional or technical workers with a year or more of college, had only 1.9 children, as against 2.4 for whites.

The impact of family size on the life chances of children and the strength of the family can be measured by a number of statistics. The Task Force on Manpower Conservation (1963) studied the nation's young men who failed to pass the Selective Service written test. A passing score on this test indicates the achievement of a seventh- or eighth-grade education. Three out of four of the nonwhite young men failing the test came from families with four or more children. One out of two came from families with six or more children.

A Negro child born to a large family is more likely to be reared in a broken family. Such are the strains of rearing large families with marginal incomes and unemployed fathers. In the urban U.S. in 1960 there were 154,000 one-child nonwhite families headed by married men age twenty to twenty-four with wives present. There were 19,000 such families headed by women separated from their husbands, one-eighth as many as whole families. There were a similar number of such husband-wife families with four or more children, 152,000; but there were 39,000 headed by married women separated from their husbands—one fourth the number with both husband and wife. Poor families break under the responsibilities imposed by a large number of children. Children from these families become the nation's draft rejectees, because—among other reasons—they have spent a basic learning period in an institution too large for its resources and often with one of the instructors missing.

Poverty is both the cause and the result. In 1963 the median income of nonwhite families was $3,465, about half the $6,548 median of whites. The magnitude of the income gap is illustrated by the fact that incomes were lower in nonwhite families with employed heads than in white families with unemployed heads. What the long trend of the gap will be is not, of course, clear, but from 1960 to 1963 the nonwhite median family income as a percent of white declined from 55 to 53.

In March 1964 nearly 20 million persons fourteen years and over were living in families with annual incomes under $3,000. Nonwhite persons accounted for a quarter of those living in such families. But nearly half of all nonwhite youths under fourteen are living in families with incomes under $3,000. Nonwhites make up 40 percent of the children living in such families. Using a flexible scale that relates required family income to family size, the Department of Health, Education, and Welfare has estimated that 60 percent of the Negro children in America today are growing up in poverty-striken families. In these circumstances the stability of the Negro family, still grievously impaired by the heritage of slavery and segregation, would seem to have been weakened still further.

The fundamental problem is the position of the male. To begin with, the Negro father tends to hold jobs with a minimum of either prestige or income. In 1963, fully one third of the nonwhite family heads who worked at all had their longest (or only) job in farming, domestic service, or laboring occupations. For these persons, income was well under half that of all families with working heads. In addition to low income and low prestige, the Negro father is burdened with savage rates of unemployment at precisely that moment in his life when family responsibilities are most heavy. The ratio of nonwhite to white unemployment is highest among men between the ages of twenty-five to thirty-four—2.57. This compares with a ratio of 2.17 for all men fourteen and over. The next highest ratio for men was 2.48, at thirty-five to forty-four years of age. In 1963, 29 percent of nonwhite males in the work force were unemployed at one time or another. Three out of ten nonwhite men who were unemployed in 1963 had three or more periods of unemployment; one-fifth of all unemployed nonwhites were out of work half the year or more.

A measure of the distress of Negro men in their middle years is that they disappear—literally. In 1964 for every 100 white and nonwhite women age thirty to thirty-four years, there were 99.4 white, but only 86.7 nonwhite, men. The Negroes had not died—they begin to reappear after forty—they had simply become invisible. (An interesting question is whether an accurate enumeration of these missing males would not significantly increase current unemployment rates for Negro males.)

It is in the perspective of the underemployment of the Negro father that we must regard the Negro mother as being overemployed. From 1957 to 1964 the civilian labor-force participation rate of nonwhite men dropped from 80.8 percent to 75.6 percent. The ratio of nonwhite to white labor-force participation rates dropped from .99 to .97. During this period, the civilian labor force participation of nonwhite women rose somewhat overall. It rose particularly in ages twenty to twenty-four, from 46.6 percent in 1957 to 53.6 percent in 1964; in ages twenty-five to thirty-four years, from 50.4 percent in 1957 to 52.8 percent in 1964; and in ages forty-five to fifty-four where it reached 62.3 percent in that year. Typically, the nonwhite/white ratio of labor-force participation for women is highest in the middle years, reaching 1.50 for age twenty-five to thirty-four, a stark contrast with the male situation. Striking, also, is the fact that the unemployment ratio of nonwhite to white women is lower than average in just those middle years when it is highest for nonwhite males. In 1964 it was only 1.73 for women thirty-five to forty-four years of age, compared with 2.48 for men of the same age and 1.96 for all women.

Inevitably, the underemployment of the Negro father has led to the break-up of the Negro family. In 1964, among unemployed white men twenty years and over there were 859,000 married with wife present and only 147,000 of "other marital status" (excluding men never married), the former group being six times the size of the latter. But among nonwhites, for 168,000 unemployed males with wives present, there were 76,000 of "other marital status." Nonwhites made up 34.1 percent of all unemployed males of "other marital status." These are the men who first lose their jobs and then lose their families.

The first effect is simply that of broken homes. Nearly a quarter of the Negro women living in cities who have ever married are divorced, separated, or living apart from their husbands. These rates have been steadily rising and are approaching one third in, for example, New York City. Almost one quarter of nonwhite families are headed by a woman, a rate that also continues to rise. At any given moment some 36 percent of Negro children are living in homes where one or both parents are missing. It is probable that not much more than one third of Negro youth reach eighteen having lived all their lives with both their parents. The second effect of the deterioration of the position of the Negro male worker has been a sharp increase in welfare dependence among Negro families. It would appear that a majority of Negro youth sooner or later are supported by the Aid to Families of Dependent Children program. In 1961 not quite half of all children receiving AFDC aid were Negro (1,112,106) and half of these were in cities of 250,000 population, where they made up three quarters of the AFDC recipients. Nonwhites account for almost two thirds of the increase in AFDC families between 1948 and 1961. The third effect that must be associated with the deteriorating position of the Negro male is the phenomenon Kenneth Clark has described as the tangle of pathology—the complex of interrelated disabilities and disadvantages that feed on each other and seem to make matters steadily worse for the individuals and communities caught up in it.

The cycle begins and ends with the children. A disastrous number begin their lives with no fathers present. Many, in some communities nearly half or more, are illegitimate. In 1963, 24 percent of all nonwhite births in the nation were illegitimate. Too few live their early years in the presence of a respected and responsible male figure. The mothers, as often as not magnificent women, go to work too soon—if indeed they ever stop. This situation is getting worse, not better. In March 1958, 29.3 percent of nonwhite women with children under six years of age were in the work force. By March 1964 this proportion had increased to 36.1 percent! At that moment 56.7 percent of nonwhite women with children six to seventeen years of age were in the work force—a higher percentage than that of nonwhite women with no children under eighteen years of age, which was 50.5 percent. Although these movements were matched among white women, they clearly have gotten out of proportion among Negroes.

Negro children are going to school in nearly the same proportions as whites in the years from seven to nineteen, when free education is available more or less everywhere in the United States. But after having once closed the gap also in the crucial years on either side of that age span, they have begun to fall back again when education often is not free. In 1953, 18.1 percent more of the white population than of the nonwhite were in school between the ages of five and six. By 1958 this gap had narrowed to 7.5. By 1963 it had widened again to 13.1. The conclusion must be that Negroes are falling behind once more in terms of the number of students who enter the main grades with advance preparation. Similarly the gap in population enrolled in school age twenty to twenty-four narrowed from 6.5 points in 1953 to 5.4 in 1958, but spread to 8.1 in 1963.

As they go through school, the economic pressures begin to mount. In a survey made in February 1963, half of the white male dropouts, but only one third of the nonwhite, attributed their leaving school before graduation from high school to school-connected reasons, such as lack of interest in school, poor grades, or difficulties with school authorities. In contrast, more nonwhite males than white gave economic reasons for leaving school.[5]

A pressing question is whether the impact of economic disadvantage on the Negro community has gone on so long that genuine structural damage has occurred, so that a reversal in the course of economic events will no longer produce the expected response in social areas. There are several combinations of social and economic data which make it reasonable to ask both of these questions. They prove little, but they suggest a great deal. More importantly, they raise questions researchers should attempt to answer, for many of the answers we are looking for will, in my opinion, be found in the

[5]The pinch of poverty is felt early. Negro families can save very little. In 1960–61 Negro families and single consumers living in cities averaged $23 in savings. White groups saved almost nine times that much.

Table 4. Percent of Nonwhite Married Women Separated from Husbands, and Unemployment Rates of Nonwhite Males Aged 20 and Over

	Nonwhite Married Women Separated from Their Husbands March of Each Year		Unemployment Rate of Nonwhite Males 20 and Over 9 Months Prior to April 1 of Each Year	
	Per Cent	Deviation from Linear Trend	Per Cent	Deviation from Linear Trend
1953	10.6	−2.4	4.1	−2.1
1954	12.7	−0.6	5.6	−1.1
1955	15.1	1.6	9.3	2.2
1956	14.2	0.5	6.8	0.8
1957	13.1	−0.9	6.8	−1.3
1958	16.0	1.8	9.8	1.3
1959	17.6	3.2	12.3	3.3
1960	13.8	−0.9	10.2	0.7
1961	14.3	−0.6	10.7	0.8
1962	14.9	−0.2	11.2	0.8
1963	14.6	−0.7	9.8	−1.1
1964	14.8	−0.8	8.6	−2.7

Source: Bureau of Labor Statistics.

interplay between the economic environment and the social structure.

The relationship between the nonwhite male unemployment rate and the number of new AFDC cases opened each year since 1948 (excluding cases under the program begun in some states since 1961 under which fathers may be present but unemployed) is one example. The curves rise and fall together. Between 1948 (when, it will be recalled, the nonwhite unemployment rate first became available) and 1962, they have the remarkable correlation of .91.[6] Between 1955 and 1956, however, the unemployment rate dropped, but the number of new cases went up slightly, from 256,881 to 261,663. Unemployment in 1960 was lower than in 1959, but new cases were higher, 338,730 as compared to 329,815. (Note the rising level of new cases.) In 1963 unemployment was down, but new cases were up. In 1964 it went down, but new cases went up again—sharply now, reaching the highest point ever: 429,000.

While the two lines on the chart go hand in hand, the situation is more complex than it first appears. Some of the increase in AFDC cases is the result of white dependency, not Negro. However, almost two thirds of the increase in the AFDC rolls between 1948 and 1961 is attributable to non-white families. While the unemployment rate for nonwhite males is used for comparison, the unemployment rate for all males would show similar changes. Some of the changes in AFDC families among nonwhites are also due to unemployment problems among families headed by females, families

[6]A correlation was also computed for the deviations from the linear trends of the two series. With the trend removed, the correlation was .82, thereby ruling out the possibility that a similar but unrelated trend was responsible for the high correlation.

broken long ago. At present, these components cannot be isolated completely and we look to corroboration from additional approaches.

The statistics are available by which we can observe the year-to-year changes in the percent of nonwhite married women who are separated from their husbands. The period from 1953 to 1964 was one of generally rising unemployment for Negro men with marked fluctuations corresponding to the rise and fall of the nation's economic activity in this period. This was also a period when the number of broken Negro families was rising with fluctuations up and down.

Table 4 shows the percent of nonwhite married women separated from thier husbands (as of March of each year) and the unemployment rate (for the nine months preceding separation rate) of nonwhite men twenty years of age and over. The two lines rise and fall together, with both having an upward trend. The bottom half of Table 4 shows the yearly fluctuations from the trend, and again, the lines rise and fall together. The correlation between the deviations of the two series from their respective trends is .81.

As in the comparison of AFDC cases and unemployment, the strength of the relationship between unemployment and separation is considerably less after 1959 than it was before, at least in the limited period of time we are able to examine it. After 1962, unemployment dropped sharply, but the increase in employment opportunities for Negro men was not accompanied by a decline in broken marriages.

It would be troubling indeed to learn that until several years ago employment opportunity made a great deal of difference in the rate of Negro dependency and family disorganization, but that the situation has so deteriorated that the problem is now feeding on itself—that measures which once would have worked will henceforth not work as well, or work at all.

The important point is not that we do not know whether this is or is not the case. It is rather that until now we have never seriously asked such a question. Obviously an answer, or set of answers, can be had, and public policy can be guided accordingly. Time, not method, is our enemy. In the next six years the nonwhite work force will increase by 20 percent, about twice the rate of the past decade and the rate for the whites in the coming same six years. The crisis of commitment is at hand.

Harold Sheppard and Herbert Striner: Family Structure and Employment Problems

This report placed strong emphasis upon the relationship of family structure and size to the problems of employment and job status for many Negroes. At the outset, it should be stressed that there is no such thing as *the* Negro family and that there is nothing intrinsically pathological about different family structures or sizes. Because of the great lack of research and data concerning the relationship of family structure and size to employment and economic opportunity, much of what follows is necessarily inferential. There is great need for gathering data explicitly for the purpose of more systematic research on this subject. Recent discussions of this topic have tended to engender acrimonious debate instead of needed research. Unless a calmer, more empirical analysis is undertaken, a solution to the employment problems of Negroes will not be found.

The large-scale migration of Negroes during the forties and fifties has had a profound effect on their families. This impact on the families is heaped upon repercussions from the plantation and slavery system. In any evaluation of differences between the Negro family and the white family, it is quickly apparent that the former is much more frequently identified with the poverty population. But an even closer look is required. Nonwhite poverty families have, on the average, more children than white poverty families. There is a direct relationship between a large number of children in a family and frustrating experience; and this correlation provides a pessimism base, an unconscious or conscious disposition to believe that "we just can't beat the game." The problem of planning family size, unfortunately, is being faced very late. But it is being faced at last; and the issue of employment and economic security cannot be divorced from the outcome of present and future family planning programs.

The following table presents the comparative distribution of large size families among whites and Negroes, and the relationship of size to poverty.

Such comparisons show that the larger the family the greater the poverty. Furthermore, there is a greater proportion of larger families among Negroes than among whites. *Given the continuing differential in birth rates between poor whites and Negroes, it is possible for the problem to become even more acute among Negroes.* As Philip Hauser has pointed out, "The Negro, like the inhabitant of the developing regions in Asia, Latin America, and Africa, in his new exposure to amenities of twentieth-century living, is experiencing rapidly declining mortality while fertility rates either remain high or, as in urban areas, actually increase."[1]

Reprinted with permission of the authors and The W. E. UpJohn Institute for Employment Research. This report was prepared for the U.S. Civil Rights Commission. Harold Sheppard is a staff member of W. E. UpJohn Institute for Employment Research. Herbert Striner is Director of Program Development for The W. E. UpJohn Institute for Employment Research.

[1]"Demographic Factors in the Integration of the Negro," *Daedalus*, Fall 1965, p. 864.

Distribution of Negro and White Families in Poverty, by Number of Children under 18, 1963*

All Families with Children under 18 (Percent)	Families with 1 Child (Percent)		Families with 6 or More Children (Percent)	
	Negro	White	Negro	White
22	33	10	77	35

*Based on the less rigorous "economy" level criteria established by the Social Security Administration (Mollie Orshansky, "Counting the Poor: Another Look at the Poverty Profile," Social Security Bulletin, January 1965).

Furthermore, for every 100 Negroes between the ages of 20 and 64 in 1960, there were 94 under 20, while the corresponding ratio for whites in the same year was only 75. In other words, Negroes of working ages carry a greater burden of dependency than whites. As of 1965, there were 103 Negroes under 20 for every 100 aged 20–64.

In 1960, one-third of all nonwhite children under the age of 14—as contrasted to only one-twelfth of white children in the same age group— were living and being reared in the absence of one or both parents, usually the absence of the father. About 20 percent of all nonwhite children were living with mothers only, as contrasted with less than 6 percent of white children. There are no data on how many Negroes have lived in fatherless families during all of their childhood. Living in a fatherless family is especially difficult for boys in their developmental years. The emergence of this type of pattern as an urban phenomenon is suggested by the fact that, in 1965, 25.5 percent of nonfarm Negro families were headed by females, in contrast to only 15.3 percent among farm families, according to the Bureau of the Census.

With one-third of Negro children under 14 being reared in families with one or both parents absent, economic equality with whites for large numbers of Negroes (perhaps growing numbers) can only be a pious wish. There is nothing intrinsically immoral about fatherless or motherless family structures—unless we view as immoral in our type of society and economy high unemployment rates, low income, and exhausting occupations. Nor is there anything intrinsically immoral about matriarchal families if there is an adequate role for the husband and son to perform in such families and in the general society.

As long as there are large families in low-income, low-skilled, poorly schooled populations—white or Negro—we must strive to design more effective means of attaining progress in income and occupational status. Low-income rural-origin families with large numbers of children have a high rate of dropouts. And dropouts have a higher unemployment rate than high school graduates. Thus, there seems to be a definite correlation between birth in a large low-income, rural-origin family and low job status and high unemployment. In other words, the nature and size of the family can become a condition for poor jobs and unemployment. Generally speaking, birth rates actually have declined in periods of unemployment in our history; that is, extended unemployment has tended to be followed by declines in birth rates. It would be interesting, incidentally, to trace historically white-Negro differences, if any, in birth rate "adjustments" to changes in nonfarm unemployment rates.

The fact that in urban centers Negroes currently have a higher proportion of low-income recent migrant persons and larger families than whites creates the impression of a "Negro problem." Many Negroes become sensitive to such a description. Many whites use the description as a defense against any action that would change such a fact, thus indulging in a self-fulfilling prophecy. It may also be possible that some Negro leaders, by refusing to cope with these facts, are also participating in self-fulfilling of the prophecy.

In years past, we witnessed the reluctance on the part of whites and Negroes alike to accept the proposition that education is a crucial variable in the life chances of Negroes. Prejudiced whites insisted that biology was the sole underlying cause of Negro inequality, while many Negroes insisted that discrimination was the sole cause. Biology certainly was not and is not the explanation, but discrimination on the basis of skin color alone is no longer as crucial as it was in the past (although it is far from being eradicated). The main point, however, is that Negroes and whites now accept the importance of educational improvements as one of the means or conditions for equality.

Since education and training are recognized today as making a difference between success and failure in the world of work, it has become almost trite and platitudinous to state that Negroes must be given better and more education and training. What has not been recognized sufficiently is that one—and *only one*—of the obstacles to rapid progress toward this goal for more Negroes is the nature of the family structure in a significant minority of the Negro population in urban areas. This minority has a greater birth rate, and it may thus be on the way to becoming a larger minority than before—*the result of which can be a perpetuation of the very crisis we are trying to prevent or mitigate*. One statistical aspect of this differential birth rate is that 64 percent of all the nonfarm, nonwhite poor population living in families are 21 years of age or younger—a proportion 21 percent higher than that among white poor persons living in nonfarm families. Among the nonwhites who were not poor, about one-half were 21 or younger.

The modern American urban world encompasses a caste system that has emerged out of the migrations of the descendants of 19th century slavery. As St. Clair Drake has pointed out:

. . . the character of the Black Ghetto is not set by the newer "gilded," not-yet run down portions of it, but by the older sections where unemployment rates are high and the masses of people work with their hands—where the median level of education is just above graduation from grade school and many of the people are likely to be recent migrants from rural areas.

The "ghettoization" of the Negro has resulted in the emergence of a ghetto subculture with a distinctive ethos, most pronounced, perhaps, in Harlem, but recognizable in all Negro neighborhoods . . . . The spontaneous vigor of the children who crowd streets and playgrounds . . . and the cheerful rushing about of adults, free from the occupational pressures of the "white world" in which they work, create an atmosphere of warmth and superficial intimacy which obscures the unpleasant facts of life in the overcrowded rooms behind the doors, the lack of adequate maintenance standards, and the too prevalent vermin and rats.[2]

About 60 percent of Negro families in the United States earn less than $4,000 per year, while 60 percent of white families earn more than that amount. Within the Negro low-income segment there is naturally a heterogeneity of social strata and styles of life. Many low-income Negroes behave within a system of what has come to be called "middle-class" values, including a stress on respectability and decorum; getting an education (if not for themselves, at least for their children); family stability; and a reasonable family size. To quote Drake, "For both men and women, owning a home and going into business are highly desired goals, the former often being a realistic one, the latter a mere fantasy."[3]

But within this same income category there are other types of families and individuals. This part of the urban Negro population and its style of life provide the flesh-and-blood world from which spring the statistics of the "Moynihan" Report:

. . . an "unorganized" lower class exists whose members tend always to become disorganized—functioning in an anomic situation where gambling, excessive drinking, the use of narcotics, and sexual promiscuity are prevalent forms of behavior, and violent interpersonal relations reflect an ethos of suspicion and resentment which suffuses this deviant subculture. It is within this milieu that criminal and semicriminal activities burgeon.[4]

The maintenance of a middle-class style of life requires more than sheer perseverance and willpower. It also calls for a certain level of income (more precisely, a certain level of purchasing power) and perhaps even a certain kind of family structure. Purchasing power is not distributed and occupational and family structure are not organized among Negroes to the same degree as they are among whites. The issue is, can one be changed without changing the others?

In this respect, a vicious circle continues to pervade the social world of many Negroes in which the number of families without fathers and a lower prestige of males among their female associates and their children are dominant features. The pattern of Negro male insecurity, sustained by other current conditions, continues to be a major obstacle to effectuating a distinct break from the disadvantaged position of a large part of the Negro population today. For one thing, "An impressive body of evidence indicates that

[2]"The Social and Economic Status of the Negro in the United States," *Daedalus*, Fall 1965, pp. 771–772.
[3]*Ibid.*, p. 779.
[4]*Loc. cit.*

rather serious personality distortions result from the female dominance so prevalent in the Negro subculture. . . ."[5] What is not sufficiently recognized is the link between the nature of the social status of many Negro males today and their problems of employment and occupational status. Indeed, this link is often vehemently denied.

The low esteem of the Negro male, especially in the lower income strata, must be given prime attention in any serious effort to change the social structure of American Negro society, which is much more like a pyramid than the white social structure. Negro occupational structure, for example, consists of a miniscule capstone of upper-class families, a larger stratum of middle-class families under that, and the largest class at the bottom. Conversely, white social structure is shaped more like a diamond, with a large middle-class bulge.

This situation of a large number of Negro males warrants further comment. For example, Negro boys in lower-income families receive less and even inferior education compared to Negro girls. Smaller proportions enroll in college-preparatory and commercial classes in the high schools. Even if the girls in such classes do not actually enter college, they at least become more qualified for white-collar jobs—the occupational sector which is expanding at a greater rate than manual jobs. As one study has pointed out:

> When more white-collar occupations open up for Negroes, the girls will be better prepared and more motivated to fill them than the boys. This is true for clerical and sales positions, but also for semi-professional and professional ones. Under these conditions Negro girls, especially those of a working class background, can be expected to achieve higher occupational status than the boys from their socioeconomic category. This kind of development would tend to perpetuate the high prestige position of Negro women with the Negro group.[6]

The author of that study also confirms one of the major theses of this bulletin, namely, that the disadvantaged position of Negroes can persist even when discrimination itself declines or is actually eliminated, especially in the case of Negro males. If this is so, the civil rights movement and the drive for equal job status face some severe frustrations. Unless major changes can be brought about in the demography, sociology, and psychology of lower-income Negro families, and of males in particular, civil rights legislation for fair employment practices will not soon achieve its goal. At best, the only kinds of jobs available for unskilled Negro males born and reared in such family settings are actually declining, and the large numbers involved cannot possibly be absorbed.

The adverse character of families in substantial parts of the Negro population is certainly due in large part to (1) the heritage of past decades and (2)

---

[5] *Ibid.,* p. 787.

[6] Jetse Sprey, "Sex Differences in Occupational Choice Patterns among Negro Adolescents," *Social Problems,* Summer 1962, p. 22.

the nature of their present environmental setting. In other words, it may be looked upon as an effect, a result. But effects can assume a causative role in human affairs.[7] Illegitimacy, many children in a family, and unstable parental relations have their effects, too; they should not be looked upon merely as results of other factors if we intend to deal with the problem and not just continue to look for someone or something to blame.

A large number of children is obviously an insuperable burden for a low-income family, regardless of racial background. In this particular instance, just on the aggregate level, the average income of Negro families is about 50 percent of the average income of white families, but the average number of children in Negro families is 30 percent more than in white families. Putting it even more dramatically, while the average number of children in upper-income nonwhite families has fallen below that of whites with comparable economic characteristics, the average number of children for lower nonwhites is above that for comparable whites. According to the 1960 Census, for every 1,000 nonwhite females aged 15–19 who had ever been married, 1,247 children had been born unto them. For comparable white females, the corresponding figure was 725.

The basic point is that the growth in the Negro population is concentrated among those with low income, inadequate education, employment insecurity, and unstable family structure.

If we are sincere in our statements about the crisis nature of Negro income, employment, and occupational status, it is not enough to be comforted by long-run predictions that, like others before them, Negroes will decrease their rural exodus to urban areas and thus eventually produce a population "increasingly similar to others in the areas to which they have come."[8] For one thing, there is nothing inevitable about such a prediction. Even if it were inevitable, the current rate of change is actually so slow that it could take more than 100 years to reach "parity." Certainly, recent trends in income and occupational status do not point to any optimistic conclusion about the future.

Hauser points to the impact of the higher birth rate among Negroes on their socioeconomic status:

High fertility with its consequent large family size handicaps the Negro by limiting the investment the family can make in human resources—that is, in the education and training of the child. Under economic pressure the Negro child, on the one hand, has little incentive to remain in school and, on the other, is often forced to leave even when he desires to obtain an education. Thus, the Negro child tends to be the high school drop-out rather than the high school graduate. Even if much more is done to remove the Negro family from the bitter consequences of raw poverty, large numbers of children will tend to set limits on the education each child in the Negro

---

[7] The family problem does exist and also does affect efforts to move the Negro into the economy and the society on a comparable footing with the white. But to be really effective, one must see the family factor not as the sole or major focus of our efforts, but as one of many crucial focuses. We are faced with a social simultaneous equation where the solution can only result if all factors are dealt with in the solving process.

[8] Hauser, *Daedalus*, Fall 1965, p. 85.

community will receive. Certainly, the family with two or three children will, for some time to come, be in a better position to support its children through high school than the family with six or more children.

The poverty of the Negro family must rank as the single most important factor preventing the Negro from developing those abilities which could help him to assume both the rights and obligations of being a first-class American citizen . . . . The large proportion of Negro children now under eighteen cannot possibly be expected to participate fully in the mainstream of American life so long as they are steeped in the morass of poverty.[9]

Since education is becoming a much more important requirement for eliminating Negro-white economic differentials and for increasing job opportunities, and since "large numbers of children will tend to set limits on the education each child in the Negro community will receive," we must come face to face with the subject of family structure and size. This matter is more than a spurious factor in the issue of Negro progress in employment and occupational status. To put it more directly by quoting Hauser, "As a result of a high birth rate, the Negro population retains characteristics such as inferior occupations, low income, and a style of life precluding association and social interaction with the dominant white society—all of which retard assimilation."[10] This statement underscores the authors' view that a high birth rate among low-income families can itself serve to perpetuate inferior occupations and high unemployment rates.

The vicious circle of poverty, large family size, poor education and skills, and high unemployment rates must be broken. It *can* be broken. And a vicious circle can be entered and broken at many points of its circumference. One of these points of entry relates to family size. We need a massive effective program aimed at helping "the relatively uneducated and impoverished Negro family to restrict its size." If all Negroes were in the upper 5 percent of the income distribution, concern about family size would, of course, be irrelevant (or indicative of fears of Negro dominance). Millionaires—Negro or white—can afford to have families of six or more children. The only adverse effect would be smaller inheritances for each child. Low-income persons—Negro or white—cannot afford large families, at least in the current stage of human history.

Poverty, poor education, punitive welfare policies (such as the "man-in-the-house" rule), and even pathological discrimination, have all contributed to the economic and social-psychological frustrations of our Negro citizens. Such frustrations are a result of these and other patterns created and sustained by dominant white beliefs and practices. But again, results can, in turn, become causes. Today, the inferior role and status of low-income Negro males contribute to the perpetuation of Negro inequality in general. "There is a great need for special efforts to enhance the role of the Negro

[9] *Ibid.*, pp. 865–866.
[10] *Ibid.*, p. 866.

male in the family, to concentrate on providing him with the capabilities of taking on his expected functions, responsibilities, and obligations as husband, father, and provider."[11] These capabilities also depend on the less understood, but nevertheless real, psychological phenomena such as self-identity, ego strength, etc. These factors are among the causes, as well as among the effects, of the employment problem.

The psychological literature is replete with findings about the unique personality problems of Negro males from lower-income families. Department of Labor and Bureau of the Census data on economic and demographic characteristics offer only partial—and hence inadequate—information and "explanations" about the employment problem of Negroes. Furthermore, the data too frequently understate the problem by being reported in the category of nonwhites instead of Negroes specifically and exclusively.

The research findings on Negro males in particular, as well as on the impact of fatherless situations on the basic behavior patterns and motivations, have been summarized by Thomas Pettigrew. One of his passages supports the authors' position that the employment problems of Negroes (males in particular) cannot be separated from family structure.

. . . eight- and nine-year-old children whose fathers are absent seek immediate gratification far more than children whose fathers are present in the home. For example, when offered their choice of receiving a tiny candy bar immediately or a large bar a week later, fatherless children typically take the small bar while other children prefer to wait for the larger bar. This hunger for immediate gratification among fatherless children seems to have serious implications. Regardless of race, children manifesting this trait also tend to be less accurate in judging time, less "socially responsible," less oriented toward achievement and more prone to delinquency. Indeed, two psychologists maintain that the inability to delay gratification is a critical factor in immature, criminal, and neurotic behavior.

. . . Various studies have demonstrated the crucial importance of the father in the socialization of boys. Mothers raising their children in homes without fathers are frequently overprotective, sometimes even smothering, in their compensatory attempts to be a combined father and mother . . . boys whose fathers are not present have initially identified with their mothers and must later, in America's relatively patrifocal society, develop a conflicting, secondary identification with males . . . .

Several studies point to the applicability of this sex-identity problem to lower-class Negro males.[12]

Lower-income Negroes have experienced difficulty in the learning process, as Martin Deutsch pointed out.[13] He also described how the economic and social experiences of the low-income Negro male have influenced his "con-

[11] *Ibid.,* p. 867.

[12] *A Profile of the Negro American* (Princeton: Van Nostrand, 1964), pp. 17–19.

[13] "The Disadvantaged Child and the Learning Process," in A. H. Passow, ed., *Education in Depressed Areas* (New York: Teachers College, Columbia University, 1963), pp. 163–179.

cept of himself and his general motivation to succeed in competitive areas of society where the rewards are the greatest.... The lower-class Negro child entering school often has had no experience with a 'successful' male model or thereby with a psychological framework in which effort can result in at least the possibility of achievement.... A child from any circumstance who has been deprived of a substantial portion of the variety of stimuli which he is maturationally capable of responding to is likely to be deficient in the equipment required for learning." Deutsch and Brown have also shown that even when income is held constant, the IQ's of Negro pupils from families without a father present are lower than the IQ's of those from families with a father.[14]

The large urban areas of the United States are fostering and are subject to a set of adverse social conditions affecting young Negroes—especially the males. These boys are too frequently in fatherless and/or unemployed families; they lack adequate stimulation for achievement, adequate occupational guidance (often nonexistent) in the families and the schools and sufficient occupational training; and they obtain only blind-end jobs, if any. The "choice" of a first job is itself a vital variable; an unskilled (or nonskilled) worker typically takes the only job he knows about when entering the labor market, and this job is stigmatized by a low wage and/or frequent spells of layoffs. If young Negroes are not poorly motivated to begin with, they inevitably lower their aspirations and efforts at self-improvement as a result of the syndrome of environmental insults. Even the pernicious system of easy credit and exorbitant interest operates to discourage their active job-seeking once unemployed, since their income from jobs would only be garnished by their creditors. The unemployed have their own version of cost-benefit analysis too.

David McClelland, of Harvard University, who has studied extensively the role of motivation in economic behavior, has pointed out that the conditions of slavery influenced the nature of American Negro adjustment conducive to obedience but not to achievement and self-betterment; and that it should not be surprising to find that many of the descendants of slavery—even though "free"—still show the effects of such adjustment. It is significant that for those few Negroes who have become middle and upper class, their achievement motivation (as measured by McClelland's projective test approach) is conspicuously high—"reflecting once again the fact that individuals who have managed to move out of a low ... achievement [motivation] group tend to have exceptionally high motivation."[15]

The relevance of the family structure to the individual's motivations to succeed—to aspire to and obtain better jobs, more education, and training—should be made clear to persons concerned with the job and income status of Negroes. A number of studies have indicated that people whose fathers were

[14]Martin Deutsch and Bert Brown, "Social Influences in Negro-White Intelligence Differences," *Social Issues*, April 1964, p. 27.

[15]*The Achieving Society* (Princeton: Van Nostrand, 1961), p. 377.

absent during their childhood tend not to develop such motivations.[16] Neither Negroes nor the nation as a whole will benefit if we create the conditions for greater opportunities in employment without preparing Negroes to take actual advantage of these conditions and opportunities. Part of this preparation must include a full-scale program of restructuring the motivational conditions of Negroes, again especially Negro males. This attack must enlist the active leadership of Negroes themselves, with the financial and organizational support from public and private sources. Some Negro leaders have already taken the initiative in the formulation of part of the issue in these terms, notably Whitney Young, Jr., of the Urban League. Since he has professional background in the field of social work and community organization, this is to be expected. We must, however, persuade others that these considerations are involved in the economic problems of Negroes, not merely as effects but as causes.

In a 1963 study, in Philadelphia,[17] it was found that lower status Negro mothers had lower educational and job aspirations for their sons than did higher status Negro mothers; they were less certain about aspirations for their sons than for their daughters (which was not true of higher status mothers). Compared to higher status mothers, a much higher percentage of these mothers said that 21 years of age or under is the best age for their sons to marry and 19 years of age for their daughters. This finding is crucial because "if a mother holds high educational and occupational aspirations for her children and at the same time thinks they should marry young and have a large family, there is often, by implication, a contradiction in her aspirations." And the younger the age at marriage, the greater the chances for bearing more children. If one keeps in mind the high percentage of mother-dominated families (even in families where the father is present) in Negro urban lower income groups, these findings have a significant bearing on the occupational and employment progress of Negro males. Given the importance of the mother in Negro lower income urban families, her aspirations can adversely influence the future of her offspring—even in the face of rising job opportunities as a result of economic growth and fair employment legislation:

. . . the relative positions of Negro mothers in the lower class may be related to different aspirational values transmitted to their children, and may also contribute to a way of life which makes any alternative aspirational levels difficult for their children to internalize and possibly achieve.[18]

---

[16]For example, W. Mischel, "Father-Absence and Delay of Gratification," *Journal of Abnormal and Social Psychology*, Vol. 63 (1961), pp. 116–124; R. L. Nuttall, "Some Correlates of High Need for Achievement among Urban Northern Negroes," *Journal of Abnormal and Social Psychology*, Vol. 68 (1964), pp. 593–600.

[17]Robert R. Bell, "Lower Class Negro Mothers' Aspirations for Their Children," *Social Forces*, May 1965, pp. 493–500.

[18]*Ibid.*, p. 500.

If such lower aspirations operate at the lower end of the lower income group's values system, the greater is the need for agencies and institutions to exercise a positive role in reshaping the goals of Negro youths who lack such motivation. The schools, training programs, the employment service, OEO, and other agencies in the community have much to do. If they fail, the less likely will it be that values conducive to occupational upgrading can be injected into the thinking and behavior of these groups of Negroes, especially the males. Negro adults must not be excluded from such attention, either.

Much of this reshaping must be carried out by the larger society, too. Once opportunities are available, the larger society and the government in general cannot simply stand aside and watch. What whites do in addition will also play a role in the motivational environment of Negroes. What motivation is there for a young Negro to graduate from high school when he sees that whites with high school diplomas earn one-third more than Negroes with similar schooling? How can a young Negro aspire to enter an apprenticeship program when he might be required to serve for four to seven years before he enjoys the fruits of such training? How can a young Negro adult with a family to support enter a training program, instead of taking a job as a laborer, for 16 to 52 weeks if the training allowance is less than the immediate income as a common laborer, and if the job for which he may be trained seems to be a dead-end one?

The responsibility for helping low-motivated Negroes to improve themselves lies partly in community institutions such as the schools. But the teachers are not yet equipped with the appropriate techniques to perform this task. Any program aimed at raising the motivations and aspirations of those Negro youths who are frustrated, and who often have ample reason for frustration, will in and of itself be a motivating factor in their lives. If someone pays attention to them and is sincerely concerned about their future, a large number of them will respond favorably. There is a great urgency for a vast program to train large numbers of Negro male "motivators" to serve in this role.[19]

[19]In this connection, David McClelland now believes that he and his associates at Harvard (Sterling Livingston, George Litwin, and others) have techniques for increasing the achievement motivation of individuals. His proposals deserve serious consideration by public and private agencies concerned with the issue of employment progress among Negroes. See "Achievement Motivation Can Be Developed," *Harvard Business Review*, November–December 1965.

The National Advisory Commission on Civil Disorders: Unemployment and the Family

The Magnitude of Poverty in Disadvantaged Neighborhoods

The chronic unemployment problem in the central city, aggravated by the constant arrival of new unemployed migrants, is the fundamental cause of the persistent poverty in disadvantaged Negro areas.

"Poverty" in the affluent society is more than absolute deprivation. Many of the poor in the United States would be well-off in other societies. Relative deprivation—inequality—is a more useful concept of poverty with respect to the Negro in America because it encompasses social and political exclusion as well as economic inequality. Because of the lack of data of this type, we have had to focus our analysis on a measure of poverty which is both economic and absolute—the Social Security Administration's "poverty level"[1] concept. It is clear, however, that broader measures of poverty would substantiate the conclusions that follow.

In 1966 there were 29.7 million persons in the United States—15.3 percent of the nation's population—with incomes below the "poverty level," as defined by the Social Security Administration. Of these, 20.3 million were white (68.3 percent), and 9.3 million nonwhite (31.7 percent). Thus, about 11.9 percent of the nation's whites and 40.6 percent of its nonwhites were poor under the Social Security definition.

The location of the nation's poor is best shown from 1964 data as indicated by the following table [below].

The following facts concerning poverty are relevant to an understanding of the problems faced by people living in disadvantaged neighborhoods.[2]

30.7 percent of nonwhite families of two or more persons lived in poverty compared to only 8.8 percent of whites.

Of the 10.1 million poor persons in central cities in 1964, about 4.4 million of these (43.6 percent) were nonwhites, and 5.7 million (56.4 percent) were whites. The poor whites were much older on the average than the poor nonwhites. The proportion of poor persons 65 years old or older was 23.2 percent among whites, but only 6.8 percent among nonwhites.

Poverty was more than twice as prevalent among nonwhite families with female heads than among those with male heads, 57 percent compared to 21 percent. In

Reprinted from *Report of the National Advisory Commission on Civil Disorders* (New York: Bantam Books, 1968), pp. 258-263.

[1] Currently $3335 per year for an urban family of four.

[2] Source: Social Security Administration. Based on 1964 data.

Percentage of Those in Poverty in Each Group
Living in:

	Metropolitan Areas			
	In Central Cities	Outside Central Cities	Other Areas	Total
Whites	23.8%	21.8%	54.4%	100%
Nonwhites	41.7	10.8	47.5	100
Total	29.4	18.4	52.2	100

Source: Social Security Administration.

central cities, 26 percent of all nonwhite families of two or more persons had female heads, as compared to 12 percent of white families.

Among nonwhite families headed by a female, and having children under 6, the incidence of poverty was 81.0 percent. Moreover, there were 243,000 such families living in poverty in central cities—or over 9 percent of all nonwhite families in those cities.

Among all children living in poverty within central cities, nonwhites outnumbered whites by over 400,000. The number of poor nonwhite children equalled or surpassed the number of white poor children in every age group.

Number of Children Living in Poverty (Millions)

Age Group	White	Nonwhite	Percent of Total Nonwhite
Under 6	0.9	1.0	53%
6–15	1.0	1.3	57
16–21	0.4	0.4	50
Total	2.3	2.7	54%

Two stark facts emerge:

1. 54 percent of all poor children in central cities in 1964 were nonwhites;

2. Of the 4.4 million nonwhites living in poverty within central cities in 1964, 52 percent were children under 16, and 61 percent were under 21.

Since 1964, the number of nonwhite families living in poverty within central cities has remained about the same; hence, these poverty conditions are probably still prevalent in central cities in terms of absolute numbers of persons, although the proportion of persons in poverty may have dropped slightly.[3]

[3] For the nation as a whole, the proportion of nonwhite families living in poverty dropped from 39 percent to 35 percent from 1964 to 1966 (defining "family" somewhat differently from the definition used in the data above). The number of such families declined from 1.9 million to 1.7 million. However, the number and proportion of all nonwhites living in central cities rose in the same period. As a result, the number of nonwhite families living in so-called "poverty areas" of large cities actually rose from 1,561,000 in 1960 to 1,588,000 in 1966.

The Social Impact of Employment
Problems in Disadvantaged Negro Areas

The high rates of unemployment and underemployment in racial ghettos are evidence, in part, that many men living in these areas are seeking but cannot obtain jobs which will support a family. Perhaps equally important, most jobs they can get are at the low end of the occupational scale, and often lack the necessary status to sustain a worker's self-respect, or the respect of his family and friends. These same men are also constantly confronted with the message of discrimination: "You are inferior because of a trait you did not cause and cannot change." This message reinforces feelings of inadequacy arising from repeated failure to obtain and keep decent jobs.

Wives of these men are forced to work, and usually produce more money. If men stay at home without working, their inadequacies constantly confront them and tensions arise between them and their wives and children. Under these pressures, it is not surprising that many of these men flee their responsibilities as husbands and fathers, leaving home, and drifting from city to city, or adopting the style of "street corner men."

Statistical evidence tends to document this. A close correlation exists between the number of nonwhite married women separated from their husbands each year and the unemployment rate among nonwhite males 20 years old and over. Similarly, from 1948 to 1962, the number of new Aid to Families with Dependent Children cases rose and fell with the nonwhite male unemployment rate. Since 1963, however, the number of new cases—most of them Negro children—has steadily increased even though the unemployment rate among nonwhite males has declined. The impact of marital status on employment among Negroes is shown by the fact that in 1967 the proportion of married men either divorced or separated from their wives was more than twice as high among unemployed nonwhite men as among employed nonwhite men. Moreover, among those participating in the labor force, there was a higher proportion of married men with wives present than with wives absent.

Unemployment Rate and Participation in Total Labor Force, 25- to 54-Year-Old Nonwhite Men, by Marital Status, March, 1967

	Unemployment Rate Nonwhite	Labor Force Participation (%) Nonwhite
Married, wife present	3.7	96.7
Other (Separated, Divorced, Widowed)	8.7	77.6

Fatherless Families

The abandonment of the home by many Negro males affects a great many children growing up in the racial ghetto. As previously indicated, most

Proportion of Families of Various Types

	Husband-Wife		Female Head	
	White	Nonwhite	White	Nonwhite
1950	88.0%	77.7%	8.5%	17.6%
1960	88.7	73.6	8.7	22.4
1966	88.8	72.7	8.9	23.7

American Negro families are headed by men, just like most other American families. Yet the proportion of families with female heads is much greater among Negroes than among whites at all income levels, and has been rising in recent years.

This disparity between white and nonwhite families is far greater among the lowest income families—those most likely to reside in disadvantaged big-city neighborhoods—than among higher income families. Among families with incomes under $3,000 in 1966, the proportion with female heads was 42 percent for Negroes but only 23 percent for whites. In contrast, among families with incomes of $7,000 or more, 8 percent of Negro families had female heads compared to 4 percent of whites.

The problems of fatherless families are aggravated by the tendency of Negroes to have large families. This is characteristic of poor families generally. The average poor, urban nonwhite family contains 4.8 persons as compared with 3.7 for the average poor, urban white family. This is one of the primary factors in the poverty status of nonwhite households in large cities.

The proportion of fatherless families appears to be increasing in the poorest Negro neighborhoods. In the Hough section of Cleveland, the proportion of families with female heads rose from 23 to 32 percent from 1960 to 1965. In the Watts section of Los Angeles it rose from 36 to 39 percent during the same period.

The handicap imposed on children growing up without fathers, in an atmosphere of poverty and deprivation, is increased because many mothers must work to provide support. The following table [below] illustrates the disparity between the proportion of nonwhite women in the child-rearing ages who are in the labor force and the comparable proportion of white women:

	Percentage of Women in the Labor Force	
Age Group	Nonwhite	White
20–24	56%	51%
25–34	55	38
35–44	61	45

With the father absent and the mother working, many ghetto children spend the bulk of their time on the streets—the streets of a crime-ridden, violence-prone and poverty-stricken world. The image of success in this world is not that of the "solid citizen," the responsible husband and father, but rather that of the "hustler" who takes care of himself by exploiting others. The dope sellers and the numbers runners are the "successful" men because their earnings far outstrip those men who try to climb the economic ladder in honest ways.

Young people in the ghetto are acutely conscious of a system which appears to offer rewards to those who illegally exploit others, and failure to those who struggle under traditional responsibilities. Under these circumstances, many adopt exploitation and the "hustle" as a way of life, disclaiming both work and marriage in favor of casual and temporary liaisons. This pattern reinforces itself from one generation to the next, creating a "culture of poverty" and an ingrained cynicism about society and its institutions.

The "Jungle"

The culture of poverty that results from unemployment and family disorganization generates a system of ruthless, exploitative relationships within the ghetto. Prostitution, dope addiction, casual sexual affairs, and crime create an environmental jungle characterized by personal insecurity and tension. The effects of this development are stark:

The rate of illegitimate births among nonwhite women has risen sharply in the past two decades. In 1940, 16.8 percent of all nonwhite births were illegitimate. By 1950 this proportion was 18 percent; by 1960, 21.6 percent; by 1966, 26.3 percent. In the ghettos of many large cities, illegitimacy rates exceed 50 percent.

The rate of illegitimacy among nonwhite women is closely related to low income and high unemployment. In Washington, D.C., for example, an analysis of 1960 census tracts shows that in tracts with unemployment rates of 12 percent or more among nonwhite men, illegitimacy was over 40 percent. But in tracts with unemployment rates of 2.9 percent and below among nonwhite men, reported illegitimacy was under 20 percent. A similar contrast existed between tracts in which median nonwhite income was under $4,000 (where illegitimacy was 38 percent) and those in which it was $8,000 and over (where illegitimacy was 11 percent).

Social Distress—Major Predominantly Negro Neighborhoods in New York City and the City as a Whole

	Juvenile Delinquency*	Venereal Disease†	ADC‡	Public Assistance§
Brownsville	125.3	609.9	459.0	265.8
East New York	98.6	207.5	148.6	71.8
Bedford Stuyvesant	115.2	771.3	337.1	197.2
Harlem	110.8	1,603.5	265.7	138.1
South Bronx	84.4	308.3	278.5	165.5
New York City	52.2	269.1	120.7	60.8

*Number of offenses per 1,000 persons 7–20 years (1965).

†Number of cases per 100,000 persons under 21 years (1964).

‡Number of children in Aid to Dependent Children cases per 1,000 under 18 years, using 1960 population as base (1965).

§Welfare Assistance recipients per 1,000 persons, using 1960 population as base (1965).

Narcotics addiction is also heavily concentrated in low-income Negro neighborhoods, particularly in New York City. Of the 59,720 addicts known to the U.S. Bureau of Narcotics at the end of 1966, just over 50 percent were Negroes. Over 52 percent of all known addicts lived within New York State, mostly in Harlem and other Negro neighborhoods. These figures undoubtedly greatly understate the actual number of persons using narcotics regularly—especially those under 21.

Not surprisingly, at every age from 6 through 19, the proportion of children from homes with both parents present who actually attend school is higher than the proportion of children from homes with only one parent or neither present.

Rates of juvenile delinquency, venereal disease, dependency upon AFDC support, and use of public assistance in general are much higher in disadvantaged Negro areas than in other parts of large cities. Data taken from New York City contrasting predominantly Negro neighborhoods with the city as a whole clearly illustrate this fact.

In conclusion: in 1965, 1.2 million nonwhite children under 16 lived in central city families headed by a woman under 65. The great majority of these children were growing up in poverty under conditions that make them better candidates for crime and civil disorder than for jobs providing an entry into American society. . . .

13

Family Disorganization and Reorganization

C. Eric Lincoln: The Absent
Father Haunts the Negro Family

Under pressure of law, public opinion, and Negro militancy, progress in civil rights has reached the point where many Americans assume that the practical end of discrimination is only a matter of time. But even the end of formal discrimination falls short of the distant goal: full integration of the Negro into American life. Nor can true integration be achieved until the nation—and the Negro—solves a crucial and immediate problem: how to "Americanize" the fragile, fractured Negro family.

The Negro in America was never a "black Anglo-Saxon," though sometimes he tried to be. He was never simply "another ethnic group" to be assimilated into the mainstream. His family structure is unique in American society.

The U.S. family is primarily patriarchal. The husband and father is the chief breadwinner, carrying the responsibility for his wife and children. Even in families where husband and wife supposedly share equally in making decisions, our society regards the male as "more equal." The law defines this relationship; custom supports and rewards it. But the majority of Negro families do not follow the U.S. custom and are appropriately penal-

Reprinted from *The New York Times Magazine*, November 28, 1965, with permission of the author. Dr. Lincoln is a member of the faculty of Union Theological Seminary in New York City.

ized. Because women have assumed primary responsibility as head of the family, the matriarchal Negro household is at a distinct disadvantage in competing for its rightful share of benefits offered by American society.

About 25 percent of Negro families are headed by women who have no husbands. These are families where the male is absent because of divorce, separation, or desertion, and do not include families with illegitimate children which have never included a male parent.

The easy explanation of the shattered Negro family puts the blame on the Negro male, caricatured as shiftless and lazy. A more socially acceptable reason attributes the matriarchal family structure to super-aggressive females. In fact, the blame rests on the horrors of a slave society which stripped the Negro male of his masculinity and condemned him to a eunuch-like existence in a culture which venerates masculine primacy.

There are no discontinuities in history. Negroes today (like any other people) are largely the product of yesterday. And American slavery, the "yesterday" of the American Negro, ended only a hundred years ago. For 250 years before emancipation, slavery ordered the lives, the thinking, and the behavior of white people in one way and of Negroes in quite another.

American slavery was a different institution from contemporary slavery in South America, Portugal, Africa, or from ancient slavery in Greece and Rome. It developed its own institutionalized values uniquely designed to promote its own ends. Its peculiar impingement upon the Negro in America inescapably conditioned his values, his behavior, and his future.

When Negroes were slaves, neither the law nor the slave owners recognized marriage between slaves. Males of prime physical condition were mated with females, like so many cattle. Children were left with the mother, giving the Negro mother an early, exclusive interest in the family and forcing upon her full responsibility for its care. In those instances where a male and female were permitted to live together longer than necessary for procreation, the Negro father (he could hardly be called a husband) had absolutely no control over his family or its fortunes. Children were seized and sold. Often the father himself was sold away from his family, never to see them again.

The psychology of castration was viciously applied in other ways too. No Negro man was given a title of respect, a practice which continues in much of the rural South today. A Negro man was simply "Sam," "Jim," or frequently "boy," no matter what his age. He was never "Mister." If he was living with a woman—the nearest thing to marriage—he was known as "Hattie's Sam" or "Mandy's Jim," again denying him a position as head of the family. And if the white man wanted Hattie or Mandy for himself, the Negro male had to step aside; interference as a "husband" meant severe punishment and, not infrequently, death.

When the Negro was freed from bondage all the laws Congress could muster were not effective in wholly transferring him from the category of slave to the category of citizen.

The slaves were freed without any provision for their economic or social well-being. They were almost totally uneducated, for to have educated a slave was a criminal offense. They had no money and no homes. And they were concentrated in a politically and economically distressed society hostile to their presence as freedmen. Even those who made their way to the North quickly found themselves unwelcome, for as indigents with low skills they threatened to glut the unskilled labor market and become a burden on the tax-paying citizenry.

Because of her peculiar relationship to the white woman as a servant, and because she was frequently the white man's mistress, the Negro woman occasionally flouted the rules of segregation. Her immunity was by no means absolute, but because she often reigned supreme in the white man's kitchen and nursery she could, in times of crisis, "talk to the man" and get concessions that made life a little more bearable for herself and her children.

The practice of sending the Negro woman to do business with the white man became quickly established in the Negro-white pattern of relations. In the ruptured economy of the postwar South, Negro women were frequently paid more than their menfolk and they could ordinarily find jobs in domestic service while their men walked the streets looking for work.

"Freedom" did not improve the image of the Negro male or give him a sense of security as head of the family. He remained a semi-slave, and his slavery was rooted in the centuries he had spent in America.

If you want to understand his hatreds, his resentments, his castration as a husband and father, look back a hundred years. And if you ask why in one hundred years he has not overcome the past, it is because the past has never died: every day, every hour of that hundred years of semi-freedom has had to be rewon day by day from the prejudice which still promotes, openly or covertly, the old ways of slavery. The Negro did not earn rewards for being manly, courageous, or assertive, but for being accommodating—for fulfilling the stereotype of what he has been forced to be.

We may note, in the interest of keeping perspective, that some stable Negro families with male heads existed before and after slavery. Before the Civil War some free Negroes in the South and North maintained family structures and customs as closely analogous to those in the prevailing white culture as circumstances would permit. A few upper-class Negro families, mostly along the Atlantic Coast, have an unbroken tradition of more than a hundred years of social stability and cultural progress. And in the Deep South a handful of Negro families that date to slavery, or the first decades after emancipation, testify to the Negro's determined attempt to overcome the scars of thralldom.

The symptoms of the Negro family's enduring sickness are everywhere evident today.

The Negro crime rate is higher by far than the national average. The rate of illegitimacy is higher—regardless of the inconsistency of reporting procedures—and may be as high as 25 percent. Negro drug addiction, especially among juveniles, is much higher than among whites—dramatic evidence of the attempt to escape the rigors of living in a society which for them bears little promise for a better future. The percentage of Negro high-school dropouts, again far above the national average, reflects the same sense of Negro hopelessness.

This is social sickness of epidemic proportions, and it spreads with the steady deterioration of the Negro family.

As the basic unit of socialization for the young, the family needs the presence of both parents if children are to learn the values and expectations of society. But socialization is a continuing experience which affects not only children but parents as well. A "family man" is much less likely to lapse into criminal activity than one without ties and responsibilities.

The absent father has not been, until recently, a particularly disturbing factor among Negroes themselves (except for educated Negroes who were particularly sensitive to the white man's blanket charge of racial immorality). Any male in the average Negro family might function as a father-figure: uncles, older brothers, grandfather, even cousins. Similarly a grandmother or aunt was frequently "mama" to a brood of children not biologically her own.

Television has been one factor in sensitizing the Negro child to the fact that his family is different. Another increasingly important factor is the integrated school. In their association with white children from complete families, Negro kids learn early that something is different about their own households. This awareness is sharpened even further by white teachers who have Negro pupils for the first time. As a Negro teacher in a newly integrated school explained it: "My white colleagues get *so* frustrated when they ask little brown Johnny, 'What does your father do?' and Johnny says he doesn't know. Then they ask, 'Well, Johnny, what does your father look like? Is he big and tall?' and Johnny says he doesn't know. And finally they say, 'Well, all right, Johnny, what is your father's name?' and Johnny says he doesn't know."

The divorce rate among Negro families is 5.1 percent, compared to 3.8 percent among whites. But divorces are expensive, and the rate of desertion—the poor man's divorce—is even higher. In many cases the psychological strain of being a member of a family he cannot support because of unemployment or lack of skills is too much for the Negro husband, and he simply disappears. More often he "deserts" so that his family may become eligible for relief payments, since the family is often better off on relief than depending on the uncertainties of a job. In any event, only a minority of Negro children will complete high school in a two-parent home.

Among middle-class Negroes the battered male ego is frequently a factor in divorce or separation. The Negro professional is in actual or vicarious contact with the American mainstream. He knows his white counterpart is the chief breadwinner and head of the family in *his* home, and the Negro is acutely sensitive to the possibility of his own failings in these respects.

As tangible goods accumulate and increasingly important decisions are made, most Negro men become restive and uncomfortable if they are married to women who outearn them and who assume the prerogatives of family leadership as corollary to their earning power. In Atlanta, for example, I asked a young Negro woman, a teacher, "Who is head of the family at your house?" She thought for a moment, then answered: "Well, Jack is now, but when I get my raise, I'll be head, because I'll be making twenty-seven dollars more than he will."

The problem is considerably more formidable than such naiveté, I assure you. The Negro female has had the responsibility of the Negro family for so many generations that she accepts it, or assumes it, as second nature. Many older women have forgotten why the responsibility devolved upon the Negro woman in the first place, or why it later became institutionalized. And young Negro women do not think it is absurd to reduce the relationship to a matter of money since many of them probably grew up in families where the only income was earned by their mothers: their fathers may not have been in evidence at all.

Even in middle-class Negro families where the husband earns more than his wife, the real cement holding the marriage may be status and "appearances" rather than a more fundamental attachment. The Negro wife who grew up in a matriarchal home finds it difficult to assent to male leadership in the family; the Negro husband with a similar family history may be overanxiously insistent on male prerogatives in order to align his family in what he conceives to be the American tradition.

I know a prominent professor in Atlanta who has taught there for fifteen years while his wife worked as a teacher in her hometown several hundred miles away. They see each other at Christmas and for a brief period at the end of his summer term. This respectable arrangement obviates, or at least postpones, the problem of who will be head of the family—at the price of maintaining a one-parent household.

The task of giving the Negro husband and father a status in keeping with the larger society requires a basic change in established patterns of Negro education, training, and employment.

More Negro women go to college than men, just the reverse of the white educational pattern. Six percent of all female professionals are Negroes, while just a shadow over 1 percent of the male professionals are Negroes. Negro females do better in school, too, probably reflecting the low incentive of the Negro male who frequently feels that even if he graduates, he still won't be getting anywhere.

The long tradition of educating the girls in the Negro families is rooted in the system of segregated employment which limited sharply the Negro male's prospects of finding a job commensurate with college training. In the typical Negro family the boys leave school and go to work early, frequently pooling their earnings for the education of their sisters. The process inevitably produces a pronounced imbalance in the ratio of educated women to educated men, reinforcing the disproportionate power and prestige of the Negro woman in the family.

Having to "marry down," if she marries at all, is a common experience of the Negro woman and one which perpetuates the matriarchal pattern while fostering dissatisfaction, desertion, and divorce. For that reason, certain Negro colleges are famous as hunting grounds for eligible men, and the tuition of many an indigent medical school student has been paid by the doting parents of aspiring daughters.

The ratio of Negro college men to women is changing slowly as employment opportunities for Negro men are broadened. In time the existing disparity as a distinctive feature of Negro life may disappear, but not until Negroes can try for success in fields closed to them for so long, and not until the incentives of Negro youth can be sharply increased.

The problem of education is, of course, interwoven with the question of jobs. Since 1930 the ratio of Negro unemployment to white employment has hovered steadily at about two to one.

The working husband of any race is usually the key to family stability; when the husband loses his job it represents the point at which the family may begin to deteriorate. His loss of self-esteem, the inability to support his family, dependence upon some social agency or the wife's earnings—all these factors generally presage more difficult problems to come. In the case of the Negro family, with its historic weaknesses and the tentative nature of male leadership, a prolonged period of unemployment can be disastrous. The family may break up completely and in the long run society has to pay.

The problem is far larger than the individual Negro family; it is bigger than the limited resources of the Negro lower class, which is most affected. The Johnson Administration, using the pioneering report on the Negro family by Daniel P. Moynihan as a point of departure, has recognized the dimensions of the crisis and inaugurated the most comprehensive series of social rehabilitation programs ever designed by the federal establishment.

Even that will not be enough. The government can make available better schools, better housing, and better opportunities for employment. It can enforce the laws protecting the franchise and the right to public accommodations. But the government cannot establish a pattern of family relationships which will foster the values needed to make all this meaningful and effective. Only the Negro can save his family. The substantive help of law and the government is essential, of course, but the incentive, the motivation which can transform the Negro predicament into a shining achievement of the Great Society, must come from within the group.

The white man destroyed the Negro family and kept it weak by preserving the psychology of slavery, thinly disguised as racial discrimination and prejudice. But the white man cannot give back the values he took away.

For years myopic but well-meaning whites have been challenging the Negro to pull himself up by his own bootstraps, even though the Negro didn't have either boots or straps. The white man was looking at his own boots and imagining the Negro owned a pair too. The "straps" of the Negro's family problem are not encouraging, but he must work with what he has.

Hallowell Pope: Unwed Mothers
and Their Sex Partners

In his ground-breaking book on unwed motherhood, Vincent pointed out that different theories of causation of illegitimacy have been popular at different times. For example, during the 1930's the emphasis was on "ecological" or environmental causes of illegitimacy and in the late 1930's and early 1940's on cultural causes. Then in the 1940's and early 1950's, psychological and psychiatric theories took over, and so forth.[1] All these approaches have assumed that there must be salient differences defined in terms of their theoretical perspectives—maybe even a single important difference—between those women who have illegitimate children and those who do not. These perspectives encouraged the view that it takes a very deprived, a very immoral, a very stupid, a very deviant, or perhaps a very exploited girl to make such a disatrous mistake as to have an illegitimate child. Folk wisdom put it: there's no such thing as being half-pregnant. Some obvious causal factor was looked for, because such an obviously important result—the illegitimate child—seemed necessarily the consequence of some clear-cut initial difference.

Both the folk saying and the various research perspectives may have been making erroneous assumptions. The probability of a girl having a birth out of wedlock is related to many interconnected factors, among them: the composition of her field of eligibles, the nature of her heterosexual partnerships, frequency of premarital intercourse, her fecundity, her knowledge and use of contraception; and, if she becomes premaritally pregnant, her attitudes toward and the availability of abortion, her possiblilities of getting married before giving birth, etc. There is no reason to believe that a "normal" person in a "normal" relationship might not become premaritally pregnant—*if we avoid the tautology* of arguing that a relationship is abnormal or deviant *because* it results in a premarital pregnancy for the girl. The premarital pregnancy may indicate a prior deviant act as defined by traditional moral standards, but it is a mistake nowadays to assume that such an act must have been committed by an abnormal person, within a deviant relationship, and in an unusual social setting. We also must avoid the mistake of using single-cause theories and common-sense research categories in trying to account for illegitmacy.

In this period of ill-defined and shifting sexual standards, the criteria are blurred by which one would classify a premarital heterosexual relationship as deviant. The difference between those couples that do and do not make the decisions and perform the acts that lead to unwed motherhood may be subtle and not easily identified. For example, as the distinction between

Reprinted from *Journal of Marriage and the Family*, 29 (August 1967), pp. 555-567, by permission of the National Council on Family Relations and the author. Hallowell Pope is in the Department of Sociology at the University of Iowa.

[1] Clark E. Vincent, *Unmarried Mothers*, New York: The Free Press, 1961, pp. 17-21.

chastity and its absence diminishes in importance, the distinction between intercourse with and without appropriate contraceptive precautions has not developed apace. Linkages between social characteristics, attitudes, and patterns of behavior previously associated with illegitimacy may now be attenuated. We may be unable to comprehend these linkages in the terms we have been employing up to this time. However, we must continue to search them out. We must also search for relevant and theoretically grounded variables and develop explanatory models that allow the analysis of interaction among these variables and of the sequence of events that results in unwed parenthood.

This paper cannot hope to unravel even a portion of the complex problems mentioned above; it can only point out the likelihood of a large overlap in the nature of the prepregnancy relationship and the context within which it occurs between those girls who do and those who do not eventually become unwed mothers. This paper, then, has the following purposes: (1) the presentation of data on the nature of the prepregnancy relationship between sex partners who later had illegitimate children; (2) the presentation of data on the similarity of their social characteristics; (3) the discussion of whether the prepregnancy relationships can be considered deviant, not subject to social controls, and characterized by exploitation; and (4) the discussion of some of the racial differences that are indicated in the data.

Research Procedures

The universe sampled consisted of all those women in selected counties of North Carolina who were recorded on birth certificates as mothers of illegitimate children during 1960 and 1961—North Carolina had about 1,700 white and 8,200 nonwhite, live illegitimate births for each of these years. (The illegitimacy ratio for 1960 was 9.0 percent overall: 2.2 percent for whites and 23.8 percent for nonwhites.[2] Counties in each of the state's major socioeconomic regions were chosen so that interviews in them might complete a sample that would be reasonably representative for the state. The goal was to contact all officially recorded white unwed mothers and a one-third sample of Negro unwed mothers in each county selected.

The completed sample included over 1,000 interviews, including 939 with women who had never before been married. The completed cases represent 32 percent of the white cases in sampled counties and 42 percent of those cases actually sought by interviewers. (Because of time limitations and other factors, we were unable to try to contact all sampled white subjects.) For Negroes, 65 percent of the cases in the sampled counties brought completed

---

[2] Among the 34 states reporting, in 1960 North Carolina ranked seventeenth from the highest in white illegitimacy ratio (2.2%) and thirteenth from the highest in nonwhite illegitimacy ratio (23.8%). The 11 former Confederate states ranked from fifth (Tennessee and Florida, 2.7%) to thirty-second (Mississippi, 1.4%) in white illegitimacy ratios and from second (Tennessee, 29.5%) to eighteenth (Louisiana, 20.4%) in nonwhite illegitimacy ratios. See *Vital Statistics of the United States: 1960*, Vol. 1, Washington, D.C.: Government Printing Office, 1962, Table 1-U, pp. 1–31.

interviews or 67 percent of the respondents actually sought. In the sampled counties, the completion rates varied from a high of 70 percent in one county to a low of 24 percent in another county (where a maternity home for white unwed mothers-to-be was used as an address by its former residents). Ten percent of the white and two percent of the Negro women with whom personal contact was made refused interviews.

There are probable biases in our completed sample: in the official records from which the sample was drawn, in the counties selected, through variations in interviewer location skills, and in the type of respondents who were inaccessible or who refused interviews. The completed sample overrepresents urban cases and is limited in the number of cases from the upper socioeconomic groups, particularly for whites. However, this is the only study of unwed mothers that has employed sampling from some known universe.

Each respondent was interviewed by a female interviewer of the same race during the summer of 1962—a time period of from 6 months to 2½ years after the woman had borne her illegitimate child. The interview schedule included a number of open- and closed-end questions. The interviews averaged 75 minutes in length and were conducted in the respondents' homes, in private.

Some characteristics of the women in the sample are: about one-half are under 21; over two-fifths have completed less than the tenth grade in school; almost one-half of the whites and three-quarters of the Negroes are daughters of semi- and unskilled workers, farm laborers, or sharecroppers; 19 percent of the whites and 54 percent of the Negroes had borne more than one illegitimate child; and, finally, two-thirds live in urban areas (U.S. Census definition), even though North Carolina has no large metropolitan areas.

This paper will deal only with the 552 Negro and 387 white never-married primiparas—that is, those unwed mothers each of whom at the time of the birth of her first child in 1960 or 1961 had never yet been married. For the most part the generalizations for the primiparas also hold for the multiparas.

Results

The Social Context

What was the social context within which the fathers and these primiparous unwed mothers associated? Two-thirds of the white and over four-fifths of the Negro unwed mothers had sex partners who were living in the same localities as they did (same town or "place"—see Table 1 for question used). In addition, in Table 2 over one-half of the white and three-quarters of the Negro unwed mothers' families knew the alleged father well; on the other hand, one-fifth of the white and one-tenth of the Negro families of the unwed mothers did not know the father at the time the woman became

Table 1. Comparison of the Place Where the Father and Unwed Mother Lived When She
Met Him, by Race

| | Place Where the Father Lived* | | |
| | Same as | Different from | |
Race	Unwed Mother	Unwed Mother	Total
White	68%	32%	100%
	(212)	(101)	(313)
Negro	85%	15%	100%
	(216)	(38)	(254)

$X^2 = 22.8$; df = 1; P < .001; ϕ = .20.

*The question used: "Where was he living when you met him—in the same town or place you were, or did he usually live in (come from) a different place?"

pregnant. Among the younger girls (aged 16–20) of both races, the proportion of parents who did not know the father before the pregnancy was even less. Parents of both races apparently had an opportunity to become acquainted with their daughters' sex partners, and, consequently, it may be assumed that they had an opportunity to exercise control over the relationship.

As Table 3 indicates, many of the unwed mothers and their sex partners were in a group of mutual associates; seven-tenths of the white and four-fifths of the Negro unwed mothers knew many of the same people that their sex partners did and knew them at least "pretty well." However, over one-quarter of the white and just under one-fifth of the Negro women did not have many mutual friends with their sex partners at the time the women became pregnant. From the evidence it appears that the Negro more often than the white woman is bound into a network of relationships that includes her family, friends, and the friends of her sex partner. In addition, these findings indicate that only a minority of women have a liaison that results in unwed motherhood while they are in isolation from their normal social ties. Most of these unwed mothers had partners who were from their home towns and were known by their families and members of their peer groups.

Table 2. Degree to Which the Unwed Mother's Family Knew the Father at the Time She
Became Pregnant, by Race

Degree to Which the Unwed Mother's Family Knew the Father*

| | | Knew Him But Had Seen Him No More | | |
| | Knew Him and Had | Than | Did Not Know | |
Race	Seen Him a Lot	Now and Then	Him	Total
White	55%	27%	18%	100%
	(172)	(83)	(57)	(312)
Negro	77%	15%	9%	101%
	(193)	(37)	(22)	(252)

$X^2 = 28.2$; df = 2; P < .001; ϕ = .22.

*The question used: "Did your family know him?" (If yes) "How well did they know him—had seen him very much?"

Table 3. Number and Strength of Mutual Friendships Held by the Father and Unwed Mother at the Time She Became Pregnant, by Race

Mutual Friendships of Unwed Mother and Father*

Race	Knew Many of the Same People Very Well	Knew Many of the Same People, but Knew Them No More Than Pretty Well	Did Not Know Many of the Same People	Total
White	28%	44%	28%	100%
	(88)	(137)	(86)	(311)
Negro	39%	47%	15%	101%
	(96)	(147)	(36)	(246)

$X^2 = 15.6$; df = 2; P < .001; $\phi = .17$.

*The question used: "At the time you became pregnant, did you know many of the same people?" (if knew many of the same people) "Would you say you both knew these people a little bit, or would you say you both knew them very well?"

The Prepregnancy Relationship between the Father and the Unwed Mother

There is inevitable distortion in the following data, because they deal with the prepregnancy relationship between the father and the unwed mother as subsequently reported by the woman in an interview situation. But after checking the internal consistency of the interviews, we believe it is largely reliable and valid.

We tapped the extent of promiscuity on the part of the unwed mothers and their sex partners in several different ways. By all these measures the amount of promiscuity—both concurrent and serial—was limited.

1. Most of the women had "gone with" their sex partners *exclusively* for at least six months *before* becoming pregnant; few had never gone with their sex partners exclusively (Table 4).

2. Most of the women were, at the time of their pregnancies, either planning to marry their sex partners or were going with them regularly

Table 4. Length of Time Unwed Mother Had "Gone with" the Father Exclusively before She Became Pregnant, by Race

Time Gone with the Father Exclusively*

Race	More Than 2 Years	6 Months– 2 Years	Less Than 6 Months	Never	Total
White	21%	39%	23%	18%	101%
	(64)	(119)	(70)	(54)	(307)
Negro	32%	46%	9%	14%	101%
	(78)	(112)	(21)	(34)	(245)

$X^2 = 25.9$; df = 3; P < .001; $\phi = .22$.

*The questions used: (a) "Had you ever gone with the father of your child—I mean gone with him fairly regularly—even if you saw other men at the same time, too?" (b) "Before you got pregnant, for how long had you gone with him fairly regularly?" (c) "During this time did you go out with other men also?" (d) "Did you ever go out with just the father of your child and no one else?"

Table 5. Commitment between the Father and Unwed Mother before Her Pregnancy, by Race

Commitment between the Father and Unwed
Mother before Her Pregnancy*

Race	Seeing Each Other No More Than Now and Then	Going Together Regularly	Planning to Be Married	Total
White	14%	45%	41%	100%
	(44)	(139)	(125)	(308)
Negro	12%	57%	32%	101%
	(29)	(142)	(80)	(251)

$X^2 = 7.3$; df = 2; P < .05; $\phi = .11$.
*The question used: "Just before you became pregnant, were you and he (the father of your child) seeing one another now and then, going together regularly, planning to get married, or what?"

(Table 5). Less than 15 percent of women of both races were only seeing their sex partners "now and then."

3. Our respondents were asked how they had felt about the father before becoming pregnant, that is, were they in love with him, did they like him a lot, were they friendly toward him, didn't they care very much for him, etc. Over four-fifths of the white and three-quarters of the Negro unwed mothers reported they either were or thought they were in love with their sex partners (Table 6). Almost none of the women in our entire sample expressed any hatred toward the father in answering this question.

4. Over seven-tenths of the whites and over two-fifths of the Negroes reported that they had had intercourse with *one man only* (the alleged father); less than 5 percent of the whites and less than 15 percent of the Negroes had had intercourse with four or more men. Because the sample is predominantly young women (over one-half of them under 21), these facts might lead one to characterize them as "loose." However, this is true only in the sense that they began sex relations while young and eventually had illegitimate children; most of them were not serially or concurrently promiscuous.[3] By all of the four indicators presented above, the amount of concurrent as well as serial promiscuity was limited among our sample; the relationship between the unwed mothers and the fathers was much more often close than not.

[3] The linkage of sex to purposes other than gratification of sexual drives is basic to the institution of marriage. Therefore, the factor that characterizes a promiscuous woman is not her exchange of sexual favors for economic security and other rewards (received as well by married women) or her emotional indifference to the sexual act (an attitude found among many wives). Rather, it is indifference to her partner and the consequent lack of selectivity and exclusivity that characterize the "loose" woman. In the promiscuous sexual relationship, sexual intercourse is divorced from any stable or affectional social relationship; it is made contingent neither on genuine affection nor on the possibility of marriage. See Kingsley Davis, "Sexual Behavior," in *Contemporary Social Problems*, ed. by R. K. Merton and R. A. Nisbet, New York: Harcourt, Brace and World, 2nd ed., 1966, pp. 322–372.

Many of the white women were well aware of traditional chastity standards and professed belief in them. Eighty-three percent among the whites answered that premarital sexual relations were never all right (even with a man whom one planned to marry soon). The comparable figure for Negroes was 28 percent. Thus, a majority of the white women now held personal sexual codes that they, in the past, had violated. (We, of course, have no data on what standards they held before they became pregnant.) We will not stress data on self-reported standards for behavior, because they are subject to more bias in reporting than the data presented in the body of the paper.

Table 6. Unwed Mother's Involvement with the Father Before Her Pregnancy, by Race

Involvement with the Father*

Race	In Love	Thought Was in Love	Liked Him a Lot	Friendly toward Him	Neutral	Total
White	49%	35%	10%	3%	3%	100%
	(153)	(110)	(32)	(8)	(8)	(311)
Negro	50%	24%	23%	2%	1%	100%
	(127)	(60)	(58)	(4)	(3)	(252)

*The question used: "Thinking back to before you became pregnant, how did you used to feel about the father of your child—were you in love with him; like him a lot; friendly toward him; not care very much for him; or what?"

Comparative Social Status of the Father and Unwed Mother

Thus far, we have characterized the unmarried mother's relationship to the father of the child from two perspectives: first, the degree to which both partners were members of the same social setting; and second, the amount of the unmarried mother's involvement with and commitment to her sex partner. We will now compare the partners' social statuses using age, socioeconomic status, education, and marital status. These comparisons determine the extent to which the sex partners came from similar social backgrounds.

As Table 7 shows, a high proportion of the unwed mothers had partners no more than three years their senior—53 percent for white, 67 percent for Negroes. Among the white unwed mothers, 28 percent had sex partners who were six or more years older; the comparable figure for Negroes was only 12 percent. The older more often than the younger unwed mothers, particularly among the Negroes, had partners who were close in age or even younger than themselves. For example, among the Negroes who were over 20, almost one-half had sex partners no more than one year their senior.

Considering education (Table 8), we find that about one-half of the unwed mothers of both races have the same general level of education as

Table 7. Age Difference between Unwed Mother and the Father, by Race

Age Difference between Unwed Mother and the Father

Race	Male No More Than 1 year Older Than Female	Male 2–3 Years Older Than Female	Male 4–5 Years Older Than Female	Male 6 or More Years Older Than Female	Total
White	30%	23%	19%	28%	100%
	(92)	(71)	(60)	(86)	(309)
Negro	31%	36%	20%	12%	99%
	(77)	(89)	(50)	(30)	(246)

$X^2 = 25.7$; $df = 3$; $P < .001$; $\phi = .21$.

Table 8. Comparison of the Education of Unwed Mother and the Father, by Race

Education of the Father

Education of Unwed Mother	Eighth Grade or Less	Some High School	High-School Graduate	Total
White				
Eighth grade or less	56%	25%	19%	100%
	(33)	(15)	(11)	(59)
Some high school	26%	38%	36%	100%
	(37)	(53)	(51)	(141)
High-school graduate or beyond	6%	24%	70%	100%
	(7)	(26)	(77)	(110)
Negro				
Eighth grade or less	49%	38%	13%	100%
	(31)	(24)	(8)	(63)
Some high school	19%	39%	43%	101%
	(23)	(47)	(52)	(122)
High-school graduate or beyond	7%	26%	67%	100%
	(5)	(18)	(46)	(69)

Education of the Father in Comparison to That of the Unwed Mother

	Father More	Same	Father Less	Total
White	25%	53%	23%	101%
	(77)	(163)	(70)	(310)
Negro	33%	49%	18%	100%
	(84)	(124)	(46)	(254)

X^2 (for lower portion of table) = 5.1; df = 2; P > .05; ϕ = .09.

their sex partners (when educational levels are grouped into no high school, some high school, and high school or beyond). One-quarter of the white and one-third of the Negro women had less education than their sex partners, whereas one-quarter of the whites and one-fifth of the Negroes had more education than did their partners. In our data there is a tendency for the younger women to have sex partners who had had more education than themselves. For example, among the whites, 31 percent of the 16–20-year-old women, as contrasted with 16 percent of the 21-year-old and older women, had sex partners with at least the next higher level of education.

Another check on the degree of social-status similarity of the unmarried mothers and their sex partners is the comparison of their respective socioeconomic statuses. Only two stratum levels were distinguished—white-collar and upper blue-collar versus lower blue-collar. One-half of the whites and three-fifths of the Negroes were in the same stratum as their sex partners (Table 9). About one-third of the white and one-quarter of the Negro unwed mothers had sex partners from the higher of the two strata, and only 14 percent of the unwed mothers of each race were from a higher stratum than their sex partners. As is the case with married pairs, the women more often "chose" upward in social status, the men downward. Admittedly, the measurement here is crude—partly because many of the respondents did not

Table 9. Comparison of the Socioeconomic Status of the Father and Unwed Mother, by Race*

| Race | Socioeconomic Status of the Father in Comparison to That of the Unwed Mother | | | Total |
	Father Higher	Same	Father Lower	
White	31%	55%	14%	100%
	(60)	(105)	(26)	(191)
Negro	24%	61%	14%	99%
	(39)	(98)	(23)	(160)

$X^2 = 2.1$; df=2; P > .05; $\phi = .03$.

*In computing figures for this table, we cross-classified the cases by socioeconomic class of the unwed mother and of the child's father. The occupational statuses of their respective fathers were used as the best measure of their statuses. We used two status levels for our computations: white-collar and upper blue-collar vs. lower blue-collar.

There is a large number of not ascertained cases. This is because many of the unwed mothers did not know the occupation of the sex partner's father.

know enough about their sex partners' parents to allow reliable coding of status.

One aspect of the social location of the fathers in relation to the unwed mothers remains to be examined: the father's marital status at the time of the woman's pregnancy, as reported by the women. As Table 10 indicates, nine-tenths of the Negro unwed mothers had sex partners whom they believed had never been married; only 2 percent of them had sex partners whom they knew were married and living with their wives. The situation was distinctly different among the white unwed mothers. Only 61 percent of them were impregnated by men who had never before been married, 10 percent by previously married men who were divorced or widowed, 16 percent by men who were married but separated, and, finally, 13 percent by men who were married and living with their wives. This last figure—13 percent of white unwed mothers impregnated by men they knew to be married and still living with their wives—does not vary between the younger and older unwed mothers; but the women over 20 years of age more often

Table 10. Marital Status of the Father at Time Unwed Mother Became Pregnant, by Race of Unwed Mother

| Race | Marital Status of the Father | | | | Total |
	Never Married	Ever Married, but Divorced or Widowed	Married, but Separated	Married and Living With His Wife	
White	61%	10%	16%	13%	100%
	(189)	(31)	(51)	(40)	(311)
Negro	91%	4%	4%	2%	101%
	(230)	(9)	(9)	(6)	(254)

$X^2 = 50.4$; df=2; P < .001; $\phi = .30$. (The "ever-married" columns were combined in computing X^2.)

Table 11. Marital History of the Father and Age Differences between Him and Unwed
Mother, by Race
Marital History of the Father and Age Difference
between Him and Unwed Mother

Race	Ever Married*		Never Married		Total
	Male 4 or More Years Older	Male Less Than 4 Years Older	Male 4 or More Years Older	Male Less Than 4 Years Older	
White	28%	12%	20%	40%	100%
	(85)	(37)	(61)	(124)	(307)
Negro	5%	4%	28%	63%	100%
	(12)	(10)	(68)	(155)	(245)

*Now married or has been married at some time in the past.

than those 20 or younger associated with men who were formerly married
but now separated, widowed, or divorced (38 percent versus 18 percent). For
the Negroes a comparable difference for the younger and older women
exists, but the differences are smaller (14 percent versus 4 percent).

Table 11 tabulates the marital history of the father as well as his age in
comparison to the unwed mother to further check the social similarity of the
sex partners, particularly among the whites. Over one-quarter of the white
women had a sex partner who had both been previously married and was 4
or more years older; on the other hand, two-fifths had sex partners close to
their own ages who had never been married. Those few Negroes who had
never-married partners about equally divided themselves between those
partners who were near their ages and those who were four or more years
older.

Discussion

The data have been presented, and we turn to their implications. We wish
to ask whether the heterosexual relationships experienced by our sample can
be considered deviant, not subject to social control, and characterized by
exploitation. Is the deviant outcome—an illegitimate birth and unwed motherhood—the consequence of an atypical and deviant relationship? Our data
cannot directly answer this question because: (1) we have no comparable
sample of women who were dating or courting and whose relationship
resulted in marriage or was terminated without childbirth; (2) we do not
have results directly bearing on all the questions we seek to answer—for
example, we lack firsthand information from the fathers—and (3) we were
unable to gain an unbiased sample from our universe of women who were
officially recorded as unwed mothers. The reader is reminded that the
sample on which our data is based is not representative of all officially
recorded illegitimacies. It underrepresents those middle- and upper-status
women, particularly the whites, who were not interviewed because they had
moved, did not give home addresses on birth certificates, etc. It may be that

these very women, those who most carefully guarded against public acknowledgment of their illegitimacies, were the same women who were not included in our sample. They may be among those most deviant, most exploited or exploitative, and most subject to certain forms of social control, for example, pressures to maintain family honor. If this is true, our data overestimate the extent of similarity between courtship for our sample and courting couples in general. However, even if this is so, the data from the cases that were obtained would heavily weight the final results in the direction herein reported, particularly for the Negroes, for whom almost two-thirds of the sampled cases resulted in completed interviews. The probable sample deficiencies, because they are more pronounced for the whites, cause our data to understate Negro-white differences. In sum: the deficiencies of the sample cause overestimation of the similarity between courtship practices in the sample and the general population, but cause underestimation of Negro-white differences.

Do our data indicate that these relationships between the women in our sample and their sex partners were deviant? Deviancy must be considered relative to some set of normative standards. Our sample was composed mostly of lower-class Negroes and whites, and we can consider the question of deviancy from both lower-class and dominant middle-class standards.[4] Also, the differences that exist between Negroes and whites with regard to sexual standards and standards governing family life must be recognized.[5] An integral part of deviancy is the social control mechanisms utilized to reorient deviant behavior and tendencies toward it. If deviant tendencies did exist among our sample of women, we must investigate whether they were isolated from those agents of social control who could have applied the appropriate sanctions.

Tables 4-6, which give data on the duration and levels of involvement and commitment between the unwed mother and her sex partner, strongly indicate that even according to middle class normative standards only a small proportion of these women could be considered promiscuous. This is true of both racial groups, with the Negroes showing a higher proportion with a long-term (six months or more) exclusive relationship with the alleged father before pregnancy. Having sex relations with a man whom one has been dating exclusively for six months, for whom one feels deep affection, and with whom one may have discussed marriage does not severely violate sexual standards of the present youthful generation. There is reason to believe that one of the dominant standards of the future will be permis-

[4] See Clark E. Vincent, *op. cit.*, pp. 1-30, for a discussion of social attitudes toward illegitimacy in the United States as well as some of the shifts that have occurred in these attitudes. For a convenient collection of articles on unwed motherhood, see Robert W. Roberts (ed.), *The Unwed Mother*, New York: Harper and Row, 1966.

[5] See Jessie Bernard, *Marriage and Family among Negroes*, Englewood Cliffs, N.J.: Prentice-Hall, 1966, for a recent summary of literature on the Negro. Bernard warns against oversimplification about Negro subculture. Note especially her discussion in chapter 2 of the "acculturated" and "externally adapted" cultures and, within this context, her section on Negro attitudes toward out-of-wedlock births. Also see the work on sexual standards cited in footnote 6 below.

siveness-with-affection.[6] Of course, the crux of the societal reaction expressed through parents, schools, the mass media, etc., is not premarital intercourse but premarital pregnancy and illegitimate childbirth.[7] For some time a large proportion of men of diverse social categories have engaged in premarital intercourse, as have a significant proportion of women.[8] This behavior is becoming increasingly tolerated normatively if it occurs within the context of a "close" relationship. However, the continuing public clamor about the rise in illegitimacy rates indicates that, although illicit coitus is being more openly discussed, illegitimacy is still condemned by the "official" morality. In addition, it is not an acceptable state of affairs in any group.[9] The women in our sample were deviant mainly by becoming unwed mothers, not by the nature of their relationships with the fathers of their children.

[6]In this recent work, Ira L. Reiss has provided data on the sexual *standards* of American adults and youth. His general findings may be summarized as follows: men are more permissive than women (permissiveness being characteristic of those who accept premarital coitus); Negroes are more permissive than whites; youth (high-school and college age) are more permissive than adults; and there is no relationship between permissiveness and social class (however, his analysis suggests that in a liberal attitudinal setting the social class and permissiveness relation is positive, whereas in a conservative setting it is negative). See his following articles for further interesting analysis of the above zero-order relationships: "The Scaling of Premarital Sexual Permissiveness," *Journal of Marriage and the Family*, 26 (May, 1964), pp. 188–198; "Premarital Sexual Permissiveness among Negroes and Whites," *American Sociological Review*, 29 (October, 1964), pp. 688–698; and "Social Class and Premarital Sexual Permissiveness: A Re-examination," *American Sociological Review*, 30 (October, 1965), pp. 747–756. Also see his "Sexual Codes in Teen-Age Culture," *Annals*, Vol. 338 (November, 1961), pp. 53–62.

In an earlier work Reiss has discussed the various sexual standards in the United States. For a discussion of the emergence of the permissiveness-with-affection standard, see I. L. Reiss, *Premarital Sexual Standards in America*, New York: The Free Press, 1960, especially chap. 10. For a cautionary view on the past and likely future rates of change in American sexual standards, see Hallowell Pope and Dean D. Knudsen, "Premarital Sexual Norms, the Family, and Social Change," *Journal of Marriage and the Family*, 37 (August, 1965), pp. 314–323. See Winston Ehrmann, *Premarital Dating Behavior*, New York: Henry Holt, Bantam ed., 1960, for a detailed study of the sexual standards and behavior of college students. In a recent *Journal of Social Issues* (Vol. 22, April, 1966), Reiss has served as editor for articles on "The Sexual Renaissance in America." See especially the article by Lee Rainwater, "Some Aspects of Lower Class Sexual Behavior," pp. 96–108.

[7]See William J. Goode, *The Family*, Englewood Cliffs, N.J.: Prentice-Hall, 1964, pp. 19–30; and H. Pope and D. D. Knudsen, *op. cit.*

[8]See W. Ehrmann, *op. cit.*, pp. 39–44, for a summary of the incidence of premarital intercourse among college and high-school sample populations as reported by various investigators. Clifford Kirkpatrick, *The Family as Process and Institution*, New York: Ronald Press, 2nd ed., 1963, Table 28, pp. 351–353, presents the "evidence of sexual nonconformity" from the Kinsey findings for both males and females.

[8]The use of contraceptive techniques may be the only significant difference between the courting behavior of the women in our sample and courtships in which premarital intercourse takes place but in which no pregnancy occurs. We collected limited data on the contraceptive practices of our sample (but have no comparative data on the contraceptive practice of "typical" courtships). That 64 percent of the Negro and only 39 percent of the white women reported use of some contraceptive technique again indicates that our white sample was particularly biased toward those women who had the least concern about unwed motherhood. Of those women who reported use of a contraceptive technique, almost all (92 percent for Negroes and 84 percent for whites) said that their sex partners only employed the technique (exclusively the condom in over seven-tenths of the cases). Only 28 percent of the white and 14 percent of the Negro women who reported use of some technique said that it was used "every time" they had sex relations. It is clear that the women in our sample reduced the risk of pregnancy only minimally through contraception. And it is striking that, even when contraception was used, the female partner so often relied exclusively on the male. Although the woman might be expected to insist on the use of contraception or to employ some technique herself, her inabilities here are linked to her cultural position. She is expected to be subordinate to the male and not obviously aggressive in sexual matters. However, taking responsibility for contraceptive techniques violates both of these norms. Thus, though the majority of women in our sample reported concern about having an illegitimate child as a result of premarital sex relations, very few employed contraceptive techniques of their own—only six percent among the whites and five percent among the Negroes.

[9]See William J. Goode, "Illegitimacy in the Caribbean Social Structure," *American Sociological Review*, 25 (February, 1960), pp. 21–30.

Now we may consider the degree to which the women in our sample were subject to the normal mechanisms of social control. Because sexual intercourse can be accomplished briefly and secretly, the most effective controls are internalized ones. Short of these, persons of close acquaintance—family, friends, neighbors—are the most likely effective agents of control. Were the women in our sample subject to surveillance and possible sanctioning by such persons? The evidence indicates that by and large they probably were. Parents and peer groups were acquainted with the sex partners and could have applied sanctions if they had wished to do so and if they had the necessary knowledge. However, it is doubtful if members of peer groups would desire to sanction negatively these women and their sex partners; most of the relationships involved were of fairly long duration and of a high level of commitment. (Whether intercourse preceded or followed the development of commitment was not ascertained in this study.) Consequently, they conformed to the standard of permissiveness-with-affection. Parents may suspect what their children are doing heterosexually, but they usually do not have proof and may find it difficult to control sexual behavior in the face of possible support from their children's peer group for the more liberal standards. However, most parents of both races apparently had an opportunity to become acquainted with their daughters' sex partners and, in all probability, often had an opportunity to attempt to exercise control over the relationship. That they did not may reflect a lack of intense moral concern on their part as well as the feeling that no effective action could be taken. But note that a significant proportion of the couples, particularly among the whites, were not subject to controls from those persons most likely to administer them.

We may now shift perspective slightly and ask how likely it is that exploitation characterized the relationships between the sex partners. One exploits when he attempts to get more than he gives; he forgoes reciprocity. In an exploitative relationship there is no identification of ends, and the exploiting partner intrinsically values neither the relation nor the other person. The exploiting partner uses some lever of interpersonal influence—such as a "line," sophistication, status, etc.—to manipulate his partner into acts that the person does not wish to commit. For example, an older male may give promise of affection and security to a younger woman through his "line" and his worldliness; he bargains with these for sexual favors, but returns no real lasting affection and breaks off the liaison after the girl becomes pregnant.

Because we have no direct evidence concerning exploitation, a subtle determination at best, we will compare the partners' social status using marital status, age, education, and socioeconomic status. This comparison will determine the extent to which the sex partners came from similar social backgrounds and indicate their comparative bargaining power in the heterosexual relationship. If their backgrounds are similar (at least to the same extent as normally married couples), this supports the conclusion that the relationships might best be considered as courtships punctuated by an atypical event—the pregnancy. If, on the other hand, there is a marked dissimilarity in social background between the sex partners (for example, the men are much older than the women), we might conclude from this indirect evidence that these relationships were extraordinary and characterized by potential exploitation.[10]

As Table 7 shows, most of the unwed mothers had partners no more than three years their senior.[11] These data indicate that exploitation due to age differences was minimal, particularly among the Negroes. However, fully one-quarter of the white women (31 percent for women 20 years old or younger) were involved with males six or more years their senior; these women were potentially subject to exploitation.

When considering the social-status similarity of the sex partners on education and social class, our data show that the younger women (under 21) quite frequently had partners with the next highest level of education (31 percent for whites and 38 percent for the Negroes). However, this pattern of women going with older and more-schooled men is not uncommon in the United States. Of course, the intent of such women at the time may be to finish their schooling (e.g., graduate from high school) and thereby catch up to the men who have already finished their education, but such plans may be interrupted by pregnancy and/or marriage. Even so, there is a tendency on the part of the younger women to have associated with better-educated men; perhaps some exploitation based on the male's greater sophistication took place in this minority of cases. Before reaching this conclusion, however, two questions must be answered: (1) Is there more educational differential among these couples than among other courting couples? If not, the relationships under consideration may have produced no more exploitation than is usual. (2) Does the greater education and age of one partner increase the potential of exploitation when the male is the older and more-schooled partner? It is commonly assumed that women attain social sophistication at a faster pace during the teenage years than do men. If this is the case, the age and schooling of the men may be counterbalanced by the greater social sophistication of the women.

A majority of the women had partners homogamous with them on socioeconomic status. And even though our measurement of status was relatively crude, it indicates that the proportion of women who were dating "up" is not high (less than one-third for the whites and less than one-quarter for the Negroes) when one notes that in courting and married pairs the woman is the one that more often chooses "up" than the man. The evidence presented thus far indicates that the heterosexual associations that result in illegitimate children are usually between partners who are similar in social status and that there is no clear-cut evidence of more status discrepancy between the partners in these couples than between the members of those

---

[10]Cf. C. E. Vincent's discussion, *op. cit.*, chap. 4.

[11] Comparable figures for white married couples are very closely similar. C. E. Vincent, using data from the 1950 U.S. Census on 1,763,000 white wives between the ages of 14 and 22 who had been married less than three years, found that 53 percent of these wives were within three years of the same age as their husbands. *Ibid.*, p. 76.

couples who marry before having children—although the data necessary to make this comparison properly are unavailable.

A married man who is living with his wife and who has an illegitimate child with a single girl as mother likely represents an exploitative or, at least, a reckless relationship; the girl has little chance to escape unwed motherhood through marriage, and the man may be exposed as an adulterer. Table 10 shows that this was an infrequent occurrence among Negroes, but not uncommon among whites. Coupled with evidence in Table 11 showing that white, prior-married men who were four or more years older than their female partners was an even more frequent occurrence, this leads us to surmise that exploitation of some of our sample of white women was a distinct possibility. However, it may be that the women involved understood the risks they were taking and accepted them.

Because the deficiencies of the completed sample tend to minimize rather than maximize the Negro-white differences manifest in the data, they are worth discussion. We shall now consider whether the white or Negro prepregnancy relationship would be more likely to lead to marriage. Presumably, the more the alleged father is part of the unwed mother's social network, the closer the relationship between them; and the greater their status equivalence, the more likely a marriage would follow a premarital pregnancy. Although none of the Negro-white differences are pronounced, the Negro more often than the white alleged father was integrated into the unwed mother's social life (Tables 1–3). As mentioned above in the discussion of exploitative relationships, the Negro alleged father was less frequently much older than the unwed mother (six or more years). He was also more frequently legally available to marry: 95 percent versus 71 percent for the whites. Given these differences coupled with the higher proportion of the Negro couples that had been going together six months or more, we might expect the Negroes to be more frequently highly involved and committed than the whites. However, the whites were more often involved or committed in a way that would lead to marriage. Over two-fifths of the white couples were planning to be married (before the pregnancy), whereas this was true for less than one-third of the Negro couples. Also, five-sixths of the white women were (or, in retrospect, thought they were) in love with the alleged fathers; this was true for three-quarters of the Negro women.

We must try to account for this relative lack of marital plans and involvement on the part of the Negroes, even though, in comparison to the whites, they were more frequently in a long-term courting relationship of which their families and friends were aware. Two related reasons have been advanced in the literature: (1) Negroes have a lesser commitment to the norm of legitimacy than do whites; (2) Negro women have less reason and desire than white women to form a stable marriage, pregnant or not. The explanation of these two facts is based on the social and cultural situation of the Negro in the United States, both presently and historically.

Goode argues that populations such as the American Negro that were denuded of their culture and then "kept from either being integrated into the Western cultural and social systems *or* establishing independent, *internally* integrated cultural and social systems of their own" manifest a low commitment to the norm of legitimacy.[12] The dominant white (or Iberian) society maintained caste barriers and so did not provide the rewards necessary for effective acculturation, nor did it allow Negroes to develop cohesive communities with the accompanying control over sanctions to enforce their own norms. Although the Negro is now being integrated into the national culture, this process has not proceeded far enough to foster development of a high commitment to the norm of legitimacy among Negroes or to arm the Negro with the sanctions necessary to enforce conformity to this norm.

Along with Goode's conclusions, we may place the analysis of why the Negro less often than the white female has the desire to get married (even though pregnant). Such a practice, of course, frequently results in a matrifocal family in which the female head of household is the dominant member.[13] Some account for the matrifocal family pattern among Negroes mainly as a result of historical factors, treating it as a holdover from the past by noting that the woman was the center of the slave family. They also note that the Negro was unlikely to institutionalize a stable male-dominated family during the social disruption brought about by Reconstruction and Negro rural-urban migration. However, certain current conditions of Negro life may be considered as either supplementary factors or even sufficient in themselves to produce the matrifocal family pattern. We suggest that, in strata living under the following conditions, the woman has lessened motivation to marry and that a relatively high proportion of matrifocal families is the result.

1. It holds class position at the lowest rank of the society.

2. It has limited chance for upward vertical social mobility.

3. Its members have a high degree of job insecurity.

4. However, opportunity exists for women to engage in money-making activities (in low paying jobs—for example as domestics, farm or factory laborers).

5. The male is expected (by the dominant cultural ethos) to be the family's main money-earner.[14]

---

[12]See William J. Goode, "Illegitimacy, Anomie and Cultural Penetration," *American Sociological Review*, 26 (December, 1961), pp. 910–925 at p. 918. I. L. Reiss, "Premarital Sexual Permissiveness among Whites and Negroes,"*op. cit.*, gives data showing that Negroes are more often permissive than whites in their attitudes toward premarital sexual behavior.

[13]The matrifocal family also includes an emphasis on kin relations in the female line and perhaps the assumption by the maternal grandmother of the head of household. The father of the children may be totally absent, or there might be a succession of temporary fathers. A "weak" but stable father might even be present, but then his importance and authority are marginal to the primary sphere of mother-child relationships.

The U.S. Census provides figures giving some indication of the proportion of matrifocal families. For North Carolina in 1960, 21 percent of the Negro and 8 percent of the white families had female heads. U.S. Bureau of the Census, *U.S. Census of Population: 1960*, Vol. I, Characteristics of the Population, Part 35, North Carolina, Table 109, p. 381. For a brief comparison of the Negro and white family structure in the United States as a whole, see U.S. Department of Labor, *The Negro Family: The Case for National Action*, Washington, D.C.: Government Printing Office, 1965 (the "Moynihan Report").

[14]The most influential discussion of the historical factors generating the matrifocal family form among Negroes is E. Franklin Frazier, *The Negro Family in the United States*, Chicago: University of Chicago Press,

In strata faced with this social situation, the female has lessened economic motivation for seeking marriage and lessened respect for men as marital partners; if sanctions are not forthcoming to support legitimacy, pressures to marry even after premarital pregnancy are limited. The combination of these two factors—lessened stress on the norm of legitimacy and the lessened motivation for the woman to marry—may account for the Negro-white differences shown in our data.

Summary

The data on this sample of unwed mothers indicate that the prepregnancy relationship with the alleged father was in most cases like that of courting couples in general. Though these courtships produced illegitimate children, they cannot be described as deviant, exploitative, or lacking exposure to the normal social controls. The firmness of this conclusion is reduced because of the low completion rate for the sample of white unwed mothers. The Negro-white differences, probably underestimated in our data, are consistent with the interpretations that Negroes in comparison to whites have more permissive premarital sexual attitudes, are less committed to legitimate childbirth, and that the Negro female is less desirous of getting married than the white female. These factors help explain the findings that the Negro in comparison to the white unwed mother was more often in a long-term relationship, but yet less often planning marriage.

That some courtships produce illegitimate births is not surprising in a period in which American youth exercise much control over their courtship activity, given a culture that emphasizes the importance of sexual attractiveness. Many couples engage in premarital sexual relations, and yet some unknown proportion of these avoid having children—either through contraception or abortion or because they are not fertile. Others get married after a premarital pregnancy but before a premarital birth. Why some couples have illegitimate children and others do not awaits an investigation in which couples are followed through time to see which couples have illicit sexual relations and, among those that do, which have illegitimate births and which do not. By conducting rigorous longitudinal studies, we can more adequately unravel the factors associated with illegitimate childbirth.

1939. For more recent discussions, see Bernard, *op. cit.*; and Andrew and Amy Tate Billingsley, "Illegitimacy and Patterns of Negro Family Life," in R. W. Roberts (ed.), *op. cit.*, pp.133–157. For insightful analyses of the forces that create the matrifocal family, see Raymond T. Smith, *The Negro Family in British Guiana*, London: Routledge and Kegan Paul, 1956; and Helen M. Icken, *From Shanty Town to Public Housing: A Comparison of Family Structure in Two Urban Neighborhoods in Puerto Rico*, unpublished Ph.D. dissertation, New York: Columbia University, 1962. Also relevant are the data and discussion in Robert O. Blood, Jr., and Donald M. Wolfe, *Husbands and Wives*, New York: The Free Press, 1960, pp. 11–46.

Robert Staples: The Black
Prostitute in White America

Throughout the ages, all over the world, women have bestowed their sexual favors on men who were not their husbands for money as well as for other reasons. Primitive peoples yielded their women to transient guests. In the fifth century B. C. each Babylonian woman was in duty bound once in her lifetime to yield herself to a stranger in the temple of Mylitta for money, which she contributed to the wealth of the temple. In those days the role of prostitute was an honorable one, or at least a tolerable occupation. Later the functions of prostitutes were assigned to members of wretched castes who were segregated in ghettos or in restricted quarters. They were forced to wear distinctive signs on their clothing and were vulnerable to the capricious whims of the police.[1]

Prostitution has arisen in Western society partly because of our hypocritical attitude toward sexual behavior. Theoretically, we have a single code of sexual conduct—that sexual relations are to take place only between a man and a woman married to each other. In reality, men are permitted sexual activity with a variety of women both before marriage and after marriage. Prostitutes usually provide the male with his illicit sexual pleasure and usually receive money or its equivalent for doing so. In turn, they are denied community respect and make themselves ineligible for a "respectable" marriage.

Because these disadvantages attend the role of prostitute, most women reject the job. Women who become prostitutes usually do so because they are impoverished or because they are forced to do so. Black women were originally prostitutes for the latter reason; as slaves they had to submit to their masters and received no compensation. However, some white slavemasters saw the opportunity for commercial profit in peddling the bodies of their female slaves. As a result, there was in the South a considerable traffic in Black women for prostitution. Particularly desirable was the mulatto woman, herself a result of earlier miscegenation between a white man and Black woman.

In the ante-bellum South, large numbers of mulatto girls were carried to the cities and sold at enormous prices into private prostitution. Little respect was shown for kinship ties, as white men sold their Black daughters to other men for prostitution. In one such case,

A planter had two beautiful daughters by a slave. They were educated in England and introduced as his daughters, but he failed to emancipate them; so that on his

A revised version of a paper presented to The North Central Voters League, St. Paul, Minnesota, May 1967. This is the first publication of this article. All rights reserved. Permission to reprint must be obtained from the publisher.

[1]Simone de Beauvoir, *The Second Sex* (New York: Bantam Books, 1961), p. 83.

death they were snatched away by the creditors and sold to a purchaser who was to reap his gain from their prostitution.[2]

Although the dual elements of bondage and force impelled most Black women into prostitution, some Black females were brought up by their mothers for the career of concubine. If the white men had wealth or standing, Black girls frequently preferred such an arrangement to marriage to a Black male. In the role of a concubine to a wealthy white man, she received not only greater social status but protection from the unwanted attentions of other white men.[3]

One disadvantage in becoming a concubine to a white man, particularly a married white man, was the resentment of white women. A man who was having his sexual needs satisfied by a Black concubine was less likely to want a wife. During this period of widespread concubinage, the South had an inordinate number of bachelors. This meant that some white women who desperately desired marriage had to remain single. One white woman, decrying the sexual relationship between white men and Black women, wrote: "Like the patriarchs of old, our men live all in one house with their wives and their concubines, and the mulattos one sees in every family partly resemble the white children. Any lady is ready to tell you who is the father of all the mulatto children in everybody's household but her own."[4]

With reason, some white women feared the competition of Black females for their husband's affection. Frazier notes that "the white woman often saw in the colored woman not only a rival for her husband's affection but also a possible competitor for a share in his property."[5] Some white men became so enamoured of their Black mistresses that they disinherited their wives and children. White women who faced this problem were known to vent their jealousy in savage ways. One such white woman had slaves hold a Black girl down while she cut off the forepart of the victim's feet. Then the girl was thrown into the woods to die.[6]

Most Black women did not represent a threat to the marital status of white women. White men rarely considered marriage with their dark sexual companions. In fact, men of the master class often justified their sexual excursions with Black women with the declaration that doing so preserved the virginity of white women for marriage. Whether they accepted this explanation or not, most Southern white women endured their husbands' infidelity because they had no choice. Economically dependent on the male for support, few girls refused a man who possessed a goodly number of slaves,

---

[2] Arthur J. Calhoun, *A Social History of the American Family* (New York: Barnes and Noble, 1960), p. 229.

[3] *Ibid.*, pp. 296–297.

[4] Ben Ames Williams, *A Diary from Dixie* (Boston: Houghton Mifflin, 1949).

[5] E. Franklin Frazier, *The Negro Family in the United States* (Chicago: University of Chicago Press, 1939).

[6] Calhoun, *op. cit.*, p. 304.

though they were sure his affections would be shared by the best looking of the females.[7]

After emancipation, the flagrant sexual abuse of Black women by white men decreased. However, the amount of organized prostitution among Black women increased because prostitution was the only means that some Black women had of supporting their families.[8] And Black women had a certain function for white men. As one writer asserted:

For the young white man, Negro or mulatto girls existed to initiate him into sexual experience. Later he might set up one such girl as a concubine and produce a family. Or he might continue to indulge himself throughout life whenever an opportunity presented itself. The point to bear in mind is that despite legislation, official sexual propriety, and Christianity itself, the Southern white had embarked upon the systematic prostitution of Negro women.[9]

Although many factors compelled Black women to become prostitutes, the most important one was usually the need for money. A Black woman who gets two to four dollars a week as a cook is sorely tempted by the offer of five dollars from the man of the house for sexual intercourse. Most likely she has a family to support and bills to pay.[10]

But other variables do enter into the Black woman's decision to become a prostitute, assuming that she does decide and is not forced into the role. Included in her reasons may be a desire to get back at white women. A woman with this motive revealed: "Well, these white women may high-hat us, but we sleep with their men just the same. We may have to cook for them, but we get back at them in this way."[11] If their vengeance is not directed toward white women, it may be aimed at what they consider pulling the white man down. Sex relations, it is said, strips the male of any claim to immortality.[12]

It is also quite possible that Black women enjoy their sexual liaisons with white men. With cultural restrictions on their sexual behavior very weak, Black women may receive transitory gratification from their sexual relations with white men. Unlike white women in the South, for whom chastity is a cultural imperative, Black females can articulate the sexual impulse more freely. Prostitution, although socially degrading, may thus give Black women sexual pleasure while being paid for the experience.[13]

Yet whatever advantage the Black woman may have gained is canceled out by the loss of social esteem. Everywhere, the women who play for pay

[7] *Ibid.*, p. 310.

[8] Fernando Henriques, *Prostitution in Europe and the Americas* (New York: Citadel Press, 1965), p. 262.

[9] *Ibid.*, p. 252.

[10] John Dollard, *Caste and Class in a Southern Town* (New York: Doubleday, 1937), p. 152.

[11] *Ibid.*, p. 153.

[12] *Ibid.*

[13] *Ibid.*, p. 154.

are looked down on. Although she often performs a service for chaste white women by allowing white men to release their pre-nuptial sexual urges upon her, opprobrium is all she receives. Universally despised, she makes herself ineligible for marriage by her sale of passion. A tragic example of her plight is recorded thus:

A Black once told me of a childhood sweetheart whom he had once wanted to marry. He left town for a time and when he returned met this girl again. She had become a prostitute. He asked her if she had known what was in his mind when they were boy and girl together, and told her he thought then that she would make a good wife for some man someday. The girl regretted that she had gone too far now ever to be able to marry, and said it was the fault of her godmother, who turned her over to men before she was grown up.[14]

The disrespect that the Black male has for prostitutes of his own race is frequently reciprocated by dusky ladies of the streets. One Black prostitute stated to an observer:

A nigger don't treat you with as much respect as a white man. The white man treats you courteous-like, and leaves you free to yourself most of the time. Those white men will pay you five and ten dollars and likely won't bother you but once a week. That's all they want, and they don't think they have the right to beat you when they want to.[15]

Black women who perform the role of concubine fare somewhat better than their fellow streetwalkers. The bond between her and her lover is closer because their relationship is more permanent. While such associations are few, and getting rarer every day, they were part and parcel of the post-bellum South. This is particularly true of Louisiana, where formal balls were given to acquaint white men with Black women for whom they could bargain. Children born of such relationships were often treated by their father as though they were his legitimate brood. In some cases, the men clothed and educated their children and even provided for them in their wills.[16]

In one Southern town a number of white men have Black mistresses. Most of these men are segregationists who believe that Blacks are inferior and preach that Blacks should have their own life, separate from that of whites.[17] Whereas this may seem paradoxical in view of their sexual liaison with Black women, it is not more paradoxical than the violation of their marriage

[14] *Ibid.*, p. 159.

[15] Allison Davis et al., *Deep South* (Chicago: University of Chicago Press, 1941), p. 33.

[16] Calhoun, *op. cit.*, p. 297.

[17] Dollard, *op. cit.*, p. 143.

vows. Perhaps the losers in this situation are the women of the South—Black
and white alike—who are the unwilling victims of a Southern value system
which demeans their humanity and subjects them to exploitation by the
white males.

The Prostitute Moves North

Most authorities agree that around the turn of the century most prostitutes in the South were Black, while the prostitutes of the North were white.
That is, as one writer states, "In the North, prostitutes were a social and
professional group, while in the South they were a racial group."[18] In other
words, even lower class white women of the South were allowed to retain
their virginity until marriage, whereas some middle class Black women were
sacrificed to the white man's lust.

Along with the general immigration of Blacks from the South to the
urban areas of the North went large numbers of Black prostitutes. This is
reflected in the statistics of arrests for prostitution by racial ancestry. For
instance, in Chicago Black women constituted 16 percent of the total number appearing in the morals court caseload in 1914. In 1929, Black women
totaled 70 percent of the women arraigned. Viewing these figures, one writer
concluded that "if the percentage of colored women in the total load of the
morals court continues to increase, the court will in a few years become
practically an agency dealing with Negro female sex delinquents."[19] Without knowing the exact figures, one could speculate that this is precisely what
has happened.

That Black women are rapidly becoming the nation's prostitutes is reflected in a number of studies. One such survey found that 54 percent of the
arrests of all women for prostitution in New York City were Black women,
and that the rate for Black women was ten times that for white women.[20]
When the Kinsey group interviewed 390 Black prison women, they discovered that 56 percent of these women admitted to or had been convicted of
prostitution prior to their confinement.[21]

"Problems of poverty have made prostitution more common among Black
women than among white women."[22] But differences in the degree of prostitution among Black and white women tend to be hidden by their different
sphere of activity. With sufficient accuracy, we can designate the Black
prostitute as a streetwalker and the white prostitute as a call girl.

Call girls are described by one writer as the "aristocrats of prostitution."
They live in the most expensive residential sections of our large cities, they
dress in rich, good taste, and they charge a minimum of twenty dollars per

---

[18]Hortense Powdermaker, *After Freedom* (New York: Viking Press, 1939), p. 182.

[19]Walter C. Reckless, *Vice in Chicago* (Chicago: University of Chicago Press, 1933), pp. 26–28.

[20]Gunnar Myrdal, *An American Dilemma* (New York: Harper & Row, 1944), p. 974.

[21]Paul Gebhard et al., *Pregnancy, Birth and Abortion* (New York: Harper & Row, 1958), p. 187.

[22]Myrdal, *op. cit.*, p. 976.

sexual contact. "Unlike the streetwalker, she is selective about her customers; entertains clients in their homes or her apartment; and assiduously avoids bars and restaurants patronized by other prostitutes."[23]

Black women are much more subject to arrest than white call girls. As one observer comments,

Since it is easier to observe immoral conditions among poor and unprotected people, colored prostitutes are much more liable for arrest than white prostitutes. White women may use the big hotels or private apartments for their illicit trade, but the colored women are more commonly forced to walk the streets.[24]

The low status of Black women generally prevents them from becoming call girls. Since white men are primarily the clientele of call girls, the social life of a call girl almost automatically excludes Black prostitutes. Often these clients require an entire night of a girl's time, maybe taking her out to a night club as part of the arrangement.[25] The taboo on social relations between whites and blacks means that most call girls are found in the better cocktail lounges and restaurants, where the presence of a Black woman is usually suspect. Police officers are known to arrest Black females solely because they find them in the company of white men, whereas white women can approach white men without being conspicuous.[26]

Life as a prostitute in a society with a rigid moral code is difficult enough, but Black women have additional difficulties imposed on them by the racist attitudes of white people. A morals court official states, "I think that Negro women as a class are dealt with more harshly here in the court than the whites."[27] Restricted to a certain area of the city, she is forced to compete with other Black women for customers. Because she is in an overcrowded profession in her particular area, she must charge less than her white counterpart. One report revealed that prices for Black prostitutes range from twenty-five cents to two dollars, while those for whites were one to five dollars.[28]

One of the greatest problems faced by the Black prostitute is the racial character of her clientele. Usually she must sell her body to white men, as Black men frequently cannot afford to pay for her sexual services—nor in many cases do they need to. Judge Murtagh describes the case of Melissa Jane, a Black prostitute in New York City. She walks the streets of Harlem trying to find a Black customer or two. "But colored men do not seem to like

[23] Harold Greenwald, *The Call Girl* (New York: Ballantine Books, 1958).

[24] Harold Gasnell, *Negro Politicians* (Chicago: University of Chicago Press, 1935), pp. 120–121.

[25] Greenwald, *op. cit.*, p. 15.

[26] Myrdal, *loc. cit.*

[27] St. Clair Drake and Horace Cayton, *Black Metropolis* (Chicago: University of Chicago Press, 1945), p. 596.

[28] Myrdal, *loc. cit.*

her, and so she goes with white tricks against her will." He goes on to report Melissa Jane's feeling of shame when she undresses before a white man, her feeling of remorse when he touches her dusky skin, and her fear of the perverted sexual urges he may vent on her.[29]

Another of Judge Murtagh's examples is Jean Ford, a tall, slender Black girl. She explains the desirability of Black prostitutes for white men by saying:

A colored girl who plays her cards right and isn't too bad looking can practically write her own tickets with them. They seem to feel that, because some of us have remote ancestors who lived in Africa once, we are primitives at heart when it comes to sex. Actually, most of them are a lot more primitive than we are.[30]

This remark reflects the widespread belief that the sexual tastes of white men are uncommon among her own group. This is frequently a class difference, as Kinsey noted. "Both high school and college boys want something that is usually foreign to the prostitute's background. For the sake of her trade, she may agree to such overt activity as these males desire but, interesting to note, she still would refuse to use such techniques with her husband or boyfriend."[31] When asked about her attitude toward perverted practices, a Black prostitute responded that "girls showed her the easiest way but you never get used to it."[32]

Some of the sexual tastes of the prostitute's clients are reserved especially for women of the night. Sadists and masochists form a part of the prostitute's clientele. Beatings administered by a sadist are a common activity of the prostitute, though sometimes the beating is purely symbolic and not carried to the extent of causing pain.[33] A Black prostitute remarked that men tried to hurt her only once in a while and it was usually white men who did it.[34]

Beatings bring a higher price, and some impoverished Black women are forced to undergo such treatment for their bread and butter. One Black hustler explained that white tricks pay a hundred dollars to beat a prostitute. "Sometimes," she said, "they hit you so hard you land in the hospital."[35] Other men, who request sexual gratifications so bizarre as to defy description, usually have a need to degrade the woman before they can enjoy her.[36]

---

[29] Judge Murtagh and Sara Harris, *Cast the First Stone* (New York: McGraw-Hill, 1957), p. 89.

[30] *Ibid.*, pp. 14–15.

[31] Alfred Kinsey et al., *Sexual Behavior in the Human Female* (Philadelphia: W. B. Saunders Company, 1953), p. 604.

[32] Reckless, *op. cit.*, p. 278.

[33] Greenwald, *op. cit.*, p. 162.

[34] Murtagh and Harris, *op. cit.*, p. 103.

[35] *Ibid.*, p. 182.

[36] Greenwald, *op. cit.* p. 163.

And it is probably easier for them to vent their pernicious sexual urges upon Black women, since they can be considered less than human. As one white man told a Black prostitute, "Gal, there's two places where niggers is as good as white folks—the bedroom an' the graveyard."[37]

Black men's only relationship with the prostitute is often pimping. The pimp is a paid companion to whom the prostitute gives her earnings. He frequently provides the only human relationship with affection, continuity, and meaning for her. In addition, her status in the ingroup of prostitutes often depends on the way she keeps her pimp. Whether he drives a Cadillac or a Ford is important to the way the prostitute is regarded by her fellow streetwalkers.[38]

Black men serve as pimps to white prostitutes as well. Judge Murtagh describes pimping as a colored man's occupation. Like domestic service, he says, the job of pimping is so low that white men do not want it.[39] Yet without the pimp, few Black prostitutes would receive any affection. Their customers generally look down upon them, and they have the lowest status of any group in the Black community. So it is not surprising to hear a prostitute say: "Pimps are always handy and you fall for that sugar somehow. I guess I liked the notoriety of being a pimp's woman . . . they'd take you around in big cars and show you off and introduce you as their woman. That was exciting and you think you are somebody."[40]

But pimps also represent a destructive influence on the prostitute. He may pressure his girl to accept beatings from customers so that she can give him more money. Moreover, in many instances, the pimp himself beats the prostitute. A great number of girls have suffered beatings or have been knifed at the hands of their pimps. One girl said about her pimp, "He used to beat me up bad all the time. I loved him at first but I got to hate him after a while. One day I decided to work for him no more. When I told him, he got his knife and began slashing me all over my arms and face."[41]

Considering the hardships encountered by the Black prostitute, does she at least achieve sexual satisfaction from her pimp or even her customers? The evidence available indicates that she does not. Greenwald's prostitutes received more satisfaction from their pimps than from their clients, but few of them spoke of their pimps as being great lovers.[42] Needless to say, the prostitute is not sexually gratified by her clients. One psychoanalyst has even stated that frigidity is an indispensable element in prostitution.[43]

Many men, of course, believe prostitutes to be oversexed women who are thrilled at the sexual prowess of their clients. One prostitute, who admitted to rarely receiving sexual satisfaction, had this to say about her act of

---

[37] Murtagh and Harris, *op. cit.*, p. 104.

[38] Greenwald, *op. cit.*, p. 27.

[39] Murtagh and Harris, *op. cit.*, p. 159.

[40] Reckless, *op. cit.*, p. 278.

[41] Murtagh and Harris, *op. cit.*, p. 137.

[42] Greenwald, *op. cit.*, p. 148.

[43] Karl Abraham, *Selected Papers on Psychoanalysis* (New York: Basic Books, 1953), p. 36.

experiencing sexual pleasure with her clients: "I don't let the men know it though. I make them think they're hell on wheels. I act woooo! As though they're doing something. But they really ain't doing nothing. I never get no kicks out of it."[44]

Even though they receive little besides money for being a prostitute, thousands of Black women are attracted annually to the second oldest profession. While poverty is a key factor, discrimination against Black women in employment plays its part. High school graduates have gone into prostitution because the only work that they could get was as domestics or waitresses. One young woman who lost her white collar job during the Depression explained that she could not tolerate scrubbing floors at this late date and so turned to prostitution.[45]

An unstable family life is a common background of many Black prostitutes. Lack of a two-parent home or failure to receive love and acceptance from parents sometimes pushes Black girls into prostitution. The case histories of most Black prostitutes do show an unhappy family background. Such was the case of one Black woman whose father died when she was three years old. Her mother died when she was only nine. Her stepfather deserted, and she went to live with her married sister. This woman says her childhood was not happy and believes that life would have been different if her father had lived.[46]

Despite their knowledge of the life prostitutes must live, some authorities have asserted that prostitutes are safeguards of the sanctity of the home and of the innocence of other men's wives and daughters. One sociologist has even declared that prostitutes receive money for not only their sexual services but also their loss of status in the community.[47] What these people fail to consider is that prostitution is a crime punishable by imprisonment in this country and that in most cases only the woman is arrested.

Because the streetwalker is predominantly Black, much of the only open prostitution left in the United States is in the Negro ghettos. *Fortune* magazine describes Harlem as "Reefer pads, gambling houses, and countless houses of prostitution. Most hotels are brothels, and it is a usual sight to see a dozen streetwalkers on every corner in lower Harlem."[48]

This situation has made the Black ghettos of America a frequent haunt of sex-seeking white men. Recently, Detroit attorney Lawrence Massey appeared on behalf of Black prostitutes who were arrested and hauled into court on charges of accosting and soliciting. He filed a motion with the court, declaring the police are using discriminatory practices in arresting the prostitutes and refusing to arrest the white men who invade Black neighbor-

---

[44]Abram Kardiner and Lionel Ovesey, *The Mark of Oppression* (New York: W. W. Norton, 1951), p. 230.

[45]Drake and Cayton, *op. cit.*, p. 598.

[46]Reckless, p. 277.

[47]Kingsley Davis, "Prostitution," in *Contemporary Social Problems*, First Ed., Robert K. Merton and Robert A. Nesbit, eds. (New York: Harcourt, Brace and World, 1966), pp. 262–288.

[48]"Harlem," *Fortune*, July 1939, p. 170.

hoods looking for prostitutes.[49] In Los Angeles Black ghettos, it is known that white men driving around in certain areas are looking for the pay-for-play girls. Often they accost Black women who are not prostitutes and make walking the streets at night unsafe for respectable Black women.

Women who become prostitutes face a multitude of problems. Men have been known to declare that females never face starvation because if they cannot do anything else, they can always sell sex. Such statements ignore the realities of the prostitute's life. Not infrequently, it is the pimp who gets the greatest monetary gain from the sale of the prostitute's body. From him, she gets the only love and understanding she has probably known. And even though prostitution may be lucrative for a while, the prostitute becomes less desirable as a sex object to most men as she grows older. Then, if she stays in the hustler's underworld, she must resort to performing those degrading services for emotionally disturbed men that all other women refuse to perform.

As a woman who shares her body with all types of men, she also inevitably encounters the occupational hazard peculiar to sexually active women—venereal disease. It has been authoritatively reported that one out of every six women appearing in New York City's Women's Court is infected with a venereal disease.[50] It is to be expected that Black prostitutes will face this problem. Some 58 percent of the Black prison women in the Kinsey sample, many of them former prostitutes, had syphilis.[51]

Prostitution has been called the world's second oldest profession because women have lacked the sexual freedom of men from time immemorial. A society that allows men sexual expression before marriage and outside marriage, yet relegates the majority of women to chastity and marital fidelity, must have some women who will supply their bodies for the unrestrained sexual urges of the male gender. Prostitutes have long played this role. What is more important is, who will be the prostitutes and why? Impoverished women of all races have historically played this role. More and more, the role of prostitute in the United States is synonymous with the word "Black." Although white women still enact the role of prostitute, they are paid more and persecuted less. In all endeavors, the Black woman faces the liability of a black skin. It is just as true in the prostitute's world as anywhere else.

---

[49] *Jet*, May 26, 1966, p. 44.

[50] Murtagh and Harris, *op. cit.*, p. 191.

[51] Gebhard, *op. cit.*, p. 186.

Harry Edwards: Black Muslim and
Negro Christian Family
Relationships

The notion that the Nation of Islam has possibly exerted positive as well as negative influences upon its members became the originating idea out of which the major questions for this study emerged. Specifically, the study focused upon a comparison between Muslim and lower-class Negro Christian families.

Due largely to the work of Frazier, many Americans became aware of the chaos and instability extant within many lower-class American Negro families. Frazier portrays the lower-class Negro family as matriarchal in structure, often common-law in nature, and characterized by an adult male figure functioning almost solely in a procreative capacity.[1]

Although there have been many studies that have enlarged upon some of the specific aspects of Frazier's work, in the nearly two decades since its publication, there has been no study done on the lower-class American Negro of comparable scope or sociological import. Since the surprisingly rapid expansion of an isolated incident aboard a bus in Montgomery, Alabama, into what has become known as the "Negro Revolt" and the occurrence of other significant events, it is doubtful that the nature and structure of the lower-class Negro family, as described by Frazier, have remained unchanged. Indeed there is some recent evidence, albeit controversial, that tends to substantiate the oft-voiced speculation that the Negro family is in the process of still further deterioration.[2] Many students of the race problem in America are becoming more aware of the role the instability of the lower-class Negro family plays in hindering the implementation of some practical solutions to the problems involved.

Although the civil rights movement has, for the most part, had as a goal integration of the black American into the existing social fabric, it has also given rise to an abundance of what have been termed "black Nationalist" organizations. These organizations have not stressed the need for a racially integrated society but have advocated the development of a racially and socially plural society—as in the case of several so-called Afro-American organizations—or they have pushed for complete racial separatism—physical and social—as is the case with the Nation of Islam. Most of these black Nationalist organizations have developed special programs of study and training to prepare themselves to assume roles in their unique version of the

[1] E. F. Frazier, *The Negro Family in the United States*, Chicago: University of Chicago Press, 1939.

[2] Evans and Novak column entitled "The Moynihan Report," *New York Herald Tribune*, August 18, 1965; Benjamin F. Payton, "The President, the Social Experts, and the Ghetto: An Analysis of an Emerging Strategy in Civil Rights," unpublished paper, pp. 1–9; Peter Goldman, "The Splintering Negro Family—A Confidential Report," *Newsweek*, August 9, 1965.

Reprinted from *Journal of Marriage and the Family*, 30 (November 1968), pp. 604–611, by permission of the National Council on Family Relations and the author. Harry Edwards is a member of the Department of Sociology, University of California, Berkeley.

"great society." One aspect of this training and preparation has been the attempt to alter the pattern of family relationships characterizing the lower-class Negro family. There are increasing signs, particularly in large urban centers, that these attempts have been at least partially successful.

Methodology

The basic design for the study involved the comparison of matched pairs of families—one group of families affiliated with the Nation of Islam, the other group affiliated with lower-class Negro Christian Churches. The major technique employed was the focused interview supplemented by a great deal of participant observation and the occasional use of informants. The interviews focused on four specific areas of family relations: husband-wife, extended kinships, parent-child, and family-community.

The sample consisted of 14 families from each group. They were matched for mean spouse educational attainment, mean spouse income, race, and the factor of having a minimum mean time of four years in active affiliation with their respective religious organizations. The highest level of educational attainment for the families was twelve and one-half years. Most were considerably lower. The bulk of the spouses were educated in southern public schools. The yearly family income ranged from about $2,000 to a high of $5,500. All members of the sample lived in the same geographical area and were phenotypically Negroid.[3] Each family had at least a minimum mean time in active affiliation with its church or mosque of four years; however, the Muslims as a group averaged five and one-half years while the Christians' average was 11 years. The lesser mean active affiliation time among families of the former group may be due to a number of factors among which are the traditional religious posture of the American Negro and the more recent proselytizing success of the Nation of Islam.

Although detailed information on all of the families involved in this study is not presently readily available, there are sufficient data to substantiate the following brief statements regarding the general occupational and family profiles of the Muslim and Christian groups.

On the whole, Muslim families were wage-earning families in contrast to Christian families, which tended to be non-wage-earners. The types of jobs held by Muslims ranged from low-income jobs—selling papers and manual part-time labor—to relatively high-income jobs—steady factory work and fork-lift operations. Those Muslims holding low-income or part-time jobs usually held more than one job. For instance, it was not unusual to find a Muslim selling papers during morning work hours and busing dishes during the afternoon work hours.

In the Christian families, by contrast, the model condition was one of unemployment. The female spouses typically earned what steady wage in-

---

[3] Both the Muslim and Christian religious bodies, however, numbered among their memberships persons of other racial extraction.

come came into these families. The jobs held were low-income ones; part-time jobs were held also. These were usually jobs of a service nature—waitress, domestic, and hair-straightener. In the cases of both Muslim and Christian families, the higher paying jobs were held by persons with relatively high rank in the two religious organizations (e.g., incomes over $4,000 were earned by assistant ministers and student ministers in the Christian and Muslim groups, respectively).

The Christian spouses were, on the average, older than the Muslim spouses. They also had a greater number of children than did the Muslims. However, the Muslim families were characterized by a stair-step succession of births, whereas the Christian families were less intensively prolific. There is evidence to support the contention that the discrepancy between these two contrasting birth patterns may have been due to differing attitudes toward birth control. Also, the fact that working female spouses would have been considerably inconvenienced by a continuous succession of nine-month gestation periods was probably a factor of some impact in determining this discrepancy.

All of the families involved in this study lived in the same geographical area—an area characterized by dilapidated housing, rats, or high unemployment rate, as well as other conditions typical of the black ghettos across the United States.

Results

The results will be reported for each of the four areas of family relations. In each instance, the responses of the Muslim group will be compared to those of the Christian group.

Husband-Wife Relationships

The questions in the area of husband-wife relationships were directed toward ascertaining those role functions of each spouse that involved work, money authority, decision making, and the use of leisure time. The literature is replete with references to the characteristic tendency toward the use of physical expression, often in the form of violence, among lower-class Negroes. This violence is often also present in husband-wife relationships, particularly as these relationships revolve around such fiscal problems as the procurement and allocation of money.

For the Christian families, the state of one spouse's financial and material affluence as perceived by the other played a greater role in determining the degree of stability of their relationship than did the same situation among the Muslims. All but one Christian case responded with at least a qualified "yes" to the question of whether they thought the female spouse should work. They indicated a "balance of authority" between themselves and their spouses. Through contributing a portion of money to the family income equal to or greater than that of their husbands', the Christian females felt themselves to be more justified and secure in expressing or seeking the realization of their own individual desires, opinion, and decisions in the marriage situation. Though not all of the Christian females worked, the majority did bring money into the family. This was primarily due to welfare and child support payments from previous relationships. In light of this, it would appear that the welfare system is indirectly perpetuating the matriarchal family structure among these lower-class Negroes by making welfare aid and child support payments payable directly to the female spouse in the household.

The Muslims' opinions regarding the desirability of married females working were the exact opposite of those expressed by the Christian groups. In fact, the Muslims were against any female holding an income-producing job, whether married or not. They felt that a woman's place was in the home and the task of earning a living was the sole responsibility of the adult male. This conviction was expressed adamantly by both male and female spouses. The majority of these Muslim women seemed to believe that their main task in life was to be good wives and mothers ("good" being synonymous with Muslim). Most, if not all, authority was vested in the role of the male. Consonant with this authority, the Muslims reported that all major decisions affecting the family were made by the male. In the majority of cases, such decisions as where to live and what purchases to make, as well as when to make them, were made by the Muslim male. This is in contrast to the Christian families, wherein the females made these decisions. The responses of the Christian families relative to decision making and authority, both of which were anchored in the female's role because of income production, tended to lend substantial validity to the notion that the lower-class Christian families functioned within a matriarchal structure. The Muslim families, by contrast, through family role definition prescribed by Black Muslim dogma, have established for themselves a more patriarchal family system. This role clarity appeared to reduce intrafamily conflict considerably for the Muslim families.

For the most part, Muslim respondents regarded intrafamily conflict of any type as totally unnecessary and avoidable. By contrast, the Christian respondents thought such conflict to be unavoidable and some physical violence inevitable "if two people lived together long enough." The Muslim mechanism for avoiding trouble involved a use of the fundamental teachings of their religion in the face of impending conflict. Statements were often made to the effect that, when conflict threatened, the spouses concerned merely "got on the side of Islam" and the wrong fell of its own weight. No such responses came from the Christian, nor was there any evidence of their gravitating toward religious fundamentals in time of impending conflict between spouses.

The duties of each Muslim spouse in the marriage situation were outlined in astonishingly minute detail and taught in training sessions held specifically for this purpose. The female was trained to fulfill her principal duties—

those of mother and housewife. She was taught, among other things, how to cook, what to cook, how often to cook, how to sew, and how to keep house. She was trained in home economy and maintenance. The male spouse likewise was taught his responsibilities and how to fulfill them. These predetermined responsibilities and the activities that they generate were so calculated as to avoid a conflict. They further placed the Muslim male spouse in the position of the productive, contributing breadwinner and protector of his family. By contrast, the typical Christian response to questions as to who held what responsibilities was: "It depends."

Another contrast between the two types of families was in the extent of "idling" activity. The Christian male spouses participated in this "idling" or "killing time" far more than did the Muslims. Not once did the author find a Muslim male in any of the local "hangouts" or in an idling situation. First of all, most of the idling places were also places where drinking and smoking were common pastimes. Muslim ideology forbids the use of either alcohol or tobacco. There were two other factors which contributed to this lack of an idling custom among Muslims. First, due to the Muslims' overt enthusiasm for their religion, they were often unwelcome at idling places. Their constant tendency to emphasize the decadent and useless behavior of the "regulars" of such places made them unwelcome, even on the occasional "fishing expeditions" to hangouts frequented by the "dead" (see below). Secondly, the Muslims did not have free time to participate in idling. After fulfilling a predetermined schedule of activities, the Muslim males would spend a great proportion of their leisure time on "fishing expeditions." These expeditions were considered part of their duties as Muslims. They believed that the final hour for North America was near. They, likewise, believed it to be their duty to save as many black men as possible.[4] Not to make an attempt to do so was considered behavior unworthy of a Muslim.

Family-Extended Kin Relationships

A number of situations determined the break between the Muslim spouses and their relatives. In those cases where the parents and in-laws of the Muslim spouses lived within the area, "uniting with" the Nation of Islam was contrary to the wishes of these relations. This assumes added significance, since the majority of these parents and in-laws belonged to Christian churches. Also of significance in the break between Muslim spouses and their parents was the inflexibility of the Muslim spouses in their adherence to the behavioral codes of the Nation of Islam. It was found that conscientious Muslims did not smoke, drink, or curse, nor did they tolerate these prohibited indulgences within their homes. Since many of the Muslims' relatives did in fact indulge in these habits, a situation of mutual intolerance

---

[4]The Muslims ignore completely the traditional grouping of homo sapiens by race. Hence, any nonwhite by Muslim definition is a "black brother" (these racial brothers include such racially diversified people as Chinese, Filipinos, Mexicans, Indians [Eastern], North American Indians, Arabs, Negroes, Africans, Japanese, Eskimos, etc.).

and estrangement soon followed. Of relevance here also were the reactions of the parents and in-laws to the Muslims, particularly as these reactions focused upon the behavior and activities of the Muslim female spouse. Muslim females never straightened their hair or wore make-up of any kind. The resulting appearance of the female was often a point of criticism and mockery from relatives, particularly it seemed from the female spouse's mother. This situation, too, was intolerable. No Muslim tolerated criticism or mockery of moral directives emanating from the Honorable Elijah Muhammed—especially not in his own home, which is next to the mosque in its sanctity.

The Christians, by contrast, maintained continual, if not stable, relationships with their relatives. Generational ties were particularly characteristic of the Christian female spouses and their mothers. In only a few cases did the mothers of the female spouses actually live in the same homes with them. However, even though the physical propinquity was not there, psychosocial closeness was very much in evidence. The telephone was the major medium for contact. The majority of Christian females indicated that their primary confidants, creditors, and advisers were their mothers. Several Christian female spouses noted that their mothers were the first to learn of their pregnancies, plans to work, and other such important occurrences.

Among the Muslims, no such relationships existed. In discussions with the female spouses at the mosque, it was made abundantly clear that the primary, and often the only, confidants for these women were their husbands. There were apparently never any occasions for these Muslim females to borrow goods or money from anyone, since such decisions were typically made by the male spouse. And for the female to do so "over the head" of the male spouse would have been in direct opposition to Muslim directives regarding her proper role in the family.

Parent-Child Relationships

The responses of the Christian spouses show that they conformed more closely to the generally held lower-class Negro subcultural attitudes and practices with regard to children and child rearing than did the Muslim spouses. The differences between the two groups' relationships with their children did not begin with the actual socializing effects of home life on the child, but with the parents' attitudes towards birth control.

The Muslim subjects expressed indignation and disgust at the queries on birth control methods. Not a single Muslim respondent reported that any methods of birth control, "natural" or otherwise, had been used by either spouse since they became serious adherents to the ideology of the Nation of Islam. The Christian respondents, on the other hand, not only stated that they had used or were using various birth control devices, but several subjects also reported that they regretted not having practiced birth control more often and more consistently. While the Christians had more children than did the Muslims, the spacing of the children in the latter group was characterized by a stair-step succession of births, whereas child births in the former group were erratically spaced. Apparently the desire for children also helped determine to a large extent parents' interaction with the child. By removing any question of the desirability of children, regardless of circumstance, the Muslims also removed one potential source from which a child's emotional and social maladjustment might arise. In doing so, they quite possibly may have opened the door to other problems, such as poverty-stricken families and lack of adequate living space, which could have equally as damaging effects on the child as the lack of proper parent-child emotional relationship. However, the Muslims felt that poverty and "over-population" were merely manifestations of what they considered to be the white man's intrinsically evil nature and his criminal use of the world's resources. As such, these afflictions would pass away with him. The act of practicing birth control because one does not desire children was, on the other hand, viewed as an act against the Nation of Islam and, therefore, against Allah.

Given the birth of a child, the Muslim and Christian groups also exhibited differing attitudes with regard to child-rearing practices. These differences involved the acceptability and effectiveness of various disciplinary practices as well as the manner in which these practices should be carried out. The Christians had few reservations concerning the use of physical punishment. Generally they held the opinion that, after the age when a child knows that what he is doing is wrong, other forms of punishment are only minimally effective.

The Muslims generally indicated that they held the use of physical punishment in close reserve, to be used only at those times when all other forms of chastisement failed. The reasons were very similar to those given for not advocating the use of physically coercive measures between spouses. They also indicated that there was seldom any need for physical punishment because of the effectiveness of Muslim child-rearing methods and the example of proper behavior provided by the parents.

Of significance in the area of disciplinary practices were the subjects' responses to questions pertaining to youths who get into trouble. Their differing points of view began with their ideas concerning the concept of "trouble" itself. The Christians' responses tended to indicate that they considered a child to be in trouble when (and if) he was caught in a compromising situation. The Muslims, on the other hand, considered any individual to be in trouble when a transgression was conceived, regardless of whether he actually committed the act, much less whether he was caught. They reasoned that such an idea was indicative of a more deep-seated anomaly which at best could give rise to more un-Muslimlike behavior. In short, the Christians considered the onset of trouble to be the point at which relevant authority figures become aware of the act and the person responsible for it, whereas the Muslims considered the commencement of trouble to be that point at which the idea for the act was consciously conceived. Consistent with their varying conceptions of trouble were the two groups' opinions as to what types of trouble young people "inevitably" get into. The Christians felt that it was inevitable that youth would get into trouble because of a spirit of curiosity and the need to experiment. Among these acts were included sexual offenses and thefts of varying degrees of seriousness. The Muslims, on the other hand, considered only one type of trouble as inevitable—that which a black man might encounter as a Muslim in a white man's society. They saw sexual offenses, thefts, and other law violations as inexcusable and, hence, intolerable. They argued that such behavior was only the consequence of the black man's attempt to imitate the white man.

While the Christian respondents did not endorse premarital sexual relations, neither did they express violent opposition to it. Instead, their responses indicated that their main effort was directed towards the preparation of their offspring to "protect themselves because you sure can't stop them." The Christians also permitted their offspring to begin the use of cosmetics and other such accoutrements at an earlier age than the general society would consider as appropriate. The Muslims abhorred the use of any cosmetics at any time and any age.

Although the Christian subjects, as a group, had greater educational aspirations for their children than did the Muslims, the latter group took more positive steps toward the fulfillment of their more limited aspirations. The Muslims expressed an intense determination that their children should finish school. This determination originated primarily from the Muslims' belief that knowledge, from whatever source, is "the key to all things." They felt that knowledge acquired within the walls of the white man's schools had value when interpreted within the context of Muslim ideology. Their respect for the law and their determination to adhere to its dictates were also chief factors underlying their efforts to keep their children in school. However, they were extremely hostile towards higher education and its more specialized knowledge. While adamantly insisting on an absence of truancy and on rigorous study habits for their offspring through high school, they felt just as strongly against their children continuing in the existing system of higher education. Among the reasons for these anti-college feelings were criticisms of the curriculum in history and science. It was felt that these subject areas did not acknowledge the works of Allah and the original black man before the dawn of the white man's recorded history. It was also thought that the white man has left out of his history and science books those contributions and achievements made by black individuals and nations and, in some cases, that he had even claimed these achievements and contributions as his own. Finally, the Muslims reported that the black youth who was away from his own people while attending these institutions would find it difficult not to believe "the white man's lies," primarily because he would have no one to explain to him how and why these lies were being propagated.

The Christians by comparison, who were much less strict about the school attendance and study habits of their children, placed a high value on college for their offspring. However, they apparently had little notion of the sacrifices necessary if these aspirations were to be realized.

Though the Muslims' educational aspirations for their children were more limited than those of the Christians, the Muslims' aspirations were, nevertheless, more realistic with respect to their prevailing economic and social situations. The probability of their attaining these limited goals would appear to be much higher than the Christian group's chances of realizing the educational goals to which they aspire for their offspring. In general, then, the Christians advocated the use of the severest form of punishment for their offspring, but were very lenient and permissive with regard to their children's engaging in the illicit forms of behavior which, at the very least, might prompt such punishment. Their only justification for this inconsistency would appear to be that the punishment is not administered for the commitment of the act, but for being caught. They also held high educational goals for their offspring but did little to attain them.

Family-Community Relationships

An analysis of responses pertaining to family-community relations revealed that the Muslim families had almost no contact with any institution other than that to which they maintained religious ties. The Christians, by comparison, reported an array of extra-religious institutional contacts and commitments. Overwhelmingly, the most common contact was that reported to have taken place with various welfare institutions. Of the Christian families, 93 percent had applied for and received some type of public aid within a three-year period as opposed to 21 percent of the Muslim families. Likewise, 64 percent of the Christian families reported that they had had contact with some branch of the local law enforcement system as opposed to 21 percent of the Muslim group.

Considering the Christian families' reports as to their attitudes towards "trouble"—especially that most characteristic of juveniles—and these families' economic situations and work habits, their reports of institutional contact with respect to welfare and law enforcement agencies were strikingly consistent. Likewise, the Muslims' institutional contacts of the sort discussed above followed more or less consistently from their expressed views on trouble and their values on industriousness and the economic independence of the family.

The two groups were diametrically opposed to one another on the question of the desirability of social clubs for either adults or youths. While the Christians thought that such clubs were highly beneficial, the Muslims viewed any type of social club with intense suspicion and distrust. Not all of the Christians belonged to social clubs, only a little over one half. However, even among those Christians not belonging to clubs, such membership was not considered undesirable. While no Muslims belonged to any social club, neither was there any consistent answer given as to why such was the case. This suggests that the Muslims possibly had no direct policy against such affiliation but may have discouraged it through more indirect means. Among these means might have been the prohibition against the consumption of liquor, the preparation of relatively rigid activity schedules for members, and the declaration that time should not be used wastefully ("wasted time" being defined as all of that time not used in Muslim goal attainment).

The Muslims were also concerned with economic and social "welfare." There were two facets to the Nation of Islam's approach to changing the economic and social situation of the black man in the ghetto. First of all, there was no need for the potential Muslim to apply separately for material aid and then for aid in adjusting socially and psychologically to his responsibilities. When a person applied to and was accepted by the Nation of Islam, as a Muslim, regardless of what the precipitating factor behind his decision to apply was (be it economic hardship or the need for spiritual security), he was exposed to the entire program. That is, efforts were immediately initiated by the Muslims to ascertain and at least partially satisfy his economic needs; efforts were made to secure work for him that he was qualified to do or to train him for the types of jobs that were available; and he was resocialized to the Muslim orientation to life. Secondly an attempt was made by the Muslims to show the convert that his social and psychological orientations to life were inextricably interconnected with his poverty stricken or socially deteriorating situation and that to change the latter would inevitably change the former. This task was made easier by the fact that the same individuals who gave him aid and found him a job were also the people who attempted to resocialize him—his "Muslim brothers." Material aid and resocialization were both administered by the same people, under the same roof, and at the same time. It is perhaps through this technique that the Muslim convert may have come to see economic betterment and security as part and parcel of religious, social, and psychological change.

Discussion

In the family relationships of the two groups, there is evidence of two differing foundations for authority. The first of these foundations is manifest in the relationships observed among Muslim families. It derives its legitimization from a basis of respect on the part of the female spouse for the role and position of her husband and the acceptance of her role as a supporting one. This female role is not, however, without its relative advantages. Since, traditionally, the lower-class Negro family has not been organized on a foundation of primary authority, it would appear that the Nation of Islam has had some success in narrowing the gap between the family structure and interactional patterns of its members and those of American middle-class society.

The Christians' family relationships may be characterized as deriving from a second basis of authority. These relationships appear to have been grounded in the spouses' desires for physical comfort, economic security, and a subtle type of respect that emerges from conflict situations. As the economic situation changed, there apparently also occurred commensurate changes in the balance of authority and the overall status of the marriage relationship.

The Muslims approximated the dominant group's values concerning family relationships to a far greater extent than did the Christians. The same general statement holds for the Muslims' relationships with their children. It seems that the Muslims anchored the appropriate role characteristics with the appropriate sexes as prescribed within the context of traditional American values. The Muslim male earned a living, protected his family, and was chief representative of his family in outside social dealings, while the Muslim female concentrated her efforts primarily in the area of child rearing and housekeeping. This is in contrast to the typical lower-class American Negro family life style, where, because of the social heritage and the disadvantaged position of Negroes in American society, there developed a matriarchal family type which has become extremely unstable. If we are in fact moving more and more toward an urban, neolocal, nuclear family type, the Muslims would appear to be less deviant than the lower-class Negro Christians. Also in the area of family-community relationships, the Muslims typified the wage-earning, noncriminal, middle-class ideal to a greater extent than did the Christians.

On the basis of these findings, there would appear to be some questions as to the accuracy of the popular notion concerning the degree of social and psychological nonconformity extant within the Nation of Islam. From the perspective of the uninformed public, the Muslims are seen as in a state of rebellion—as totally rejecting the values and goals of this society and replacing them with their own values and goals. Because of their separatist ideology and their refusal to participate in various institutions of the society, persons who are fairly well informed might view the Muslims as an organized group of either rebels or retreatists. However, the results of this study tend to portray the Muslims as, again in Merton's terminology, primarily ritualists who have adopted and "black-washed" a version of American middle-class values and goals while simultaneously rejecting the institutionalized means to their attainment.

Although the Muslims are shown to be lower class in terms of income, education, and general environment, they are very middle class in many other respects—especially with regard to such issues as sex practices, the value put upon education (with some qualifications), personal hygiene and grooming, the high value placed upon work and industriousness, and their intense interest in developing and maintaining a high degree of mental and physical alertness. These are clearly not the characteristics typically found to exist throughout the lower-class Negro subculture.

In conclusion it seems clear that the Muslims were not only more conforming than the Christians in their adherence to what appear to be traditional American values regarding intrafamily behavior, but also that there exists a narrower gap between the Muslims' ideational values and their normative behavior.

Although a severe access problem exists with regard to researching the Nation of Islam and its membership, it is hoped that much research will be forthcoming, particularly since it is only through this means that accurate social and psychological portraits of this significant group can be obtained.

Selected Bibliography

Aldous, Joan. "Wives' Employment Status and Lower-Class Men as Husband-Fathers: Support for the Moynihan Thesis." *Journal of Marriage and the Family*, 31 (August 1969), pp. 469–476.

Anderson, C. S., and Joseph Himes. "Dating Values and Norms on a Negro College Campus." *Marriage and Family Living*, 21 (April 1959), pp. 227–229.

Andrew, Gwen. "Determinants of Negro Family Decisions in Management of Retardation." *Journal of Marriage and the Family*, 30 (November 1968), pp. 612–617.

Bell, Robert. "The Lower-Class Negro Mother's Aspirations for Her Children." *Social Forces*, 43 (May 1965), pp. 493–500.

Bernard, Jessie. *Marriage and Family among Negroes*. Englewood Cliffs, N.J.: Prentice-Hall, 1966.

Billingsley, Andrew, and Amy Tate Billingsley. "Negro Family Life in America." *Social Service Review*, 39 (September 1965), pp. 310–319.

Blau, Zena Smith. "Exposure to Child-Rearing Experts: A Structural Interpretation of Class Color Differences." *American Journal of Sociology*, 69 (May 1964), pp. 596–608.

Bowie, C. C. "The Meaning of the Marriage Contract to 674 Negro Male Veterans." *International Journal of Sexology*, 2 (1948), pp. 42–43.

Brody, Eugene B. "Color and Identity Conflict in Young Boys; Observations of Negro Mothers and Sons in Urban Baltimore." *Psychiatry*, 26 (May 1963), pp. 188–201.

Cavan, Ruth Shonle. "Negro Family Disorganization and Juvenile Delinquency." *Journal of Negro Education*, 28 (Summer 1959), pp. 230–239.

Clark, Kenneth, and Talcott Parsons (eds.). *The Negro American*. Boston: Houghton-Mifflin, 1966.

Coles, Robert. *Children of Crisis*. Boston: Little, Brown and Co., 1964.

_____. "Racial Identity in School Children." *Saturday Review*, 46 (October 19, 1963), pp. 56–57.

Cox, O. C. "Sex Ratio and Marital Status among Negroes." *American Sociological Review*, 5 (1940), pp. 937–947.

Davis, Allison, and John Dollard. *Children of Bondage*. Washington, D.C.: American Council on Education, 1940.

_____, Burleigh B. Gardner, and Mary K. Gardiner. *Deep South*. Chicago: University of Chicago Press, 1941.

_____, and Robert J. Havighurst. *The Father of the Man: How Your Child Gets His Personality*. Boston: Houghton Mifflin, 1947.

Day, C. B., and E. A. Hooton. *A Study of Some Negro and White Families in the United States*. Cambridge, Mass.: Peabody Museum, Harvard University, 1932.

Deasy, Leila C., and Olive W. Quinn. "The Urban Negro and Adoption of Children." *Child Welfare*, 49 (November 1962).

Drake, St. Clair, and Horace Cayton. *Black Metropolis*. Chicago: University of Chicago Press, 1945.

DuBois, W. E. *The Negro American Family*. Atlanta: Atlanta University Press, 1908.

Duncan, Beverly, and Otis Dudley Duncan. "Family and Occupational Success." *Social Problems*, 16 (Winter 1969), pp. 273–285.

Edwards, G. Franklin. "Marriage and Family Life among Negroes." *Journal of Negro Education*, 32 (Fall 1963), pp. 451–465.

Erikson, Erik. "Memorandum on Identity and Negro Youth." *Journal of Social Issues*, 20 (October 1964), pp. 29–41.

Frazier, E. Franklin. *Black Bourgeoisie*. New York: Collier Books, 1957.

_____. "Ethnic Family Patterns: The Negro Family in the United States." *American Journal of Sociology*, 54 (May 1948), pp. 433–438.

_____. *The Free Negro Family*. Nashville, Tenn.: Fisk University Press, 1932.

_____. *The Negro Family in Chicago*. Chicago: University of Chicago Press, 1932.

_____. *The Negro Family in the United States*. Chicago: University of Chicago Press, 1939.

_____. "The Negro Slave Family." *The Journal of Negro History*, 15 (April 1930), pp. 198–206.

_____. *Negro Youth at the Crossway*. Washington, D.C.: American Council on Education, 1941.

_____. "Problems and Needs of Negro Children and Youth Resulting from Family Disorganization." *The Journal of Negro Education*, 19 (1950), pp. 269–277.

Frumkin, Robert M. "Attitude of Negro College Students toward Intrafamily Leadership and Control." *Marriage and Family Living*, 16 (August 1954), pp. 252–253.

Gans, Herbert. "The Negro Family: Reflections on the Moynihan Report." *Commonwealth*, 83 (October 1965), pp. 47–51.

Gebhard, Paul, et al. *Pregnancy, Birth, and Abortion*. New York: Harper & Row, 1958.

Glazer, Nonay, and Carol F. Creedon (eds.). *Children and Poverty*. Chicago: Rand McNally, 1968.

Gordon, Joan. *The Poor of Harlem: Social Functioning in the Underclass*. New York: Office of the Mayor, 1965.

Gottlieb, David, and Warren D. Tenhouten. "Racial Composition and the Social Systems of Three High Schools." *Journal of Marriage and the Family*, 27 (May 1965), pp. 204–212.

Grier, William, and Price Cobbs. *Black Rage*. New York: Basic Books, 1968.

Hammond, Boone, and Joyce Ladner. "Socialization into Sexual Behavior in a Negro Slum Ghetto," in *The Individual, Sex, and Society*, Carlfred Broderick and Jessie Bernard, eds. Baltimore: John Hopkins University Press, 1969, pp. 41–52.

Hart, H. 'Differential Negro Fertility." *American Sociological Review*, 18 (June 1953), pp. 192–194.

Herskovits, Melville J. *The American Negro*. New York: Harper & Row, 1928.

———. *Dahomey: An Ancient West African Kingdom*. New York: J. J. Augustin, 1938.

———. *The Myths of the Negro Past*. Boston: Beacon Press, 1958.

Hertz, Hilda, and Sue Warren Little. "Unmarried Negro Mothers in a Southern Urban Community." *Social Forces*, 23 (October 1944), pp. 73–79.

Herzog, Elizabeth. "Is There a Breakdown of the Negro Family?" *Social Work*, 11 (January 1966), pp. 1–8.

Hill, Mozell, et al. "Research on the Negro Family." *Marriage and Family Living*, 19 (February 1957), pp. 25–31.

Himes, Joseph S. "The Factor of Social Mobility in Teaching Marriage Courses in Negro Colleges." *Social Forces*, 30 (May 1962), pp. 439–443.

———. "Interrelation of Occupational and Spousal Roles in a Middle Class Negro Neighborhood." *Marriage and Family Living*, 22 (November 1960), pp. 262–263.

———. "Some Reactions to a Hypothetical Premarital Pregnancy by 100 Negro College Women." *Marriage and Family Living*, 26 (August 1964), pp. 344–349.

———, and R. E. Edwards. "Hair Texture and Skin Color in Mate Selection among Negroes." *Midwest Journal*, 4 (1952), pp. 80–85.

Jeffers, Camille. *Living Poor*. Ann Arbor, Mich.: Ann Arbor Publisher, 1967.

Johnson, Charles. *Growing Up in the Black Belt*. Washington, D.C.: The American Council on Education, 1941.

———. *Shadow of the Plantation*. Chicago: University of Chicago Press, 1934.

Kardiner, Abram, and Lionel Ovesey. *The Mark of Oppression*. New York: W. W. Norton and Co., 1951.

King, Charles E. "The Sex Factor in Marital Adjustment." *Marriage and Family Living*, 16 (August 1954), pp. 237–240.

Lewis, Hylan. "The Changing Negro Family," in Eli Ginzberg, ed., *The Nation's Children.* Vol. I. New York: Columbia University Press, 1960.

Liebow, Elliot. *Tally's Corner.* Boston: Little, Brown and Co., 1966.

Lincoln, C. Eric. "A Look Beyond the Matriarchy." *Ebony,* August 1966, pp. 111–116.

Lystad, M. H. "Family Patterns, Achievements, and Aspirations of Urban Negroes." *Sociology and Social Research,* 45 (1961), pp. 281–288.

Mercer, Charles V. "Interrelations among Family Stability, Family Composition, Residence, and Race." *Journal of Marriage and the Family,* 28 (August 1967), pp. 456–460.

Middleton, Russell, and Snell Putney. "Dominance in Decisions in the Family: Race and Class Differences." *American Journal of Sociology,* 29 (May 1960), pp. 605–609.

Miller, Elizabeth W. *The Negro in America: A Bibliography.* Cambridge, Mass: Harvard University Press, 1966.

Parker, Seymour, and Robert J. Kleiner. "Characteristics of Negro Mothers in Single Headed Households." *Journal of Marriage and the Family,* 28 (November 1966), pp. 507–513.

_____. "Social and Psychological Dimensions of the Family Role Performance of the Negro Male." *Journal of Marriage and the Family,* 33 (August 1969), pp. 500–506.

Pettigrew, Thomas. *A Profile of the Negro American.* Princeton, N.J.: D. Van Nostrand Co., 1964.

_____. et al. "Color Gradations and Attitudes among Middle Income Negroes." *American Sociological Review,* 31 (June 1966), pp. 365–374.

Pierce, Ponchetta. "Divorce and the Negro Woman." *Ebony,* July 1967, pp. 84–92.

Powdermaker, Hortense. *After Freedom: A Cultural Study in the Deep South.* New York: Viking Press, 1939.

Radin, Norma, and Constance K. Kamii. "The Child-Rearing Attitudes of Disadvantaged Negro Mothers and Some Educational Implications." *Journal of Negro Education,* 34 (Spring 1965), pp. 138–146.

Rainwater, Lee, and William Yancey. *The Moynihan Report and the Politics of Controversy.* Cambridge, Mass.: MIT Press, 1967.

Reid, Ira D. A. *In a Minor Key: Negro Youth in Story and Fact.* Washington, D.C.: American Council on Education, 1940.

Schulz, David. "Some Aspects of the Policeman's Role As It Impinges upon Family Life in a Negro Ghetto." *Sociological Focus* (September 1969), pp. 63–71.

Schwartz, M. "Northern United States Negro Matriarchy: Status versus Authority." *Phylon,* 261 (Spring 1965), pp. 18–24.

Smith, Howard P., and Marcia Abramson. "Racial and Family Experience Correlates of Mobility Aspirations." *Journal of Negro Education,* 31 (Spring 1962), pp. 117–124.

Smith, Mary. "Birth Control and the Negro Woman." *Ebony,* March 1968, pp. 29–37.

Staples, Robert. *The Lower Income Negro Family in Saint Paul.* St. Paul: St. Paul Urban League, 1967.

———. "Reconstruction of the Black Lower Class Family: The Role of the Social Worker." *Bayviewer,* 5 (July 1969), pp. 14–18.

———. "Research on the Negro Family: A Source for Family Practitioners." *The Family Coordinator,* 18 (July 1969), pp. 202–210.

———. "Sex Behavior of Lower Income Negroes." *Sexology,* 34 (October 1967), pp. 52–55.

———. "Sex Life of Middle-Class Negroes." *Sexology,* 33 (September 1966), pp. 86–89.

———. "What's Wrong with the Negro Family." *Progressive World,* 20 (October 1966), pp. 32–37.

Sussman, Marvin, and H. C. Yeager, Jr. "Mate Selection among Negro and White College Students." *Sociology and Social Research,* 35 (September-October 1950), pp. 46–49.

Thursz, Daniel. *Where Are They Now?* Washington, D.C.: Health and Welfare Council of the National Capital Area, 1966.

Tietze, C., and S. Lewit. "Patterns of Family Limitation in a Rural Negro Community." *American Sociological Review,* 18 (1953), pp. 563–564.

Valien, Preston, and Alberta Fitzgerald. "Attitudes of the Negro Mother toward Birth Control." *American Journal of Sociology,* 55 (1949), pp. 279–283.

Vincent, Clark. "Ego Involvement in Sexual Relations." *American Journal of Sociology,* 65 (November 1959), pp. 287–296.

Wakin, E. *Portrait of a Middle-Class Negro Family at the Edge of Harlem.* New York: Morrow, 1965.

Warner, Lloyd W., Buford H. Junker, and Walter A. Adams. *Color and Human Nature.* Washington, D.C.: American Council on Education, 1941.

Woods, Sister Frances Jerome, and Alice Cunningham Lancanter. "Cultural Factors in Negro Adoptive Parenthood." *Social Work* (October 1962), pp. 14–21.

73

P 31